Dissonant Worlds

Roger Vandersteene
Among the Cree

Dissonant Worlds

Roger Vandersteene
Among the Cree

Earle H. Waugh

Wilfrid Laurier University Press

This book has been published with the help of a grant from the Humanities and Social Sciences Federation of Canada, using funds provided by the Social Sciences and Humanities Research Council of Canada. A grant in aid of publication was also given by the Canada Council.

Canadian Cataloguing in Publication Data

Waugh, Earle H., 1936-
  Dissonant worlds

Includes bibliographical references and index.
ISBN 0-88920-259-1

1. Vandersteene, Roger, 1918-1976.   2. Cree Indians –
Alberta, Northern – Missions.   3. Indians of North
America – Alberta, Northern – Missions.   4. Oblates
of Mary Immaculate – Missions – Alberta, Northern.
5. Oblates of Mary Immaculate – Biography.
6. Missionaries – Alberta, Northern – Biography.
7. Missionaries – Belgium – Biography.   I. Title.

E99.C88W38 1996   266'.271231   C95-932856-4

Copyright © 1996
WILFRID LAURIER UNIVERSITY PRESS
Waterloo, Ontario, Canada   N2L 3C5

Cover design by Leslie Macredie using a painting by
Roger Vandersteene

Printed in Canada

Respectfully dedicated to my mother,
Erma English Waugh
And to my late father,
Howard Cecil Waugh
Who taught me the burdens and the glories of
the inner life called religion

They that wait
upon the Lord
Shall mount up on wings of eagles . . .
— Psalm 103:5

Contents

Preface and Acknowledgments

Night Chorus

Suddenly
    Yap-plaint of dogs
And whining,
        Coyote-cries
Through howling
    Of wolves.

Homesickness
        Unawares
                Smarting
Through the night
And through my marrow.
                — Vandersteene, 2 June 1974

This book is about a man haunted by a vision. He pursued it because it was reality-laden, yet, strangely, its essence always seemed to elude him, despite the many talents he brought to bear in its pursuit.

Rogier (originally Roger; his Canadian colleagues used the altered form, which he preferred in Canada) Vandersteene was born on 15 June 1918, in Marke, a town deep in the heart of Flemish Belgium; he died on 7 August 1976 in the priest's house in Slave Lake, a northern Alberta town on the fringes of his Cree mission station east of Peace River, Alberta. Between those two stark bookends is a life imbued with two great loves: Flanders and the Cree people — and a religious vision that united them at a very deep level.

Flanders was the root of the man. Flanders bequeathed to him many of the principle concerns of his life: language and rights, feeling for minority status, piety toward Mary, the power of the forces of history, an Oblate heritage, which we will have occasion to explore during his colourful life. As time went on, he was more and more consumed by his other love: the Cree people. It was a passion that moved him to reject the implant of a Euro-Canadian church among his Cree friends. What he really sought was the deep veins of Cree culture, because therein he hoped to germinate a genuine Cree Christianity. Only traditional values could be recognized as the basis for a specifically Cree way of life; Vandersteene sought to bring into actuality his vision of a strong, spiritually powerful Cree church, based on Cree conceptions of reality. What others held to be ephemeral, he held to be real: a magnificent Cree formulation of Christian life.

Like any figure larger than life, Vandersteene raises questions about ourselves. Hence this is not just a study about who he was. Any gripping biography is partly an attempt to translate personality into a flesh-and-blood person. I have found that Vandersteene cannot be dismissed as "just a priest" or "just a missionary" or "just" whatever, despite my training that values categorizing and "objectivity." Somehow he articulates essential elements about our world and the way we are integrated into it. On the other hand, this is not a tale; I have tried to configure his life as he grasped it. Even if you think, after you have dipped into its description, that the attempt falls short, my hope is that something beyond the mundane would still be important to you.

Vandersteene lived and worked in an environment quite different from ours today. Not the least of these differences is the concept of acceptable language. Some references in this text will appear patronizing. I wrestled often with this issue, finally electing to express the words as they were, rather than what we would think appropriate today. The reader will surely be aware that repeating such phrases is not to condone them.

I am very grateful to those who have supported this research. I should first indicate that the Boreal Institute (now the Canadian Circumpolar Institute) at the University of Alberta provided a seed grant; this was supplemented from time to time by the Faculty of Arts through its Endowment Fund for the Future and the Research Fund of the Vice-President (Research). At a critical point, I received funding from the Alberta Historical Society for a research trip to Belgium, which helped me see the whole project in another light.

The number of people who have made a contribution to this book is so great it resists counting. Over the thirteen years of collecting and interviewing, scores have made comments that have become part of the book, either consciously or unconsciously. One fears the inevitable: someone will surely be left out. I hope they will accept that no slight was ever intended. Rather, the book is a testimony to their contribution and our joint collaboration.

I received impressive assistance from the Catholic hierarchy, including Archbishop Legaré in MacLennan, Alberta. The Oblate Museum in Girouxville and the Oblate archives in St. Albert were very helpful. All of the poems and most of the artwork are here courtesy of the Oblates of Mary Immaculate, and Fr. Jacques Johnson, Provincial.

None of this could have been achieved without the support and continual contribution of Father Paul Hernou, better known in the north as Maskwa (bear), who carries on the work of Vandersteene in the mission stations east of Peace River. A large note of appreciation is owed to the sisters in the various missions. A considerable number of the Cree people I consulted are listed in Appendix 2, but many more made comments that were never recorded, but became, in one way or other, part of my understanding.

I found all of Rogier's clerical colleagues to be forthright and helpful. During my Belgian sojourn, Rev. Omer Tanghe provided wonderful assistance, and subsequently approval to quote from his voluminous sources. The Vandersteene family, especially Pol and Mietje Dewaegheneire opened their home and hospitality to me and my wife so that we could interview the extensive family and associates of Rogier in Kortrijk. Later Pol Dewaegheneire, Willy Vander Steene (Rogier's cousin) and Walter Zinzen penned valuable comments on the text. The sculptor and folk singer Willem Vermandere drew a fascinating study of Vandersteene in interviews, presenting him through popular Flemish eyes. The Cree people from Garden Creek, Jean D'Or Prairie, Fort Vermilion, Slave Lake and Wabasca have all made a special contribution, suggesting insights about Vandersteene the man, as well as Vandersteene the legend. Many of the sisters with whom Rogier served, including Sister Gloria (d. 1983), and Sisters Bernadette and Lorraine were the source of much important information.

Right from the beginning Dr. William Krynen was supportive of this effort, and he kindly translated large sections of Rogier's poetry and literary material. Gordon Verburg, Thelma Habgood and the late Elly Englefield also assisted with some translations. Nancy Hannemann's skills as a research assistant and translator were sorely tried as she chased down obscure and sometimes non-existent letters, etc. Her talent has made this a better-documented book. Most of the best art photos were taken by Donald Spence, now of Video Video Productions on the campus of the University of Alberta. Some appreciation of his thoroughness can be gauged by noting that there remain around three hundred slides of Vandersteene's material in my files.

Early in the collecting process, Lois Larson and Marg Bolt heroically typed out the many hours of interviews I had, providing me with the textual base upon which this book is built. Both Miss Larson and Judy Springings contributed greatly with their computer skills throughout. Preliminary maps were kindly sketched by Catherine Boyd of

Edmonton; the final map was redrawn by Pam Schaus of the Department of Geography, Wilfrid Laurier University. Dan Gleason, my colleague while at St. Thomas University in Fredericton, New Brunswick, graciously provided my photo.

I am grateful to the staff at Wilfrid Laurier University Press and particularly its vigorous director, Sandra Woolfrey, and the editor, Maura Brown, for their fine activity on behalf of *Dissonant Worlds*. They have made it a much better book than I had dared conceive.

Finally, to my wife Mary-Ellen, whose critical evaluation aided immensely in sharpening what I wanted to say, and who provided much-needed inspiration and assistance along the way, I owe a huge debt. Whatever problems remain derive from my own imperfect ability to see what should have been seen, recorded and commented upon. I hope Steentje will forgive me for that . . .

Roger (Rogier) Vandersteene, 1918-1976

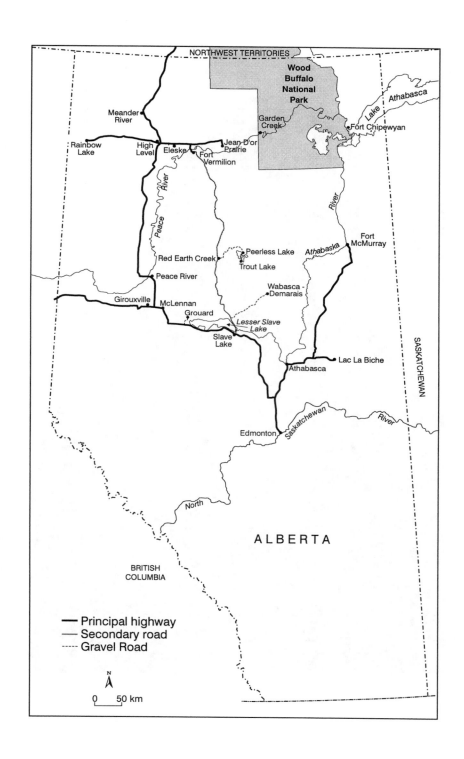

NORTHWEST TERRITORIES

Wood Buffalo National Park

Meander River

Rainbow Lake

High Level

Eleske

Fort Vermilion

Jean D'or Prairie

Garden Creek

Lake Athabasca

Fort Chipewyan

Peace River

Peerless Lake

Trout Lake

Red Earth Creek

Peace River

Athabaska

Fort McMurray

Girouxville

McLennan

Grouard

Wabasca - Demarais

Lesser Slave Lake

Slave Lake

Lac La Biche

Athabasca

Edmonton

Saskatchewan River

North

ALBERTA

BRITISH COLUMBIA

SASKATCHEWAN

— Principal highway
— Secondary road
---- Gravel Road

N

0   50 km

Introduction

> The world of the Native American, spiritual and other-
> wise, is not to be understood by assuming that it can be
> described easily in the English language, and in religious
> terms.
> — Wabanaki Elder Eunice Baumann-Nelson, 1991

I never met Rogier Vandersteene, although I had heard about him often, and had read his *Wabasca*. I promised myself I would learn more about him, go talk to him, perhaps ask him about his insights into native peoples whose stories sat respectably on the margins every-where in Canada. Then he died. Unannounced, too early. I had banked on years, bewitched by other old Oblates I had met, who sit, seemingly eternal, in discrete, rumpled clusters at Catholic gatherings.

Despite this setback, I determined to press on, and after some dozen years the book you now hold in your hands is my meeting with Van-dersteene. It is a story — actually more like a drama — of a deeply reli-gious Fleming, steeped in European citied culture, moving beyond his European assumptions to face the conflict and alienation of living in remote bush-camps of a completely different cultural world, and then labouring to piece together a new religious reality. At the heart of his attempt was the sheer authority of his personality, and his overwhelm-ing conviction of the power of ritual.

I have not written about a saint, I think, but about a kind of religious Ernest Hemingway. One's life is many things, and Vandersteene is no exception. The story told here involves several interacting themes: con-ceiving mission, trying to comprehend religion from a different per-spective, framing a special kind of leadership, wrestling with the role of immigrant and relating to the "other" in Canada. Some of them are treated more thoroughly than others, but I have tried to let Vander-steene shine through in all his complexity. He has, I think, something very important to say to all of us, and I have tried to convey that in this book.

Behind Vandersteene lay almost twenty centuries of mission his-tory, a history that reflects many twists and turns in conceptual modifi-cation. Origen (182-251) apparently believed that the Church was in

---

Notes to this Introduction are on p. 6.

1

the minority, even within the Roman Empire, and seemed to regard that as normal.[1] Much later, during the fifteenth and sixteenth centuries, the discoveries by Europeans of non-Christian peoples all over the world led to aggressive notions of converting the inhabitants to Christ, a considerably different task than the scriptural injunction to "Go ... teach."[2] Vatican II,[3] of which we will have more to say shortly, removed the word conversion from the language of its discussion on non-Christian religions, relying more on eschatological hope for the reconciliation of all peoples. Thus Vatican II's fourth statement of the *Declaration on the Relationship of the Church to Non-Christian Religions* states: "In company with the prophets and the Apostle Paul, the Church awaits that day, known to God alone, on which all peoples will address the Lord in a single voice and serve him with one accord."[4] The tone and spirit is dramatically different from forthright conversion.

Change is not new to the Church, but this declaration indicates that during Vandersteene's time the Church underwent a sea change. Since he and the Oblates were central to that concern, we will see in Vandersteene's life some of the stresses and tensions of modifying what was at one time a massive program to convert aboriginal people to Christ, in effect, a program of cultural destruction. He could not have foreseen all of them, but he himself made some contribution to the eventual radical modification of mission policy that emanated from the Oblates: a profound apology to the Native People of Canada.[5]

Vandersteene was first and foremost an Oblate, with all that entails in terms of predisposition to ritual protocols. In many ways, his lifework is a metaphor for understanding the processes of rites and the roles of acts of religious significance within an institution whose forms have been permanently imprinted upon Western civilization. Very early he saw ritual comportment as one way of escaping the deadening hand of cultural conflict with aboriginals. It is a trend that reaches well beyond the Church.

Religious ritual is the vehicle through which many leading Western scholars have studied aboriginals throughout the world in their encounter with spiritual realities; for such scholars, rituals set up the possibility of interaction with transcendence. The process is a series of postures toward unnamed and uncharted powers. This sort of ritual is a fundamentally normative and assertive act.

Vandersteene accepted this pattern of thinking about aboriginal life; for him it was *the* way into a genuine Cree-encoded Christianity. His quest was for a religious experience that was beyond the current form of Church ritual, but which encompassed Christianity's true meaning — except it was *based on Cree tradition itself*. In order to properly distinguish this vision, we have called this religion *interstitial*, because, in some sense, it operates in a domain beyond previous conceptions of either Christian or Cree traditions, yet depends upon them.

Such an encounter with religious reality implies that, while the organization believes the access to divinity or transcendence is strictly encoded and manipulated by its authorities, the ritual moment itself is not so fettered. It is the moment of delivering the powers to the believers, and the experience of those powers by definition cannot be fettered. Because of that, transcendence cannot be definitively conceptualized; continuous inspiration is ritual's sustenance.

Whoever knows how the gods may be reached becomes the key figure in the ritual moment. Thus, the organization remains stable, the roles remain fixed, but the ritual situation is ideal for the provisional and dynamic input of a charismatic person who can introduce the believer to the gods in a convincing and enervating manner. The ritual moment thus provides a potent environment for a special kind of leadership, called here interstitial leadership.

Such a person has insight into the experience of transcendence that is the goal of the corporate effort. At the same time, ritual specialists — priests, officiants and the like — do not have the same encounter goals as their flock. It is they who, so to speak, introduce the gods and the believers to each other, providing an entry into the spiritual world. They are the gatekeepers and the signal interpreters. Their experience of the powers is thus markedly different than that accorded the participating believer.

Ritual officials strive to generate a kind of experience that is formulaic, in that it is generated out of the rituals of the tradition. Yet the innovators want to free the worshipper from the specifics of the formula, so that the individual will encounter the reality of the powers without routinization. Only when the worshipper encounters the powers directly is the formula validated. If this is not accomplished, the ritual becomes a form, with its own beauty, but without the encounter with divinity deemed essential to empower the ritual expression.

This book is concerned with these officials, at least the role of Vandersteene as one of these gatekeepers. Officials, as we will see, are special kinds of worshippers. They activate the formulae, and assure that the possibilities of encounter are available, yet they do not believe that they *create* the reality the individual worshipper encounters. The officials *sense* the reality, perhaps manipulate the formulae toward the potential encounter and evaluate the power of the experience. Evidently their abilities are provisional, for the encounter depends upon religious sensitivities which they can lose or obfuscate, or which affairs beyond their control may destroy, depending upon a delicate balance that is religiously encoded. These are really individuals who operate beyond the formula, in the betwixt and between world of interstitial reality.

Rogier Vandersteene was a man with such an interstitial vision. Well known in northern Alberta, and in circles dealing with the Cree-speaking peoples, this Oblate had served among that nation since 1946; he had built up a significant relationship with them, and, along the way, a considerable reputation within the Apostolic Vicariate of Grouard of the Roman Catholic Church. Outsiders wondered whether he represented a fifth column within the Church: in conferences and press statements he appeared to argue that the Church had largely failed the people among whom he laboured. Moreover he suggested that leadership like his could only succeed if a radical change came about — a Church had to be fashioned out of Cree tradition rather than adding a little Cree tradition to Christianity. Cree had to fashion their own church, effectively eliminating the missionary's role entirely.

Here was an individual who worked within the Church, but who really saw its raison d'être defeated by its own cultural underpinnings. If this line of reasoning were taken to its logical end, one would have to conclude that the very organization to which he belonged militated against the success of his Christian goals. Yet he never appeared to go to that length. What he laboured to construct was a church that would be properly Cree. Within his worldview, he felt he had to have the concept of church necessary to assist God in building a genuine Cree Church.

At the same time, his role in that proposed Cree Church, and even his role in the Church as it existed was either unclear or not satisfactory to him. This seemed to spur him on. When he celebrated mass, or moved among the Cree, he carried on as if he had a special warrant to carry the Church beyond what it was at this point. His authority did not seem to derive solely or even principally from the authority of the Roman Catholic hierarchy, despite his being a faithful son of that organization. Rather, it arose from the vision he had of a genuine Cree-Christian reality, which gave him special inspiration and power. Part of that came from the religious roles bestowed upon him by the Cree people themselves. How he perceived himself within these two dissonant systems is never spelled out clearly in his writings or letters, but it is evident he felt their tensions. We will feel them too as we try to understand what he faced.

What he worked towards was provisionary in another sense; he did not know the ramifications for the Church. He believed that a special leadership was necessary, one that would unite both Christian and Cree dimensions. Such a unification had wide repercussions for the

Cree, for the present Church and for white-aboriginal relations. His vision thus had implications for many social levels.

Vandersteene was extremely talented in ways that were usually not considered necessary for one committed to the conversion of aboriginals; some of them may even have been peripheral to his carrying out his missionary obligations. For example, he acquired considerable horticulturalist skills from his father. He also painted with no little talent and wrote delightful poetry. Later we will sample some of his talents.

None of these would seem essential to a missionary. Yet all three elements were to be pressed into service in shaping his Cree Catholic Church in interesting ways. Some of the results of these talents were not always welcomed by his colleagues or his Church. It should not surprise us, then, that Vandersteene exhibited dimensions of rebellion as he actively pursued his role. There is no doubt that his individual genius and how he put it to work helped shape a distinctive interstitial leadership.

This leadership is obviously different from that which Weber had configured. That analyst talked about charisma as a key ingredient in religious leadership. Yet, while charisma plays a role in the construction of religious reality, it does not rely entirely upon it. Rather, there was an organizational component which provided a base from which the leadership of Vandersteene then grew. Such a fact moulds leadership in ways other than the classic cases studied by that great sociologist. For example, despite the prophetic nuances in Vandersteene's religious world, the significant element is that he never conspires to move outside the structure which provides his base. He is quite mindful of the need for the support and contribution of the socio-religious framework around him. In the final analysis, Vandersteene was very much a product of his existing structure, and made no attempt to go radically beyond that organization *in a theoretical or rationally defined manner*. This factor constrains the organizational radicalism that would ordinarily attract the interest of the analyst; it also reveals a kind of religious experience that needs the security of the standard organization to operate as a bedrock so that its ritualized experience can dramatically supersede the conventional.

Moreover, in my view, the independent little priest from Marke opens to us another dimension of religious understanding, in addition to providing us with a creative and fascinating life. Religion in Canada is really a very distinctive creation. Attempting to conceptualize the formulas within which it operates is a fledgling undertaking, and likely quite complex. Mindful that not everyone is enthused by such matters, this material has been diverted to a theoretical epilogue.

There is a further theme here, perhaps distinctively Canadian; the
continuing impact of minority status which an immigrant brings. In
Vandersteene's case, this "minority-ness" derives first from his Belgian
roots and the situation of the Flemish-speaking peoples in Belgian history and second from his work among the Cree in Canada. It is striking
that Canada's emphasis on multiculturalism also contributes to this
phenomenon: the immigrants who on the surface are made welcome
for the contribution they can make, but really are forever not of this
country. Nor are they of their own "home." Strangely, Vandersteene
may have been considered as Canadian as any other, but that very *being Canadian* divided him from home as surely as it divided him from
the Cree. Vandersteene's sense of minority played a key role in his perception of the Cree, both in regard to his striving to become one with
the Cree people and his sensitivity to their minority situation in Canada. The attempt to bridge the gap between Canada's first people and
Euro-Canadians was a religious project that took him to the heart of a
moral dilemma: Canadian "colonialism" leaves Euro-Canadians without moral authority in constructing the country. Worse still, perhaps, it
leaves aboriginal people without a commitment to the current nature
of Canada. Thus, in some ways, this book is the exploration of the immigrant phenomenon and its impact on the life of a bright and talented
individual and on a diversified country.

All of this is by way of preparing you for the highly nuanced life of
Rogier Vandersteene, a preparation that you may safely set aside for
the moment as we reach into the nexus out of which this extraordinary
individual arose, and the journey that he saw as a trip down the great
river of life.

Notes

1 Joseph Schmidlin, *Catholic Mission History*, translated by Matthias Braun, S.V.D.
(Techny, IL: Mission Press, 1933), p. 91.
2 For example, the charter work on missiology of the seventeenth century by Thomas à
Jesu explicitly linked spreading the faith all over the world to conversion of the masses
(Thomas à Jesu, *De Procuranda Salute Omnium Gentium* [Antverpiae, 1613], Lib. III, Cap.).
3 Vatican II is the council of the Roman Catholic Church called by Pope John XXIII for
1962-65; it was notable for its openness to other religions and Christian traditions.
4 See Ronan Hoffman, "Conversion and the Mission of the Church," *Journal of Ecumenical Studies*, 5, 1 (Winter 1968): 7, n. 10, where the passage is quoted.
5 The apology was given at Lac Ste. Anne, 20 July 1991, by Rev. Douglas Crosby, the
president of the Oblate Conference of Canada. It read in part: "We apologize for the
part we played in the cultural, ethnic, and religious imperialism that was part of the
mentality with which the peoples of Europe first met the aboriginal peoples and
which consistently has lurked behind the way the Native people of Canada have been
treated by civil governments and Churches" (press release from the Missionary Oblates of Mary Immaculate, Edmonton, 24 July 1991).

One

Flemish Matrix: Blood, Art and Piety

> I cannot thrust my hand into the fire for another.
> — Flemish Proverb

D awn spread like a misty shroud across Marke, Belgium, that rainy day on 15 July 1918, and little Roger, first child of Julia Kerkhove and Adolph Joris (George) Vandersteene, eased into the midwife's hands. He was not robust, and from the beginning he was plagued by lung problems. Julia feared for her son, quickly rising from the natal bed to church for his baptism so he could be committed to the gentle care of the Blessed Mary. She feared lest hesitation weaken little Roger's resources further. From such inauspicious moments did one of Flander's most talented and enigmatic missionaries spring.

At our point in time, it is hard not think of war and blood when Belgium is mentioned. Indeed, for her own citizens, Belgium's identity is solidly rooted to some critical event of the past. Yet for many people around the world, Belgium *is primarily* a kind of memory, perhaps a memory of conflict, which has been an integral part of Belgian history. Every child in the English-speaking world almost immediately associates "In Flanders' Fields" with rows upon rows of crosses. Field after field. Wandering among them is still a bewildering experience. The bitterness of both the First and Second World Wars flares up every Remembrance Day, scarring again the minds of every soldier who watched colleagues fall in that boggy land. Driving through verdant fields, or walking by placid, grass-lined waterways, or squinting through the gauzey morning light, the contrast between such a pleasant, fertile atmosphere and its bloody past strikes one like a cold hand. Wherever one goes, the dampness is present. The quality that seems to abide in the Belgian soul is not violence, however, but history — a

---

Notes to this chapter are on pp. 18-19.

sense of survival despite its bitter past. A tough destiny, to survive when the odds looked impossible. It is a quality that walked with Vandersteene.

Belgium itself is a recent country by European standards, having come into existence after various power struggles and concessions within the last two centuries. A century before Vandersteene's birth, the lowland countries of north and south had been brought together at the Congress of Vienna; this was one of those projects that looked fine on paper — after all, they once had been part of a larger country before the war — but there were deep divisions between them. To the north, Protestant Holland was dynamic and economically aggressive. For many Flemish, the accord had ignored the religious factor — the southern people feared because there were no safeguards against the Protestant religion of the Dutch being imposed upon the less-developed Catholic regions. To make matters worse, the Flemish-speaking people of the land, even if they did speak a regional dialect of Dutch, had little intellectual or artistic tradition to stand against their more vigorous northern compatriots. For their part, the Walloons (the French-speaking inhabitants of the south of Belgium), and the French-speaking aristocracy in Flanders, looked to France and its religious traditions for their inspiration. The hapless unification fell apart fifteen years later, and from its ashes arose the French-language-dominated independent country called Belgium.[1]

From its inception, the independence movement featured two key elements. They were a cohesion of liberal ideas of state, including the belief that the national will is expressed through the people as a whole, (along with an independent press, trial by jury, liberal education, etc., i.e., those characteristics identified with Western democratic governments) *and* a national Catholic sensitivity, represented by the clergy, committed to the goals of a free and independent Belgium. Within this new country, both Flemish and Walloon identities were to be integral to the whole. August Vermeylen (1872-1945), modernist writer and nationalist, put the Flemish case clearly: "In order to be something, we must be Flemings; we want to be Flemings in order to be Europeans."[2] In this way Flemish identity was connected to French-speaking fellow Belgians by religion and liberal perceptions of government.

Belgian statehood and particularly Flemish national awareness flowered in the arts and literature; it developed particularly strongly in Flemish-speaking areas after 1860 when Guido Gezelle (1830-99) broke the dearth of literary achievement with his first book of realist poetry.[3] The young student Vandersteene especially looked to Gezelle as one of his models. Gezelle had also been a priest, and, while assigned to a teaching post, he launched into writing a remarkable kind of poetry. It was charged with a nature-consciousness, one could almost say a particular countryside nature consciousnesss, and it contrasted dramatically with the landscape depicted by the romantics. It was sensitive to Flemish experience, particularly that of the common and the poor. At its heart was a strong ethical nationalism. God and Flanders' natural environment were blended into a seamless whole. In addition, with Gezelle, the close relationship between literary expression, religion and nationalism came to the fore, a trait that touched many writers both inside and outside the movement. Sotemann describes the relationship: "Writing becomes a form of positive mysticism. . . . The word of the poet conceals a final form of 're-ligion' in the etymological sense of the word, a religion of reality, a sensory incarnation of what has been seen."[4]

In retrospect one can see the elements that contributed to this remarkable movement. Earlier in the century, Domiens Sleeckx (1818-1901) wrote with a sharp sense of observation, particularly in his description of local haunts and the common people; he was joined by such nationalists as Hugo Verriest (1840-1922) and Jan Van Beers (1821-88). A militant edge was added by the great epics of Albrecht Rodenbach (1856-80), who also wrote Flemish songs of marked passion that were quite influential in Flemish nationalism. By the turn of the century, the Flemish national cause was etched with both Christian and personalist symbolism: the first by means of the vigorous Augustinianism of the priest Cyriel Verschaeve (1874-1949), the second through the complicated psychological vision of Karel Van de Woestijne (1872-1945). The "Flemish Movement," as it was known, was deepened immensely by Stijn Streuvels' (1871-1969) stories. The most powerful is his classic *Langs de Wegen (Along the Roads)*, a work that paints the Flanders landscape as a microcosm of human existence, and confirms Flemish writing as a critical ingredient in European prose.[5]

This movement arose, in part, from the precarious situation in which Flemish speakers found themselves in their own country. Vandersteene grew up in the shadow of this conflict, once incurring the wrath of his school principal when he refused to wave the national flag for visiting dignitaries because the national government was dominated by French speakers little concerned about Flemish language rights. Many are the stories told during the First World War of Flemish-speaking soldiers under the command of French-speaking officers who either could not or would not acknowledge the language of the soldiers in communicating with them. The consequences? Confusion and tragedy. Following the war, Flemish nationalism flared anew, spurred on by stories of discrimination within the army and the government. The outraged cry of the soldiers and other Flemish nationalists found expression in a text scratched on a stone by an unknown soldier:

> Here our blood
> When our rights?

Similar sentiments found expression in Cyrile Verschaeve's poem:

> Here their bodies lie as seeds in the sand,
> Hope in the harvest, O Flanderland.

Such nationalist emotions were not new. Long before the First World War, Albrecht Rodenbach had been a key figure at the origin of the Flemish Movement. He was considered a young radical in 1875 when he formed the Blauwvoeterij or Stormy Seagull Movement, a loose organization of students dedicated to Flemish independence. The movement was roundly condemned by the government and went underground. But Rodenbach's poem *Flies the Seagull, Storm at Sea* became the rallying cry of young Flemish nationalists of all stripes from that time on. The sentiments of the poem are that the Flemish people, in the symbol of the seagull, will rise above the storm, survive and thrive. On Rodenbach's statue are inscribed the following lines:

> Uit houwe trouwe wordt moereland herboren
> En Vlaanderen's sonne is aan het daghen.

> Out of strong fidelity, Our Motherland is being reborn
> The sun of Flanders is rising.

From such sentiments grew the Flemish language/nationalist movement. It goes without saying that it did not play the same role all over Belgium. It did not even play the same part for all Flanders' citizens.

As has been noted, the Flemish language is a regional dialect of Dutch. The Flemish Movement was undecided about whether to develop Flanders' own standard language, different from that of Holland, or to commit the Flemish speakers to modern Dutch, for which standards had already been established. Those who favoured the latter approach within the Flemish Movement included powerful leaders like Jan Frans Willems, August Snellaert and Philip Marie Blommaert. The "Flanders Only," or the "Particularists" as they were called, were identified with Gezelle, but it remained a minority viewpoint that more and more lost ground to the Dutch contingent. Nationalists who prize the independence and uniqueness of Flemish identity tend to opt for the distinctive individuality of Flanders' language; those who are content with state sovereignty and recognition of Flemish linguistic rights within Belgium accept the connections of Flemish with Dutch.

The issue is a contentious one, fostering much debate.[6] While Vandersteene does not indicate in my sources any stated preference, it is clear
from his youth to which group he belonged: the Particularists. All of
his writings begin with or contain a monogram

a

v   v   k

v

meaning All for Flanders, Flanders for Christ. Designed by Joe English,
Flemish nationalist, the lettering was incised on the Celtic cross and
placed on the grave of every Flemish soldier who died in the famous
Ijzer front during the First World War. It is a ritual formula expressed
on the famous Flemish national shrine at Diksmuide, which now has
become the site of an annual Flemish pilgrimage;[7] Vandersteene used it
throughout all periods of his life. As we shall see, the direction (or lack
thereof) of the Flemish individuality caused him great dismay towards
the end of his career.

The language issue is not one-dimensional. For one thing, it cuts
across the religious dimension. There is a religiously vigorous component to Flemish national meaning, and it comes in the form of a deep
commitment to the Virgin Mary, who is held to be the national protec-
tor of the Flemish people and the guardian of their interests. Mary was
associated with the decidedly second-place ranking Flemish speakers
were given in the First World War, and was the patron saint promoted
by the nationalist priest Cyriel Verschaeve. He firmly asserted that
Mary piety was a factor in the survival of the Flemish people despite
Walloon attempts to reduce the credibility of the claim. In some areas
of Flanders, priests have developed a Flemish piety towards the Virgin
Mary, identifying their souls with that of the Mother of God with special prayers. Such piety is reflected, too, in the ubiquitous shrines to
Mary throughout Flanders. A popular song states it bluntly: "When we
travel on Flemish roads, we everywhere meet you, O Mary." It will
take more than a virulent secularism to winnow mariology from the
Flemish soul; Flemish identity has deep, holy roots.

Vandersteene was also affected by another kind of piety which, in its
own way, represents something very special about Flanders. This is the
role of the great orders in Flemish history. This role dates back to the
Crusades and the Catholic traditions which cultivated crusading.
Among them is the Hospitaller's Order of St. John of Jerusalem, which
founded an important hospital at Brugge whose buildings can still be
visited today. The most significant organization for the development
of western Canada is the Oblates of Mary Immaculate (O.M.I.), a con-

gregation begun by Eugène de Mazenod (d. 1861). When De Mazenod, the only son of a noble family, announced his decision to be a priest, his family resisted, pointing out that the family would die out without heirs. His reply was a question: "Would it not be more beautiful if it finished with a priest?" His family relented, and he began preaching small missions around southern France. Eventually his congregation was approved by Rome and given the name "Oblates of Mary Immaculate" from Latin words meaning "an offering to sinless Mary." De Mazenod was distinctive in that he utilized the local language of the people, preaching in the vernacular and urging his priests to go to the poorest and to dare to bring the least attractive to Christ. The Oblates flourished, eventually founding small colleges where students could learn to be missionaries for the Oblates. These schools, called "juniorates" were an important part of Belgian education. It is to one of these schools that Vandersteene was sent.

Of all the regions in Flanders famous for its missionaries, the area around Marke has a special significance. Literally scores of priests and missionaries came from the surrounding countryside, partially because of the forward-looking bishops who sponsored a college for training priests, but partly because of a mystical connection between Flemish nationalism and Catholic piety; the linkage was echoed by Vandersteene when he addressed the local congregation when he returned from the Canadian mission field on his first furlow: "I serve my country by going on this mission."

Flemish clerics had a formidable reputation among the heads of orders: St. Francis Xavier was said to have asked for Flemish priests for the Jesuits because "they are not afraid of anything."[8] The ideology about the hardship of mission life became part of Oblate rationale, and, consequently, because of the "wildness" and tough demands of the north, Canada was regarded as a prime environment for carrying out the mandate of the great founder. For this reason Oblates have had a strong impact on Canadian development.[9] Their reputation for being dedicated missionaries doggedly committed to converting the poor was attractive to many young men. Both Frs. Mariman and Hernou, Vandersteene's Belgian colleagues, credit this dedication to the toughest missions as a key element in Vandersteene's commitment to the Oblates and his desire to come to Canada.

The Church in Flanders and indeed in Europe generally was in a state of flux just at the time when Vandersteene was growing up. Two movements from this period almost surely had considerable impact on him: the Liturgical and *aggiornamento* movements. The Liturgical Movement actually began in the mid-nineteenth century at the Abbey of Solesmes in France under the reforming hand of Dom Guéranger (1805-75) who proposed an enthusiastic return to the medieval liturgy as the means to revive the Church and eliminate aspects of liturgy that came from other than pure "Roman" sources. The movement was to shift later to Germany and, more powerfully to Belgium, where it came under the influence of Dom Lambert Beauduin who had been a pastor in a workers' parish before delivering a paper at a Catholic Conference in Malines, Belgium, in 1909, what Bouyer has called "the decisive turning point for the Liturgical Movement."[10] Beauduin had retreated to a monastery before the paper, but he sounded the note that was to become a key to the movement. The liturgy was to be returned to the people, where it was to become the basis of true prayer and the meeting place between the believer and God. The liturgy was for the participation of the congregation, not the occasion for spectacle or the celebration of an elite. His little book *La Piété de l'Église* (1914) affirmed the simplicity of the Church's mission to conduct liturgy for the people as it is found among them, not as formalized from above. He urged that Gregorian chant be reintroduced, that choirs be given retreats in liturgy, that the Roman missal be translated and that the Church abandon its many other roles and return to its true calling.[11] Between the war years, his work was continued by Brugge's famous monk Dom Gaspar Lefebvre, who sent the movement far and wide. In particular, the movement attracted the interest of members of Catholic Action,[12] especially its youth. Vandersteene was an active participant in this wing of the movement.

With Vatican II, many of these themes came together, resulting in a wholesale change in Church policy. The work on liturgy was conceived as a "restoration" of the original freedom associated with the Church's celebration of worship, a restoration that wished to affirm the unchanging elements of liturgy, but, at the same time, wished to promote the Church to change those non-permanent aspects. Vatican II said:

> In this restoration, both texts and rites should be drawn up so that they express more clearly the holy things which they signify. Christian people, as far as possible should be able to understand them with ease and to take part in them fully, actively, and as befits a community.[13]

The possibility of changing the liturgy to reflect local or cultural differences with these parameters opened up new possibilities for those working in mission fields, and Vandersteene was excited and motivated for change by the possibilities. His desire to do promotional work at the diocesan level would be one factor that drew him away from his beloved missions.

The second movement, called *aggiornamento*, is identified with the contemporary renewal of the Church, and is usually associated with Vatican II. Vandersteene's connection with this movement is complex. One of his favourite authors was John Henry Newman, whose books were sources of inspiration throughout his life. Newman's published works appeared in the German edition under the hand of a young Jesuit, Otto Karrer, and Fr. Erich Przywara (1922), and it was the version edited by these clerics that was treasured by Vandersteene. The linkage is not just by happenstance, for Vandersteene was also conversant with Karrer's other work.[14] Karrer was established in Lucerne during the interwar years, and wrote extensively (some 718 articles and books) on such subjects as the mystic Meister Eckhart, women in the Church and spirituality.[15] He was instrumental in forming ecumenical organizations during the war, and his work in this regard, while inspired by Rudolf Otto's *Das Heilige* (1917), really comes out of the tradition that non-Christian religions are necessary stages in revelation's plan. This universal perspective asserted that Christianity has to face the fact of other religions since the world was now far smaller than it had been. Vandersteene, as we shall see, was very much in tune with this perspective. These ideas were to find a permanent place in Vatican II's initiatives towards other religions.[16] Karrer also stressed the notion of the Eucharistic celebration as an act of thanksgiving and praise to God, not as the repetition of Christ's sacrifice, which he held to be unique, so that "when we confess that the Saviour himself, with all that he is and does for us, [He] becomes present in us and fills us in the course of the eucharistic celebration." The result is a sense of "the Real Presence" of Christ.[17] One finds echoes of these notions in Vandersteene's mature work.

Vandersteene was also an artist of some ability. He came into the world at a time when the artistic life of Europe was in turmoil. Two movements vied for position at the turn of the century in Belgium: symbolism and impressionism. The symbolist movement arose out of the French poets Mallarmé (1842-98), Verlaine (1844-96) and Rimbaud (1854-91). "To *name* an object," said Mallarmé, "is to suppress three quarters of the poem's pleasure ... to *suggest* it, that is the dream."[18] There were symbols, signs, significances which could deliver a message to the unsophisticated public, but whose real meaning was known to a few initiates. It was this power to suggest meanings to those who did not know that attracted these poets to symbolist writing. Up to this time the symbol had been viewed as a different type of analogy, by which a truth was encapsulated in a kind of shorthand form. The understanding was that there was a direct connection between the intellectual content of the truth and the understood meaning in the symbol. The symbolist saw that could not be so. For example, if the number seven could elicit certain feelings without being connected to any observable reality, then a whole language of meaning could be explored without empirical connections. Dutch painter Vincent Van Gogh (1853-90), whose father had been a clergyman in the countryside of Holland, wrestled as a young man with the decision to pursue a religious or artistic career. Having failed as a theological student, he turned to painting, developing a style that built upon the symbolist philosophy; in a letter to his art-dealer brother, he said: "Instead of trying to render exactly what was before my eyes, I use colour more arbitrarily in order to express myself more powerfully."[19] Colour became the primary medium for plumbing the emotional language of a painting, for tapping into the symbolic world where meaning could be delivered without recourse to the "realism" of the material world. He and Paul Gauguin (1848-1903) represent the artist at the most alienated; the former sold only one painting during his lifetime, and the latter only a few. Van Gogh, driven by a recurring madness, committed suicide; Gauguin died in despair on the remote Tahitian island of Marquesas. Their style of painting, along with the spatial experiments of Cézanne and Seurat, led directly to the artistic movement known as expressionism.

The other artistic influence was impressionism. Impressionism attempted to catch the visual moment in an exquisite recreation of reality. Landscapes were the favoured topic because colour could indicate seasonal characteristics, and mood and tone could be delivered by the shape of the brush stroke. The everyday, contemporary setting, without artifice or idealizing, was a central motif in this art. Camille Pissarro (1830-1903), Edgar Degas (1834-1917), Claude Monet (1840-1926) and Pierre Auguste Renoir (1841-1919) were leading lights of the movement who exhibited in the first series of non-conformist, anti-Salon showings in Paris between 1874 and 1886. Despite the poverty of the group, they never abandoned the ideology of raising the unsuspecting moment to classical proportions. It was a movement that would celebrate the commonest of subjects, leading them to become part of the artist public, and it lent itself well to the power and drama of the primitive world, now becoming more dominant through studies in the more remote areas of the globe and its art.

In Belgium, too, impressionism had its practitioners. Rik Wouters, Henri Evenepoel and Louis Thévenet all painted with similar tendencies. But the First World War destroyed all that. The blood and terror of that conflict pushed the painter to try to capture ugliness — to try to tone down the violence sufficiently to paint it as ugliness on canvas. Out of the trauma of the war came painters who returned to the simple values of Flanders, but who did so in a form close to the new movement called expressionism that arose after the turn of the century. For example James Ensor (1860-1949) addressed the poverty, misery and folly of human life with sarcasm; he saw things with a deep philosophical sense of humour. Like Rubens, however, he had a rich sense of colour and had profound sensitivity to the iridescent glow of the Flemish environment. At the same time, he could paint as if what he saw was pure visionary landscapes. Hubert Malfait (1898-1971) was more properly an expressionist, and he, too, valued the ordinariness of life. He liked plain things, and is sometimes regarded as an animist because he saw nature imbued with a kind of glow. But of even greater significance for the study of Vandersteene was Constant Permeke. Permeke was one of Flander's greatest modern painters. Nature is not just a background for human activity, but pregnant with meaning. The cosmos is alive, vital and monumental. A process is at work here: the cycle of decay to death to new life. Expressing humans' encounter with this process in art was Permeke's great calling. Another Flemish artist of interest is Albert Servaes. Servaes was keenly aware of peasant life and work. His painting was also strongly mystical, but, in contrast to other impressionists, his was a mysticism drawn from the Church and the power of religious images, such as the Blessed Virgin Mary. Many of Vandersteene's works reflect the influence of Servaes.

Vandersteene grew up to expressionism. Six years before his birth, Wassily Kandinsky (1866-1944) had written *Concerning the Spiritual in Art*, a work that has since been regarded as "the most important single expressionist theoretical statement."[20] In reality, however, Kandinsky had been inspired some years earlier when, returning home one evening and in the dark, he did not recognize one of his paintings lying flat. He had then, he said, the instantaneous revelation of the power of colour and design when released or separated from identifiable subject matter.[21] The element that can only be described as religious inspiration is found in most expressionist painters. For example, Ludwig Meidner (1884-1966), considered to be the most typical, was to recall,

> In December, 1912, I had a thorough-going religious experience for the first time. Suddenly, while I was painting one evening, I noticed that I could get nothing right. I just couldn't paint. Then all at once I succeeded to such a degree that I actually watched myself as I painted. I painted. My arm was writing on its own and I was taken by surprise completely. Then something came over me: The Holy Ghost. . . . I noticed that it was what people call ecstasy.[22]

Expressionism sought an art that would express the emotional veri-
ties of human existence without having to rely upon the Church and
formal religion for their definition; often there was a link between
strong feelings for a geographical and cultural environment (for Kandinsky it was folk Russia, for Émile Nolde (1867-1956) north German
landscape) and a native idealism. Sometimes, as in the case of Franz
Marc (1880-1916), the apocalyptic vision became part of the abstract
language of art. Nature is no longer the constructor of reality. Rather, it
is only the starting point, the vehicle by which humans formulate their
own world. As the poet Gottfried Benn wrote: "There is no outer reality, there is only human consciousness, constantly building, modifying,
rebuilding new worlds out of its own creativity."[23] At the same time,
there was an urge to cut away the superfluousness of modern civilization and to reduce it to its absolute essential, to its most primitive. With
such trends swirling about, young Vandersteene and the Belgian
people survived the First World War, and began the long, slow process
that would take them to the Second.

One final influence should be mentioned: Belgium and the Nazis.
The controversy surrounding Belgium's relationship with Germany
and the German people is still unfolding; a recent book suggested that
King Leopold of Belgium had even conspired with the Nazis during
the Second World War.[24] The fact is that Verschaeve and several other
activist Flemish were heavily influenced by German culture and politics. Throughout the latter part of the nineteenth century the Flemish
nationalists used German culture as a counterweight to French culture.
When the Germans occupied Belgium in 1914, those with pro-German
sympathies allied themselves with the group called the Young Flemings, who argued that the Flemish-speaking parts of Belgium should
become an independent state within the German empire; Germany
fanned this nationalism by responding to a long-time desire for a Flemish university by turning Ghent into a Flemish-speaking institution.[25]
Belgium's Nazi experience was thus one more complicated result of its
location in the map of Europe. Vandersteene's old friend and fellow
priest Fr. Platteeuw saw Roger becoming more and more involved in
the student movement which arose following the First World War, and
his reliance on Germany continued throughout the Second, because
Vandersteene saw no way that Flemish nationalism would receive fair
treatment under Walloon hegemony. Consequently, his stance was politically oriented, based upon his Flemish nationalist goals. As we shall
see Vandersteene's attitude toward Nazism was a source of some concern to his relatives and friends. The German presence in Vander-

steene's young life left a lasting legacy that will require further examination.

From such a rich background came Vandersteene: a world of idealism, Belgian statism, Flemish nationalism, Catholic piety, nature-mysticism, Mary adoration, poetic genius, artistic flourish and German political machinations. A young man of this variegated background confronted an entirely different world in Canada.

Notes

1 See V.J. Dossogne, S.J., "From Caesar to 1814," in Jan-Albert Goris, ed., *Belgium* (Berkeley: University of California Press, 1946), pp. 15-36, and Ernest H. Kossman, *The Low Countries, 1780-1940* (New York: Oxford University Press, 1978).
2 Quoted in Jan Greshoff, "Belgian Literature in the Dutch Language," in Goris, ed., *Belgium*, p. 292.
3 *Lyrica Belgica: Guido Gezelle, Karel van de Woestijne, etc.*, translated into English by Clark and Frances Stillman (New York: Belgium Information Centre, 1963).
4 See A.L. Sotemann, "Martinus Nijhoff's Poetry in Its European Context," in Francis Bulhof, ed., *Nijhoff, Van Ostaijen, "De Stijl": Modernism in the Netherlands and Belgium in the First Quarter of the 20th Century* (The Hague: Martinus Nijhoff, 1976), p. 108.
5 Stijn Streuvels, *Langs de Wegen (Along the Roads)*, translated by Edward Crankshaw (Boston, MA: Twayne Publishers, 1976).
6 Details of the debate are found in R.P. Meijer, *Dutch and Flemish: Two Literatures or One?* (London: University College of London, 1973).
7 See Manu Ruys, *The Flemings: A People on the Move, A Nation in Being*, translated by Henri Schoup (Belgium: Lannoo, Tielt and Bussum, 1981), pp. 71-79.
8 This report has become so much part of the heroic mythology of the Belgian Oblates that I heard it several times. Fr. Mariman, Vandersteene's compatriot from Belgium, reported it to me first in 1979.
9 Gaston Carrière, *Histoire documentaire de la Congrégation des missionnaires Oblates de Marie-Immaculée dans l'Est du Canada* (Ottawa: Éditions de l'Université d'Ottawa, 1957-75), pp. 1-12.
10 Louis Bouyer, *Liturgical Piety* (Notre Dame, IN: University of Notre Dame Press, 1954), p. 58. There is a rich literature on this movement; see, among others, Dom Olivier Rousseau, O.S.B., *Histoire de mouvement liturgique* (Paris, 1945), in English, *Progress of the Liturgy* (Westminster, MD: Newman Press, 1951); Joseph A. Jungmann, S.J., *The Mass of the Roman Rite, Its Origins and Development* (Missarum solemnia), translated by F.A. Brunner, C.S.S.R., 2 vols. (New York: Benzinger, 1951 and 1955); and The Sacerdotal Communities of Saint-Severin of Paris and Saint-Joseph of Nice, *The Liturgical Movement*, translated by Lancelot Sheppard (New York: Hawthorn Books, 1964), and the bibliography found therein.
11 Bouyer, *Liturgical Piety*, p. 61.
12 Catholic action in the first instance was any action in conformity with the principles of Roman Catholic tradition, but it became action by laymembers which they carried out under the direct supervision of the Roman Catholic ecclesiastical authority for the benefit of the Church. In 1922 Pope Pius XI summoned Christians to lend their efforts to christianize local folk. Belgium was quick to respond to the call and the clergy created action groups for each social group. Within a few years, the number of organizations mushroomed in Belgium.
13 Walter M. Abbott, S.J., ed., *The Documents of Vatican II* (New York: Guild Press, 1966), p. 146.
14 Personal conversation with Fr. Paul Hernou.

15 Material for Karrer is derived from Victor Conzemius, "Otto Karrer (1888-1976): Theological Forerunner of *Aggiornamento*," *The Catholic Historical Review*, 85, 1 (January 1989): 55-72.

16 Among the trends is the so-called transcendental anthropology, especially in the writings of Karl Rahner, *Lexicon für Theologie und Kirche*, 11 vols. (Frieburg, 1957-67).

17 O. Karrer, "Die Eucharistie im Gespräch der Konfessionen, Vortrag 6.8.1960 beim Eucharistischen Weltkongress München," *Una Sancta*, 15 (1960): 229-50; and Conzemius, "Otto Karrer," p. 66.

18 Frank Whitford, *Expressionism: Movements of Modern Art* (London: Hamlyn Publishing Group, 1970), p. 27.

19 Ibid., p. 28.

20 Ibid., p. 103.

21 George H. Hamilton, *19th and 20th Century Art* (New York: Harry N. Abrams, 1970), p. 232.

22 Whitford, *Expressionism*, p. 147.

23 Ibid., p. 177.

24 See *De Standaard* during November 1990, Groot-Bijgaarden, Belgium, series section.

25 See Ruys, *The Flemings*, pp. 62ff.

Two

"Steentje's" Beginnings: Between Family and Flanders

> When the soul listens, everything on earth has a living
> language.   — Guido Gezelle, *Tijokans III* (1883)

One evening when our Blessed Lady was still a very little girl, she was sleeping in her cot, warmly tucked in, sleeping like a little rose. It was just around the time that father and mother were going to sleep. In the kitchen there was the light clatter of pot against pan, then the creaking of the stairs and the light of a candle climbing hesitantly to the room.

Saint Joachim and the Holy Anna tiptoed to the tiny bed of the child and carefully, so as not to waken her, they kissed her little red face. "Our little angel," said father, but the tickling of his beard made the child hit at the flies, and then father and mother turned into their own room.

"She is a little angel," mother said quietly while she pulled back the blankets. "She plays and romps like a kitten, she laughs and is happy as a bird, and she can look so deeply into your eyes as if to say: 'Mother, I do love to see you.' "

"Whatever may the Lord have planned for this child?," mused Joachim.

T his is the beginning of Vandersteene's unpublished story of the life of Mary.[1] Naive, perhaps, showing a strikingly solid peasant lifestyle. What distinguishes it is that he completely transformed Mary into a poor, blond-headed Flemish maiden, and one who lived not next door, but in the Vandersteene household. From the tiptoeing parents to the climbing candle and the single-minded piety, we are really

---

Notes to this chapter are on pp. 36-37.

glimpsing life in the Vandersteene home. Roger was the first of 13 children to fill this home.

George Vandersteene was a horticulturalist, who cultivated a small garden and had a hothouse business in tiny Marke, next door to the town of Kortrijk. Kortrijk (written as Coutrai in French atlases) sits in the rolling countryside in the southern part of West Flanders. The area is at the intersection of sandy and loam agricultural land types and is regarded as good farming country, but the median size of the farms, at least at the time of the 1930 census, was less than 2.47 acres.[2] The Vandersteene nursery business centred around flowers, vegetables and potted plants.

Kortrijk is also rich in Flemish history; the area was the scene of the famous Battle of the Golden Spurs where local Flemish militiamen fought and defeated the troops of Philip the Fair of France on 11 July 1302. Flanders became independent because of the victory, and there was considerable pride that the commoners had prevailed.[3] George and his family thus lived and worked in a region that melded together the honest work ethic of farming life with the sense of Flemish history and tradition.

George was a blunt, hard-working man. The business was passed down to him from his father, and while it supported his growing family, household affairs for him always seemed to be marginal. Years later, family and friends would note that Julia Vandersteene was the soul of the operation; she was pleasant, organized and competent, and was well liked by the community. What George lacked, Julia made up for abundantly. But George did have a real botanist's heart. He loved plants and the soil, and bequeathed the joy he found in the science of horticulture to his children, particularly to Roger, whom he hoped would take over his business. The soil was heavy in Marke, requiring constant manure and fertilizing; it was also difficult to maintain, so George spent all his time outdoors attending to the gardening. He had little time to spend in the activities of his multiplying brood.

Julia's hand on the family was generally very strong, and over Roger exceptional. For the first six years of his life Roger was very sickly, and she hovered over him, lavishing her generous spirit on his tousled red head. She took every precaution for her son's chronic lung problems: Roger was dressed in blue and white for those first years because blue and white were the colours of the Virgin. Partly because he was her firstborn, partly because she felt him to have a special gift, Julia protected him from the demands of George, or the accusations of the other children. A very devoted relationship grew between them. Roger almost reverenced her; he had what was called a "holy devotion" to her. Although she never permitted him to see her breast-feeding, she and Roger had a very affectionate relationship, and they shared the joy of newly arrived children together. Indeed, all the children arrived and flourished in a vigorously pious household. Mindful of a nineteenth-century priest, Gezelle, who wrote a Flemish poem of a child learning to ask for the sign of the cross on his head before bed-time even before he learned to talk, Julia and George used the tradition. Hence every morning, the little ones were given a benediction with the sign on their foreheads, and the last touch they received at night was the cross on their forehead. Years later Roger would recall to his fellow priest Paul Hernou that the children would be so upset they could not sleep if father was angry at them and did not give them the sign of the cross before bed.

The children came like clockwork: Etienne, Anaïs, Jaak, Trees, Willy, Walter, Wilfried, Renaat, Jos, Mietje, Eric and Johan, and the house re-sounded to their laughter and pranks. When the children grew, Julia insisted that they stay close to home; she objected to the children visit-ing other families and playing in other yards. Even years later Roger's brothers and sisters would recall the turmoil in the yard, when 20 to 30 children would be playing and shouting. Roger honoured that time in his story of Mary's early life:

> About five years later, little Maria was sitting on a wooden bench in father's garden, amid her tiny girlfriends, tired out from playing. Mother did not like to see her children wandering in the streets, and so the children from the streets wandered in mother's house and garden. Father was a gardener, and in his garden all the furnishings of a chidren's paradise could be found: lots of space, a swing, a wooden bench, grass, fine, loose earth and as much water as you could ever want. Ruth was still swinging a bit, her skirts flattening like flags around her thin legs. Those legs! They were black with dirt, and the hands, the faces! They shone with the fun of it all, while the long braids came down from the playing.
>
> "Maria, come along it's time."
>
> "Mother calls," said Maria, "Goodbye Suzie, Lia, Ruth, good-night everyone!"
>
> "I'll have to give you a good scrubbing, " said mother, "You're black from the top of your head, and tomorrow is Sunday!"
>
> The cool water quickly rinsed away the dust and dirt in the metal tub, and soon little Maria was sitting on a chair in her nightgown, while her mother dried her brown legs.

An interesting sidelight to the Vandersteene family is provided by Fr. Césare Mariman, O.M.I., fellow countryman and northern Alberta missionary. He tells a story widely known as part of the "Vandersteene lore." When Roger was about seven, he and Etienne were chagrined that a neighbouring lady had given birth to a boy, and there was no evidence that they, too, would have another brother. Consequently, they decided to go to the nearby River Lys (also known as the Leie), to look for the children boat. There is a local legend that children arrive in the area via a special boat that plies the river. Every time the boys went to the river, someone would tell them that the children's boat would arrive at night, so they decided there was not much hope to get a baby boy directly. However, they did hear that doctors could go and get babies from the boat. So the young Vandersteenes approached the back door of the doctor's office. They carefully removed their little caps when the doctor came to the door.

"Please, Mr. Doctor, you brought a little baby to our neighbours, and we, too, would like one little brother."

"Well," said the doctor, "I will see whether I can serve you," and he took out his little notebook. "Dear, dear, I have quite a few who have asked for a little baby." He diligently read through his notes.

"Perhaps I can delay this lady; she is not very fond of children, so I will postpone her. Maybe I could put your mother there. Yes I will serve you soon. It will not be very long."

"Thank you, Mr. Doctor," said the boys, and as they turned to go, they said, "We are not going to tell our mother; it must be a surprise."

Some time later the doctor was riding his bicycle past the school grounds, and he called Roger over to the fence. "Roger, you have a little brother," he announced.

Roger related how the boys tore home after school and said to their mother, "We knew it, but we didn't want to tell you, because we wanted it to be a surprise for you!"

Such moments endeared Roger to his mother. In turn she spent the best of her short life nurturing and building a pleasant homelife. Christmas was a wonderful time. Neighbours dropped by at all times, and there was always a place and a drink for them at the kitchen table. The house was filled with the songs and smells of the season. Flemish cooking, cakes and special little liturgies of making the crèche for the baby Jesus were highlights of the time. The texture of such a homelife is still felt among the brothers and sisters today.

Despite Roger's fragile health, his mother's ministrations and the great attention of his godmother and paternal grandmother Mietje (Julia Maria Kerkhove) helped him flourish. He assumed the role of the elder brother, with all the authority that implied in the traditional Flemish family. It is here that he learned a skill that would stand him in good stead: to direct conversation so that the littlest could participate. As number one son, he became very confident of his place in the family, and his place in his mother's heart, but he learned the discipline that comes with making each person part of the whole. He also learned the value of solidarity of the family and each member's importance for the common good. He told stories to the younger ones at their level, providing them with a sense of belonging and stability. His warm concern for his tiny siblings would be remembered long afterwards.

But the family faced an even greater challenge to their security than the rapidly growing family. They had again to contemplate the terror of the German armies. George well remembered the disruption and anguish that had come with the first assault from the German army; on 4 August 1914, having been rebuffed in its request for free passage across Belgium to attack France, Germany invaded the country. Announcing that "Necessity knows no law," the Germans decided to strike before Belgium and France could properly respond, hoping thereby to secure their rear line for when they eventually would have to turn towards the Russian army. Belgium attracted such a move because it had ample roads, streets and lanes, certainly sufficient to move a million men. When the Germans finally attacked they brought massive 12-cm howitzers, of a size previously unknown, and the light Belgian forces were driven from Liège, Namur and Antwerp. Then began the race for the sea by the remaining elements of the army. Halting at the Ijzer river, the Belgians flooded the low-lying land, with the result that the Germans constantly but unsuccessfully tried to break through.[4] But they turned aside and ploughed through West Flanders. The stories of the valiant stand taken by Flemish soldiers, some of whom had to serve under French-speaking officers who refused to speak their language or to acknowledge their cultural differences, sparked a Flemish backlash, known as the Front Movement. This independence movement was to have a dramatic effect on Roger and his perception of the world.

All these memories swirled around Flanders with the new invasion of the homeland. On 10 May 1940 the German army with its speedy tanks swept around Belgium. The speed and efficiency of the army was in marked contrast with the earlier war. The Belgian forces offered what resistance they could, but the Germans roared around the Belgian army with amazing precision, heading for the French coast near Dunkirk. The Belgian army was surrounded and had to surrender. It was during this period that a touching story from the Vandersteene family was told. The Germans and Belgian forces were fighting almost daily in the region. Shells and artillery hit Marke. The house rocked from nearby explosions. Belgian soldiers fought and died in the streets.

George hustled his little family to the basement whenever the fighting erupted, hoping they would be safe even if the upper part of the house collapsed from the shelling. The impact on the family was traumatic. Trees was terrified. With the shelling she began screaming and running back and forth, trying to get away. Julia comforted her with prayers and admonitions that the statue of the Virgin Mary was right there in the house. This was of small consolation to Trees. She was not even mollified when they took the statue to the cellar and set her up in one corner.

"Maybe she'll run away like I want to do right now," said Trees sobbing.

"No, no, she won't," said mother. "Look! We'll tie her down right here." So saying she tied a rope around the statue and fastened it to the table. Trees, calmed that the Mother of God was firmly fixed, relaxed. Eventually, half-convinced, she said, "There will be no danger now."

Roger was an inveterate story-teller, and particularly liked to tell stories about his family, especially his father. George liked his beer, and felt that one of the strengths of the Flemish people was their breweries. Roger later was to jokingly comment that he never knew what water tasted like. One time, while accompanying his father, the neighbours gave the boy gin instead of water. They really wanted to see how much he could drink and still get home. Roger left in a very wobbly state; when he arrived home, his mother was astonished to see his nose bloody and his head scratched. "Whatever happened to you? You little rascal, have you been fighting again?" she chided. "Mother," said Roger, "I walked between two poles, but I didn't see the third in front of me, and it flattened my nose," explained the obviously tipsy boy.

Roger had a far less pleasant relationship with his father. George worked hard, and expected everyone to work hard too. He was less sympathetic than Julia to his son's fragile health. As his son grew, George's personality had more and more effect on him. George was an oppositional character; he often took a position just to play the devil's advocate. Cantankerous, moody, and in some ways a very weak man, he openly chided Roger on his contribution to the family. He was an ardent Flanders nationalist, however, so the two did agree on some fundamentals. Later, during Roger's teens, George espoused a pro-German approach, only to switch it when it became evident that Roger would also move in that direction. The two clashed on several levels of their personalities.

At the same time, George suffered from criticism for his large family. The most voluble foe was Julia's brother-in-law Joseph, who seemed to be able to rile George at the drop of a hat. Joseph caustically asked George how he was going to feed so many children. He saw his sister-in-law's health slowly deteriorate under the flood of children. Later he was to scathingly comment that, with the beginning of the Second World War appearing on the horizon, "We shall see who starves first, you with 13 children or me with two!" George was continually on the run, and his business suffered from the constant disruption caused by local politics and his own inability to organize properly. He was willing to turn over the centre of the family life to his wife, who, although frequently sick or pregnant, still maintained a positive outlook on life. George more and more took solace in alcohol.

Like all active boys, Roger found ways to be troublesome. Family stories relate how on one occasion Roger and his brothers went on a frog hunt. Once the house was settled down for the night, the girls came screaming out of their room; somehow the frogs had ended up in their beds. Early on he developed a keen sense of humour, and he was well known for being a practical joker, as the priests in secondary school were to learn. But it is the symbolic refusal to hold the flag that his brothers and sisters remember most.

The event was the one hundredth anniversary of the founding of Belgium, celebrated in May 1926. Roger was in primary school at the School of St. Martens Latem in Marke, and, along with his schoolmates, was given a Belgian flag to wave when the visiting dignitaries from Brussels came on the platform. Primed ahead of time to hold it out front and to wave it with vigour, Roger refused. Instead he held it behind him. His mother was very upset, as were the bishops. When scolded about his actions, Roger was adamant: "They won't let me speak Flemish, so why should I wave their flag?" In fact, even when Roger knew French, he refused to speak it. The flag incident was the harbinger of future attitudes.

Roger was a diligently religious boy, attending church twice on Sundays, especially since his mother stressed the gift of health that the Virgin had given him. In 1925, at the age of seven, he received his First Communion. At age 11, he had his solemn communion, and in 1930 he was confirmed. After finishing his primary education, he went in June 1931 to the College of St. Amand in Kortrijk for his secondary studies. The curriculum of the time was the wide-ranging classical model, incorporating the traditional subjects like religion, history, geography, mathematics, biology and chemistry as well as poetry and rhetoric. In the fine arts, he studied music and drawing. Besides the classical languages of Greek and Latin, he was trained in modern Dutch / Flemish, French, German and English.

He was a clever student, always among the leaders in the class and usually first. It was here he came in contact with the great nationalist writers of the previous century, especially the priest and poet Gezelle. He was particularly attracted to the poets, and, although he did not write poetry at the time, many of the themes he would later explore arose from his study.

His educational progress was hampered, however, by his ill health. Two years into his training his health collapsed and his parents were forced to keep him home. His lungs filled with phlegm, and they feared that he would die of tuberculosis. Although expensive, they arranged for him to receive gold injections every week, the current cure for his condition. Slowly, under the careful nurturing of his mother and family, Roger came around. He lost a year of schooling, and perhaps even worse, the illness left him with weakened lungs. But he was able to return to school for the final two years and finish his secondary studies. The years from 1930 to 1937 deeply affected him. The die was set for his life, too. He decided he would study to become a priest.

His father was livid. His first reaction was blunt: "You want to become a priest. Here's a rope, go hang yourself!" When he calmed down, George rightly pointed out that the family had supported him a great deal in his sicknesses, and that the business required his skills just to keep the family going. Roger knew full well that his mother was not well, and could not provide the long-term strength needed to keep the florist business thriving. Just maintaining the family would require everyone to contribute. Such arguments, however, fell on deaf ears. His choice had the old tradition of large families behind it: the firstborn was always given to the Church. Julia rallied the family around and with a keen eye for shifting attention to unifying activities, suggested they build a new house to accommodate the growing family. Roger agreed, contributing as he could outside his studies. When the house was completed, his mother celebrated his sixteenth birthday and the completion of the house with a present: his first pipe. It was an acknowledgement that she accepted his independence of mind.

Thus, despite his father, Roger accepted the invitation to become a member of the Missionary Oblates of Mary Immaculate (O.M.I.) congregation. As was customary, young priests had a year of novitiate, during which time their religious and moral mettle would be evaluated by the authorities; Vandersteene took one year of novitiate at Korbeek-loo, near Leuven-Louvain. Following this, he moved to the O.M.I. Belgian scholasticate of Velaines, and he took his first vows as an Oblate on 29 September 1938.[5] For two years he studied at Velaines, and was there when the German army invaded in 1940. This prompted the authorities to close the school, and the students were dispersed; Roger returned home. He was drafted into the medical corps of the army, a position he did not immediately take up because of family responsibilities. He spent a few months in the interim at the secondary Holy Heart college in Waregem, where he taught religion and a variety of humanities courses.

Meanwhile the Flemish Oblates started their own seminary at Waregem,[6] and eventually Roger joined them. Despite his earlier weak health and the workload, he plunged into his studies. This section of his training focussed particularly on theology, church dogma, morality and ethics, canon law, church history and catechetics, all considered essential by the Church of the time for missionaries and priests. All subjects with the exception of church history were taught in Latin. It was during this time at Waregem that he finally decided to give himself to the missionary life (29 September 1942).

The Superior at the time was Fr. D. Albers, who was in charge of both Velaines and Waregem from 1938 to 1944. Albers would later remember him as a very "sympathetic young man, a very religious man, that managed to bring together many talents and synthesize them in a beautiful manner."[7]

Life in the college brought many changes. Most noticably, he began the process of withdrawing from his family, a process that he insisted had to be done if he was to follow Jesus' declaration that "He who does not leave father and mother is not of me." Although he could have visitors, he discouraged his family from coming to see him, and he returned home only every six months. This separation was particularly hard on the younger members and his mother. When he was home, she was amazingly rejuvenated; when he left, she slipped back into illness and withdrawal. Financially, the business was suffering, and with war clouds looming, everyone felt great anxiety for the family's future.

If Vandersteene was aware of the strain, he did not let on. He did return home for the birth of the last child, Johan, because he took the young ones from home for a picnic where he organized games and stories until, at the prearranged sign of the white flag in the window, he knew the child had been born and they could return. It was, however, with the birth of the earlier child Jos that his ties to the family became more formal. He agreed to become the godfather for Jos, and the liturgy of baptism set up a special relationship with the boy that was to bear strange fruit many years hence.

In the absence of his family, Roger developed a substitute family: his colleagues in the seminary. Omer Devos, who was killed while serving in Africa, became a lasting friend, and was the subject of this note in a letter to a religious in Belgium many years later:

> Thanks for the memorial card of Omer Devos — Oblate, martyr, neighbour, and one who had helped a great deal in making me an Oblate! Thank God I visited him on my last leave. To be a missionary remains a dangerous undertaking: three of my acquaintances have been murdered . . . one entered a year ahead of me, one a year after, and now Omer, from my own village.[8]

Roger was not of imposing stature, probably just a little more than a metre and a half, but what he lacked in size he made up for in dynamism. His colleagues grew to like him very much. They even consecrated him with a new name, "Steentje," a play on the last phrase of his name, which literally meant "little stone," but which had the endearing notions of being a tough little character along with the irritation of a pebble in one's shoe. The name stuck.

His mischievous nature had something to do with this. Fr. Mariman recalls hearing of Roger organizing his little band of colleagues into a brigade, trading on the "Soldiers of Christ" theme. Roger marched them lock-step into the classroom, where the professor, Rev. Emmanuel De Baenst stared in disbelief.

"So, boys, do you pray to St. Dymphna too?" asked the professor. When the contingent looked confused, he noted: "She's the patron saint of crazy people, who have nervous diseases and are locked up in asylums. You would do well to invoke her so you may not end up losing your minds completely!"[9]

Later, as the war dragged on and the meals became ever more skimpy, Roger and his friends decided to snare a rabbit.[10] Finally they were successful, and with rabbit in hand they went downstairs where the laybrother was working on supper. He agreed to clean it and cook it for the boys. Later the Superior came in, saw the rabbit and told the brother not to prepare it for the students but for the priests. The old brother, realizing this would be a real problem, informed the boys what he had to do. The boys held a council of war. Since there were plenty of cats in the seminary, one of the boys caught and skinned a cat, went to the kitchen and switched the body of the rabbit for that of the cat, but he placed the head of the rabbit with the body of the cat.

The special treat for the priests was bruited about among them, and at supper, they noisily enjoyed the treat. One old priest, however, who had nearly starved during the First World War knew differently. He asked whether any of the priests knew what rabbit ribs looked like, and then, with a suspicious look at the boys, asked them if they knew what the priests had eaten. When the boys confirmed that it was cat, the entire table of priests erupted, vomiting. Later the boys snuck out and roasted the rabbit over a fire. However, since everyone knew the Superior had switched meals to begin with, there were no reprisals.

Steentje's extraordinary intellectual abilities began to come to the fore. His reading and interests ranged widely, from tropical plants and cactii to psychology and Protestant theology. The isolated lifestyle of the seminary seemed to be ideal for him, and he developed sophisticated tastes in music, art and theology. He read deeply in Flemish history, literature and studied extensively Belgium's artistic tradition. Like many Flemings, he developed a deep and abiding reverence for his country's culture, as was common in his day, as a rival to that of the ancient Greeks. His writing skills flourished, and he learned the value of correspondence, a mode of communication that he was to nurture all his life.

While at seminary he met several very talented young men. One such individual was both a musician and an artist, and the story is told of the young musician martialling Roger and some friends to cut down some trees and level a place in the nearby woods so they could hold a concert. The Superior was outraged when he saw the results of this creativity, and was only mollified when the boys told him the concert was to be in celebration of his namesake, St. Paul. Under the influence of several students, including his close friend and artist Stefaan Van Gheluwe, Roger began to flourish as a painter, and, as the Flemings have done since the beginning of time, they formed an association. Really more of a handful of like-minded colleagues, it nevertheless became the basis for artistic expression. The seminary artists' group tried every style — primitivist, symbolist, impressionist, expressionist. Eventually, they became known for an ultra-realist style.[11] A kind of freedom to experiment flooded the young students and painting allowed them to try their hand at just about any kind of representation, including nudes. In a letter to his family at the end of this period, Roger wrote that "Painting is a mirror in which man is God," reflecting the wedding of Flemish landscape and common folk painting with a deep religious piety. The group received permission to leave the seminary for a few days so they could visit with Door Albert Servaes, whose Flemish paintings inspired nationalism among the young artists. The association was also heavily influenced by Constant Permeke, his dark brooding colours setting a sombre, deathlike vigil; Roger's paintings from the period were often dark and meditative. It is also likely that this was the period he came into contact with woodcut art, a form he was to use with religious purpose later in his missionary career, although there is no evidence surviving from that early phase. Art seemed one way of expressing his views without risking subdual by the discipline of the Church.

In other ways Vandersteene was not so fortunate. However loyal he may have been to Flemish causes, they were not shared by the priests and superiors of the school. Mindful that Fr. Cyriel Verschaeve had been the inspiration and driving force in the Front Movement at the Ijzer River in 1918, Roger and his friends agitated for a Flemish identity and Flemish clergy for Flanders. His associates followed the model of Rodenbach's First World War student associations, maintaining political objects, especially in language and cultural rights for Flemish-speaking people. Roger became a leader in the Katholieke Studenten Actie (KSA), the Catholic Student Action group, a religiously oriented association lobbying for Flemish language and culture.[12] During the interwar period, the Catholic hierarchy had treated the nationalism of the Flemish youth with restrained disdain; they regarded these nationalist urgings as activities threatening to the security of the state, and destructive for the Catholic Party, which had the overwhelming support of the Catholic hierarchy. Moreover, as part of the favoured French-speaking group, the priesthood was not about to make amends for the demographics; the hierarchy did little to spur opportunities for Flemings, knowing the advanced education required and the social-economic class to which most Flemish-speaking people belonged. In short, the Flemish people were too poor and too poorly educated to be able to meet the demands of the priesthood.

But if the Church hierarchy was slow to react, the political situation was rendering the view outmoded. As early as 1940 the Flemish National League (Vlaams Nationaal Verbond — VNV), the primary organization dedicated to Flemish concerns, believed that a new European order was coming into existence under Hitler and the Nazis, and members agitated for some kind of accommodation with the Germans to secure Flemish independence.[13] Roger and his friends seesawed dramatically between being Belgian patriotists, Flemish nationalists and/or socialists dedicated to the benefit of the ordinary citizen; they scrambled to adjust themselves to the führer's power. Dominican J. Callewaert, a well-respected member of the hierarchy, however, took a different tack. He argued that the VNV should back away from so close an association with the dreams of the Third Reich, and by 1943, he was writing openly against collaboration. The pro-collaborationist group, known as DeVlag, and famous for the "Black Shirts" uniform reminiscent of the Nazi SS, actively began to search out resistance fighters, and the result was the infamous street fights of the "blacks" and the "whites." The Church was split over the issue; some priests like the Flemish activist Verschaeve openly supported the notion of Flemings and Walloons in separate and independent states within a greater German empire. Even some Walloons had supported the collaborationist position. But the hierarchy in Flanders had desperately tried to contain the radical elements on both sides, arguing that neither socialism nor Nazism had any place for the Church in its scheme of things and that there was no evidence that the führer would support true independence anyway.

During this period Vandersteene underwent the various orders leading to priesthood: first tonsure[14] on 5 June 1941, minor orders for priesthood in Tournai on 12 July 1941 (by Bishop L. Delmotte), final minor orders 20 December 1941 in Brugge under Bishop Lamiroy, sub-diaconate in Waregem 19 July 1942 and diaconate 19 December 1942 in Brugge. Bishop A. Clabaut conferred on him the order of priesthood on 11 July 1943 at his home church in Kortrijk.

He had for some time been inspired to emulate the life of Fr. Damien de Veuster (1840-89) who worked among the lepers with great dedication and extreme personal cost, but he also wanted to dedicate his life to the most abject mission station. He wanted to follow the public image of the toughest Oblate missionary to the *nth* degree, and he ardently believed in de Mazenod's idealism of high-level training in order to serve among the poorest. Among missionaries, the posting to the Arctic was regarded as the most difficult. Roger applied to the Superior of the Oblates in Rome to serve among the Eskimos. He read everything he could get his hands on. The French Oblates published *Amidst Ice and Snow*, a book that dramatized the life of missionaries working among the people in the north of Canada, and Fr. Mariman, writing in the local missionary magazine *Flemish Echoes*, had suggested that there were linguistic connections between Beaver, Chipewyan, Slavey and Flemish. Whether true or not, the possibility intrigued Roger. Later, following the war, Fr. Mariman had returned home on furlough and had lectured in the churches around Kortrijk about his missions. He had even shown some primitive black-and-white slides of the missions in Alberta. Roger was excited that the Indians still travelled with dogteams, and that one needed snowshoes. Mariman recounts that Roger was "happy to hear that the Indians in the south still wore head-dresses with feathers, but he was also glad to hear that the Indians in the north were too poor to dress this way."[15] It appears, however, that Fr. Mariman had stretched the facts somewhat, since the main reason for the variation in dress was cultural difference. On 29 October 1945, for whatever reasons, Rome replied by assigning Vandersteene to the Vicariate of Grouard in northwestern Alberta. Despite Mariman's positive propaganda, Roger was despondent. He wanted the far north.

There was little possibility of him going immediately anyway. Canada had very stringent immigration rules during the war, and there were few opportunities to travel to North America. All missionaries needed the approval of the bishop under whom they would serve, because the government of Canada would not approve a visa unless the Church agreed to be responsible for the missionaries' expenses. All of this took time. Roger had been assigned to Sacred Heart College in Waregem as a professor; Sacred Heart was a juniorate school originally church-sponsored for training boys who eventually desired to be missionaries and priests, but it had fallen on hard times. Few young men wanted to do this any more. The school became a general public school, albeit under Catholic control. Roger taught languages and pastoral studies for those who were still committed to serving the Flemish church. At the same time, he taught those youngsters whose goals were more secular: doctors, accountants and teachers.

The times were unsettling. He made a point of going on the pilgrimage to the Ijzer site, spending time at the nationalist shrine even though his superiors were not in favour of it. When he stood at the front of the shrine, he meditated for quite some time, and often criticized the young people who ran around, laughing and shouting. He thought it a sacred place, and he told them they should be serious. His pro-Flemish politics inevitably placed him in the pro-German camp. The policy of the Church was to keep French-speaking Oblates in Belgium but to encourage the Flemish-speaking priests to move elsewhere, and he realized that his loyalty to Flemish nationalism was working against any long-term service to his beloved Flanders in the Church. During the spring of 1945, as the war wore on and he awaited news of his missionary posting, Vandersteene became known as the "Priest with the Black Heart," especially among those who eschewed any hint of collaboration. His father attacked his politics and continued his opposition to his choice of career. Even though George had somewhat relented from his

earlier castigation of Roger for going into the priesthood (he did fund
the purchase of his cassock and participated in the party at his ordination), he made every effort to support those in the family, like Etienne,
who wanted Roger to give up the missionary life, at least for the time
being and take a church in Flanders. Business was poor, Julia was not
well and the additional funds would have greatly helped the family.
Roger refused.

Activist politics fitted his temperament. He relished the resistance of
people like his father, who appeared to project a solid front against
him. He throve in that environment. But it would prove to have a bitter
aftertaste. In 1940, Etienne was called up to the Belgian army, to be sent
to France to fight against the German army. Etienne refused to go. After the victory of the Allies, the collaborationists were hounded on
every front. Etienne ended up in jail. Suddenly everyone had been a
resister, all except, of course, Roger and his friends. Many of them were
thrown in jail. Roger took the shift in fortune in stride and began working with those who were discriminated against for alleged "collaboration," sometimes in ways that could have landed him in jail himself.
One day he appeared in court on behalf of some of his friends accused
of collaboration. When the court case was complete, Roger hurried
from the building, forgetting his black satchel. A court official ran after
him, "Father, Father, you've forgotten your bag." Luckily the official
had not looked inside. Roger had 15 false passports in the bag. He
dressed a woman as a priest in order to get her through anti-collabora-
tionist lines, but he realized when they were almost at the lines that he
had forgotten about the woman's rings. Quickly he signalled to her to
cover her hands, and they passed through without difficulty. At other
times, he represented himself as an ordinary citizen who wanted to
visit the collaborationists in prison so he could taunt them, only to
bring them food. He also hid people in his room until searchers were
gone. One day he barred the doorway of an artist's house when it was
beseiged by irate anti-collaborationists. "You'll have to go over my
dead body!" he chided them, as he stared them down. His family and
friends feared for his safety, and, especially with the mood immediately after liberation, they anticipated that he would run afoul of the
government with his well-known support of those accused of collaboration. Mariman linked Vandersteene's activist politics with his desire
to get quickly out of Belgium after the war was over, and he recounted
the story circulating of how Roger had even tried to hire a fishing boat
to take him to North America without a visa, a doubtful legend at best.

Early in December 1945, Archbishop H. Routhier from the archdiocese in MacLennan wrote to him assigning him his position in Grouard

and welcoming him to take up his duties. Roger answered on 29 December 1945 that he would come as soon as he could arrange passage and tie up family affairs. Roger planned to leave as soon as he completed his teaching for the year in June, and thus began finishing off his activities in Flanders. He immediately began reducing the amount of clothes he wore, so that he would toughen his resistance to the cold. His mother doubled her prayers on hearing this, since she was sure he would die of pneumonia before he had a chance to go to Canada. As is traditional, the family threw a big farewell party for him, inviting his friends and acquaintances from his college days, and supporting him while he preached his farewell sermon in the cathedral in Kortrijk. So grand was the celebration that Roger later wrote to a friend that these traditional sendoffs "may well be the real reason for Flemish vocations to the Oblates and other religious congregations." He was set to take a boat from Antwerp on his birthday, 15 June 1946. Then tragedy struck. He was informed just before boarding that Julia had died of a heart attack at the age of 49 on 14 June 1946.

The family was dumbstruck. The centre was gone. George did not know how to face the future alone. He turned to drink. Business failed. The children feared for their future, especially Eric and Mietje, who now had to look to the older children for their care. Roger remained unmoved in his resolve to leave. His stubbornness was beyond his family. They pointed out that he could work out his priestly calling just as ably among the common peasants of Flanders if he wished. That way he could be nearby to help the family over this critical moment. Some local priests thought his dedication to the missions misplaced, a result of Oblate propaganda to paint missions as incredibly difficult, appealing to the heroic Flemish ideal. They sided with the family against Roger. Even the Oblates thought him a touch on the enthusiastic side. After all, under the circumstances, they were willing to grant him up to six months relief for family affairs before he had to leave. Roger rejected all options.

Besides, he felt he had been away from the family situation too long to do much good. Legitimately he pointed out that he could not cook and take over his mother's position. Anaïs had more and more been doing these duties, and quite effectively. What he had not counted on was Anaïs' marriage, which took place the same year. He had secretly hoped that she would put off her marriage, perhaps indefinitely, so that she could look after the family. He reasoned that a quick departure would force her to chose that option. He argued that he did not see how he, a bachelor, could do much for the family anyway. In so doing, he ignored the fact that, as the eldest, it was his responsibility in Flemish culture to take care of the family. The family was proud and very reluctant to ask neighbours and relatives for assistance. Roger opted to read the situation in a purely religious manner: if you do not give up mother and family, you are not of me. The bitterness is still to be felt among the family.

Early in September, he returned to the port, embarking on a ship bound for America.

Notes

1 The text was part of Vandersteene's files after his death; this portion was translated by Elly Englefield of Edmonton, with minor modifications by the author. I have been unable to trace the whereabouts of the original, although it may well be in Flanders.
2 E.G. Misner, "The Agriculture of Belgium," in Goris, ed., *Belgium*, pp. 148, 156-60.
3 The Flemish commoners revolted against their French feudal lords and murdered several French or pro-French lords. Philip sent a cavalry composed primarily of nobles, whose accoutrements were richly ornamented, including, it is said, gold spurs on their boots. Unfortunately their mounts were unable to move in Flanders' mud. Contemporary Flemish nationalists delight that the story seldom seems to be included in French histories. I owe it to Fr. Charles N. Deharveng, O.M.I.
4 See George Theunis, "In the First World War," in Goris, ed., *Belgium*, pp. 53-65.
5 This information comes in a personal note (May 1994) from Fr. Charles Deharveng, who was one year ahead of Vandersteene in his studies.
6 Fr. Deharveng, whose mother was Flemish and father Walloon, reports that his grandfather, great-uncle and two uncles on his mother's side were French-speaking but had strong Flemish roots. Indeed, the family was bilingual. He notes that the Flemish-speaking Catholic clergy were at the forefront of an "avant garde" minority who used the old motto of "Our language, our faith"; he draws parallels between them and the French Canadians in Western Canada in the last century and their similar rallying cry: "Notre langue, notre foi" (personal note, May 1994).
7 Personal testimony at the time of Vandersteene's death.
8 From Roger Vandersteene, *Wanneer gij uw ogen op God gericht houdt: Brieven aan een religieuze* (Kortrijk, Belgium: De Riemaeker pvba, 1977), chap. 29, Garden River, 9/5/75, pp. 91-92.
9 St. Dymphna was an Irish maiden whose father persecuted her because of her faith. She fled to Flanders, where she was martyred at Mol, in the province of Antwerp. According to Mariman, she was invoked "against mental sicknesses, nervous breakdowns, and plain crazy behaviour, most probably because her own father acted foolishly toward her because she wanted to keep her virginity" (from a note received on 22 July 1978).
10 The veracity of this story is not beyond doubt. Fr. Mariman said he heard it told of Vandersteene, but Fr. Deharveng said he had heard the same story when he was in school about students during the First World War. If not precisely true about Vandersteene, the application of it to him and his friends still indicates the kind of impressions they made.
11 Fr. Deharveng, note, May 1994.
12 The KSA in the province of West Flanders was created through the work of the charismatic teaching-priest Karel Dubois (1895-1956) who toured the colleges and challenged the students to form KSA groups. Part of their modus operandi was to develop entertainment in the evenings that would promote the idea of "Flanders for Christ," a concept based on both the Holy See's call to action and Flemish nationalism. It was also developed as an alternative to the more radical group known as Het

Katholiek Vlaams Studentenverband (AKVS—The Catholic Flemish League of Students) who organized meetings and cultural events promoting Flemish consciousness. The AKVS collided head-on with the Belgian Episcopate, which was largely French, and were condemned by them. Sympathizers, both students and priests, were suspended. Beginning in 1928, each diocese started its own KSA movement in order to keep students from joining AKVS (personal note from Eric Calenbier, a current leader in KSA, in Brugge, 4 March 1996). One measure of the depth of Flemish-speaking Catholic priests' commitment to Flemish language and culture is their policy in the Congo; they established schools with Flemish as the official language (personal note, Fr. Deharveng, May 1994).

13 There are now revisionist interpretations of the role King Leopold played with regard to the Nazis. Eminent historian Albert De Jonghe, in several interviews with Gaston Durnez, argues that when King Leopold went to "talk" with Hitler on 19 November 1940 in Berchtesgaden, he went "at his own invitation" and not "under force" as the King had originally said. De Jonghe maintains that he has evidence to prove that the King went over the line between passive resistance to collaboration. See *De Standaard*, November 1990, Groot-Bijgaarden, Belgium, published as a series throughout the month. Fr. Deharveng for one does not accept this revisionist view, and affirms that the King had absolutely no interest in furthering Nazi claims; moreover, he believes that most Belgians, both Flemish and Walloon, remained steadfastly royalist, from the time when the revisionist theories were first propounded (personal note, May 1994). For a recent evaluation of collaboration, including an analysis of the differences between seeing the Third Reich as a military force and as a racial-ideological goal, see Gerhard Hirschfeld, *Nazi Rule and Dutch Collaboration*, translated by Louise Willmot (Oxford: Berg Publishers, 1988). For an earlier work of significance see J.-A. Goris, ed., *Belgium under Occupation* (New York: Belgium Government Information Centre, 1947).

14 First tonsure, according to Roman canon law, was the ritual by which a man is set apart from the laity. He was, by that rite, enrolled as a cleric in his diocese. It was the first step towards ordination and took place after theological studies began. The practice was abolished in 1972 by Pope Paul VI.

15 Personal interview, 20 July 1978.

Three

Grouard before Vandersteene: Cree, Catholic, Canadian

> This is a ravaged people. You have to be a Breton, or a Catalan, or from the Alsace, or a Fleming in order to understand them, to love them, and to be a missionary here.
> — Rogier Vandersteene to Joris Fenaux

R oger Vandersteene apparently left Marke believing that he was to work among isolated aboriginals whose culture and language he had to learn as the Oblates had done for hundreds of years. He brought with him expectations that the reality he would encounter in Alberta would be relatively unitary, that is, a *Cree* culture basically unmediated by either Church or Canadian elements. That is the ideology one finds in his first published response to his labour, in his book *Wabasca*.[1]

> I just want to tell you about my own share in the great missionary offensive. To be a scout in a no man's land, who struggles through the skirmishes before a major frontal attack; whose victories and defeats will be absorbed by that front, but who feels the heavy responsibility that each shot does not just strengthen our front or weaken the enemy, but that each shot can give life. Eternal life.

He would later wince at this as hopelessly romantic.[2] Indeed, he refused to have the book published in English. Yet, even when he came to realize how complicated Cree culture was, and how riddled it was with modern elements, there remained a pre-contact shadow, a haunting conviction of an original Cree tradition. A Canada-as-no-man's-land notion framed their wildness, the vastness a cipher of unknownness in his mission. This certainly fits well with the precontact-postcontact model that many, including not a few scholars of aboriginal culture from social science disciplines, have assumed. It still imbues popular culture in Canada, and certainly enlivens past travel tales: Julian Ralph, intrepid traveller from the United States towards

---

Notes to this chapter are on pp. 78-85.

the end of the nineteenth century would catch it perfectly: Hudson's Bay Company posts flew the flag with "HBC" emblazoned on the field. Old hunters said the initials stood for "Here before Christ."[3] A fine phrase to titillate the good folks back in New York.

It is now evident that the model is inadequate, or as Fisher more strongly puts it, "spurious."[4] Vandersteene, perhaps unconsciously, as we shall see, eventually grew beyond it. One reason that he and others found it a difficult process from which to escape may be the Euro-American romance with origins. Among students of aboriginal peoples in the past, however, it has formed the foundation for a whole plethora of understandings, from the nature of early religions to acculturation ideology.[5] Admittedly it is a simple and easy model. But the notion that religious traditions can be understood as serial worlds along a continuum masks their more proper meaning, which might better be described as converging streams of various colours. This notion stresses the merging and jostling that goes on, with new hues and shades the result. Unfortunately we are never able to examine the "original" colours, because the merging has been going on for some time, and we have no reliable description of the "original" colours.

Moreover, we must ask how was it possible, after more than a century of the Church working among the Cree, even after the internationally famous pioneer missionary Fr. Albert Lacombe (to name only one — see below, p. 67) had been known to labour among them, could young Vandersteene hope for "true" Cree tradition to be still evident? The easiest and least profitable position would be to dismiss him as a dreamer. There are a few who think that. Could he have been just composing a propaganda piece in *Wabasca* for the folks back home? A few of his Canadian Catholic colleagues tend to this interpretation. Would this clever man have been that duplicitous? It's possible, but still doubtful. Perhaps something more important was going on. The Cree traditions he did encounter were real enough. He just thought, in true nostalgic style, that getting back to the original would allow him to build the proper structure; it is the "proper" that is the key. What he found was a people who had been in contact with European culture for over 200 years and who did not seem any closer to participating in the religious values of that culture. Christ had to be made to relate to those religious values or no "proper" structure could ever be built.

The very fact that he was able to find an alternate tradition would seem to indicate that Cree tradition persisted. Yet even if one were to take a thoroughly conservative view about Cree culture, could it still be argued that it was exactly the same? Surely what Cree culture meant would be different because of its modifications in the Canadian religious environment. Not even the most dewy-eyed romanticist could ignore that fact, and Vandersteene was not dewy-eyed. So something else was at work in this clever young priest. In order to understand what he saw, we have to note what was available to him when he came to Alberta in 1946. And we must situate that world in its Cree, and Catholic-Canadian context.

The Cree People

Cree History: A Sketch

Just who were the Cree among whom Vandersteene lived and worked? The little communities he served had, themselves, been part of several surges from the eastern regions of Canada whose migrations patterns are still a matter of some debate.[6] Hlady gathered what was known in an article in 1960, and basically says that the Cree were the first aboriginal group encountered by a party from the fort at the Nelson and Hayes Rivers at Hudson's Bay in 1682. Subsequently they were found at various rendezvous across what is now Saskatchewan and into Alberta. He places the first documented date of Cree settlement in Alberta between 1725 and 1760.[7] Ray suggests that the Cree and their allies the Assiniboine had been linked to the "Ottawa-Indian-French trading network," and that they were the most important suppliers of furs during the mid-1600s.[8] The Cree and Assiniboine,[9] along with the Ojibwa, waged war against the Sioux using the guns they received from York Factory. It has been conventional wisdom since the time of Mackenzie[10] that the Cree-Assiniboine alliance gave them a virtual headlock on all trade throughout the region during the eighteenth century, because this is what motivated their movement west.

Russell breaks completely with this theory, saying Mackenzie's contemporaries and writers since then have misinterpreted his words. He argues that small groups of Cree were in the west before the establishment of the Hudson's Bay Company post at York Factory, and that throughout the 1700s they appeared to live at peace with their neighbours; it was not until the following century that they began raiding the Blackfoot, etc.[11] Cree history is thus far more stable than had been supposed, and the reference to "Plains Cree" has predisposed us to think that the Cree moved onto the grassland permanently, where the evidence suggests that they have always been a parkland people.[12] When the French tried to break the monopoly of York Factory, the Cree temporarily shifted to the French because they did not have to haul the furs to the Bay. But some of them continued their go-between practice, for they bartered equipment for the furs with tribes who did the trapping.[13] Eventually they tried operating independently, trading with either the French or the English, whichever provided them with the best value. They also pushed back competitors, such as the Chipewyans in the north and the Gros Ventres in the south. Some of them began raiding, especially when resources began drying up in their territory, encroaching on and forcing back with their superior arms the Blackfoot of southern Alberta. Some Cree migrated to the forest in the winter to trap and trade in furs and then lived in the shadow of the trading post in the summer, or moved to the grasslands with the HBC traders where the bison were found; these Cree no longer could claim the resources or the skills to become fur producers. When the Blackfoot finally were able to reach trading posts and replace their bows and arrows with guns, the pushing ceased.

As for the Cree themselves, they currently distinguish either three or four "Cree-speaking peoples," depending upon the sources: all appear to agree that there are Plains, Swamp and Woods Cree. Only some of these three accept a fourth, the Rock Cree.[14] The fact is, however, that even the identity of Cree has come about largely through the impositon of a label for a group of aboriginals who were linguistically related, with whom the French first made contact in New France and who continued to have interaction with the fur trade as it and the HBC began moving west. At the time, these people had distinctive names for themselves, often recorded by the HBC factors, such as "Athapuskow" (Athabascan), "Nahathaway," "Michinipee," etc. The contemporary divisions between the groups are not strictly by dialect. One can find representatives of the n, th, r and y dialects intermixed at various points throughout Canada. Lacombe's dictionary, published in 1874, also lists an l dialect which he says is found among the Cree of Labrador, but which has no impact in the region of our study.[15] Contemporary Manitoba Rock Cree state that one group of Cree usually travelled from Alberta to the Bay regularly,[16] even before contact so that the territory was well known to that group. This would suggest that migration back and forth was a fixture even before the fur trade, and that linguistic mixing must have been familiar. Cree, therefore, served as something like a lingua franca in pre-contact central and western Canada, and must have been the principal language for early western explorers and the development of the fur trade.

By 1763, however, the Cree traders/go-betweens were being bypassed by both Hudson's Bay Company and the Montreal traders because both these trading companies built posts directly within the country of the trappers. Many of the Cree, the entrepreneurial life of the go-between at an end, had no alternative but to turn to the bison on the plains for their provisions. Their westward boundary was established by a treaty with the "Slaves" (probably the Beaver) at the Peace River in 1787, and that effectively ended their migration patterns within Alberta, although there was movement from the east to make up for the devastation by the smallpox epidemic. By the turn of the nineteenth century, they had become increasingly dependent on the trading system for their livelihood and for many of the staples of life; cut out of the system, they had nowhere to go to find the resources they needed to retain their position. With furs drying up, and competition between the companies at an end by 1821, the fur trade moved away from the Cree to the Ojibwa, who knew their region better and could husband the resources. In addition, the Cree suffered from smallpox epidemics, which depleted their numbers, and ultimately led them to settle in areas where they could reach whatever resources were still available, away from the disease. By the mid-1800s the migration patterned-living was at an end, the fur trade only required a minimum number of traders, and the bison were localized to the regions dominated by the Blackfoot people. Once the Hudson's Bay Company began to supply food stocks such as flour and biscuits, they were able to subsist with local trapping, but they no longer had the skills to provide for a wide range of hunting and trapping. Even those who had retained the skills, however, found that the fur-bearing animal resource base had been depleted by the fur trade.

Meanwhile European settlers were flooding in, and governments were anxious to accommodate them. Between 1871 and 1876 all native claims in the central area of grassland, parkland and local woodlands had been extinguished by Treaties 1 through 7. Further to the north, in Wabasca, where Vandersteene first served, a somewhat larger agglomeration of Cree, known as the Bigstone Band, agreed to Treaty 8 in 1899, deeding land to the government in exchange for a reserve, education and other services. In retrospect, the reserves were one way of holding on while they regrouped after the rejection of their fur-trading liaison skills by the fur-trading companies. They were also a way of turning inward, away from people with whom they had little in common, and who regarded them as inferior.

Not all Cree were covered by treaties. In general in the Peace River region (parts of which comprised Vandersteene's Grouard Vicariate), the Cree had adapted to the area by organizing into hunting bands of two to five families, which accommodated themselves to variability by learning to shift from one kind of local food source to another as the resources rose and fell, that is, to fishing, hunting, trapping, gathering and harvesting as the resources allowed. They no longer moved, but used the adaptive and entrepreneurial skills that had been the hallmark of the Cree migration from Hudson's Bay to Alberta. They were adept at utilizing local resources, although the lack of resources tended to keep them regionalized in their small bands. From about 1850 on they no longer met in the traditional summer tribal meetings, perhaps because of the decline of the bison, which had been the basis of the food for the group, but also because of a changed lifestyle and white law: the "sundance" was banned by the federal government. Besides, whites were moving into the region en masse, and they felt safer keeping to themselves in their own little communities.

The terrain and wildlife in the region also fostered the isolation of the Cree communities. The rolling geography is dotted with small lakes, waterways and their tributaries and sloughs.[17] On those areas not cleared for agriculture, dense stands of aspen poplar are to be found, laced with willows and tough prairie grass. Open fields are apt to be dominated by fireweed, a plant that turns blood-red in the summer, and makes a dramatic impact on the landscape. Polar air dominates the weather, and the growing period is scarcely more than three months. The Peace River basin is the staging area for bird migrations throughout North America, so ducks, swans and ptarmigan thrive on the shallow waters, while muskrat, beaver, otter, mink and lynx are the principal furbearers. The most important fish is lake trout, with whitefish providing the locals with nutritious food sources. Rabbits are abundant. The relationship between the small bands and the natural habitat has evolved slowly, and a kind of ecological balance developed between the size of the families and the natural resources from which they drew. The lifestyle was one built on resource supply, and even to today, most small-band diet still retains a connection to the resources available in the streams, lakes, bush and grassland around settlements.

The Athabasca sub-basin region covers some 24,255 square kilometres, slightly larger than the British Isles, so lack of adequate transportation facilities is endemic, including access to the urban areas via automobile. In pre-WWII times movement was confined to the summer months by canoes on the rivers, or wagons and horses on bush trails. Trappers sometimes had dogteams for winter transportation, but they were not universal because of the expense of the animals, the difficulty in obtaining them and the cost of maintenance. Today bush travel in the winter is by skidoo. But at that time, isolated communities like Garden River could only be reached during some times of the year by small plane.

Accessibility has been a contentious issue among northerners, both native and non-native in Alberta. Little Red River, the first site of Vandersteene's missions among a small band of Cree, was moved by the government in the mid-1950s from south of the Athabasca to Fox Lake on the north side, ostensibly to make it easier for government and policing services to serve them, but widely regarded by Cree as an attempt at a land grab by the government for its natural resources. The Hudson's Bay Company still buys furs in the region, and the Alberta Fur Marketing Board is also active.

Nevertheless the size of the region they live in is massive; Cree are in an area whose size militates against easy interaction with whites. But we should not then conclude that Cree are isolationist. In reality the Cree tendency since the advent of European exploration has been interaction, and the current fur trade, even if minuscule in comparison with what it once was, is symbolic of that linkage. This suggests that a complete isolationist position was not and is not consistent with Cree history.

That Haunting Reality: "Original" Cree Tradition

What can be said about Cree religious tradition? If religions, like primary colours, appear as cohesive, they nevertheless have dominant and recessive elements. To return to our metaphor of colours flowing together, we may still determine what primary colours existed even after they have been blended. Clearly, however, we can never hope to precisely recover the "original," if for no other reason than that our sources are never "pure." For example, Diamond Jenness claimed that the Cree had a "weak culture of their own." As a consequence, he supposed them to have acquired their religious customs from the Assiniboine and the Ojibwa; even so he allowed that "most of the Cree societies were more definitely religious than the Assiniboine."[18]

This is probably a misjudgment, since we already know how adaptive the Cree were to white traders and businessmen, and how close they were to the Assiniboine people, so it is better to think that their culture was more adaptive and open than others. In fact, we know that there was a high degree of individualism allowed within the Cree structure, and people from one band could move to another, or new bands could form under the influence of a powerful chief. It appears that they also incorporated aspects from other religions into their own in ways reflecting their own values. Hence the Cree appear to have had a different view of religious boundaries and how these functioned than Jenness conceived. In fact, the tribes appeared to have been vigorous enough and strong enough to integrate outside influences without disrupting socio-religious structures. One could contend that it is precisely the flexible nature of the religious category that allowed the Cree to adapt and integrate outside rituals and symbols. Vital aspects from other peoples were recognized for what they were: powerful. They accepted that the sacred came to them from many directions. In short, religious boundaries were not comprehended in terms of either a tribal, people or a "nation" consciousness. This fact, incidentally, may well have made it easier for Christian missions, since missionaries did not have to worry about the Cree resisting conversion on the grounds that their enemies had become Christian. Such an argument is only found within inter-Christian aboriginal rivalry.[19] The net result of all this is that, since essentialist statements have missed the mark, sometimes badly, very little credibility can be given to declarations about either the character of "original" Cree religious tradition or its evolution.

It does not follow that we can say nothing at all about the shape of Cree religion at the time of contact. We do know that the Cree did share some of the great ceremonies of their neighbours; the key was that their own medicine men had to have received the authorization to put on the ceremonies. They obtained it from spiritual sources, sometimes conceived as non-human persons, or spirit helpers, either through a dream seen at least three times, or through its purchase from someone who owned the rites and transferred the songs and ritual forms through a transfer ceremony. Some of these authorizations concerned public rites, others related to individual achievements. The former constituted the primary ceremonial life of the tribe, while the latter encompassed abilities like healing, medicine provider, war leadership or special teacher. While, in theory, all rituals could be transferred, and could be treated like commodities, in reality, status and spiritual legitimacy functioned behind the scenes. It was part of the legacy of ownership that the medicine man could reject anyone who was not considered properly prepared or spiritually endowed.

Ritual forms graced Cree culture because those forms rested upon interaction with specially endowed entities, in a perpetual movement to engage those "persons." The word for these powers was *manitowok*, usually translated as "many gods"; the word is referred to here as "endowed entities" to signal a shift away from a Western conception of a permanently embodied deity. Very often they constituted only a special quality residing in a sacred object. The movement to engage these powers was seen to be present in all aspects of life, in the bear that gave himself for meat, in the frightful scurry of rabbit from coyote, and submissive behaviour of the dog rolling on its back, or lowering its ears in acknowledgment of power. One could not be neutral in relating to the reality represented by this quality, for it was stuff out of which one's own self was constructed. No matter how ghastly the situation, the fury that raged towards the people was a sign of belonging, cut from the same mysterious cloth as the world around. Even as it raged, it was *their* world, imparting new lessons. The people had to learn how to react to its forces.

There was no natural order apart from the supernatural, nor supernatural from natural. There was no simple dichotomy, as the Europeans would contend. That did not square with reality. The rituals of deliberations around a council fire, the stories passed on in the dead of winter, the passing on of pipes, the songs learned in the sweat lodge, the lessons bestowed upon young girls at puberty, the giving of the dead back to the earth, the token gifts to the *manitokan* (object endowed with sacred power, i.e., a totem pole) by the time-worn hunter in the bush, all were considered sacred, but could be more sacred at one moment than another. Context and human interaction determined how significant the moment was to be perceived. Broken taboos could lessen the sacred, as could inattention, lack of focus or loss of power through disobedience or cowardice. The sacred was not an absolute, unlike the European word, which seems to have no room in it for slippage, nor the possibility it could be terrifying at one moment, ordinary the next.

Ritual speaks through sets of postures and gestures one takes toward this powerful quality; these sets act very much like frames that give an entirely different perspective when adjusted. Rituals might well be changed under the spell of new insights, or by appropriating elements from another band. They could be adjusted, created, revitalized with new visions, new gifts, new powers, new authorities. The ritual "form" belongs to the people, but the "content" depends upon the spiritual life of the owners of the ritual, the participants and their own encounters with the reality. Lest the form be lost, it had to be handed on properly, through the instigation of the guides, that is, the elders, the men and women who had spent a lifetime in contemplating the universe and understanding its moods.

This does not mean, however, that Cree elders' views will always agree. The perspectives from different experiences will likely be contentious or even conflicting. No conceptually logical structure can come out of trying to place such elements together. The logic of one will not always hold in another. Besides, trying to piece things together logically is another way of acting, another kind of ritual, another frame. It is because framing cannot be done in more than a provisional manner that there are limitations to authorities, special talents only for special events, significant little contributions from a wide range of people, a consensus culture.

Given the provisional nature of relating to spiritually endowed entities, the possibility was open for individual accomplishments that were
then honoured as an expression of the corporate being of the Cree
people. Social activity affirming the solidarity of tribal/band/group
consciousness called for the celebratory event, a time of ritually significant Cree cohesion. No gift, whether the ability to steal horses or to
perform the shaking tent healing ceremony could ultimately be validated by the solitary individual's claim. Group approbation gave it
power. Thus ritual, though a gift to the spiritually accomplished,
required an acceptance and validation from the group; there existed
a delicate balance between the spiritually gifted and the receiving
people.

The Cree ceremony drawing the bands together in the late spring
was the great Thunderbird dance (sometimes called sundance, a term
that more justly applies to a similar ceremony among the Sioux and
other Plains people). Hultkrantz calls this dance "a thank-offering to
the Great Spirit for the reawakening of all nature after the silence of
winter." He then affirms that it is a sacred recreation of the world.[20]
But the Cree word for the dance is *piyesiwomowin*, which is literally
thunder dance, underlining the notion that the dance was to the great
Thunderbird, who provided rain, growth and fertility.[21] This powerful
spirit plays an important role in religious beliefs of the Cree in the
Peace River region. Madeleine Sewepagaham related how the Thunderbird tried to carry off her baby while she was canoeing. She shot in
the air, knowing she could not kill the Thunderbird, but hoping to express her reluctance at giving up her child, and the great bird flew
away. Only a few feathers drifted to earth (interview, June 1976). Fr.
Virgilio Baratto related that some Cree children, who have been to
school and know the scientific cause of thunder, still refer to it as the
Thunderbirds beating their wings. There seems to be a general cultural
belief that people have been alone in the bush during thunderstorms
and have been attacked by the Thunderbirds. There is no "theological"
explanation which relates the Thunderbirds to Kisemanitou (usually
translated as Great Spirit or God),[22] although Kisemanitou would seem
to be related to a more general notion of positive fate, personal assistance, health and blessings.

Thus, while Kisemanitou might be understood as the great positive
quality/power behind all that can be encountered in the world, it is
clear the Thunderbird dance was not directly performed in Kisemanitou's honour, even if s/he was invoked during the course of these rites.
Rather, a shaman constructed a small, sweat-lodge type building to
which petitioners came seeking the assistance of the spiritual man for

some personal cause or to validate some vow or offer some votive offering to the spirits. It is true that the shaman could call upon Kisemanitou to help the petitioners, but it was more likely to be his personal
spirit helpers or the other greater-than-human beings, the grandfathers. They were the spiritually endowed entities in the purification
rites.[23]

The main rituals took place in a carefully constructed circular lodge,
whose centre pole, called the medicine pole, was selected with special
ceremonies and propitiation of the spirits. Once cut, the tree could not
touch the ground, since it was held to be the sacred conduit for the
spirit-forces with humans. The lower branches were lopped off, and
the Thunderbird's nest was prepared at the top of the tree, where petitioners and worshippers tied prayer clothes. The tree was then lowered
into the ground, becoming the centre pole for the round lodge. Upright
poles circled the centre pole, about thirty feet back from the pole, in an
off-centred fashion. Cree did not thatch the entire roof of the lodge, as,
for example, was the case among the Blackfoot. Rather, a fairly solid
backdrop, behind the medicine pole, was built against which the elder
and drummers would sit. They faced looking east through an opening
in the circular poles. Within this outer circle and forming a semi-circle
ending next to the medicine pole area was a fence of stakes about four
feet high and tightly woven. During some of the ceremonies, singers
and whistlers crouched behind this fence, standing then crouching in a
pattern of appearing and disappearing during the songs, much like an
animated call-response choir. Men were on the left, women on the
right side of the pole from the perspective of the entrance.

There are strong cosmic meanings reflected in the lodge's symbolic
construction, that is, the four cardinal directions, along with above and
below.[24] The best short description of such a dance by an eyewitness in
a related region to that of Vandersteene is that of Fr. Pierre Moulin,
who related the following to some white women in Wetaskiwin, in January 1928. The ritual took place in Hobbema, not far from Edmonton,
sometime after his arrival in 1903. It is possible that Cree from Peace
River participated.

> Once a year, in the early days of the summer, about the middle of the
> month of June, they celebrated their Sundance, or rather for our Cree,
> the thirst dance. You have heard of it, most probably and perhaps your
> curiosity took you to one of these dances for a few moments, and cer-
> tainly you did not see in it much more than a great celebration, a great
> meeting of Indians. In the olden days—and today, yet to a certain
> extent—it was strictly a religious ceremony; one of extreme penance
> and fasting to make propitiation to the divinity. It was celebrated in
> honour of the Bird of Thunder, to ask also Manito to burst asunder the

clouds and give rain to the people and to the earth. It must have origi-
nated in warmer countries and deserts where the need for water is of extreme necessity. According to their legend, the thunder is the voice of a
bird, of a very white bird. An old man once has seen millions of these
birds in the mountains over a field of snow. They were playing, and at
once rose up in the sky; the noise was thunder and the moving of the air
would kill the audacious who would go near and brave them.

Our Cree, by that ceremony, asked the great spirit Manito, to be preserved of sickness, of sudden death and generally success in hunting or
in war.

From February, they prepared for that dance and sent invitations far
and near. Indians, men and women, had made a kind of vow to join in
the dance. Then when the tent was built with trees and branches, all
those who had promised to join would go there and at the sound of the
drum and tamtams would start to dance. For two nights and three days,
they would dance and dance, stopping only now and then; during that
time, they would keep a very rigorous fast, not being permitted even to
take a mouthful of water, they could only receive the rain in their mouth
if any fell during those days. To make the sacrifice more complete they
give away their possessions: horses, cattle, house, field, garments,
clothes; in old days, they even mutilated their bodies.[25]

Moulin may not have all the details correct, but the form and description is in keeping with Cree ceremonial.[26] There were other collective ceremonies of the Cree people. The Cree in northern Alberta did
not use sweet grass as the purifying element during their rituals as
their southern brothers and Plains tribes; rather they burned *weh-
kamasikan*, a special species of fungus. Traditionally Cree utilized the
calumet or sacred pipe as a central feature of their worship services.
The tobacco carried the prayers of the people to the spirit world, sometimes called the realm of the grandfathers. Once a year, according to
Jenness, a smoke-offering was held to honour Kisemanitou.[27]

At the same time, an aspect of collective ceremonies that has surely
been overlooked by observers is the role of the drum and drumming.
Bewitched by an understanding of ritual acts as discrete and formal ingredients, they may have missed the entire significance of regulated
sound. Yet just about any ritual of any sort will in some way involve
the drum. The drum and its sound relates not just to a certain syncopa-
tion, but to cosmic sound, a concept that affirms that there is a "speaking" tone of the universe as surely as there are noises in the world. The
drum thus speaks, structuring the understanding of the reality in
which humans are submerged. This is the reason why drumming and
singing go together. *Drumming is a ritual form of significant depth and
richness for the Cree and its importance can hardly be overstated.* It is further evidence of a religiosity whose expression was quite different in

form than the Europeans, but surely just as complicated and empowering.[28]

The other great tribal ceremony, focussing more on localized tribal identity, was held in the winter. Designed to beseech the non-human persons to bless and provide animals for trapping, it featured the honouring of the ancestors, who had a key place in the rites in the form of spirit dolls. The ceremonies involved a corporate dinner, at which a place was left for the participation of the dead. Called *wikokewin* (also spelled as *wikkottowin*), it was the centrepiece of the Cree ancestoral spirit belief. The fact that part of the celebration underlines the contiguity of the alive and the dead has important repercussions for our story, because the ceremony became Vandersteene's entrée into Cree life. Since it is very important for his theological understanding, his entire description is translated here:[29]

> I hardly expected to find so many people; my whole parish, out in full strength! As well, many of the Protestant Indians, why there were even people here from Desmarais!
>
> I feared that my arrival might cast a chill over things, but on the contrary, the people seemed flattered, honoured, and comfortable with my presence. I unloaded my contributions [comprising two grouse, three rabbits and five pounds of loaf sugar] from the wagon, and as for the rest, I could do nothing . . . willing hands unhitched my horses and fed them. In the cabin and immediate surroundings, exuberant activity reminded me of an ant-hill. Long rows of perspiring women were busy cooking bannock, that is, bread without yeast, and outside, over several fires, large pots boiled. Full and empty buckets came and went. The sounds of axe-blows all around. Constant crackling of dead branches. Screams of laughter. A crossfire of orders and jokes. Whinnying horses. Whining children. The *wikkottowin* tent rises dignified and calm in the midst of all this tumult. It is shaped like a distended sphere. The walls are covered with different canvas tarpaulins, and at the top, like an ordinary *mikiwap* (tipi), the roof is open, with smoke curling from it.
>
> In front of the tent stands rows of peeled tops of spruce, all painted. Their parallel arrangement forms a triumphal way towards the entrance. Just at the moment when the sun disappears, the signal is given . . . *Ekwa!* and the drum begins to entone, te-tom, te-tom. Each person takes his utensils for the feast, a plate and a cup, and heads for the tent. I am shown to a place at the centre of a half-circle at the back of the tent, like a kind of apse. On the bear-skin spread out before me are pipes, dolls, drums, and small medicine-bundles.

On my right, the old men crouched on bear skins, and on my left, the drummers immediately began to tune up their drums by warming them at the fire. All along the sides right to the doorway was a swarm of men, women and children, each jostling for an advantageous spot on the thick carpet of spruce branches. There must be almost 250 people in this tent; I have never seen so many Indians gathered at one place before.

The sacred fire sits right in front of me. Beyond the fire stands a thin *manitokkan* (totem pole), decorated with rings and ribbons. Set around the fire are the boiling pots I saw a few moments ago, steaming away. Masses of bannock are piled up. Behind the *manitokkan*, I see a series of four fires. Four young men are designated as ritual accessory bearers; they are to bring them at the right time and maintain the fires.

The guests have finally found their places and a gentle whisper hangs over the tent. Outside everything is in complete darkness, save for a vague luminosity from the fires. People and things are bathed in the warm intimacy of semi-darkness.

Ayamihewasow begins to beat his drum rapidly, very rapidly, tom, tom, te-tom, te-tom, te-tom, and begins to sing. While chanting and drumming, he turns towards the tent-pegs which form the corners of the central nave, and having indicated the four directions, he anoints them with bear grease. Finished, he returns to crouch with the old men. I let nothing escape me because everything is new to me. It is touching to see how the old men mutually refresh their memories of those dead for many long years. They enumerate names; they quote deeds done by so and so. This is not idle gossip, but a ceremonial remembrance. It is crucial that no one be forgotten. To recall the name of the dead is to invite the dead to take part in the feast. Truly a memento!

While they tell their beads of memories, the serving-men fill bowls from the pots set around the *manitokkan*. These are set one by one beside each of the old men. They contain different kinds of meats, grease, bread, water, tea, etc.

When each one has been served, Ayamihewasow gets up, takes his bowl, and goes to stand facing the sacred fire before the *manitokkan*. He raises the bowl as a sign of sacrifice and murmurs a formula which I could not hear because he spoke in a low voice with his back to me. Then he threw the sacrifice into the fire and went to sit in his place. A second old man does likewise. And the others follow until each has made his offering to the *tchipayak* (the ancestor spirits).

Meanwhile, the servers have lit the *wikkimasigan*, a kind of fragrant tinder which grows only on very old willows. The sacrifice ended, they incense the fire, the pipes, dolls, and small medicine-bundles. Then they make the round of the tent, finally bringing the incense to rest in front of the fire. This is the spot where the *tchipayak* are said to reside.

Following this ritual, a moment of waiting. People chat and smoke. Yet no one breaks the collective atmosphere, as if to allow the *tchipayak* to make their entry peacefully. Then, at a signal from Ayamihewasow, the musicians begin suddenly to beat their drums, which rumble and roll by fits and starts. Suddenly a cry: "Ahehi-yahohiyha owaka"!

A procession of young dancing men holding high the sacred dolls passes in front of the fire. Serious and dignified, they glide around the central fire nine times. Apart from the chanting and rhythmic dancing, not another sound is heard in the tent. These ritual dolls represent the spirits of the dead; they constitute reliquaries stuffed with locks of hair taken from the ancestors. Some of them are at least a hundred years old, at least their contents are.

After nine turns carried out extremely slowly, the dolls are set down near the fire, in the place of honour. The peace pipes are then lit and presented to the old men. One by one, these turn towards the fire and to *manitokkan*, where they puff three puffs of smoke . . . first to the centre, then to the right, then to the left. Then the pipe is raised to the invisible spirits. To conclude, the different pipes make the tour of the group, from mouth to mouth, beginning with the other old men. As the pipes finish their rounds, they are set down at the foot of the dolls.

These pipes are carved from rather soft red-coloured stone or slate. Some of them are really very old. Generally, they take the form of an upside-down capital T in the vertical bar of which the bowl is cut while the tube fits into one of the arms.

It is almost midnight when all the ceremonies are finished, but no one worries about the late hour. The servers then begin to distribute the food which they draw from the large pots. Until this time, everyone kept his plate and cup carefully hidden, but now that feasting-time has arrived, all hurry to place them conspicuously by their knees. Voices become animated in proportion as the servers advance, but nobody begins to eat until the last person has been served. First an enormous piece of meat, than a chunk of bear-grease, then a piece of bannock as large as a fist and a portion of loaf sugar as much as the knife can scrape up, finally tea, strong and black. Then go to it! Everyone attacks his portion.

I lose courage when I see this pile of food before me, never will I be able to finish all this grub. It is more than I could eat in three days. But I must avoid letting them think that this cooking does not please me at all cost. It's a great feast day, right?

I begin to eat like all the others. Would you like to try it? Here is the procedure: you use your fingers instead of a fork; you tear off a scrap of meat which you stuff into your mouth; you add to that a thimbleful of grease; you chew it up and swallow it. As dessert, a mouthful of bread spread with loaf-sugar and a gulp of tea to moisten everything. It's fabulous!

Despite my meritorious efforts, I was soon full, and my pile of food seemed hardly touched . . . four or five kilos! Who could swallow such a quantity? By luck some others begin also to have their fill. Wait and watch . . . what will they do? Without a shadow of embarrassment, they take a bag or piece of cloth and stuff into it what is left on their plates. Then they place everything behind them against the wall of the tent. What a relief!

When everyone has put away his leftovers, a procession is organized, but this is not a ritual . . . towards the door in the direction of the forest. Laughter bursts out, and joking. They breathe the fresh air. The night is spendid, clear and limpid, bitingly cold, lit by innumerable little stars which twinkle around a majestic moon whose coppery face seems to have been polished for the occasion. But above all, what makes the heart rejoice and the night a hundred times more enchanting, is the northern lights. They clothe the sky, the moon and the stars. Rippling like azure water here, shining like the moon over there. . . . There is a dance of coloured fans opening and shutting, lights of all shades follow other more luminous rays. If the aurora borealis, with its splendour, its hallucinating movements and its ghostliness rejoices the heart of the Indians, it is because it assures them that the deceased are present. The dead open the dance, these are their movements, their cadences, their rhythms. For in Cree, the aurora borealis is designated as *tchipayak e nimitutwaw,* that is, dancing ancestor spirits.

But it is not good to stay outside in the biting cold. Little by little, each comes back to the tent which is shining like a chinese paper lantern. Ayamihewasow begins again to beat his drum in a rhythm so abrupt that one might take it as a reproach. "Tom-te, tom-te, tom-te, tom-te," and even before everyone has settled down in his place, the musicians intone a chant, the sounds of which seethe against their palates: *Ohohiyahayahiyehaho ahohiyaho eyaho*.... The drums rumble, thump and thunder, while the singers emphasize the beat by jerky movements of the body and wail in a loud strident voice *Eyaho, eyaho!* Legs crossed or with one knee on the ground, the drummers lean their heads until the cheek touches the skin of the drum: *Aye-e, aye-e, aye-e!*

Slowly the men rise and go to dance in a row around the fires. The women slowly follow, and soon the children, too, enter into the dance. The circle is soon complete. Gravely and majestically, the row advances. The men shake their shoulders and bend their knees slightly, leaving their arms dangling alongside the body. Three steps, the point of the toe, then the heel, then the toe, and the other foot in turn makes the movement in cadence ... toe-heel-toe. The women, face towards the fire, advance slant-wise and hopping, shaking their shoulders and without raising their feet from the ground, they dance with such speed that it is impossible for me to distinguish the rhythm.

This dance is a meditation or it is conceived more or less as such. The monotonous rhythm brings about an itching of the muscles, but it calms the spirit, making it less alert and more apt for concentration. It may happen that the circle is complete. At other times the dancers are less numerous, but the drums beat uninterruptedly, their uniform cadence until dawn dissipates the northern lights, absorbs the stars, and fills the tent with a penetrating chill. At that time, Ayamihewasow gets up, and surrounded by the other old men, stands before the fire facing the *manitokkan*. Everyone sits down. The three directors rock to the sound of the drum and suddenly they leap forward towards the fire. They stretch their heads at the end of their brawny necks and stare with immoblized eyes at the sacred stake. They make several rhythmical leaps while the drums burst forth in a rhythm so savage that one cannot repress a shiver. The strident, raucous voices yelp out an incantation: *Eha, eya, eya, eyaho eyahoyeyaha!* Again several paces forward, then backwards. They chant and they pray: Thank you for the blessings of the year gone by! Help us in the months that are ahead! Spare us from your malevolent ministrations! Refrain from making our lives unbearable!

The last part of the night was the most impressive. Their chants, their entreaties, were poured forth in such a spell-binding fashion, so deeply sincere, that their accents still ring in my ears. These faces stretched toward the invisible, these voices soaring from low to high notes, these drums with syncopated beat, these dancers clinging to the world beyond! They beseeched, they gently pleaded. Their hearts, their chants, their gestures, thrust them from the depths to the heights, from dark fear to pure hope, from one pole to the other.

Without a guide to announce its coming, a pale copper-coloured sun caressed the walls of the tent. At its appearance, we were at the end: *Aye-e, aye-e.* The camp turned to blankets and slept.

Other dances also had special functions. Among the Cree in northern Alberta, the most important were the spring and fall tea dances. For example, after the winter hunting season, Cree held *meskisimowin* dances; their technical meaning is "lame dance" which derives from the distinguishing lame step of the dancers, but they are also called good-time dance because they were occasions of gift-giving. A central feature of the dance was the pleasure in honouring someone by dancing while holding his/her hand, signalling the desire to honour them with presents. Status and tribal generosity were measured by the magnanimous giving at those celebrations. Likewise, offerings to the spirits were made at these dances, thanking them for their bounty and asking for their continued assistance in providing food and health. Offerings of food, tobacco and tea were made into the fire, while the elders sang songs inviting the non-human persons to take pity on their children. The spring rite was a thank offering for the successes of the winter trapping cycle, and requests for increased numbers of animals to be sent during the coming birthing period, while the fall rite was a thank offering for the blessings of the plants and trees along with the summer bison hunts. There were also the more general thank-offering ceremonies, sometimes called smoking tipi ceremony, which apparently was once an invitation to warriors to gather for summer wars;[30] now there are smokes throughout spring, summer and autumn, in which special praise is addressed to the earth for her continual blessings of sustenance and care.[31] (Vandersteene rarely mentions such ceremonials.)

One other rite should be mentioned: the sweat-lodge rite. It is difficult to tell whether the northern Alberta Cree originally used the sweat lodge. Certainly it is present now, but it is not clear whether this presence is the result of southern Cree influence, or from the growth of pan-Indian religious rituals. Like pipes, sweat lodges probably originally came about among the Cree as a result of dreams. They were constituted by adherence to the basic rules of the cosmic system, with a sunken hole as receptacle for the hot stones, seating protocols, spirit directions, tobacco thank offerings, prayer flags and special songs to the spirit helpers of the owner. The sweat progressed through four sessions of sweat, appropriately to the spirits of the four directions in the cosmic structure, each of which ended with opening the flaps of the lodge to allow for the spirits to leave and the devotees to cool. Like all Cree ceremonials, the goals of the rite were multipurposed, but the primary focus appears to have been on confession, expiation and petition. Sometimes the owner would have prayers for healing, or perform such rites as eagle-feather doctoring. Sweats also functioned as the forerunner for more strenuous spiritual activities, such as participation in Thunderdance ceremonies or *powagan* quests.

Periodically, too, Cree held a kind of social thank-offering dance for the people. This was called a round dance, and its goal was to express appreciation to the spirits for the obvious flourishing of the people. Any kind of remarkable achievement could also elicit a round dance. They were usually held every two or three months. Sometimes they were called powwows, probably the one word most uninitiated associate with aboriginal ceremonials.

During traditional Cree celebrations, games of chance or gambling were a common ingredient. Called *astotuwin* (sometimes *asstotuwin*) these were social moments when individuals played various games of chance, testing "luck." For some, these had a fortune-telling function, reflecting how their luck would be during the next season of hunting or trapping. The concept may well live on in Cree attraction to bingo and other games of chance.

Personal Rituals and Attitudes

If the emphasis was upon Cree tribal consciousness as an arbitrator of identity, this does not mean that the individual had no place in the scheme of things. Indeed, every person had a unique place. A person is *ayisiyiniw*, a word that implies there is a certain pattern appropriate to the bearer, since *ayisicikan*, or model, comes from the same word structure. In Cree, everything that is is either animate or inanimate, which means that it either has the power to affect activity or it does not. Cree language carried out this conception, distinguishing verbal forms and word endings on the basis of this distinction.

Persons, however, share purpose with all things. Purpose is an important concept, since it covers why everything happens the way it does.[32] *Ocitaw* explains why one is large, another small, why a tree happened to fall on him, why she married him. It explains why an outcropping of rock stands the way it does, why the moon shines, and why one person is successful and the other not. If someone dies, it is *ocitaw*; there is no more than incidental value in knowing that they ate poisoned food. If you killed an animal, it was *ocitaw*; if you missed it, it was *ocitaw*. In short, each person has a distinctive *ocitaw*.

Traditionally, one gained *ocitaw*, not precisely at birth, but as the maturing process began. For young males, discovering a firm identity meant retreating to the bush, constructing a small sweat-lodge type shelter, and, without food, drink or warm clothes, seeking in contemplation a dream or vision from the non-human world.[33] When this occurred, the spirit helper was usually in the form of an animal, to whom the individual would be intimately related for life. This dependency upon an animal spirit, in essence, freed the young man from relying on his parents or on humans.[34] Among the Cree, taboos were attached to this relatedness, and one was that the individual could not eat any of the helper spirit brothers and sisters, i.e., a bear spirit meant that one could not eat bear. At the same time, the helper spirit bequeathed a certain *ocitaw* to the individual. Vandersteene himself recorded one such vision, that of Salomon:

> It had to do with three airplanes: that happened at a time when airplanes had not yet been invented. One plane was red, another blue, and the third yellow. They converged on him with dizzying speed, a real nightmare! ... "And I saw that three times," he said, "And finally I knew that the fourth time would be fatal to me. I succeeded finally in doing violence to my feelings; stuttering and stammering, I told my vision to an old man. He explained it to me and my soul found peace again." To this day, Salomon has not revealed to me the contents of that interpretation.[35]

The modern tenor of this vision should not distract from its truth: Salomon's spirit helper is an "updated" Thunderbird. This *powakan* (translated sometimes as totem, but technically one's personal animal helper spirit) gave character and personality to the individual who was believed not to have any until so endowed. Character and personality were not held to be parental constructions. They were spirit-helper formations. The interpretation of one's vision was left to the elders, who translated the meaning of the vision into practical understandings for everyday life. Vision quests were not always successful. If this were the case, the young man alternately might receive a powerful dream, in which the key to his personality was expressed.

Young women would likewise be visited by spirit helpers, but these did not depend upon the endurance of suffering; rather, around the time of puberty, girls would have recurring dreams, and a spirit helper would become part of their personality.[36] There are some suggestions that girls were not conceived to have souls, but this probably means that their souls were not constructed in the same manner as males.[37] There is no evidence that girls were considered less human because of this difference; the difference did relate, however, to legal rights within the tribe, since tribal identity tended toward the male side.[38]

The *ocitaw* of the individual animal was inviolate; in traditional Cree belief each animal, in effect, was given to the hunter. The hunter did not and could not just "kill" an animal because the hunter had greater power. This is because the individual animal was intimately connected to the *ocitaw* of all such animals, so, for example, the individual beaver came out of the great beaver spirit. This is why parts of the animal had to be offered to the spirit world before humans ate. It was a thank offering to the animal's spirit provider. In addition, the helper spirit was not the spirit of an individual animal, but its "source" spirit.

Fr. Balter of Saddle Lake records in his diary another significant aspect of that animal/human relationship — the notion of pity for a particular hunter and the power of the animal spirit. In 1907 Kakisim, one of his parishioners, dropped in for a visit, and his comments to the old priest ran like this:

> "See how thin I am? I've had a real scare, and I haven't fully recovered from it. I had been hunting for a bear's den because an Englishman had promised me a good price for a bear hide. Suddenly I found the bear's den, covered with branches. At the same time, I heard quite clearly the grunting of a bear. I was sure then that the bear was there. I cleared the branches away, and the hay that covered the opening. Then I shot through the opening, at the bear which I was sure that I had shot at. There was nothing in the hole! Scared, and nearly out of my wits, I fell on my knees and prayed to God. Then I took off a silken scarf that I had on and offered it to the bear, saying: 'Think nothing of this incident, and especially don't hold it against me. I didn't do it on purpose.' "
>
> "Really now," said the priest, "I can't see why you were so afraid, and why you excused yourself to the bear. After all, the bear wasn't there and you did him no harm."
>
> "That's precisely why I was afraid. I was afraid because I shot at the bear and he wasn't even there. If I had killed him, or at least the bear had been in his hole and I had wounded him, I wouldn't have been afraid at all."
>
> "Frankly, I don't understand."
>
> "Well, I'll tell you something and perhaps you will understand. I got this story from the old Cree people. One day, long ago, a young Cree boy became lost in the forest. The boy was close to death when the bear came along and had pity on the boy. The bear took the boy to its den and gave him something to eat. While the boy was there, the bear told him, 'There's a hunter at this moment looking for me.

He wants my body for food. But he won't kill me. It's another hunter that will kill me because I've already taken pity on this other hunter and I shall deliver up my body to him for food. Though he may appear to kill me, he won't, really. I shall still live!' "

"Now you'll surely understand why I was so afraid. The Spirit of the bear was there in the den, but his body wasn't there anymore. I had heard the bear cry and I was frightened to death to think that I had nearly shot at the *Spirit* of the bear. You see, according to these old Cree people, there are three who have power: first the Master of all things, then the Thunderbird, and then the bear. There you are!"[39]

There is another aspect of the relationship that Kakisim did not spell out: Why shoot at all if you can't see what you are shooting at? The element of chance, of the inability to read whether "this is the bear giving itself to me," and hence the occasion to try, to "go for it," because who knows whether this is it or not. Behind it is the logic of luck.

The other personal zone of religious power was the shaman or medicine man. The roles and significance of these people have been much maligned in the popular press, and even among scholars, an ethnocentric view has been taken of them.[40] Curing, spell-casting, healing, foretelling and herbal therapy was all part of Cree tradition, but the information is sketchy. McLean in 1896 said there were four different kinds of medicine men among the Cree, conjurer, bone-killer, man-of-the-day (secret revealer) and spell-destroyer,[41] but the tasks applied to each category were sketchy, and it is not known where he received his information. A medicine man/doctor, in the sense of one who provides herbal medicines or techniques is *maskikiwiyiniwiw*, which basically means that this man has the ability to doctor, but there are several other terms related to the health and information complex: *omamaskasapamohwiw*, conjurer, *mitew*, sorcerer, *aweyak kamamahawsiw*, shaman, and *okakeskihkemow*, prophet. (Abilities in these areas developed through interaction with the non-human-person world, and skills were imparted by dreams or through transfer. There seems to have been little evidence of the elaborate *midewewin* healing ceremony, even though it was present among the Ojibwa.[42])

The most spectacular of the medicine men traditionally has been the owner of the shaking tent rite, whose abilities to handle the violence and direct confrontation with the spirits set him apart, for that rite is still part of active Cree practice; he is *mitew*.[43] While that term is technically translated as sorcerer, that translation does not appear to include the genuine curative dimension of the *mitew*.

The correct term for one who owns a medicine bundle is *maskikiwiyiniwiw*, literally one with doctoring abilities. Part of the root of that word relates to lameness or being crippled, suggesting that the doctor has a basic flaw: s/he is dependent upon the spirit helper for assistance. On the other hand, the Cree also had terms for prophet or seer: *okiskiwahikew* as well as *okakeskihkemow*. An essential gift of this type of specialist is the ability to intuit deeper truths; it is based on maturity and wisdom. The word for teacher derives from the same root. Also closely related is the word for guide.

Among the Cree then, there were shamans who practised the shaking tent rite as a healing and conjuring rite. The elements in the rite identified by Cooper, who drew from Ray and Hallowell, include: shaking of the top of tent or lodge at the entrance and departure of spirit; the performer is not possessed by the spirit but only poses a question and the spirit departs for the answer; the performer is, however, concealed from the spectator or client during visitation; and participants smoke the pipe and an offering is made to the spirit. He identifies this rite as primarily a personal rite to seek information about the future or some event some distance away. This rite is still practised today, even in the city of Edmonton.[44] It apparently does not command the presence of either Kisemanitou or Micimanitou but is dependent upon the power of the conjurer's *powakan*.[45]

The tendency in European literature has been to see Kisemanitou as God and Micimanitou as the devil,[46] thus imposing Christian conceptions upon Cree notions, but it is likely that the Cree felt that good and evil forces both existed equally in the universe, and that humans were subject to the tensions created by two equal spiritual qualities, one good and one bad. The traumas of fighting potentially destructive influences were said to cause illness and even death. When smallpox destroyed as many as two-thirds of the Cree nation, Cree told white witnesses they believed that "the Great Master of Life (i.e., Kisemanitou) had delivered them over to the Evil Spirit (i.e., Micimanitou) for their wicked courses; and for many years afterward those who escaped the deadly contagion strictly conformed themselves to their own code of moral laws."[47] Escaping from the potentially destructive nature of Micimanitou's power was singularly attractive for the Cree and may have contributed to their conversion to Christianity.[48] Even today there is continuing belief in the power of evil medicine; Christianity's devil, while reduced somewhat from the power of Micimanitou, is still deemed strong enough to destroy the unprotected. Various amulets, feathers and animal sinews served and continue to serve this purpose.[49]

Finally, there are a range of values which reflect important aspects of Cree religious life. Several attitudes like consensual approval, sharing of resources, antipathy of permanent accumulation of goods, cultivation of patience, and respect for elders are far more significant than their quick statement would imply. They run very deep in the psyche of the Cree.[50] For example, far more equality exists between children and adults in Cree than in white society. Parents do not believe that children and youths should be regimented according to pre-established rules early in life as a means of integrating them into society. They are perceived to have all the spiritual requisites possessed by the parents and thus they have the means to fit into their society as they grow. Rules are intuited, not authorized.

This makes it difficult for children to adapt to white schools and their fundamentally authoritative system, a situation that exists right across the employment spectrum. Traditionally, especially after the epidemics, the Cree responded to Europeans by withdrawing to isolated communities; at the same time, the disintegration of relationships with neighbouring tribes often led to war and this weakened them. With the loss of the shell of protection afforded by distance and inadequate roads, stress has created other responses, including conflict between Treaty and Métis, alcoholism and a sense of failure.[51] A religious and moral value, identified by Vandersteene as contemplative, is also of significance; it is an attitude of anticipation of insight, of attempting to fathom deeper connections, of a passive stance with regard to the activity of the world around. Vandersteene saw it in his oldest and most loyal followers, and it was one of those elements on which he proposed building his Cree Church.[52]

Catholic and Christian Interactions

Religious Connector Factors in Cree Tradition

The basic system of Cree belief remained in place after the coming of the Christian Europeans. What cross-over elements would allow the Cree to connect the new Christian configuration with the old? Is there extrapolation out of one system into the other? The people Vandersteene took as his teachers among the Cree presented him with this kind of extrapolation. They did not give the tradition they belonged to a distinctive name, like "Thunderbird religion," because the spiritual/religious aspects of it were not seen to be separate from the natural/ordinary. If anything, they called the whole of their experience "Cree." They did not see their response to the non-human persons to be categorically different than the Christian's to God.

What seems evident is that the non-human persons were understood by the Cree to be still present, and that they had supported and
enhanced the new reality associated with Christianity after almost two
centuries of contact, and were continuing to do so when Vandersteene
arrived. To return to our converging streams of colours again, the Cree
recognized a new collectivity emerging, made up of the distinctive be-
haviours and rituals of the burned-wood people (Métis), the "blackrobes" (the name given by Western Indians to missionaries) and the
settlers.

The new force was perhaps best symbolized by the distinctive dress
of the priests. These forceful people looked enough like their old spiritual authorities to be recognized for what they were, spirit representatives connected to a religiously powerful reality. Insofar as their beliefs
were articulated to the Cree, they were an alternative source, another
expression of the powers available in the cosmos, to be related to and
tapped for whatever benefits they could provide. This scenario is quite
in keeping with Cree tradition, which, so far as we can determine, regarded the universe as a consortium of powers, which humans learned
to "read" and relate to as Christians and others relate to sacred texts. A
good example of these points is the conversion of Jean-Baptiste Sewepagaham. Jean-Baptiste was to become one of Vandersteene's great
stalwarts. The story of how he became a Christian early in the twen-
tieth century provides much insight:

> The old man thought greatly of his seventh and youngest son, in
> whom he saw a future Chief. In order to force him to make contact
> with God, who manifests Himself in nature and in solitude, the old
> Chief ordered Jean-Baptiste to leave home and to go and live in the
> forests as a wanderer for a year, with only his gun and a dog for
> companion.
>
> At the end of the year the young man returned as sceptical as
> ever. His journey through the Northwest Territories among other
> Indian tribes did not bring him closer to the faith. So one evening,
> his father, who had an exceptional faith, performed a miracle for
> him. He started praying and he sent Jean-Baptiste outside the cabin.
> He asked his son: "Do you see the moon?" The younger man said he
> did. In fact what he was seeing was an incredible spectacle: the
> moon was moving about in the sky in a fantastic dance. After a
> while, the father asked: "You believe now, don't you my son?" The
> son answered: "No, I don't."
>
> He remained firm in his unbelief until the time he had a special
> dream that moved him deeply. He saw a woman dressed like an
> Oblate priest, with long black robe, a cross hanging from the neck,

holding a book in her hand. She told him: "Go see the man, who is dressed like I am, and ask him to teach you to read the book he holds in his hand."

The Indian left for Fort Vermilion as soon as he could. When he arrived Father Habay was finishing Sunday mass. Jean-Baptiste approached him and saw, to his satisfaction, that the priest was in every point what the woman had asked him to look for. The book he had in his hand was a Cree hymnal. He immediately asked the missionary to teach him to read the book. The priest brought him home and asked him who he was. When he told him, the priest said: "Oh, so you are the one who does not want to become a Christian." Father Habay taught him the syllabic characters whereby in the matter of a few hours our man could read. He took the hymnal and left for home.

A few months later, when Father Habay went to the Little Red River mission, he met Jean-Baptiste, who asked to be received into the church along with his people. Father Habay would refuse to take any credit for the conversion: "They did it all themselves" he would say. What happened, in fact, is that Jean-Baptiste studied all the hymns which contained the whole story of salvation in Jesus Christ, his life, his death, his resurrection, the foundation of the Church, the Sacraments, The Blessed Virgin Mary that he recognized as the woman who spoke to him in a vision. It was a discovery that transformed his whole life. He shared his good news with his people who received it with joy.

J.B. Sewepagaham became a most remarkable leader to his people. He always demonstrated a very deep faith. Father Vandersteene, who narrated these facts to me last summer, told me how moved he was, when meeting the chief, then an old man, who would kneel at his feet right there in the street before everyone, and ask for the priest's blessing. To him the priest was God's envoy.[53]

The conversion involved all those ingredients classic to the vision quest — the long period alone in the forest, the failure, the dream or vision, the new spirit helper (the Virgin Mary), and the elder (Fr. Habay) confirming the vision. What is new is the different perception of proof: the book, the "European" spirit helper, and the lack of the usual personal achievement. In fact, the notion of the spirit source being human seems quite normal by Cree standards, where non-human persons of many different types interacted with humans. This reminds us that the Cree saw social interaction to be reflective of special significance, for in that nexus the quality of respect was measured out in terms of personal power. A reflection of this kind of power is found in Jefferson:

> Every Indian is not an orator, but they are all adepts at "sound-
> ing" — that is, weighing and gauging the influences that sway the per-
> son they are addressing, with a view at addressing all their efforts to the
> weakest point. Their preliminary talk is all aimed at this, and what fol-
> lows is an appeal, an argument, or a threat, as they have decided the
> occasion requires. I have watched this process over and over again, and
> wondered at it as often; first he will try to frighten you, and if he finds
> this is not working, will gradually change his tone until he has found the
> feeling you will respond to.[54]

What is important for our purposes, however, is that the narrative
shows that the new religious power (the Church) appearing on the
horizon did not redefine either the notion of power, nor the perception
of Cree "people." It did not propose a fundamentally new way of "experiencing reality" nor a new Cree "people of Israel." The universe
was still there for contemplation of its powerful qualities, and tribal
identity and "Cree-ness" still retained their traditional strength. *No
new way of comprehending reality and no new identity symbols were initially
involved in recognizing Christian powers.* One might argue that in some
ways both traditional power centres continue today.[55]

However, the new ingredient called "Indian" did arise soon after
the white men and then the blackrobes came. It is important to note
that this notion of monolithic "other" was just not held on the white
side. The Cree had a term, *moniyawiw*, with pejorative overtones, but
whose basic meaning is pale-faced man, to identify all Europeans. Tribal people were never *moniyawiw*. How were the Cree and Blackfoot
and Ojibwa, etc., to comprehend this new reality that was designating
them in a new form and which they mutually recognized as foreign?
Just what was the content of this new term? To what extent did both
Christianity and European nationalism contribute to the notion of
"Indian?"[56] Or to put the question from the other side, to what extent
did becoming Christian imply blurring the lines between Cree and
moniyaw? Were the priests, then, *moniyawiw* with a difference? These issues are important because they directly bear on how Vandersteene
progressed with his work. Several items may help to follow this development.

Authority

Leadership seems a good place to commence. New authority figures
were appearing. It is not necessary to rely solely on stories told by the
old people about their prophets foretelling the coming of great pale
medicine men to accept that religiously powerful visionaries among
them foresaw coming interruptions to traditional patterns.[57] Any kind
of political power could have religious implications, since they saw no

distinctions between the two realms. It would be common sense that they would see their position to be immediately challenged; most of them realized they were custodians of the tools and represented tribal relationships to the non-human persons.

We know that, whatever the religious attitudes of the first contact Europeans, the Cree in Alberta became involved in the international trade network[58] before they were exposed to any in-depth experience of the new religion, so they encountered the new culture through men who made no open religious claims.[59] The traders whom the Cree first encountered were probably French or more likely Métis, whose relationship with Cree was mediated by a considerable adaptation process, reflected in intermarriage, common lifestyle and tough work attitude. These Métis had been born out of the French-Canadian milieu, where far more importance was given to accommodation to native cultures. Accommodation was a factor less prominent among the English.[60] It would seem quite reasonable that some holy men, and not a few chiefs themselves, might perceive that significant religious shifts were coming from this process.

When the priests did arrive, there was essential contact but there are no stories of Cree in religious awe of the newcomers — feared and likely respected, but no great "religious" reaction to the blackrobes' aura.[61] There are, however, many stories of the bands asking the fathers to accompany them on their summer hunt, for good luck; this was particularly true of the Métis. Catholic sensibility to relics appealed to Cree religious values, because the kissing of relics implied a passing on of some kind of magical power. It is also important that only shamans had the power to give names, and in this they reflected the authority of the priests in Catholic christening ceremonies.[62] Foster believes that the relationship between the Métis Chief and the Oblate priests was a key element in the latter's success in conversions.[63]

Pipe-smoking, one of the fundamental religio-cultural validators in Cree tradition, involved patterning motions while smoking the calumet. Based on the recognition that each point of the compass involved powers with special abilities and interests in the world, the elder smoked the pipe as a means to communicate with the spirit world. For example, one such patterning motion is raising the pipe high overhead to call attention to the non-human entities of the sky, Thunderbird, perhaps; some priests saw the process of raising high the pipe as reminiscent of the priest raising the chalice during mass. The connection with the Indian status people, the chiefs, is evident because only those of wealth or power owned pipes and could initiate such ceremonies. Thus, the blackrobes followed a pattern that dovetailed with the tribe's political structure — they related directly to the head chief, who, in traditional Cree society was elected from among heads of leading families of local bands.[64]

There is a certain irony about this. The Cree chief moved up the ranks in a system that was, at least from the 1700s on, heavily influenced by a warrior ethos. The young Cree began without apparent status and moved up the social ladder by the success of his exploits as a warrior. When he became chief, he might display wisdom, or generosity or bartering ability, but he would not reach chiefdom unless he had demonstrated extraordinary leadership, of which warriorship was a key element. In the earliest period for which we have records, the warrior was the most sought-after leadership role, and dictated band headship. A man who wanted to be head could just form a new band if he could attract the support of enough families, and a prime measurement of such leadership was prowess in battle, wealth and generosity.[65]

Here again, the Cree differed somewhat from their neighbours. The warrior chief and the band chief could be separate individuals,[66] and there seems not to have been hereditary transfer of chieftainship. Bands could also have several chiefs, and personality seems to have played a role in becoming one.[67] Chieftain, however, in Cree is *okimow*, which derives from the verbal form of "give away," and seems to suggest that wealth distributed among tribespeople was of greater significance for status marking than white sources acknowledge.[68]

Cree culture was competitive.[69] Competition applied to healers and medicine men as much as to warriors, and each achievement was registered as much by the redistribution of wealth as by miracles. Prestige was also related to ownership, because owning a ceremony raised the status of the individual in the community. Hunters and trappers who excelled often became the focus for migrating families attracted by the tales of their abilities and the generosity of their wives, who were responsible for distribution of the kill. Powerful men took pride in welcoming into their homes children of the poor or orphans, so one measure of how powerful a man was was the number of non-genealogically related people who ate with the head. In general, the more healthy and cared-for the band, the greater the prestige of the leaders. Well-being did not arise out of "nature,"[70] but out of the activity and initiative of the leaders. Leadership can be said to be driven by individual initiative, but the consensus declared whether the initiative was apt in promoting the well-being of the band.

The blackrobe-chief contiguity must have been very significant for the perception the aboriginals had of the developing church; religious authority relating to the political chief gave a particular patina to church-tribal relations. Ralph records some significant material on the ramifications of this relationship:

> The good priest — for if ever there was a good man Father Lacombe is one — saw fighting enough, as he roamed with one tribe and the other, or journeyed from tribe to tribe. His mission led him to ignore tribal differences, and to preach to all the Indians of the plains. He knew the chiefs and headmen among them all, and so justly did he deal with them that he was not only able to minister to all without attracting the enmity of any, but he came to wield, as he does to-day, a formidable power over all of them. . . . He knew Old Crowfoot (Chief of the Blackfoot) in his prime, and as I saw them together they were like bosom friends. Together they had shared dreadful privations and survived frightful winters and storms. They had gone side by side through savage battles, and each respected and loved the other.[71]

The question is, why did the blackrobe not relate first and foremost to his natural equal, the medicine man? Why did white recorders like the one above only reflect the priest's relationship with the chief and not with the shaman? After all, the Cree word for priest is *ayami-hiwiyiniw*, which is a cognate of the words for man and prayer/religion, so the Cree perception recognized that there was a kind of life-pursuit fitted to those who claimed to be priests. One point seems important: This focus on priest and chief as equivalent indicates that the Church could not and would not develop a distinctive tribal identity as its converts mounted. Could not, because the priests saw membership in theological terms, i.e., as trans-tribal; would not because the priests' relationship with tribes already implied something political — they were "chiefs of the church." Besides, they had no experience in Europe in developing "tribal" churches since the Oblates all came from strong national-identity states, and therefore could not "see" such nation-states as "tribes." Johnsen Sewepagaham, grandson of Jean-Baptiste, in an interview in November 1988 addressed the issue from the Cree standpoint:

> The Church is like the government. It is too stylized, too systematized. It has had great difficulty in understanding our religiosity because of it. For over 200 years the Church regarded us as pagans, without religion. The problem was not us, it was them. The Church has great difficulty in relating to a different kind of spirituality than they propose. Not even someone as sensitive as Vandersteene understood from the start.

From the standpoint of the aboriginals, the character of the priest and his organization had a polity quite unlike anything available to them — a sort of tribe whose members were all abroad. Yet it was still

political. Where the shaman/medicine man stressed the need for integration or conciliation between humans and the positive/negative
qualities in the universe, and based their ceremonies upon that philosophy, urging reconciliation between tribal people and powers as the
true direction of the universe, the priest represented a new kind of tribal polity with an acceptance of an important sacrifice (Jesus') as the basis for reconciliation and obtaining blessings from God. It was precisely
not healing, nor conjuring nor foretelling nor doctoring nor being inspired while possessed. These were exclusively the external roles of
various medicine men/witch doctors and lesser spiritual authorities.
This new kind of role holds even if the blackrobes did heal with their
herbs and potions. The primary relationship of all churchmen, regardless of stripe, was with Cree peoples' everyday authorities, the chiefs;
hence they were chiefs from a new kind of "religious" tribe.

It is also very likely that the nature of church development has contributed to the meaning of "Indian." When the priest ministered across
tribes and/or valiantly tried to shield the Indians from the encroaching
railway and white settlers, he also gave specific content to the category
of "Indian." Yet the distinction the priest made was not just white-
Indian, for he also included the French-speaking Métis under his wing.
He was really juxtaposing those who came accepting the normative-
ness of the culture of the people in the land, and those who wished to
displace it. Most missionaries developed deep affection for "les
pauvres," and naively, perhaps, wanted to keep them Indians but
make them Christian. Unfortunately, the identity associated with the
Christian Church entailed certain cultural understandings. But the
basis of that imposed identity by the whites was neither religious nor
tribal, at least in a sense the "Indians" recognized, so it had no rootedness for the First People. And no wonder, because it really had little
following in Europe: the priest wanted a trans-tribal church out of
theological commitment, yet desired an Indian church built on the distinctive culture found among the Indians. It seems to have been entirely a church-constructed dilemma, for First Peoples saw whites as coming from different tribes, and Christianity the religious culture of the
European tribe.[72] Strangely, white settlers had little interest in "becoming native" in order to participate in the culture here. These com-
plexities were to have dire consequences for the Church. As Vandersteene was to become aware, it was precisely because the Church did
not develop along the lines of a North American tribal consciousness
that it had difficulty in building a permanent church.

Yet, because the blackrobes deigned to stand between the people of
traditional ways of life and the new European culture, because they

created a self-constructed role, they opened up a wholly new kind of religious leadership. They operated in an interstitial sector, creating a position that was neither that of a messenger presenting a new religion, nor of chief of a new tribe. This was authority without roots in either culture, fostering a group whose identity was neither rooted in traditional tribalism nor completely identified with an exploitive culture from abroad. Priests were pulled in two directions. In Vandersteene's case, as we shall see, interstitial group identity would urgently impel him towards Cree tradition, while its social meaning would repel him back to Flanders, an outsider on several levels. Significantly the Church, of whatever stripe, has never seized the nettle of this dilemma.

Social Connectors

Tribal leaders accepted the priest and ministers as protectors because they trusted their political acumen with the white government. Thus they accepted the Church's power and became dependent upon it to translate the affairs of government politics into benefits for their people. In the end, they accepted the Church as another go-between. Cree could identify with that. The missionaries were part of a barter system with another tribe. Accepting the Church and its spiritual powers were further ways of cementing their allegiance to a mediating power. It was also a way of building a bridgehead to the culture of the immigrants. On the surface one might conclude that this was a wholly new position to accept. But all these moves were *religiously* no different than bargaining with the non-human persons of the spirit world in place before contact.[73] It was really only a matter of bringing to bear the resources available to plead with these powers to have pity on the people — in this case, to accept the blackrobes' rituals as a way of relating to a new authority that had suddenly become very important in the world. Nor was it socially much different than acting as an entrepreneur between the tribes and the trading post. It was working with one's resources to procure what the tribe felt it needed, which, as always, was survival.

On the other hand, the doctrines the priests brought must have had a strong impact on Cree identity. Most of the priests condemned traditional religious practices in no uncertain terms, telling the people that they would burn in hell. The spirit-helper complex, built upon the vision/dream was undermined as the basis for individual salvation. The whole procedure was larger than just stopping some rites and ceremonials. It undercut the traditional way of building identity. Dream power opened the individual to mutually supportive inner forces, which, in turn, provided the basic distinctions between people.[74] Brightman's traditionally oriented informant had this to say:

> Usually it was the older people who knew how to do all these *mamaskac* ["wonderful" things]. When the religions — all different kinds of religions — came up north, people stopped doing those things. The priests scared them so they stopped . . . scared then by telling them all about Hell. At the time people didn't know any better so they did what the priest said. They should have kept on. Mostly they didn't hurt anybody. Mostly they used it for hunting and for doctoring sick people.
>
> God gave that *mamatawisiwin* to the Indians because they didn't have all the machines and guns that the white man has. When the priest came, he told everyone to quit everything and believe in Jesus. Especially he told everybody to get rid of their drums. So they stopped talking to their dreams (spirit guardians) and they lost all those powers they had. Indians would have a lot of money and be a hundred percent if they still kept their drums and kept up the old powers. I heard this story about G.N. at Pukatawagan. It was a bad winter there and they didn't have any meat. Couldn't kill anything. So the priest tells G. to throw away his drum and pray to God for food. G. stayed in his cabin for a week praying to God. Nearly starved to death. He went back and gave that priest hell.[75]

For our purposes, this selection appears to affirm that religion has had an important impact in separating whites from Indians. At least for this informant, the Indian was the one who had powers before the missionary said they had to get rid of them. Now they had none. It is directly tied to the position the Indian felt in the developing Church.

It really is several steps further on to accept that there is a collective power in being "Indian," at least equivalent to and perhaps even superior to the white man. Yet without the Church's intermediary role, it is doubtful that the first step could have ever been made. It is quite possible that the Church's paternal care and its missionary stance toward the First Peoples provided sufficient distance for the nation-wide sense of "Indian" to gel, providing a means to come to understand the categories imposed upon them by the Canadian public and its principal representative, the government. There is a further irony that the Church should have been so instrumental in developing the sense of Indian, which now becomes a means of asserting collective power vis-à-vis white society, as it has been done in Canada's recent constitutional debate.[76]

Church Policy and Christian Politics in the Northwest

Roman Catholic missions in Canada are divided by their historian Memorian into three distinct phases, French regime (1611-1760), British rule (1760-1840) and Inland missions (1840-1939). France received the first assignment to evangelize new France under a papal bull, *Inter Coetera*, and the first missionaries were sent by France in 1611. Following the Treaty of Paris in 1763, France was no longer obligated to send missionaries, and from that time on, Catholic missions were left very much on their own. In 1818 Abbé Norbert Provencher and Abbé Sévère Dumoulin moved to the Red River district in what is now Manitoba to evangelize among the Métis and Indians, as well as to minister to the Selkirk colonists and HBC employees. Beginning in 1840, the distant mission field of Mackenzie and the west fell to the Oblates.[77] St. Bernard had been established at Grouard in Alberta by 1872, St. Henry at Fort Vermilion by 1876, Wabasca (known by the church as St. Martin's) by 1896 and Akitameg (St. Benoit) by 1902. With schools, hospitals and chapels, the Oblates were making a dramatic impact on northern Alberta.[78]

The development of Christianity in northern Alberta and the Northwest Territories is a complicated mix of charity, politics, deprivation, hard work and stubbornness on the part of the Oblates, the leaders of the Hudson's Bay Company, the Anglican Church Missionary Society (ACMS) missionaries, the Dene and the Métis-Cree. It all began during the mid-1800s when Monsignor Alexandre-Antonin Taché, priest at Île-à-la-Crosse in what is now Saskatchewan made an inaugural journey to Fort Chipewyan on Lake Athabasca in 1847. Subsequently he sent young Fr. Henri Faraud, O.M.I., to establish the Nativity Mission at Fort Chipewyan in 1850. Faraud had his eye further afield, and requested permission to move into the great lands of the Mackenzie River that was big enough "to form a kingdom or an empire."[79] Alarmed at the aggressiveness of the Catholics, the governors of the HBC requested that the ACMS send an Anglican minister to the area. He arrived in 1855. Meanwhile, Bishop Taché sent two Oblates, Frs. Jean Tissot and Alexandre Maisonneuve, to establish Notre-Dame-des-Victoires on the shore of Lac La Biche farther south on the Athabasca because he wanted an overland centre from which supplies could be shipped to the burgeoning missionary entreprise in the north. Taché did not believe that the Church could rely on the HBC to supply the missions, and wanted a route not dependent upon them. His insistence was to set off a long-standing feud between him and Fr. Faraud.[80] In the meantime, the little mission was to set a string of firsts, including the first wheat of commercial quantity and the first residential school.[81]

The oldest mission in the northwest belongs, not to an Oblate, but to a secular (diocesan) priest, Jean-Baptiste Thibault, who was sent west by Bishop Provencher in 1843. He established a mission on Lake Manito (which was sometimes translated as Devil's Lake, but known by aboriginals as God's Lake because the water was deemed to have healing powers and was the site of pilgimage for first peoples in the region), and the lake was renamed Ste. Anne, in honour of the name of the mission. Albert Lacombe, before he became an Oblate, succeeded Thibault at the mission, and aided in the construction of the church. Monsignor Taché visited the church in 1854. It was Fr. Lacombe who was instrumental in developing missions in the Grouard area, travelling to Métis and Cree settlements from St. Paul to Lac La Biche.[82] Lacombe joined the Oblates in 1855, and he became the hero of the fledgling church in the west. Diocesan priests appear to have had little success with missions; in the west, it has been the Oblates who have implanted Christianity among the Métis and Indians.[83] According to the *Catholic Encyclopedia*, in 1845 the west had one bishop and six priests; by 1908, it had seven bishops, nearly 400 priests; there were 150,000 Catholics, 420 churches and 150 schools. It was all largely because of the Oblates.[84]

Protestant missionaries were more than disquieted by the mission program of the Catholic Church. William Cockran arrived at Red River in Manitoba in 1825, and his memoirs reflect the running battle he had with the Catholics from day one:

> He began by describing his 42 day trip carried out in 1825, between York Factory and Red River. The crew of the boats were without exception made up of Catholic Métis who, according to Cockran, carried on according to the rules of their Church, that is to say they manifested a constant repugnant attitude towards the heretic Cockran. Their hatred would come to the point where they frequently let Cockran's baggage fall into the river, completely ignoring the instructions of the minister. He accused the men of blaspheming, in English and in French, and of cursing in the name of God, the devil, the saints, the Church and divers parts of the body of the Virgin Mary.[85]

In Edmonton in 1891, Canon Newton would complain loudly about the cacophony of religions that seemed to mean that the country would never have any unified culture.[86] Indeed, the vision of various groups would not only help shape that culture, but would bring Vandersteene bitterly into conflict with the religious free-market system characteristic of Canada. Religious conflict was part of the dynamic that drove missionaries to build institutions in Canada, a process that he probably had not anticipated in the remote locations of his missions.

Despite their apparent head start, the Oblates were not content to minister only to the Métis and Cree. Both Lacombe and Grandin, and indeed all the Oblates, promoted colonialization to the northwest as a means to establish the Church in this part of the world. Taché had set out, beginning as early as 1881, to establish a chain of francophone parishes from St. Boniface, in what would become Manitoba, toward the west.[87] The first cleric with the explicit directive to head up colonization was Fr. Jean-Baptiste Morin, brought by Msgr. Grandin to Edmonton in 1890.[88] But there was more to it than just francophone believers — the Church did not appear to have a solid grip on the Indian community, and Grandin for one believed that only through establishing schools and teaching the girls would the Church have access to the family, the soul of the people. Hand in hand, of course, went the belief that Indian children in Anglican schools would be lost to the Church forever.[89] It is for those reasons that the Church moved into education as soon as missions were founded, and there is great resentment among those Oblates who are now accused of undermining native culture by their educational efforts.[90]

It is evident, however, that the Church could not have it both ways. Priest and clergy could not maintain that they wanted to retain the culture and tradition of the Cree and Métis and, at the same time, work to fill the country with Europeans or, as was the case with the Oblates, to extend francophone culture into the prairies through immigration of French-speaking people from Quebec and the New England states. They had to decide whether they would expand the Church or try to adapt Christianity to the culture of the people already here. In fairness to the Church leadership, they recognized that events were overtaking them. Already the presence of Métis groups spelled the end of Canada-wide traditional Indian culture because of intermarriage and trading interaction. Once the government moved to settle land claims through treaties, the handwriting was not only on the wall, it would soon be present in the land in the form of a railway. By 1900, it was all over. The moot point is whether the Christian missionaries ever were able to tell their Indian and Métis charges, that, from the standpoint of native culture they had completely misread what the Church should have done. Translating the hymnal into Cree and perhaps even educating the children was important, but, in retrospect, it was a rather slim manner of trying to preserve Cree culture. Developing a Cree Church would have recognized the Cree as a nation, with their own national "church," even as had been done by Christianity in Britain. The complicity of the Church in the Cree condition, then, is very real. Vandersteene saw the result, and reacted to it as a minority issue. But the issue was larger than that: the Church was not able to cope with the pull of its commitment to the Cree and the push of its need to develop the European church in Canada. Slowly the shift of loyalties would drain its stamina. Vandersteene would confront this issue when he was more seasoned, perhaps more cynical.

There is also the organic development of the Catholic Church in its Canadian setting. Vatican II appeared to herald a new openness to local hegemony; what happened with that appearance, and how far it went reflected the conservative nature of the Canadian church. Arthur Lamothe, Métis and one-time priest in the diocese, pointed to this factor for the understanding of Vandersteene's position:

> The Church is in the process of evolving from an absolute monarchy with divine right over a "colonized institution" to a form of democratic society. In this society, baptisms and sacraments will be recognized as deriving from the individual Christian community . . . from the individual's own Christian community and the authority of that community. Compared to his confreres, Vandersteene was well into the democratic movement.[91]

The amount of development that can take place is dependent upon many factors, not the least of which is how to understand the "local Christian community." Vandersteene had to contend with a Church that had regional aspirations deriving from the Canadian Church's priorities. Then, too, he had to live with the restrictions placed on liturgical, administrative and doctrinal controls arising out of Rome's own limits placed on the devolution process. Just how far would Vandersteene move away from the "traditional" Church? One way to judge this might be to scan Church mission theory.

The Cree and Church Mission Theory

The missiology[92] Vandersteene grew up on was the heroic ideology of the Oblate founder de Mazenod. As expressed by Fr. Levaque it was this:

> As envisaged by Bishop de Mazenod, the Oblate missionary vocation was first and foremost one of working amongst the poorest of the poor, wherever they might be. An Oblate missionary must live with the people, learn the language, preach the Gospel, teach Christian virtues by word and example and try to change attitudes and practices which impede the acquistion of Christian virtues. At the social level, the Oblate attempts to change the conditions of poverty which contribute to human indignity.[93]

Already the goals are more complicated than the simple message in Matthew to "Go ye into all the world, baptizing them in the name of the Father, Son and Holy Ghost." They go beyond what de Mazenod himself had envisaged when he began to give the order shape in 1815:

> By devoting the Society to the ministry of the missions, especially for the instruction and conversion of the most abandoned souls, my purpose was to have the society imitate the Apostles in their life of fervor and self-sacrifice. I was convinced that if we were to obtain the same results from our preaching, it would be necessary to follow in their footsteps and to practise as closely as possible their same virtues. I therefore regarded the evangelical counsels, to which they had been so faithful, as indispensable if our words were not to be like those of so many others I have heard preaching these self-same truths and which I recognized only too well for what they were; sounding brass and tinkling cymbal.[94]

The mode of action required for this imitation of the Apostles, nevertheless, required conforming to European ideas, that is, living among the poor meant building institutions and churches, just as had been done in Europe from the beginning.

Unfortunately carrying out such tasks would inevitably bring the Oblates into conflict with the culture in place. Just attempting to define poverty from a Cree point of view must have been difficult, at least until they were no longer able to trap sufficient animals for food, or could not rely on the great summer hunt of bison for their livelihood. Starvation was a definition of poverty that all could comprehend.

The Church was only part of a larger problem — that is, the problem known in law circles as the "theory of aboriginal rights." These derive from the fact that aboriginals have lived on Canadian soil from time immemorial and therefore have claim to it.[95] If Indians claimed that they had not received just settlement for the lands vacated by them, or if they claimed that resources found in the land but of which they were not originally aware belonged to them, it has not ordinarily been the Church's position to support their claim. Generally the Church has taken the position that treading into this minefield was not its reponsibility.[96] But the more fundamental stance by the Church, and indeed, Canadian society, was that aboriginal religion and culture needed to be replaced with something "civilized"; just such a statement involved a moral condemnation of existing beliefs and social organizations. Yet surely there is something problematic about the view that a distinctive culture, especially one that has obviously sustained people for thousands of years ought to be and could be displaced. Extinguishing aboriginal religion implied extinguishing aboriginal rights.

Those charged with the theory of missions wrestled with this problem, and one solution that may not have been available to Vandersteene when he left Belgium, but which he must have encountered at some point, for the book was in his library, heavily marked, was R.J. Möhr's *Missionethnologie: Ein Wissenschaftliches Programm*. Published in 1956, it evidently developed out of work done by Fr. Wilhelm Schmidt, especially his *Handbuch der Methode der kulturhistorischen Ethnologie*, published in Munich in 1937, and the translation into German of the British ethnologist R.R. Marett's *Faith, Hope and Charity in Primitive Religions* (1932) (*Glaube, Hoffnung und Liebe in der primitiven Religion* [Stuttgart, 1936]). Fr. Schmidt believed that there was an original High God which one could detect behind all the gods and pantheons among primitives peoples, thus implying that all religions had had the original insight of monotheism. For one reason or other, perhaps because of sin, the High God retreated to the upper reaches of the universe, and seldom was called upon. The result was that lesser gods and holy figures filled the vacuum, as we find among primitives. Even when scientific research turned up no *ur* divinity like this among all people, Schmidt maintained there must have been one. It derived from his theological commitment as a Christian and monotheist, on the one hand, but on the other, a genuine attempt to hold that all religions were ultimately valid because they were all conceptually linked to one divine being.

The key to Möhr's mission theory arising out of this ethnological approach was the distinction between civilization and culture. For Möhr, culture is formed by tendencies and values inherent in the "inner form of man's spirit." These are not accessible, for they "are the inner valuable attitudes that a person takes toward reality."[97] These attitudes give rise to two structures, the one religious, the other civilizational. The outer expression of the first is the symbols and analogical expressions of religion. The outer expression of the second is the "structural principle of magic," or, more properly, the "magical-rational structural principle." This expresses itself in terms of striving for personal power, aggrandizement and physical-technical skills. It must be carefully distinguished from culture, and should be identified clearly as civilization.[98]

These notions provide the basis for the missionary, whom Möhr sees as the individual who comprehends the difference between culture and civilization and is able to rise above his own environment to grasp the religious essence:

> From a psychological perspective, the man of religious culture is the man of reverence, who feels bound to an independent god-ordained order, who therefore integrates himself into society and subordinates himself to tradition. Contrastingly, the man of civilization, the man of self-confidence, who as an individual rises above tradition and creates his

own order. The man of culture is theocentric, the man of civilization is anthropocentric.[99]

Möhr sees Western civilization, and indeed, Western mission as destructive of primitive cultures precisely because it is concerned with the outer expression and tries various means, economic, social, political and pedagogical, to modify them. What they end up changing is not the religion, however, but the forms of civilization, which, in any case, is only another form of colonialization, of changing civilization. Indeed, he holds that missions must stop this destruction. Missions must return to the basic structures that religious life is built upon among all peoples, that is, a High God, the creation of the world by a godly creator, perhaps many gods, an opponent of god, the sinful nature of man, the origin of death, a flood, a god-human saviour, a medium between god and man, the son of god, and further life after death. These elements, along with the notion of sacrifice, are important in the life of peoples all over the world. It is those items for which the missionary must find corollaries among the primitive people and bring Christian truths to the people through them. These forms, he claims will "bring about a true integration of Christianity into the thinking, the world view, the milieu and the culture of these people."[100]

He has an interesting twist to this interpretation of Christian mission. The religions of primitives are in danger of being destroyed by the West's rationalism. Yet many of these societies are religious through and through, that is, every aspect of their culture is religiously endowed. The West has attempted to change their culture, but all it is seeking to do is change the standard of living. That is only a civilizational concern — a concern of the outward. The ethnomissionary's task is to integrate Christianity into these cultures, and thus to preserve them. "The last remainders of true culture and that which accompanies the true — the life-forming religion — are in danger of being annihilated." This is not an old form of conservatism or romanticism. It is really to point out to Western civilization that it has lost its own life-forming religion and must look to these primitive peoples to show them how they can live religiously again. "It is the cultural goal of the ethnomission to indicate to Western civilization its direction and to smooth the way to work positively for the retention of the religious."[101] We shall turn now to Vandersteene in his mission to see the extent to which he applied these ideas, and with what success.

Notes

1 Rogier Vandersteene, *Wabasca: Dix Ans de Vie Indienne*, translated from Dutch by Jacques De Deken, O.M.I. (Gemmenich, Belgium: Editions O.M.I., 1960), preface. Portions of the book have been translated by Thelma Habgood and appear as "Some Woodland Cree Traditions and Legends," *Western Canadian Journal of Anthropology* (*WCJA*), 1, 1 (1969): 40-64. Habgood has also made other translations of the book which are currently in manuscript form. See p. 106, below, for discussion.

2 Fr. Forget, a Canadian colleague and teacher responsible for native schooling, insisted that Vandersteene saw the country as "theirs," that is, that the tribes as a group owned the country, and when whites came, they unjustly took what was not theirs. Forget added that he did not always agree with Vandersteene, and on one occasion had "a civilized clash" over Indian-white government relations. He did not believe that Vandersteene ever modified his views on the injustice of whites. Obviously Steentje did not hold these views when he wrote the preface to *Wabasca* (interview, 13 November 1978).

3 Julian Ralph, *On Canada's Frontier: Sketches of History, Sport, and Adventure and of the Indians, Missionaries, Fur-Traders, and Newer Settlers of Western Canada* (New York: Harper & Brothers, 1892), p. 213.

4 "[T]he distinction between pre-contact change and post-contact change, before 1600 or after 1800, is a largely spurious distinction. . . . All we can maintain in terms of pre-contact/post-contact differences is that the environmental conditions, particularly the sociological environmental conditions became somewhat more oppressive over time" (A.D. Fisher, "The Cree of Canada: Some Ecological and Evolutionary Considerations," *Western Canadian Journal of Anthropology*, 1, 1 [1969]: 10).

5 Mircea Eliade surely alerted us to this siren song in *Cosmos and History* when he pointed out the "nostalgia for origins" that predisposes our analysis of things (quoted in Sam Gill, *Mother Earth: An American Story* [Chicago: University of Chicago Press, 1987]), where the argument of the existence of a generalized conception of Mother Goddess devolves upon whether white sources talk about it; Gill *may* be right that religionist scholars need the notion of Mother Goddess for their paradigms, but, on the issue of female spirits of the earth, the most that can be said is that we don't know. There just has been poor or insufficient documentation on female domains. R. Wolf ("American Anthropologists and American Society," *Western Canadian Journal of Anthropology*, 1, 3 [1969]: 10-18) casts the issue in terms of power, whereby traditional concepts are regarded as normative, and finds it difficult to accommodate to external power structures because the concepts presuppose a closed cultural group.

6 Arthur Joseph Ray, *Indians in the Fur Trade: Their Role as Trappers, Hunters, and Middlemen in the Lands Southwest of Hudson's Bay, 1660-1870* (Toronto: University of Toronto Press, 1974), suggests that there may have been a push by Selkirk (Cree) out of Manitoba sites before contact (p. 4), while D. Jenness, *The Indians of Canada*, Bulletin 65, Anthropological Series No. 15, 2d ed. (Ottawa: National Museum of Canada, 1958), notes that the Assiniboine-Cree alignment suggests that the Assiniboine would have to be separated off from the Dakota Sioux a few generations before the seventeenth century for this to occur (p. 308). Alan L. Bryan surveys the theories about the Cree in Alberta in "Late Protohistoric Cree Expansion into North Central Alberta," *Western Canadian Journal of Anthropology*, 1, 1 (1969): 32-37. David Mandelbaum argued that the Cree movement west came in response to the fur trade ("Changes in an Aboriginal Culture Following a Change in Environment, as Exemplified by the Plains Cree," Ph.D. dissertation, Yale University, New Haven, 1936; "The Plains Cree," *American Museum of Natural History, Anthropological Papers*, 37, 2 [1940]: 155-316; and *The Plains Cree: An Ethnographic, Historical, and Comparative Study*, Canadian Plains Studies No. 9 [Regina: Canadian Plains Research, 1979]).

7 Walter M. Hlady, "Indian Migrations in Manitoba and the West," *Historical and Scientific Society of Manitoba*, Series 3, No. 17 (1960-61): 27. Mandelbaum ("Plains Cree," p. 166) divides them into Downstream People and Upstream people, that is northwestern plains and southwestern plains, roughly corresponding to routes used by the two groups. These are not hard and fast divisions, however.
8 Ray, *Indians in the Fur Trade*, p. 12.
9 Francis Haines suggests the Algonquin stock people came up from the lower Mississippi shortly after the last Ice Age and separated into six tribes. When the Cree emerged from the forest in the east, they could not successfully attack the Assiniboine, so they set up an amicable relationship with them. One way they did this was to provide them with materials from the French. If this scenario is correct, the Cree have been entrepreneurs much longer than just with the Hudson's Bay and their rivals in the French trade (F. Haines, *The Plains Indians* [New York: Thomas Crowell, 1976], p. 52).
10 Alexander Mackenzie, *The Journals and Letters of Sir Alexander Mackenzie*, edited by W. Kaye Lamb, Extra Series No. 41 (London: Hakluyt Society; reprint, Toronto: Macmillan, 1970). His work was published in 1801, based on trips between 1789 and 1793.
11 Dale R. Russell, *Eighteenth-Century Western Cree and Their Neighbours* (Hull: Canadian Museum of Civilization, 1991). The theories and advocates are discussed on pp. 16-46.
12 Ibid., pp. 16-48 on migration and its theories.
13 See Harold A. Innis, *The Fur Trade in Canada* (Toronto: University of Toronto Press, 1930), pp. 135-45.
14 For general discussion see James G.E. Smith, "Western Woods Cree," in J. Helm, ed., *Handbook of North American Indians*, Vol. 6: *Subarctic* (Washington, DC: Smithsonian Institution, 1981); for distinctions which Rock Cree make, see his "On the Territorial Distribution of the Western Woods Cree," *Papers of the Seventh Algonquian Conference*, edited by W. Cowan (Ottawa: Carleton University Press, 1976) and his "Preliminary Notes on the Rocky Cree of Reindeer Lake," in *Contributions to Canadian Ethnology*, edited by D.B. Carlisle, Mercury Series, Canadian Ethnology Service Paper No. 31 (Ottawa: National Museum of Man, 1975), pp. 171-89; David Pentland found other Cree did not distinguish the Rock as separate ("A Historical Overview of Cree Dialects," in *Papers of the Ninth Algonquian Conference*, edited by W. Cowan [Ottawa: Carleton University Press, 1979]).
15 Fr. Albert Lacombe, "Introduction," in *Dictionnaire de la langue des Cris* (Montreal: C.O. Beauchemin & Valois, 1874), p. xv.
16 Robert A. Brightman, *ACAOOHKIWINA and ACIMOWINA: Traditional Narratives of the Rock Cree Indians*, Mercury Series, Canadian Ethnology Service Paper No. 113 (Ottawa: Canadian Museum of Civilization, 1989), pp. 2-3.
17 Material for the following facts was drawn from *The Mackenzie Basin: Proceedings of the Intergovernmental Seminar Held at Inuvik, N.W.T., 24-27 June 1972* (Ottawa: Inland Waters Directorate, 1973).
18 Jenness, *The Indians of Canada*, p. 315.
19 The rivalry between Huron and Iroquois involved Iroquois-British-Anglicans and Huron-French-Catholics after the British triumphed in 1634. Up to that date the Protestant Huguenot traders had restricted Recollets for obvious religious reasons. See John W. Grant, *Moon of Wintertime* (Toronto: University of Toronto Press, 1984), pp. 7-8.
20 Åke Hultkrantz, *Prairie and Plains Indians* (Leiden: E.J. Brill, 1973), p. 9.
21 Jenness, *The Indians of Canada*, indicates this in a footnote (p. 317), but many sources speak of a thirst dance, e.g., Hultkrantz, *Prairie* (p. 9), where it refers to a fasting and drink-abstinence aspect of the dance by the Shoshonean and Algonquin tribes. I have heard it spoken of as a raindance by some Saskatchewan Cree, and this is con-

firmed by Koozma J. Tarasoff's *Persistent Ceremonialism: The Plains Cree and Saul-teaux*, Mercury Series, Canadian Ethnology Service Paper No. 69 (Ottawa: National Museum of Man, 1980), pp. 20-25. Ahenakew, on the other hand, insists there are sundances as well as dances for rain. See Edward Ahenakew, *Voices of the Plains Cree*, edited with an Introduction by Ruth M. Buck (Toronto: McClelland & Stewart, 1973), where the Cree name given is *Nepakwasemowin* or All-night thirst dance (pp. 68-70 and 179). It is also not clear whether all Cree thirst dances involved torture rites or the name derived from the fasting aspect of a general thirst dance. It is possible that the fasting aspect derived from their closeness to the Sioux, who practise the sun-dance as a self-torture rite de passage for young males. There is confusion among my sources in the north about just what the ceremony should be called; my most reli-able informants, speaking in English, called it a thirst dance. I am convinced that, among the Cree, it was first and foremost a fertility dance, or, in anthropological terms, an increase rite. See also J.C.H. King, *Thunderbird and Lightning: Indian Life in Northeastern North America* (London: British Museum Publications, 1982).

22 Despite the popularity of "The Great Spirit" in many texts, it is doubtful the term should be used, at least not of Cree conceptions, since the term seems to suggest a monotheism of the Judeo-Christian sort. The Cree conception was far more a dy-namic between fundamental positive and negative qualities or energies in the uni-verse. See Jordan Paper, "The Post-Contact Origin of an American Indian High God: The Suppression of Female Spirituality," *American Indian Quarterly*, 7, 4 (1978): 1-24. I agree with Lee Irwin that it is preferable to utilize original words for aborigi-nal concepts where possible ("Myth, Language and Ontology among the Huron," *Studies in Religion/Sciences Religieuses*, 19, 4 [1990]: 414, note 3).

23 This is drawn from my own research among the Cree, undertaken periodically over the last 15 years, including attending and participating in thirst dances. S. Cuthand prefers to translate *Kisemanitou* as "mystery," and says it is much closer to the Hebraic notion of God (personal discussion, 8 March 1987).

24 See Hultkrantz, *Prairie*, p. 18. Some visual aspects of the Blackfoot rite can be seen in my film (*The Sacred Circle*, National Film Board/University of Alberta Production, 1979).

25 Fr. Pierre Moulin, *Bulletin, Western Oblate History Project*, 18 (January 1992): 14.

26 See Pliny Earle Goddard, "Notes on the Sundance of the Cree in Alberta," *American Museum of Natural History: Anthropological Papers*, 16, 4 (1919): 295-310, and Alanson Skinner, "The Sundance of the Plains Cree," *American Museum of Natural History: Anthropological Papers*, 16, 4 (1919): 282-93.

27 Jenness, *The Indians of Canada*, p. 317.

28 Studies of value in understanding drumming include Thomas Vennum, Jr., *The Ojibwa Drum Dance: Its History and Construction*, Smithsonian Folklife Studies, No. 2 (Washington, DC: Smithsonian Institution, 1982); Andrew Neher, " A Physiological Explanation of Unusual Behaviour in Ceremonies Involving Drums," *Human Biol-ogy*, 34 (1962): 151-60; and Gordon C. Baldwin, *Talking Drums to Written Word* (New York: Norton, 1970). It would appear to be a profound insight that the universe speaks through drumming, just as profound as the Christian notion that God speaks through the human form (Christ), or the Muslim notion that God speaks through the Book (the Qur'an). Much more research must be done on this conception among North American First Peoples.

29 From Vandersteene, *Wabasca*, pp. 182-91, translated by Thelma Habgood with amendments by the author. *Wikokewin* was technically an "asking dance," which derives from its role as a petitionary rite for the approaching trapping season. It in-volved propitiation and thanksgiving for the gifts of the bodies of the animals who had been sacrificed as food. It was one of the most critical dances of the ritual year. However, it was not primarily a sacrificial rite, as Vandersteene eventually main-tained.

30 "[M]en with presents of tobaccco, to the whole tribe . . . inviting them to meet at a specified place early in the spring, in general council. . . . The war pipe is then lighted up, and those who are willing to become soldiers in the campaign, smoke the pipe" (W.K. Lambe, ed., *Sixteen Years in the Indian Country: The Journal of Daniel William Harmon, 1800-1816* [Toronto: Macmillan, 1957], p. 223).

31 E.S. Rogers, "Plains Cree," *The Beaver* (Winter 1968), p. 58; for the argument that pipe-smoking is a pre-contact pan-tribal ceremony, see Jordan Paper, *Offering Smoke: The Sacred Pipe and Native American Religion* (Edmonton: University of Alberta Press, 1988). Paul B. Steinmetz sees it as a nativistic movement ("The Sacred Pipe in American Indian Religions," *American Indian Culture and Research Journal,* 8, 3 [1984]: 27-80).

32 Vandersteene's understanding of this word is spelled out in "Some Woodland Traditions and Legends," *Western Canadian Journal of Anthropology,* 1, 1 (1969): 41.

33 For a general treatment of guardian spirit and vision-quest relatedness, see Ruth F. Benedict, "The Concept of the Guardian Spirit in North America," *Memoirs of the American Anthroplogical Association,* 29 (1923): 28-85, especially p. 41.

34 Harmer has argued that among the Ojibwa, seeking help from a human after you have a guardian-spirit can even be dangerous. Once the dependency syndrome has been created, and the guardian has no power, the youths turn to alcohol. Thus the guardian spirit concept has left the young native open to alcohol (John H. Harmer, "Guardian Spirits, Alcohol and Cultural Defence Mechanisms," *Anthropologica,* 11, 2 [1969]: 225). If he knew of this interpretation, Vandersteene never commented upon it. Ted Parnell rejects such interpretations. He argues that Indian attitudes have largely been formed by whites who allowed the Indian no freedom to pursue whatever cultural direction appealed. Consequently, the usual response is passive resistance, withdrawal from contact, silence, feigned stupidity, irritating behaviour to whites and alcoholism ("Conclusion," in *Disposable Native* [Edmonton: Human Rights and Civil Liberties Association, 1976). On the other hand, R.C. Dailey ("The Role of Alcohol among the North American Indian Tribes as Reported in the Jesuit Relations," *Anthropologica,* 10 [1968]: 45-57) holds that the sacred dream was replaced by drunkenness as a legitimate means to encounter the "real soul," and even to have a religious experience. When the disruption of alcohol became a menace, the Indian appealed to whites to stop the liquor. Based on a code of honour and trust, the Indian thought the white man would do what was best for the Indian, even if it cost the white man. It was naive, but was a legitimate aboriginal viewpoint (p. 56).

35 Vandersteene, *Wabasca,* pp. 64-65.

36 For a modern example of this notion see my film, *The Sacred Circle.*

37 As Vandersteene noted, *Wabasca,* p. 97.

38 See Fisher, "The Cree," p. 10.

39 Collected by Fr. Paul Labelle from the diary at Saddle Lake and sent to Fr. Vandersteene at an unknown time.

40 See, for example, Robert Hood, "Some Accounts of the Cree & Other Indians, 1819," *Alberta Historical Review* (Winter 1967), pp. 12-13.

41 John McLean, *Canadian Savage Folk: The Native Tribes of Canada* (Toronto, 1896), pp. 81-82.

42 Selwyn Dewdney, *They Shared to Survive* (Toronto: Macmillan, 1975), pp. 93 f.

43 Vandersteene used this term to describe himself among the missionaries, as we shall see, but his use of this translation can hardly be accurate.

44 From information provided by Cree elder from Wabasca, George Cardinal, May 1994.

45 See John M. Cooper, "The Shaking Tent Rite among Plains and Forest Algonquians," *Primitive Man,* 17 (1944): 60-84; V.F. Ray, "Historic Backgrounds of the Conjuring Complex in the Plateau and the Plains," in L. Spier et al., eds., *Language, Culture and Personality: Essays in Memory of Edward Saper* (Menasha, WI: Sapir

Memorial Publication Fund, 1941), pp. 204-16; and A.L. Hallowell, "The Role of Conjuring in Saulteaux Society," *Philadelphia Anthropological Society*, 2 (1942): 89-96.

46 Thus we find in Fr. Lacombe's *Dictionnaire de la langue des Cris* and most other sources since then. Manitou was probably fixed upon by the Jesuits as a generic word for the mystery of the spiritual world, then elevated to the meaning of "God." The process of the term coming to have all the meanings of the Christian God is beyond the scope of this study, but certainly worth study. It goes without saying that Christian fixation upon this term and its cognates has likely skewed our understanding of Cree relationships with non-human, "divine" beings.

47 R. Cox, *Adventures on the Columbia River Including the Narrative of a Residence of Six Years on the Western Side of the Rocky Mountains among Various Tribes of Indians Hitherto Unknown: Together with a Journey across the American Continent* (New York: J. & J. Harper, 1832), quoted in John S. Milloy, *The Plains Cree: Trade, Diplomacy and War, 1790 to 1870* (Winnipeg: University of Manitoba Press, 1988), p. 71. Vandersteene says: "The supreme mystery in the life of the Cree is clearly God. Not God in his invisible essence, nor his unfathomable attributes, but God insofar as He is necessary to us; or better, God on whom we feel dependent. . . . [T]he Cree language has a very precise grammatical form to designate the activity of God with regard to men: *osisuw*. (Note also that it has no form to designate the activity of man in relation to God.) Here are some examples: *Asamikowisuw* — 'God nurtures him, etc.' " ("Some Woodland Cree Traditions and Legends," p. 60).

48 Fr. Jacques Johnson, director of missions among the natives in Grouard at the time of this research, in an interview in 1975, related the story of a young man who was sorely beset by these spirits to the point of committing suicide. When the priest anointed him and prayed over him, the spirits left and the young man was able to live a normal life. The motif is a common one in conversion stories which I have recorded.

49 Fr. Deharveng notes that many Cree still believe that the sacraments provide protection from evil (interview, June 1994); the amuletory basis of the mass seems to play a much larger role than theological discussion has acknowledged.

50 See Dewdney, *They Shared to Survive*, and comments in Parnell, "Culture Collision," in *Disposable Native*.

51 Edward R. Bhajan, "Community Development Programs in Alberta: An Analysis of Development Efforts in 5 Communities, 1964-1969" (M.A. thesis, University of Alberta, 1972). Wabasca is one community evaluated in chap. 8.

52 For an insightful article on this aspect of Cree tradition see Richard J. and Sarah C. Preston, "Death and Grieving among Northern Forest Hunters: An East Cree Example," in David R. Counts and Dorothy A. Counts, eds., *Coping with the Final Tragedy: Cultural Variation in Dying and Grieving* (Amityville, NY: Baywood, 1991), pp. 135-55, especially pp. 135-38.

53 Fr. Jacques Johnson, "Pilgrim's Reflections," *Father Record-Gazette*, 26 January 1977. Fr. Mariman had this to say of Jean-Baptiste's father: "He communed regularly with the spirits and was what we call a clairvoyant. He foresaw the first World War and prophesied many things for the future. He had a telepathic mind; he was really inspired by God and he had a great impact on his son and grandson."

54 Robert Jefferson, *Fifty Years on the Saskatchewan*, North West Historical Society Publications, Vol. 1, No. 5 (Battleford, SK, 1929), p. 53 f.

55 On the latter, it is this factor that gives questions of treaty rights, status Indians, and non-status "native" women their sharpness. Bands have apparently always been present; one is Cree and then a member of a band, as is evident by the way people were passed around from band to band, or even dropped. See John Goddard, *Last Stand of the Lubicon Cree* (Toronto: Douglas and McIntyre, 1991).

56 Being "Indian" might be just another way of not-being-white in today's world, somewhat like Worsley's perception of cargo cults in Melanesia as being methods of

reaction against foreign domination (P.M. Worsley, *The Trumpet Shall Sound: A Study of "Cargo" Cults in Melanesia* [London: MacGibbon and Kee, 1957]). Edie Scott was an Eastern Woodlands Cree who devoted her later life to Christian prayer and piety. Brought up in Montreal, she had lost all trace of Cree language. Vandersteene brought her to his mission in Garden River, the most "natural" Cree environment, because he saw in her another Kateri of the Mohawks; he hoped her piety would influence the village. The Garden River Cree had no part of her, and she ultimately left in disillusionment. In this case, band/family identity was certainly stronger than Christian or Cree ties. Somewhere in the complexity of this case was the commonness of being Indian, but like the other two, it had little influence in bringing her into the group. Omer Tanghe presents Vandersteene's perceptions of this Indian mystic, as near as we can tell, in his booklet *Little Big Man, My Brother* (Kortrijk: Lanoo, 1973).

57 The context of prophetic movements is surveyed in Joel W. Martin, "Before and Beyond the Sioux Ghost Dance: Native American Prophetic Movements and the Study of Religion," *Journal of the American Academy of Religion*, 59, 4 (1991): 677-701.

58 The first encounter by Cartier in 1534 with the Micmac resulted in the natives bartering everything, including the skins on their back. It is possible that the Cree bartered with the Montagnais who seem to be the first "go-betweens" in the fur trade. See H.P. Biggar, *The Voyage of Jacques Cartier*, No. 11 (Ottawa: Public Archives of Canada, 1924), pp. 49 f.

59 Ray, *Indians in the Fur Trade*, pp. 12, 35 and 36.

60 Ralph says pointedly: "Canada was French soil, and peopled by as hardy and adventurous a class as inhabited any part of America. The *coureurs de bois* and the *pois-brulés* (half-breeds), whose success afterwards led to the formation of rival companies, had begun a mosquito warfare, by canoeing the waters that led to Hudson Bay, and had penetrated 100 miles farther west than the English" (*On Canada's Frontier*, p. 154).

61 If the white man ever was regarded as the holy one sent from the other world, as some elders are said to have believed, and was apparently the basis of Indian-Spanish encounter, there is no indication that that held among the Cree. What seems to have been present was respect, such as would be accorded a messenger from another peaceful tribe, or a messenger from an enemy tribe that had great personal power to talk peace. Neils Winther Braroe, *Indian & White: Self-Image and Interaction in a Canadian Plains Community* (Stanford: Stanford University Press, 1975), explains the way this can be viewed: "The degree of sacredness possessed by any person in a given situation with respect to others present depends on a great many factors, all of which enter into the prevailing definitions of the situation. Rank and status, familiarity or formality, and conventional settings and occasions of interaction all influence both the varieties of regard persons extend to one another and the resulting social distance between them. Whatever the degree of respect actually offered or demanded, respect itself is necessarily a component of every social interaction" (pp. 33-34).

62 Tarasoff, *Persistent Ceremonialism*, pp. 20-21. A female healer did not have the power to do naming, according to his sources (p. 12).

63 John E. Foster, "Le Missionaire and Le Chief Métis," in *Western Oblate Studies*, Vol. 1: *Proceedings of the First Symposium on the History of the Oblates in Western and Northern Canada* (Edmonton: Western Canadian Publishers, 1990), pp. 117-27.

64 Ray notes the meeting between the assembled Cree chiefs of Alberta and the chief Factor of Edmonton region on 13 April 1781. The chief who acted as spokesman was Chief Sweet Grass. He said he had heard that their lands had been sold or traded to the government and he pointed out that they did not like this, since they had not sold any of their lands. In this case, the Chief was acting as a representative spokesperson for all the chiefs so gathered, a kind of elected spokesperson for all the

groups. The subsequent Treaties involved the same kind of leadership representative (Ray, *Indians in the Fur Trade*, pp. 227-28).

65 Milloy, *The Plains Cree*, p. 75.

66 See David Mandelbaum, *The Plains Cree: An Ethnographic, Historical, and Comparative Study*, Canadian Plains Studies No. 9 (Regina: Canadian Plains Research, 1979), pp. 224-29, and Alanson Skinner, "Political Organizations, Cults, and Ceremonies of the Plains Cree," *American Museum of Natural History: Anthropological Papers*, 11, 6 (1914): 518 ff.

67 Jefferson, *Fifty Years*, p. 64, and David Mandelbaum, "The Plains Cree," *American Museum of Natural History Anthropological Papers*, 37, 2 (1940): 222.

68 The *Plains Cree Conference* elicited a strong response from Cree to Mandelbaum's insistence on warrior culture as being the basis of leadership. Later, Mandelbaum agreed that the warrior societies might be better known as "civic organizations," although he did stress that much had changed since his study in the late 1930s ("Changes in Aboriginal Culture," p. 70).

69 Milloy, *The Plains Cree*, pp. 75-82.

70 Thus male leadership among the Cree appears to reflect the same split between male hierarchical and female cosmological statuses as noted by Bruce Lincoln in *Emerging from the Chrysalis: Studies in Rituals of Women's Initiation* (Cambridge, MA: Harvard University Press, 1981) and *Death, War and Sacrifice: Studies in Ideology and Practice* (Chicago: University of Chicago Press, 1991).

71 Ralph, *On Canada's Frontier*, p. 56.

72 See below (pp. 132-33) the touching story told of the visit of Rev. Omer Tanghe and the two conversing in Flemish, along with the response of a venerable old member of Vandersteene's flock.

73 Much the same point, but with different emphasis, has been made by Tarasoff, *Persistent Ceremonialism*, p. 25.

74 For a study on dreaming, see Robin Ridington, *Swan People: A Study of the Dunne-Za Prophet Dance*, Mercury Series, Canadian Ethnology Service Paper No. 38 (Ottawa: National Museum of Man, 1978), pp. 7 ff.

75 Brightman, *ACAOOHKIWINA*, p. 161.

76 The constitution identified "Aboriginal People," a more acceptable form for the huge diversity of First People's tribes across Canada. Yet they were identified as a group, an acceptance of the "Indians" as a different group of people, somehow cohesive (*Consensus Report on the Constitution* [Ottawa: Minister of Supply and Services Canada, 1992], pp. 16 f.).

77 Bro. Memorian, "Roman Catholic Missions in Canada," in C.T. Loram and T.F. McIllwraith, eds., *The North American Indian Today* (Toronto: University of Toronto Press, 1943), pp. 90-97.

78 *Gazetteer of Indian and Eskimo Stations of the Oblate Fathers in Canada* (Ottawa: Oblate Services, 1960), pp. 63-86.

79 Faraud to Mazenod, 29 December 1855, quoted in Mary McCarthy, "The Founding of Providence Mission," *Western Oblate Studies*, Vol. 1 (Edmonton: Western Canadian Publishers and Institut de recherche de la Faculté St. Jean, 1990), p. 39; hereafter cited as *WOS*, Vol. 1.

80 Raymond Huel, "La mission Notre-Dame-des-Victoires du Lac La Biche et l'approvisionnement des missions du nord: Le conflit entre Mgr V. Grandin et Mgr H. Faraud," *WOS*, Vol. 1, pp. 17-36.

81 See the bibliography in Thomas Maccagno, "Mission Possible: The Lac La Biche Mission Historical Society," *WOS*, Vol. 1, p. 161.

82 See Ralph, *On Canada's Frontier*, pp. 54-55.

83 Memorian, "Roman Catholic Missions," p. 96.

84 Quoted in P. Duchaussois, O.M.I., *Mid Snow and Ice* (London: Burns, Oates & Washbourne, 1923), p. 322.

85 Robert Choquette, "Les rapports entre Catholiques et Protestants dans le nord-ouest du Canada avant 1840," *WOS*, Vol. 1, p. 137 (my translation).

86 Rev. Wm. Newton, *Twenty Years on the Saskatchewan*, N.W. *Canada* (London, 1897), p. 120.

87 R. Painchaud, *Un rêve français dans le peuplement de la prairie* (Saint-Boniface: Les Éditions du Blé, 1987), p. 23.

88 Alice Trottier, ed., *Journal d'un missionaire-colonisateur, 1890-1897* (Edmonton: Le Salon d'histoire de la francophonie albertaine, 1984), p. xii; see also her "Les Oblates et la colonisation en Alberta," *WOS*, Vol. 1, pp. 107-16.

89 McCarthy, "The Founding of Providence Mission," p. 47.

90 Long-time Oblate school administrator, Yvon Levaque, O.M.I., stated it boldly: "I categorically reject the thesis that the Catholic Church, through the ministry of the Oblate missionaries, was in league with the federal government to exterminate native cultures by means of the residential school system" ("The Oblates and Indian Residential Schools," *WOS*, Vol. 1, p. 182). Despite that, the Canadian director of the Oblates officially apologized for Oblate actions towards the Indians, including the ethnocentric education, at Lac Ste. Anne in July 1991.

91 Interview, August 1978. Arthur Lamothe was a Métis from northern Alberta who became a priest in the diocese during Vandersteene's time. As we indicate below (pp. 232-33), there were various reasons why he disagreed with Vandersteene and why he left the Church.

92 For background on Christian missions and theory see L. Vriens, A. Disch and J. Wils, eds., *A Critical Bibliography of Missiology* (Nijmegen: Bestelcentrale der V.S.K.B., 1960); Msgr. S. Delacroix, *Histoire universelle des missions catholiques*, 4 vols. (Paris: Grund, 1956-59); Kenneth S. Latourette, *A History of the Expansion of Christianity*, 7 vols. (New York: Harper & Bros., 1937-45); Stephen C. Neill, *Colonialism and Christian Missions* (London: Oxford University Press, 1966); Stephen C. Neill, *A History of Christian Missions* (Harmondsworth: Penguin Books, 1964); and Alan C. Bouquet, *The Christian Faith and Non-Christian Religions* (London: Cassell, 1958).

93 Levaque, "The Oblates," p. 183.

94 Jean Leflon, *Eugène de Mazenod, Bishop of Marseilles, Founder of the Oblates of Mary Immaculate*, translated by Francis D. Flanagan, O.M.I. (New York: Fordham University Press, 1966), Vol. 2, p. 40.

95 For an excellent analysis of the legal issues see Peter A. Cumming and Neil H. Mickenberg, eds., *Native Rights in Canada*, 2nd ed. (Toronto: The Indian Association of Canada and General Publishing, 1972).

96 See generally H. Cardinal, *The Unjust Society: The Tragedy of Canada's Indians* (Edmonton: M.G. Hurtig, 1969), especially pp. 65-73.

97 R.J. Möhr, *Missionethnologie: Ein Wissenschaftliches Programm* (Nijmegen and Utrecht: Dekker & Van de Vegt N.V., 1956), p. 9: "Dieser Wert liegt eben in dem Immanenten, welches das Wesen der Kultur ausmacht. Und was ist nun dieses Immanente, dieses Geistige an der Kultur? Das is die innere wertende Haltung, die der Mensch den Wirklichkeiten gegenüber einnimmt."

98 Ibid., p. 10.

99 Ibid., pp. 9-10.

100 Ibid., p. 18.

101 Ibid., p. 21.

Four

"My Little Sisters, My Little Brothers": From Encounter to *Wabasca*

> I remember him as a little girl. He would pick me up and sit me on his great knee. Total acceptance. That was his genius. Total acceptance of the Indian people and their culture. — Beth Ann Buha, 19 November 1991

When Vandersteene finally boarded the freighter *Samuel Compers* in Antwerp, and set out for Canada, he chronicled his trip in a letter to his brother. Writing from his aunt Germaine's in Montreal, he recalled the mixed group of fellow-travellers — Indians from South America, Belgian Jews, Romanian immigrants, etc. — who joined him on the boat on 29 September 1946. The principle language of the group was not English but Dutch, and Vandersteene endured the roiling waters better than some of his confreres: despite the storm at sea he was not sick. Rather, he sat on deck, beer in hand, singing Flemish folk songs and enjoying the passage with relish. Somewhere north of Cuba, the boat turned north and headed for Baltimore, a nautical course that indicates that he took the first boat he could get to America rather than wait for a ship going directly to Montreal. Disembarking, he caught the train going north to Montreal. Later he was to joke with his Indian friends that he did not know English well enough to ask for food, so all he could say was the Flemish *melk*, sufficiently similar to milk to get him a drink. Whether this is entirely true or not, it became part of the lore the Indians told of him, and he told on himself, a tale made more believable by his affirmation that he disliked speaking English because it was so crude and harsh compared to Cree. In fact, his lack of comfort in English was a matter of some mirth for Julian Gladue, an old Cree friend of Vandersteene: Julian used to interpret from English into

Notes to this chapter are on pp. 122-25.

Cree when Vandersteene could not communicate with some English speakers. Julian thought it was the height of hilarity that a Cree should be the interpreter for two white men. Most particularly he savoured the fact that they weren't able to communicate until the old Cree talked for them.

In the year of his arrival, Vandersteene's new homeland, Canada, was still in the post-war doldrums; industry had not yet moved from its war footing, and the development that would herald the 1950s was only in the planning stages. The long winter of 1946 was a reflection of the state of the economy. While the existence of the oil sands in northern Alberta had been known since the previous century, and the tremendous potential for development much discussed, little had transpired because of the war and lack of technical processes for refining the oil from the sands. In 1947, the first oil strike at Leduc, just south of Edmonton, would begin to galvanize the provincial economy, but it was several years before that had an effect on the economy, and, anyway, no native community in the north would see much of that largesse.

Archbishop Routhier would recall the situation in the north after he retired:

> The conditions in the area were quite primitive at the time. There was no decent road into the Peace River by car. There was a gravel road passing through Slave Lake and, if it was the rainy season, you quite often got stuck in the mud going north. The war was still on in 1944 when I first arrived and there were no telephones; one could not reach Edmonton by telephone. The only way to get through was by the American forces as they were in certain parts of the diocese if we wanted to phone. One could not go too far north unless one took a boat from Peace River to Ft. Vermilion. The missionaries in the northern part of the Vicariate travelled by dog team to some extent and by boat at other times or by wagon with horses. I don't think the population as a whole was more than 25 to 35,000 people under my jurisdiction. The Catholic population was in the neighbourhood of 18,000 at that time. About 1/3 were Indian or Métis, 1/3 were French-speaking and 1/3 were of practically all nationalities.[1]

None of this seemed to have affected young Vandersteene; he does not mention it in his letters home. He expected the cold, although even he was a little shocked by −40° C according to his letters home, but he had had no way of foreseeing the poverty and hopelessness in Canada, let alone among the isolated communities to which he was bound. Besides, with his full red beard and the long-stemmed pipe his mother had given him, he cut quite a figure. The first thing he had to face, however, was a general state of malaise in the Vicariate, brought about

by the continuing health problems of Bishop Langlois. Routhier recalls
those years:

> I was sent up north to the Peace River area, as we call it, to the diocese of
> Peace River. At that time it was the Vicariate Apostolic of Grouard and it
> remained the Vicariate Apostolic until 1967, when it became an archdio-
> cese. Of course there isn't much difference between the vicariate apos-
> tolic and a diocese or archdiocese. The only difference is really in the
> title and if it's an archdiocese, then the archbishop, to some extent, pre-
> sides over meetings of bishops in his own metropolitan area. The archdi-
> ocese of Grouard would have several bishops, the Yukon, Prince George,
> and the Mackenzie. A very extensive territory, but that really doesn't
> mean much because each bishop is practically independent in his own
> diocese. When I was sent in 1944 to the Peace River area, I had previous-
> ly been Provincial of the Oblate Fathers in Edmonton. Bishop Langlois,
> who was then the Vicar Apostolic, had become quite ill and I was sent
> there to assist him. In 1945, I was appointed Acting Bishop of Grouard
> and remained not completely in charge, but under his authority; I
> worked in the diocese. In 1947 he retired, moved east, became quite ill
> and died in 1953. So I was Vicar Apostolic from 1953 until I resigned at
> the end of 1972.[2]

The lines of authority remained blurred in the diocese, a factor
which combined with the isolated state of many of the missions to create the sense of operating entirely on one's own. Vandersteene was to
find this attractive; it would allow him the freedom to experiment with
new ideas. Especially he wondered about the rumblings he heard
among the young Cree, who seemed to be indifferent to the Church despite being trained in Catholic schools. He mulled over why so few aboriginals ever saw the Church as a viable place for them to serve. His
initial reaction was that the Church had become aloof, and had taken a
typical white attitude to the Indians — superiority. He determined to
meet the Cree on their own ground, as a part of their environment. His
preliminary perception was that the Cree lived in a somewhat childlike relationship with the natural world, with a simple piety toward
God and the world. This is implicit in his first letters, which speak, in
French, of "l'ignorance" of the people of Christian doctrines, and the
"simple" type of faith they practised.[3] In time he was to see this simplicity as the very essence of Cree faith:

> "That's the home of Pol and Selapien; they are the people who taught
> me how to drive a sled and a kaboes (horse-drawn wagon). They are old
> now. They know I am bringing them the Lord. . . ."
>   "Two splendid believers," he said, when we left the cabin. "Did you
> watch their faces? There was a radiance there that witnessed not only to
> their simplicity and goodness, but *to* God, Himself."[4]

His comment at the time to Tanghe, his biographer, was: "My people are silent people, but in order to talk you do not need always your voice or words. I learned from them that affection, understanding and hospitality can be expressed in quite different ways than in Western Europe. Once they allow you to enter their world, you will soon realize how beautiful my people are."[5] But, as Vandersteene was to learn, that simplicity masked sophistication; he may have entered into the world of the Cree with notions of their childlike faith, but he was to learn how complicated the inner world was, even if behaviour toward the Manitou was one of calm and simple faith.

When he first arrived, being relatively free from the heavy hand of church bureacracy allowed him to explore his new home. He was enthralled with the vegetation in this part of Canada. The old love of botany, since it no longer involved obedience to his father's will, rose to the surface. Notebooks filled with personal observations and sketches piled up on the shelf. He rooted in whatever books on flora and fauna he could find, adding them to his growing library. His colleague Fr. Mariman from Meander River would remember him chugging down a road with his eyes searching the growth on each side for telltale plants. He found excuses to get to the Rocky Mountains so he could probe the mountainsides for new and different plants. He seemed overcome with the riches he found. His interest in botany flourished for the remainder of his life and was to bear dramatic fruit in his Trout Lake grotto.

Vandersteene was assigned to St. Bernard's Mission in Grouard, where his task from the moment he arrived on 13 November 1946 was to familiarize himself with the culture of the diocese, to become acclimatized and to begin to learn the language of the Cree. As we have seen, St. Bernard's had a long history, and was foundational to Catholic development in the north. But by the time Vandersteene arrived, it was beginning to show signs of decline. For a long time, it had struggled with the issue of staffing the residential schools. Routhier recalls:

> From 1894, the Sisters of Providence had come to the residential schools to try to give education to the Indian children. This improved conditions a great deal at the schools. Whatever can be said about residential schools, they were indispensable in those days, because the Indians were roaming all over the country and you never could have a school where the children could attend all the months. It wasn't easy to get children to school because the Indian people themselves had no experience of anything like education and particularly the interaction of being grouped together. At any rate it was during my time that Fr. Vandersteene came into the area. He was sent first to Grouard and then to Whitefish Lake (Akitameg) where he with two or three other young

priests were to learn the Cree language. In a matter of six months he was
able to speak fluently and his whole desire was not to work among the
whites, but to work among the Indians.[6]

He moved to Akitameg on 19 February 1947. St. Benedict's Mission
was under the guidance of that old warhorse of mission work among
the Cree, Fr. Yves-Marcel Floc'h. A superlative Cree speaker, he had
worked so long in the field that he almost knew Cree better than anyone in Alberta. Vandersteene took to Floc'h immediately. He liked the
old man's spirit. It related directly to his own: Fr. Floc'h had once contrived to get the Anglican priest's cows drunk, to the abundant delight
of the Cree.

Vandersteene's partner in the Cree-learning process was another
young priest from Quebec, Louis-Paul Lachance. There never was any
competition between them. Vandersteene sailed into Cree like it was a
dialect of Flemish. Hour after hour he toiled over the language, never
even stopping when he went out hunting. He recalled later that he had
found it helpful to write Cree words on bits of paper and place them on
the gunsight. He forced himself to say the word several times before he
fired a shot. Relentlessly he pursued Cree, like a besotted lover; it became a constant source of delight and consternation to him, even until
the end of his life. His skills increased so rapidly that local Cree marvelled at him, and his colleague despaired. Lachance abandoned the
field.

Even with his success, Vandersteene was dismayed, even depressed.
He had come to serve in the poorest missions, but so far his time was
spent soaking up language in a burnt-out mission. He looked around
and saw the ugly side of Indian-Canadian relations, the prejudice and
antagonism lying just below the surface of many communities. He saw
the abysmal conditions of the town Cree and Métis, with the rampant
alcoholism. More distinctly, he saw the Church's ambiguous relationship with the Cree people. Within the first year, he nearly asked to be
sent home several times. There were some very dark days.

But his success with Cree sustained him, along with his inner convictions about his calling. Vandersteene did not like to fail; he had
never done it, even when he was most ill. His love for Cree grew, along
with his pursuit of an underlying Cree character. His search mixed
well with his Flemish character and language abilities: "A Fleming un-
derstands better than anybody that the language of a people is its main
artery," he contended.[7] He was beguiled by the stories of old-timers,
their powers and their ideas. He was sure something entirely Cree
could be found behind the façade of the convoluted culture he found
himself within. His experience of the Flemish language and its cultural

significance gave him an insight into the Cree. He was entranced by the way Cree could give an instant photograph of a situation; he liked the ease with which new words could be formed, just by connecting elements of meanings together. In his meetings with colleagues, he could wax eloquent about the treasures of the Cree language. He pressed academics to study Cree for its possible relationship to German and Dutch.

In 1971 he attended a conference on Cree syllabics in Winnipeg. His comments, set in the controversies of bilingualism in Canada, nevertheless sum up the attitude he early formed toward Cree:

Cree is a beautiful language that should not be allowed to die. It is spoken, in several dialects, nearly clear across Canada and in parts of the United States. It belongs to the Algonquin family of languages. . . .

Missionaries and traders who learned it themselves and taught it to the people were doing a very wise thing. English or French taught in schools were often forgotten quickly by the native children when they returned to their communities, and those who did not forget completely did not further develop. Their reading consisted mostly in comic strips. . . .

Many books and articles were printed and still are reprinted in syllabics in Cree Montagnais and Eskimo, mostly of a religious nature. Lately, however, the state took over all education in all its ramifications and native languages started to suffer. No more Cree in schools. It has been banished locally, even from recess periods and recreational halls, and propaganda is being made to have the children speak more English at home, even when parents do not understand it. A painful spiritual poverty of the children is the result of such actions. The authority of the parents is broken, respect for their own history and culture is replaced by a false sense of superiority. Mature people and children are alienated, to the detriment of both. Undigested ideas make an unreal and unrealistic atmosphere in which dissatisfaction and frustration abound.

Reaction to this situation is coming from both the people themselves and from wiser men in school administration, church and government. There is a movement of return to the native languages among educated Indians. There is still the attitude among some officials that Cree can speak and write the language and be considered illiterate! The ideal we should aim for is that with our fellow Canadians we could [*sic*] communicate in an official language, spoken or written, while at the same time we should be so rich (and helped to be that rich!) as to learn the tongue of our community — reading and writing as well as in speech. In any case, your own language, studied, spoken, written, and read is still the very best starting point to learn to speak, write and read another one, official or not.

We do some splendid research on the origins of our planet, up to going to the moon, that may teach us something of our own earth-genesis, up to digging up old bones buried for eons, but all that is only "body"; we try to neglect the past, the spiritual development, the viewpoint of other notions concerning our inner growth and be-ing, and we even try to destroy what is not spiritually "me now." Is humanity only as rich as we are? Or are we afraid of discovering things that may upset us from our self-created pinnacle of our arche de triomphe? Many truths can only be facets of one truth, and many truths are enthroned in many languages, that come through centu-ries of wisdom, thought, experience ... and kept alive and brought to us today. We must not destroy it.

Humanity will never be one because one language is spoken! Look at those who speak English. Are they one? If unity has to be bought at the price of linguistic poverty and limitation, that unity is offensive and evil. Humanity has to be diversified, with diverse ap-proaches, diverse expressions, because humanity is too big for one pair of eyes, one pair of ears, one set of brains and one language to express it.[8]

So competent did he become in Cree that people who did not know him by name and even some parishioners referred to him simply by the epithet Ka Nihta Nehiyawet, which translates as "the one who really speaks Cree."

He very soon learned that speaking Cree was not just a way of react-ing to the world and creating a culture; he also saw how Cree could use it as a force to create an alternate world to the white Canadian. The old Cree people consciously used language to help create and maintain a different cultural world. The more he learned, the more he realized how distinctive was Cree culture.

Cree people talk differently than whites. Like the problem of com-mitting themselves. Cree never will lie because they have seven or eight different words to express doubt. If someone comes and I say "Are we going to hunt tomorrow?" he would say "Enh enh ahpo ituke" that means, "It's possible." But what if tomorrow his wife is sick. He didn't want to commit himself to me to hunt because then he would have lied to me if his wife was sick. An Indian was talking to an RCMP officer and said he would be in on such and such a day but he never showed up. They said he was a liar. . . . He should have used maybe. All this applies to things like asking people their names, knocking on doors, entertaining people, property, etc.[9]

The range of information which language introduced to him was considerable. With it came a cultural code that opened a wide range of Cree experience. Like all beginning students, Fr. Paul Hernou learned from Vandersteene how to ask someone his name. But asking someone his name is also governed by protocols, as he was to learn the hard way:

> One of the first things Vandersteene taught me, next to *kayas, tansi* and *namanandow* was to ask somebody his name. Three or four days after I arrived, an old man came to the house and Father went into the bedroom for something. I thought, "This is a good time to try out my Cree." So I said "Tansi" and he said back to me "namanandow." Then he said "How are you" and I said "fine." I asked "What's your name?" and he answered "Tanisi ituke" and afterwards I found out that this means "how . . . maybe." All the time Vandersteene was roaring with laughter in his bedroom. He told me later, "It's a good thing I wasn't long away from you because you really got nailed on that. . . . you never ask a name of a Cree, because if you don't know who he is, he's not going to tell you who he is. They believe that when you give your name you give your whole personality and you are not able to do that to just anybody. However, if you want to know the name of somebody who comes to see you and there are two of them, then you can ask the other what his friend's name is."[10]

Obviously these protocols apply to a wide range of experience. Vandersteene learned that asking for anything from a Cree standpoint required him to preserve the independence of the one he was petitioning. To ask someone directly did not allow the petitionee the freedom to say no. He discovered that if he could send someone to ask for him, that is, could find a delegate petitioner, then that was fine. He also learned that there were ways that you could make requests when you were alone with someone, but they required certain positional stances: For example, if he wanted a cigarette he could say "Smoking a cigarette would be a very pleasant thing to do with you now."

Even more complicated were power relationships. When he had to say "thank you" to someone, then he was admitting the other person was, in a very real sense, superior to him. Requesting anything put him in debt to that individual. However, if he offered, then the petitioner was not indebted. Eventually Vandersteene learned why relations between the various governments and the Cree continued to be so troubled: the government cultivated the notion that the Cree people had to say thank you for the funds it allocated to them, despite the fact that they had been owners of the land before the white came. From the Cree perspective there could be no equality when one group always must be grateful to another.

At the same time Cree taught him their meaning of sharing. One of the most important lessons arose out of naivete on his part. One time at Wabasca he stopped to see old Charlebois. It wasn't long before Vandersteene realized that Charlebois didn't have very much food to share with him. Nor did he make much attempt to do so. From a Cree standpoint, Charlebois really didn't take good care of his "brother" at all. Vandersteene shrugged it off. The next morning, Vandersteene went on his way, and a few miles down the trail, he spotted a moose. He tracked and killed the moose, cut a few pieces from the carcase and brought it back to Charlebois' wife. Then he and Charlebois went and brought the moose meat down to the cabin. They feasted on moose. Vandersteene, since he had found the moose, was in no hurry to leave. Finally in a day or two he set out on the road to Trout Lake.

The Cree who heard of this thought it a great joke. In Cree tradition, old Charlebois should have fed the priest. Instead, Vandersteene ended up doing the sharing. The Cree relished the irony in the story. From Vandersteene's point of view, he thought he was carrying out Christian charity. Only later did he learn how he had given a twist to the Cree value of sharing.

Most daunting of all were the issues of moral conflict, and when they should be dealt with and how. Issues which his culture had taught him to keep silent about were discussed; actions that would bring social and moral condemnation in white society were treated openly. Fr. Hernou has a fine illustration of an issue Vandersteene learned:

> I remember one time when Vandersteene was giving a sermon on Jesus' remark that if someone hits you on one cheek, offer him the other. Cree tradition accepted that if you forgive someone, it's over with, as compared with the general notion that well, O.K. it's forgiven but it's not forgotten. On one occasion he requested the people to formulate their prayers after the sermon. Different people requested things like "I would like you to pray for my little girl who is in hospital," etc. Well, on that occasion a guy speaks up and says, "Before I am able to pray today I would like to ask forgiveness to God and ask the priest in the name of God to forgive me, because two days ago I slept with the wife of the man who is sitting next to me." I didn't know what to expect. The guy sitting next to him showed nothing on his face, and I know for a fact that nothing ever happened because of that.[11]

Vandersteene also found that the Cree language was one way that Cree maintained a subtle control over whites. Among themselves they could use the humorous resources of the language to overcome the power differences. As Hernou points out:

> There are ways of being humorous in Cree that become the means of negating criticism, or even of undermining someone of obvious power. There is an indicative and there is a subjunctive mood in Cree. If I say to Mary Rose, teasing her, "I was working today" in the indicative mood, I would say "Nikitatoskan" and she would start laughing. If I say "Eki atoskeyan," then she is free to believe if I am working or not. You have to be sharp in Cree, because they can be pulling your leg just with a tense change.[12]

One also discovers a marked attitude to events of the past. Julian Gladue and Vandersteene crashed through a soft spot in the ice when crossing the Peace River during the winter and they nearly drowned; the crisis was remembered vividly many years later, and the story often retold whenever they came together. Yet for the Cree, the terror of the experience was gone, and the occasion became one of laughter and joviality over their appearance when they finally arrived on the riverbank. The anguish of the past was now balanced by the humour of the present. Vandersteene learned that the best use of the past was for humour, not for bitter remonstrance, nor lessons for the future. Patterns of connection were not validated in the same historical, causal sense.

The protocols of learning Cree also introduced him to Cree culinary fare. To the consternation of his fellow missionaries he plunged in to Cree diet with relish; he literally ate anything he was given. Based on the usual Cree fare, and in the light of their isolation, this often meant that none of "whiteman" food was available. So he ate everything — beef jerky, duck intestines, rabbit head soup, muskrat meat, moose nose, moose intestines, soup made from fishheads. Most amazing to his Canadian associates, he abandoned the great Flemish tradition of strong coffee, and took with delight to black tea made in an old saucepan. But he still retained his love for heels of bread, whenever such were around.

Nor was he bothered by the long silences which can be characteristic of meetings with Cree. He accepted that one didn't speak very much as a rule to start with and sometimes there could be 15 or 20 minutes go by before anyone said anything. People had to get comfortable in each other's presence before anything of significance could be said. Other missionaries found it disconcerting to sit there and not say a thing, and often they hurried away.[13]

Not Vandersteene. He acknowledged that there were other kinds of communication than verbal, and that verbal interaction required several preliminaries. Sharing a smoke was an acceptable way of beginning a discussion, because it usually established the ground by which participation could proceed. His long pipe was an important tool, because he saw clearly that smoking was a medium for communication, a factor which he urged upon his superiors as a means to relate better with the aboriginal populations.[14] Tobacco was a kind of speaking grass.

He quickly adapted to Cree ways, and strained under the limitations of his language training. He was appointed to St. Martin's in Wabasca, beginning 1 September 1947. The mission was originally established in 1896, and was the base for a number of smaller missions in the region. His reply to Routhier after his appointment reflects his current state of mind:

> Before leaving for Wabasca, I wish to thank you for the confidence you bestow upon me in sending me further in the woods towards our dear [sic] Indians. I promise, Excellency, to do my utmost for these poor people I love so much. I deeply regret my poor preparation for such a noble task, for the little Cree I do possess is insufficient to do all the good works I would like to. But I will endeavour to do my best to offset this gap as soon as possible. . . . I will leave with this Flemish proverb: Man does his best and God does the rest.[15]

As we have seen above, there were many kinds of Cree. Despite Vandersteene's love for the generic Cree, he certainly had his preferences. In truth the Cree to whom he wished to go were not the "urban" Cree of Grouard, nor the Cree who were located in larger centres like Slave Lake. Many of these were called the "jetset" Indians, a group completely co-opted by white political culture and for which he had no sympathy.[16] It was the pockets of Cree strung out in tiny groups of families whom he hungered to serve. They were partially nomadic, that is, two, three or four families who were closely related, travelled around a region together and their hunters and trappers harvested the animals. Thirty kilometres or so further on, there would be another set of families, etc. These chains of communities were the people to whom he felt urgently committed in the early years of his ministry.

Within these communities, he specially sought out the elders. He wished to engage the old chiefs he had read about in the Oblate stories. Roué notes that he found a very different picture than what appears in the books: "Of course there were also the elders, those who had the authority, and then there were the leaders, who became leaders because of their character or because of some special gift. They just recognized him as a leader. The people of Whitefish or Peerless Lakes came together maybe once or twice a year, they would celebrate at the end of the hunting or trapping season, and they celebrated this with religious ceremonies or rituals of their own. They had specific kinds of leaders for that."[17] Vandersteene learned that not everything one read about Cree, even by so-called authorities, could be trusted, a fact he was to convey to his fellow missionaries with a warning, as we shall see shortly.

Hand in hand with this understanding went his acceptance that traditional Cree status structures should not only be tolerated but preserved. He refused to accept the new youth movement that began to sweep all before it in the fifties and sixties. He harangued his colleagues with long monologues on the problems of youth-oriented culture. Citing the horrible crime statistics among youth, he asserted that the dominance of the youth culture was a modern fairy tale created by the news media. He openly scoffed at the oft-heard truism that the future of the world was with the youth. Contrarily, he argued that the future of the world and the future of the Church was with the mature people. He pointed out that only when someone had remained true for 40 or 50 years could the Church know it had a real Christian. Drawing on accepted views within traditional Cree society, he insisted that youths between 20 and 30 years of age couldn't judge well, because they were still maturing, or in Cree terms, were not yet completely persons.[18] He saw that if the youth movement succeeded among the Cree, the role and status of the elders would be completely destroyed, with crushing effect on Cree survival.

While at Wabasca,[19] Vandersteene travelled into the bush, probing the little communities stretched out in small encampments within a radius of a hundred kilometres of the town. Wabasca itself was dominated by the politics of the Bigstone Cree band, a sizeable Métis population, a vigorous Protestant Church and the Hudson's Bay store. It was not "primitive" enough for this missionary. Having given his life to the poorest, the settled environment of the Cree/Métis town was not to his taste. Besides, he did not believe that these people were the authentic groups that he had been sent to evangelize. Consequently, in a trip of several weeks duration he took a dogteam north of Wabasca, moving from cluster to cluster, hoping to determine the precise needs of these people. He wrote to Routhier with a summary of his views on the 12 April 1948. In all, he made nine stops, in each describing how many people were there, whether they participated in the mass, whether they were baptized and whether they were married or not. He also recorded whether there were any "pagans" present, and any special needs, such as Cree prayer books and missals. The following comment is somewhat typical of his assessments:

> At Chipewyan, the atmosphere is quite different (from Lake Manitou), and I think it was the best of the whole journey. . . . Here there is a serenity among the people which struck me, a facility to laughter along with its religious spirit.
>
> It is here that more of the pagan superstitions still survive along with the sins of the flesh, which consume like a fire. Despite that, the atmosphere was very lovely. There are ten houses occupied at the moment, none, save one, were of cement. There are several Protestant males, but all the children were Catholic. However, here also the (religious) ignorance is particularly great.[20]

The largest cluster of homes he found was at Chipewyan, and throughout his entire trip he must have seen between 100 and 200 people. At no place did he find a complete "pagan" family, that is, a husband and wife who did not participate in the mass, although at God's Lake, the "old pagan man and his Catholic wife" did not attend. In the whole trip, he did not record more than three people who seemed to be committed to a traditional native viewpoint. Only one woman seemed to be opposed to his presence. Vandersteene admits that he left her aside, and spent his time with her Catholic husband.

Something in his trip, however, fired his resolve. He pleaded for Routhier to commit him to these Indian missions: "I wish to go and stay with them, if you will send me. I have such pity for them and I have seen many good things which inspires a beautiful hope. I love them, Monsigneur. Grant that you will agree, Monsigneur." Monsigneur did not agree. Vandersteene remained under Fr. Benoit Guimont at Wabasca for another year, serving at the nearby mission of St. Charles.

If he did not move into the mission he wanted, he at least began exploring a number of aspects of the culture. Unable to totally communicate with the Cree, and sensing that he still was not tuned in to either Canadian or Cree culture, he took up the paint brush. Here was a language that everyone could engage. Slowly he began to stock up images from his travels, reflections of scenes and plants, meditations in pencil on sites of Cree significance. Notebook after notebook filled with these sketches. Some of them spilled over into oils, as he filled spaces in the chapel at Wabasca with scenes lifted from the community he had encountered. Purposely painting in a stilted primitivist style, he tried to give a sense of the timelessness of the Cree environment, and tried to lift the local faces and shapes to universal proportion. Each has a stylized sense, but each has a strong link with a natural cosmos, in which the figures become Cree with Christian overlay. Their tone is calm and intuitive, meditative.

Vandersteene recognized that the Cree were part of a Canadian aboriginal cultural tradition, and explored whatever he could to determine where Cree culture was going. In Sucker Creek he came upon the Cardinal family, Frank and Rose, whose young son Harold would make a significant mark in the world. Whenever he had time, he swung by Sucker Creek, talking with the Cardinals and trying to find out where the Cree community was heading.[21] It was not just enough, then, to explore the remote comunities, but to keep one's eye on the movements that were impacting on Cree consciousness from many levels.

In addition, he became an avid reader of whatever he could get his hands on about missions in Canada: the foundational days of Jean de Brébeuf, the martyrdom of the great Jesuits known as the Canadian Martyrs and the self-sacrifice of the Oblates that opened the west. Yet it was piety, Indian piety, that attracted him. He found one such expression in the work of the Mohawk saint Kateri.[22] Kateri Tekakawitha was an orphan girl from Kahnawake reserve south of Montreal, who, despite her blindness, refused to accept the security of marriage. Instead she became a convert to Christianity and spent the remainder of her life in meditation and piety. Her commitment was so compelling that a commission was established to recommend her for beatification. Vandersteene saw in her the model for the many Cree girls he found in the various settlements, girls who were not married and who demonstrated a sympathy and commitment to the Church and to prayer that was refreshing.

When Vandersteene was assigned, he was sent north to Fort Vermilion, first of all to serve in the residential school at Fort Vermilion, and later the missions that ran eastward along the Peace River, toward Garden River and south to Little Red River. He arrived there on 29 August 1953, in time for the first school term in September. The assignment to the residential school was one of those "résumé" disasters. He may have taught in schools in Flanders, and perhaps even been excellent at it, but this was a personnel mistake. Perhaps the Oblate Provincial and the Bishop thought he needed more discipline under the jurisdiction of the local church organization; Archbishop Routhier recalled in an interview that it seemed good to send him into a school near to a viable Cree mission area.

The foreshadow of what eventually occurred might have been surmised from his earlier letter to the bishop; he described the Cree mother in her own home as the basis for traditional training. Here the child learned Cree and was taught things like family values, Cree history and moral truths.[23] The school at Fort Vermilion was a long way from

this ideal. Perhaps it was the condition of the boarders at Fort Vermilion: there were about 50 of them spread over all grades from one to
ten. They were joined by about an equal number of local Cree children.
Tiny children scarcely able to understand a word of English lived side
by side with teenagers. Perhaps it was the fact that he had to deal first-
hand with the attitudes toward Cree traditions in the hands of the
three teaching sisters and Fr. Tessier, the priest charged with maintaining the government's standards on training in English within the residential school. Perhaps it was his conversation with the old people at
Wabasca and Desmarais, or his discussions with young Indian activists, both of which he had ardently sought out. Perhaps it was the
legacy of prejudice against his own language in Belgium that inflamed
his emotions. Whatever, it wasn't long before he and Tessier locked
horns.[24] After a year of it, Vandersteene could take no more. He and
Tessier had strong words:

> Vandersteene: Why is it that the Cree children can't even speak Cree
> in the hallways or on the playing field at recess? Why I've even seen
> the sisters cuff a kid for talking Cree while running outside on the
> playground. You shouldn't allow that to happen! After all that is
> their language, the language of home and parents.

> Tessier: That's our job! We're not here to teach them Cree or give
> them time to talk in Cree. They do enough of that when they go
> home. We have to maintain their attention in English. If we do not
> keep them concentrating on English, even when they are playing we
> will never be able to help them with integrating into Canadian soci-
> ety.

> Vandersteene: What difference does that make? These are students
> that should be learning to trap, learning to fish and gather roots and
> plants in the bush. What possible difference would English make to
> that?

> Tessier: Don't be silly! These kids will never learn how to trap, and
> even if they do, there are not enough animals left for them all. Don't
> bring your romantic European ideas over here! This is Canada.
> These kids have to learn how to be Canadians like everyone else.
> Otherwise they'll starve or be on pogie all their lives!

> Vandersteene: What do you know about the Cree? How long have
> you been here?

Tessier: I came here from the Yukon in 1950, and I worked in schools in the Yukon about six years. I have been in education all my life, and worked with the Indians many years. But I acknowledge that I haven't had your experience among the Cree.

Vandersteene: Well I can tell you, you better get some experience if you are going to make policy for teaching them. How can you take them completely out of their communities, slap them around when they speak their language and depreciate their hunting and trapping culture and then hope that they are going to make good Canadians? I've travelled among these people and I've seen what this does to the families. The kids go back at Christmas and they don't even know how to skin a rabbit. They couldn't survive in their own environment for five minutes. You're making these kids into nobodies . . . with nothing to live for. That's not right.

Tessier: We are paid to teach them English and a curriculum that will make them productive Canadians! How can you say that that is making them into nobodies?

Vandersteene: They don't even know their own parents when they go back home. They think they're really smart because they know a little English and the old folks back home don't know any. They can't relate to any of the traditional life going on in their own communities. They can't relate to others who stay home and work locally. This education is stripping them of all their culture. That is not only educationally wrong, that's morally wrong!

Tessier: I can't help it that our people conquered the land. I can't help it that whites are here. I can't help it that we are the majority. I can't be responsible for the fact that our culture is going to dominate. When the government wants to help these people by giving them education, why are you fighting it? The government is at least trying to help them.

Vandersteene: This is their country. We are trespassing on it. We should not be taking anything from them. We should be asking them what they want us to do.

Tessier: Look, I've worked here for 25 years. I've been involved with the university, with the Church at several levels, with the government in Ottawa, with our Order in Ottawa. I've also been at the local level, and even at the native level in Trout Lake. I think I have a pretty good grasp of what this country is. You can't go back to before the white man came. You can't get the natives to go back before white traders and settlers came. That's just hopeless. We have to work for the future as best we can.

Vandersteene: White man came and ran roughshod over the Indians, giving them nothing but tiny, useless reserves. You are a religious man. You should not stand still and allow the government to treat Indians this way. You of all people should not be part of a system that subjugates the Indians. You should reject the treaties and reject the handouts and require the government to recognize the prior claim that these people have to this country!

Tessier: So it's as simple as that, eh? Just give it back to them and we all pack up and go home? Where do I pack up to? I was born here. I don't come from someplace else like you. I'm a Canadian. You're out of touch with what's really going on here.

Vandersteene: I know the Cree! They have their own school ... it's nature. They have their own training ... it's by their parents. They have their own industry ... it's living with the natural processes of the land. They are being bulldozed into the ground by white society, by western culture. I can't, I won't support it![25]

All the fire of the young priest boiled over. Argumentive at the best of times, but brilliant when pushed to defend personal or language rights, this was an issue that caused everything inside to rebel. With summer coming on, he left the residence,[26] camping outside in a *mikiwapa* (summer tipi) as if by doing so to criticize the system that he could not support. He spent more and more time in Little Red River, an isolated community at the end of his mission district. It seemed far more humane than the environment around the school at Fort Vermilion. Thus the mission of Little Red River was entirely given over to Vandersteene's hands.

The settlement had been visited periodically in the 1920s and 1930s by the old priest Fr. Habay from his mission to the west in Assumption. It was the location associated with the famous name of old Jean-Baptiste Sewepagaham. It was approximately 200 km east of Fort Vermilion, but it lay on the south side of the Peace River so, unless the river was open water, or completely frozen over, passage to Fort Vermilion could be life-threatening. Even when the river appeared frozen, the thickness of the ice could never be assured, and Fr. Jean-Paul Vantroys (see below, p. 111), travelling by dogsled back to Fort Vermilion one April recalled that they nearly drowned several times: "I can still see Rogier calling to me from the rear, as the dog sled risked disappear-

ing in the current: 'Be careful, I've no footing, we're in the main channel!' "[27]

The missions were not only remote, but the Cree perspective on social units prevailed. Based on Vantroys' remarks when he was with
Vandersteene in 1952, the evidence for this is clear: "Would you believe
that some people at Little Red River did not know the people 90 miles
apart. . . . it was the same band, but they didn't know them. They
travelled around a certain area, but they never went to the end of the
territory. They never had any chiefs, because the chief was a white
structure brought after the treaty. The Cree were not formal people and
so if they saw a need, they responded to it and somebody led. I have
heard Indians say they don't need to stockpile food and equipment like
the white man because they had enough for today and there will be
enough for tomorrow."[28]

The territory around Little Red River was idyllic.[29] The people's lifestyle was still based upon a hunter ecology, since they were too far
from a settlement to make white fare easy to obtain. They had no possibility of a wage economy out in the bush — only later would silvicul-
ture and logging be stressed in the region. The bush itself dictated the
plant and animal life that sustained them; its spruce, poplar, pine and
birch trees were laced with scrub and brush, providing ample firewood
and small game animals. The river provided some fish, and the terrain
had sloughs, water holes and muskeg, sometimes linked by wandering
creeks, guaranteeing that water fowl would be abundant. Periodically,
the whole ecosystem would be struck by a lightning-generated fire that
would wipe out the spindly overgrowth and bring fresh green shoots.
It was a blessed place for a young priest who wanted to give himself
over to studying the language, learning from the elders and writing a
book.

It is best to let Vandersteene himself tell about the founding of the
mission:

> I commenced to build my house, after two winters. After my first
> reconnoitring trip in this beautiful upland country, two things were
> decided: 1. A priest should reside at Little Red; 2. It is thus necessary
> for him to have a house. Much later, one could construct a simple
> trapper's cabin at the 5th Meridian, at Fox Lake, at Moose Lake and
> at the Peace River Rapids; but Little Red River is certainly the centre
> where the priest should reside, and there, consequently, it was nec-
> essary to build a real house.
>
> Father Serrand, my superior, gave me lots of encouragement. The
> Indians, especially those from Moose Lake and the 5th Meridian,
> were also in favour of my project. I wanted an *Indian House*, but a

little more finished than the ordinary houses of the Indians, with a divide between the living area and the bed. This will be a house where everything will be available to them, where they can come if they want to stop, but would also have a room which permitted me from time to time to be alone, and it would have to have, above all else, another part where Our Lord could live "among us."

In the summer of 1950, I scooped out a foundation/cellar all by myself. My men were occupied with the logs, cutting them in the bush and hauling them to their place. Then three volunteers and a fourth, on salary, helped me construct the walls and the roof, to cover the roof with earth and grass, and to cut the openings for the doors and the windows.

I would come to know particularly well two of these volunteers, who worked with me all autumn for their food alone, which was composed of rabbit and bannock. They were Alexandre Laboucan and Emile Senibanikat from Moose Lake. We spent many beautiful days together. We lived in communion. It seemed to me that I had two convent brothers with me. We had prayers together in the morning, at noon and in the evening, then before and after eating. They took mass every morning and confession each evening. What beautiful day-dreams I had during those days!

The winter came very quickly, and snow also, forcing me to return on foot to Fort Vermilion. There everything proceeded like a drama, participated in by Fr. Serrand, Bro. Belcourt and our friend "Petit Caribou." My free time was spent in preparing the altar and the tabernacle for my chapel. The altar would be a simple table; the tabernacle an Indian tipi in miniature, where Our Lord Himself would dwell, and, in time, among us as one of us, since "nothing is foreign to Him," said St. Paul, "except sin." This would not be the first time that He had lived in a tent!

The house is divided into three parts: a large room, 19 1/2 feet long by 18 feet wide, comprised nearly two thirds of the entire house; the other third, divided in the middle of the 19 1/2 feet, formed the chapel and the room for the missionary.

It is into the large room that the door opened, and the interior is lighted by three windows. The right-hand part extending from the room of the priest, is set as a kitchen and dining room. It contains a stove, a table, the benches and my provisions. I like what my men bring and from which I take nourishment: it will calm their imagination and their tongues. They are besides always welcome at my table, as I am always at theirs. The other part of the big room, without separation, is like the nave of the chapel.

At the bottom of the large room, the apartment situated on the right is the room of the missionary, where is found a small office, a bedroom, a library and what ever one wanted. It is here that one finds the books, the bed, medicine, clothes, guns, fishing rods, radio, the Christmas crèche, the Easter candles and many other things.

On the left is the chapel, properly called, or the sanctuary, the altar and its tabernacle, between two cabinets, which contain the sacred linens, the decorations, etc.

I said mass for the first time in this chapel on the 23 December 1951, and I gave the first benediction of the holy Sacrament the following Christmas Day, the first benediction that had ever been given in Little Red River.

During 1952, I worked on the chapel. . . . Fr. Vantroys, whom I had several months as a companion, helped me cover the walls of the chapel with the wood that we had received in Fort Vermilion.

The altar could be found in a sort of niche made between the two cabinets. On the altar is the tabernacle where Our Lord resided. The wall-painting of the niche will also be the background for the tipi-tabernacle and it represents a scene at the convergence of the Peace and Little Red Rivers. Eight families have placed their lodges around the tipi and the cross of the altar. Pastorale of peace. The people are carrying on their normal duties, and one can see in the heavens angels praising and protecting. Crowning this tranquility are the words: *Manito Jesus witchihiwew iyininak Winahoma*.[30]

Hauling provisions back and forth was a difficult task, but it was necessary, even for a priest who liked the bush. As fraught as the journey to Fort Vermilion might be, Vandersteene looked to the town as an outpost for recreation and rejuvenation. He jokingly told Vantroys that it had the trappings of home: "I always come to it when I've lost plumpness," so finding a way between the two places took up much of his time. In winter, there just was no alternative but the dogteam. Dogs were difficult to find, especially good trail dogs; he was always on the lookout for them. An old trapper in Garden River found two wolf cubs apparently orphaned in the bush, and gave them to Vandersteene. They could not be allowed to run free like the other dogs, so he built a special cage for them and provided a special diet. Little by little they adapted to his ways and became his staunch friends. They resisted and resented being tethered with the three other sled dogs he had. Rather than pull in tandem, they preferred to pull the sled themselves. Vandersteene tried every possible way to get them to co-operate with the sled dogs. They refused. Finally he hooked the wolves behind each other, and made them the right-hand team. The three sled dogs he connected together on the other side. While the two teams were connected at the sled, there was sufficient room for them to ignore each other while running in the same direction. The wolves refused to acknowledge the sled dogs, running with their backs to them. It may not have been the dogsled team with the greatest finesse, but it worked. Vandersteene was very proud of his unorthodox team — and it was renowned throughout the region.

The isolation of Little Red provided him with the opportunity to begin *Wabasca* and, looking forward to his 10-year furlough in 1956, he began working diligently on it. The book was to sum up his first years in the field, to acquaint his supporters back in Flanders with his work and to consolidate what he had learned while in the mission field. It would introduce his readers to the collection of characters who peopled his mission, and gave colour and definition to the people among whom he worked. As he wrote, he made no attempt to be definitive, but he did assume a kind of anthropological distance in his descriptions, which lent them an authenticity and validity that a less careful depiction would not have given. Indeed, some of them were eventually translated and subsequently appeared in an anthropology journal.[31]

His world was filled with the small glories of the lonely missionary: the little mice that clambered along the partitions, silently sharing his warmth throughout the winter and peopling his world with tiny noises; the raucous squirrels who fought each other for seeds and cones, and developed racetracks around his little house; the Canada geese that announced the seasons with their comings and goings; and the zap of the brilliant northern lights in the snapping cold. He revelled in the world he shared with the Cree, in the warm joy of the mass with these remote and gentle people. Ironically, however, the more he felt a kinship with them, the farther he felt removed from them.

The very gap he wished to bridge seemed to grow larger every time he invited them to worship, and the difference was perpetuated by his surplice and his European ritual. He was restive in holding communion babbling away in Latin with his back turned on the three or four who shared the mass:

Originally I used to say Mass in the log cabins of my people with my back turned to them. I jabbered a foreign language — Latin — and wore an even stranger garment — a chasuble. My Indians thought that I played my part well, but this kind of spectacle meant nothing to them. So I had no choice but to adapt the ritual myself; I offered Mass with my face turned to the people and talked to them in their own language about the Great Spirit, about Jesus and Mary; so that the liturgy might become for them a living with God. I was reprimanded.[32]

In the sparseness of the Alberta bush, he realized that everyone had a task, and while he recognized that he brought the Lord to them, he felt strongly the need to become more involved, to know them in a more definitive manner. Cut off from sophisticated communication by the ongoing struggle with Cree, he turned to art, both as a means of expressing the Gospel to them in a more universal language, and as a way of conveying the truths in a medium arising out of his own culture. His painting of the idealized community as the backdrop for the altar was one such response, but it was not limited to this. He sketched tiny pictures of Bible stories, substituting Alberta bush decor for Middle Eastern/European. He painted Mary holding a native Jesus, a St. Joseph and Christ of iconic formulation dressed in deerskin coat and leggings, and Mary and Ste. Anne in primitivist design.[33] Once the brush was in his hand, all the joys of his earlier life swept back, and he set down in oils the great day that he had taken his final vows as an Oblate. The period reaffirmed his skill in oils.

But the palette opened up another means of communing between himself and his people. Mary, generous of breast and body, sketched with expressionist delight, became a means to penetrate into the new world. The Cree women, models for this enterprise, became more and more a touchstone for the deeper awarenesses that he was trying to unleash. The old sense of fertility, of a nature embued with a mystical overplus, so powerful in Flemish artistic and literary tradition, granted him a legitimized language for this art, and he explored it with relish and exuberance. His early paintings, sober and primitivist in style, gave way to other, more free-flowing genres, while the dark broodingness of Servaes' creations found a likeness in the richness of the northern Alberta ecology.

His skills in design inspired him to create an antler candlestick holder for the altar, and to work with the women of the settlement on an altar cloth with authentic local floral designs stitched upon it. At every moment he tried to adapt himself to the world of the Little Red Cree. He abandoned his traditional clothes except for the mass, and rejected standard felt-lined Canadian winter boots. Henceforth his parishioners would provide him with the carefully crafted porcupine-quill decorated moccasins. He never went back to shoes, even when abroad.

He found it difficult to stress the spiritual side of Cree culture without coming face to face with the material; it was precisely the pressing needs of a material world that he continually encountered: toothaches that would not go away, stomachs that were constantly upset, the thousand and one accidents that can befall one in the bush, the babies who needed help being born. He realized that Cree women never had men present for births: that was the domain of an older woman, a grandmother midwife. Yet he could see the limitations on these servants of life. The RCMP could not reach a woman dying because of a birthing problem when the river was high, or unstable. Vandersteene looked on while his parishioners died in childbirth. He explored the options and decided: he would study to be a midwife, himself. Writing to the Chicago School of Nursing, he began training that would ultimately provide him with the knowledge to intervene when a case was beyond the Cree midwife. He bought surgical tools and studied practical procedures; his contacts with Dr. Hannah Kratz[34] provided him with drug samples and other aids, some of which he recognized he should not legally have, but necessity transcended the law.

It was Vandersteene's work with the families, however, that finally allowed him to break through into the Cree community. The children were not only the future, they were *his* future. He quickly realized how proud Cree parents were of their children.[35] Regarded as gifts, they were worthy expressions of the parents' own special natural fertility; they were also signs from the spirit world that the ancestors were blessing them, were continuing their presence. Each one who came incorporated something of the great linkage of existence that knotted together Cree life. Vandersteene recalled his own family life, now made vivid in the flashing eyes and childish pranks of the little Cree children, and he reduced his discourse to the littlest among them. He delighted in going into a home, hauling tiny tousleheads onto his lap and, putting a Cree syllabics book in their chubby hand, listen to them read in Cree. He established an immediate rapport with the small children, because he addressed them in the strongest of family terms: "Come, talk to me, my little sister." "Come read to me, my little brother." The children responded in kind. He talked to them endlessly, sweeping them into his arms and blowing gusts of smoke over their heads as he teased and chided them, until he had them animated and chattering. His pleasure with children was not lost on the parents; without a trace of condescension the most ragged little urchin was a friend of the man with the big barrel chest and the wild red hair.

When children wandered about, making a racket during mass, he used their intrusion as a point of teaching; when tiny Sophie relieved herself on the floor in front of him during mass, he used it as a lesson in God's sustaining love expressed in the natural processes. Mass was a family gathering, where the emphasis was on all being part of Manitou's family.

Vandersteene adopted distinctive Cree codes of behaviour. He abandoned clerical garments. He had a special Cree necklace made of porcupine quills and moose hide, which he wore all the time. He used bear grease and other native potions to keep the savage black flies and mosquitoes from eating him alive. He expected visitors to walk in without knocking, and chewed friend and parishioner out alike if they felt awkward about doing so. It was a protocol deeply rooted in the natural rhythms of another's household, of perceiving their lifestyle and reading signs of life within and without. When in Fort Vermilion or Wabasca, he far preferred the company of the Cree than his white confreres, and would deliberately refuse invitations to white homes to take whatever was offered by a Cree acquaintance. He learned to read weather patterns, the location of plants, the smell of storms and the sounds of the night in the bush.

He became party to the petty foibles, and monstrous handicaps, that the Little Red people had to deal with, and he became an intimate to their problems and hopes. In the closely knit environment of the community, he learned the inner feelings of his confessors. He had a special gift with his women parishioners: it would become a kind of truth accepted by many that he could always relate better to women than men,[36] and he always seemed able to talk about the most difficult personal issue with the women without embarrassment and without prejudice.

He brought an entirely new tone to the isolated community. By general consensus, Vandersteene was an attractive man, full of energy and joie de vivre. Diminutive by usual European standards, he came to most peoples' shoulders, but he ploughed a hugh swath through a gathering with his personality alone. An inveterate smoker, he even puffed away in the bathtub. Ashes rained down on his clothes, leaving burned pock marks. He had that disarming characteristic which some women find appealing; he was a teddy bear of a man who needed someone to take care of him. He somehow expected it from those around him, and usually they gladly complied.

He used various settlement people as models for his paintings and sketches; various local personalities showed up in his writing. Favoured among these models was Papiwapui, Laughing Waters. Papiwapui has become the symbol for a moment that was to bring Vandersteene great pain. He painted and sketched her several times, and some of these sketches ended up in the missionary journal *Pôle et Tropiques*; none of them could be found among the paintings I sur-

veyed. She was always expressed as happy and delightful, and clearly
Vandersteene put more than his usual skills into her portrayal. She
became very important for him as he tried to come to terms with his
mission.

There are no clear sources on what happened next. Some say he
fathered her child; some deny this categorically. There was, however, a
child who died at birth, because Vandersteene wrote bitterly of the
death. Some say the experience was so transforming for him that his
painting and artistic creations would never be the same. The female
body became sensual, lush and voluptuous. Mary becomes motherly,
taking on the depth of figure of the great Flemish masters. Others see it
as the beginning of the practical Vandersteene so that the experience
inspired his move into midwifery. Whatever the results, tragedy attended the event. Papiwapui died, too.

His family knew nothing of this story, and the Flemish generally regarded it as insignificant, even if it did happen. None of his Church-
related colleagues mentioned it. Nor did his Flemish Catholic colleagues, such as Fr. Omer Tanghe, who wrote the widely read book on
his life in Flemish, say anything on the matter, in print or otherwise.
Indeed, in an interview with me he appeared surprised by the possibility. It does not appear among any Vicariate correspondence. It only
came to my attention when, several years after most of the interviews
for this book were conducted, I attended a thirst dance north of Lac
Ste. Anne and it was mentioned during a conversation.[37] Members of
the clergy then confirmed the rumour but discounted its validity.

Some have ascribed this story as a standard myth applied to priests
in isolated communities.[38] Some have said the whole story was the fab-
rication of a jealous male. Vandersteene denied the story himself, and
blamed the gossip on the fact that he had curtains on the windows in
his house. He refused to have curtains in any subsequent house. Whenever the story came up, it greatly agitated him. All of those who laboured closest with him had heard of it, but all affirmed that there
were several enemies out to get Vandersteene, for a number of reasons,
and that they believed the story derived from those with malevolent
intentions.[39]

He interpreted the story to mean that there were real spiritual forces
arrayed against the success of his mission. He began to see the costs
and limits to his familiarity with the people, and that he was not im-
mune to vicious attacks from some among the people he really loved
who apparently disliked him. At the same time, he realized how much
he had become part of the Cree people. That he should be seen to be a
natural father reflected on how much he had become one with them,

even to the point that such a story would be believed by Cree. Rather than forcing him to step back from his close relationship with them, he resolved to participate even more fully in their cultural life. The saga of the medicine pipe bundle validated it (see pp. 143-44).

There is another strange story from this period in his life. Jos, his godchild, reported that Vandersteene had been very ill while at Little Red River and that he had been cared for by the chief's wife, who had literally nursed him back from death's door. Presumably the chief's wife would be Émilie, Jean-Baptiste's wife. He had been devoted to this family, which caused some jealousy with the other families in the small community. Jos insisted that Vandersteene's early insights into Cree life had been gleaned from the old chief and his wife. The episode may be fictional, for there is no evidence in his archival letters of this happening, but it would serve to explain Vandersteene's easy move toward total Cree immersion. It would also provide some answers for how he survived such long and difficult times so far away from a normal support system.

Early in 1952, the Oblates sent another priest to work with Vandersteene in learning Cree: Fr. Jean-Paul Vantroys. There is no indication of what impact the Laughing Waters saga had on the move, but it is hard to believe it had nothing to do with it. But Fr. Vantroys had been originally sent to Grouard to learn Cree there, and had not progressed well, perhaps because of the mixed population and the dominance of English in the community, so the move solved two problems. In the remoteness of Little Red, under the control of the best Cree speaker in the region, perhaps he would do much better. Fr. Vandersteene lavished his favourite procedures for learning Cree upon Vantroys, writing out complicated grammatical and word structures, and trying to make him familiar with his growing Cree liturgical language. Unfortunately Fr. Vantroys could not plunge into learning Cree by counting the mosquitoes he killed. Despairing of learning Cree Vandersteene's way, he insisted that he plod along on his own.

In the end, the Vicariate decided to pull Vandersteene out of Little Red, and left Fr. Vantroys to struggle on himself. The move alleviated the antagonism between Fr. Vandersteene and the residential school in Fort Vermilion, a situation that was close to being volatile, and freed Vandersteene to make periodic visits to other missions, for which he saw the need. The archbishop reassigned Vandersteene to Desmarais/Wabasca beginning in July 1954 to develop the missions radiating out in the region: Peerless Lake, Trout Lake, Chipewyan Lake, etc. The assignment also meant that he could keep in touch with his friends in Slave Lake and Sucker Creek. Armed with this network of friends and

acquaintances he had made earlier, Vandersteene now began to
strengthen his personal sense of mission.

The more he wrote and tried to formulate his understanding of his
mission, the more he became upset at the policies pursued in the residential schools. He had faced the intransigence of the situation every
time he went to Fort Vermilion and visited with the children from Little
Red River. They were becoming alienated from their parents back
home. Faced with no modification of the attitude towards the Cree that
he had hoped would arise out of his discussions with Tessier and the
sisters, Vandersteene put his own career as a missionary in the Vicariate on the line. He wrote to his Provincial, Fr. Armand Boucher, and to
Archbishop Routhier on 13 December 1954. The fat was in the fire:

> Maybe this letter will hurt you, but I must speak to someone. . . . Cree
> boys should be trained in skills relevant to their cultures . . . and girls
> should receive skills of a similar nature. . . . we should be taking them to
> Little Red to train them in their environment[40] . . . the present policy is
> misguided and wrong . . . this is a continuation of imperialism . . . in-
> stead of working with the Indians on their terms, the Church becomes
> part of an imperial plan . . . gradually our relationships with the Indians
> become schematic, haughty, alien. . . . We abandon our role of yeast
> within the Indian dough to be an extension of the tool of the government
> in civilizing the Indians. . . . we are not thoroughly mixed with them but
> becoming separated from them, making ourselves foreign to them. . . .
> Physically and psychologically I feel so tired that I can no longer pray,
> nor reflect clearly and work with some spirit . . . I defy my own judge-
> ment; I do wish not to be an obstacle to the good works others can
> achieve and probably will achieve by these very means which revolt me
> so profoundly.[41]

Routhier responded:

> The hunt gives less and less sufficient revenue on which they can exist,
> and I believe that it must be the concern of all missionaries to assure for
> them a modicum of subsistence. The forest gives proportionately less
> and less as the number of Indians has expanded, and one can only con-
> sider the aid which the government agrees to make available so that
> they have a permanent means to live. I believe personally that the In-
> dians should adapt their lifestyle to one which gives them the maximum
> ability to raise feed-stock animals, and a culture at least based on grow-
> ing vegetables and forage for their animals' feedstock. This is evidently
> a far-reaching problem.
>
> Concerning the education of the children, it would be normal that
> little by little the young Indian women would pursue their studies to be-
> come schoolteachers, nurses, and perhaps technicians in our hospitals
> and then to aid in the elevation of their tribe. It seems to me that the boys
> should learn those skills which would be helpful in development and

culture, and perhaps to learn the other matters which would aid them in survival. Whether we wish it or not, I am persuaded that a very great proportion of our Indians will not be able to survive through hunting alone. A change is surely going to occur in their world and it is necessary for us to have the foresight to orient them to it. We have always believed that for their maintenance in the faith and their moral preservation, it is important that we retain them as a group, but also that they themselves will have to adapt a measure to the lifestyle of the whites in order to conserve their existence. It is very important that the Indians not live without anything to do. I hope to have a meeting with our Indian missionaries in the course of the year to discuss in depth and create between us a certain unanimity. We can then make the necessary presentations to the Indian Affairs and to have continuity in our beseechings by which we gradually improve the state of Indians' life.

. . . I believe that a certain number of Indian boys should learn skills which will be of utility to them. We cannot attempt to provide these specialized apprenticeships in each of our residential schools, because the size of the institution necessarily involves a cost which exceeds our means.[42]

While the matter appeared to be closed, it was not.[43] Vandersteene's reputation had reached Ottawa, to the headquarters of the Oblates, and it is certain that his views were taken up by the Oblate Fathers. In 1958, a new directive on residential education was issued, which, in part, said "The programs of boarding schools have been improved to serve primarily the need for secondary education. Vocational education adapted to the needs of Indian Children has received some attention. Provision has been made for the higher and technical education for Indian youth."[44] They may not have abandoned acculturative education, but they recognized Vandersteene's point about taking the small Cree children from their homes. And they did accept that the usual kind of educational facility, based on the scholastic model of education, was not viable for the Indian acculturation process. But Vandersteene could not have known in 1954 that his views would be heeded. He might have feared that he would be disciplined for his outspokenness. He must have known the high degree of residential training in Canada, which comprised about 11,000 Indians in Canada and involved four major religious organizations and 67 schools.[45] The Church had a huge investment in capital, personnel and resources in residential education.

Even though moving Vandersteene could be easily justified, no one inside the diocese was fooled: the authorities didn't quite know what to do with him. Colleagues knew where the difficulty lay. Fr. Elphège

Fillion from Desmarais said it straightly, "Vandersteene should never have been sent to Fort Vermilion to begin with."

If there is a certain amount of chutzpah in a Flemish priest coming to Canada and telling superiors that they are all wrong, events and Vandersteene's persona contrived to make it seem acceptable. Canadian government and institutions were constantly on the defensive, as civil rights activists and native activists had more in common. Nor could the Church be all that confident—despite the investment in Indian missions and schools, there didn't seem to be much accomplished. There were, relatively speaking, very few Indians in any position of authority in the Church in Alberta, although there were some Cree clergy in Saskatchewan and Manitoba in other traditions. Sister Nancy LeClaire from Hobbema seems to be the only Cree in Alberta who had stayed the religious course.[46]

Vandersteene's approach to issues lent a certain cachet to his image. He read widely, and could talk on most any subject. He often took the role of the Socratic gadfly, taking extreme views just to provoke discussion. He frequently set analysis of aboriginal issues within the context of Euro-American cultural development, arguing as if these cultures were constantly set over against each other. Fresh from the vexations of minority status in Belgium, he argued for the priority claims of the Indians to North American cultural identity, and because he saw events and movements across a larger canvas, it was difficult to undermine his viewpoint. Canadian priests who looked at matters from alternative perspectives, or argued from distinctive Canadian outlooks, tended to be swept along with his rhetoric. His conversational tone shifted to the prophetic as he took free reign in portraying the direction in which Euro-American culture was heading. His fellow priests had to agree: materialism-bashing was something they all engaged in. There was no doubt that the money washing into Alberta put the province and their aboriginal charges right into the mainstream of individual aggrandizement.

But Vandersteene's own directions during this period held personal ironies. When he finally did write his book outlining traditional aboriginal beliefs, he wrote it while in the Little Red River mission, but he gave it the name of *Wabasca*. The model of a Cree identity in an isolated settlement which breathes through the book was far more in evidence in Little Red River than in Wabasca. Moreover, there is a strange conflict arising out of the book's plea for a new Catholic ritual based on the survival of a viable Cree ritual life. Such a viable ritual life as *wikokewin* could not be carried on in remote villages distant from the large groups of people and ritual specialists. Obviously if Cree traditional ritual was as secure as he said, it must have existed in places apart from the remote villages to whom he wished to commit his life. In fact, we know that to be the case. The *wikokewin* which became the central feature of *Wabasca* probably took place in the settlement of Wabasca itself. This is interesting, because it had been served by the clergy for a very long time. Yet it is precisely in those places not served by clergy where we might have thought, because of their remoteness and lack of access, they might have had a greater potential for retaining traditional culture. As it was, Wabasca was within commuting distance from Slave Lake, one of the largest of "Cree" towns in Alberta. Slave Lake's mission has been in place since 1914.

Consisting of four chapters, the book was full of data drawn from the primitive conditions under which Vandersteene worked, and proposed to show how he hoped to build a strong Cree Church in the frozen wastes of Canada. It was, as Vandersteene later admitted fully, not a book about the Cree; it was closer to being a sophisticated platform advertising his activities. It might also make a little money for his missions. He could never have judged the far-reaching impact of the book on him or his work.

The more the realities of the Canadian land, and the anxieties of mission pressed upon Vandersteene, the more he turned his spiritual life towards the Lady of the Flemish countryside. In a poem dated 19 June 1954, called *Evening Prayer by the Campfire*, he wrote:

> My campfire is the core of the night
> Warm and living heart of the forest
> Which stands around us
> Still and cold
> Like a wall, black ringed.
> Twinkling stars are swimming
> Through misty veils of Northern Lights.
> I see the moon go floating
> Through the roof of pines.
> The dogs are sleeping in the snow
> At times a chain jingles when they,
> Shivering from the cold,
> All but awake.
> The heart of the wood is the fire:
> It crackles and nibbles and creaks.
> Around it, all is still.
>
> Because what the moon relates, she tells
> Without sound

And the stars are winking and blinking
The Northern Lights are eloquent no doubt
But I am too weary to understand.

I'm tired and still
I should pray to you, Mother Mary,
And let your rosary glide through my fingers
And say and re-say your sweet name
And greet you:
Hail, Virgin, whiter than snow;
Hail, Mother, warmer than this good fire;
Hail, campsite, rest and security in our night;
Hail, Signpost, high and immutable over the course of our life
Rising higher than this centuries-old pine;
Hail, beacon, who gives resilience to tired feet
More than sudden glow of fire through dark forest
Hail, radiant as the moon
Hail, smiling star,
Hail, lovely as the Northern Lights.

I should be praying now
And let your rosary slip
Through my fingers
And greet you.
But my teeth are clasping my pipe
And my lips only open
To let the smoke escape.
And my hands are stretching
Towards the fire . . .
I am so tired . . .
The day was hard,
And but for a brief prayer for patience
And the firm will in the Lord
Not to complain,
What prayer could I pray today?

My feet are bruised
By snowshoes far too heavy,
My body aches
From stumbling through too deep snow;
My face is mauled by the wind.
I do not know if even one part of my body
Has given me no pain . . .

> What prayer could I pray?
> My brain benumbed
> My heart a chunk of ice.
> Or is this prayer too
> To have sore feet, dear Mother?
> Then with my feet
> And my back and my burning face:
> Hail Mary,
> And hail snowshoes
> And hail snow too deep and hail biting wind.
>
> No longer is the campfire the core
> Of the night,
> But your peace, Mother, in the core
> Of my heart.[47]

Slowly he began to realize that adapting the Christian message to his Cree believers was not just a matter of utilizing local floral designs and images. Despite his quick assimilation of Cree, and the great help from the pious families like the Sewepagahams, there was a real level of understanding that he was missing. Something far more radical was needed to reach the Cree people. While writing his book, and recalling one of the most powerful of the ceremonies he had attended, the *wikokewin*, it dawned on him that this ceremony was a kind of Cree mass; he saw in it a sacrificial symbolism that would allow him to synthesize Cree and Christian tradition.[48] It was first of all a total community ritual; it involved rituals of eating together; it required a singularly important role for the leaders/priests; it required ritual drumming and dancing, a key ingredients in Cree ceremonial; it featured the spirit forces beyond the physical structure of the world; it required a significant sacrificial content. For Vandersteene, the moment was one of high enlightenment:

> Never till now had any of my explanations concerning mass seemed plausible and alive to the Indians' way of thinking. Now, I could see a way out of the dilemma Why not substitute God to the dead [the *tchipayak*]? The offerings burnt by fire are reduced to ashes and smoke, while the offerings of the Mass are transformed to the Body and Blood of Jesus, who continues to live. How evident: Everything is there! The priest, the offering, the consecration, the communion, the crucifix, the incense, the kiss of peace, the church unction, the organ, the servants, the members' participation. Then, at last, I understood how All Saints' Day and All Souls' Day could be deeply experienced by the Indians.[49]

Having accepted that Cree tradition included a strong element of sacrifice, ritually expressed and vital within the community, a sacrifice which he related to Jesus' death, he then went on to affirm why he had to come to live among them: they only had part of the message. Summing up Cree religious beliefs that he pieced together from various sources, including the German anthropologist Werner Müller,[50] he concluded in *Wabasca*:

> What is there that is truly religious in all this? And what religious elements are in the fragmentary customs which are still in use? To try to make allowances for them would be hazardous. One thing is certain: in the religious beliefs of the Cree we can discover some elements which show us that our [sic] Indians have a natural faith in the divine All-Powerful. One finds also the belief that God wishes well to man and that He will always come to our aid. If faith and hope live in the Cree beliefs, on the one hand, very few traces of love can be detected. It was necessary that the Catholic priest come to reveal to them that God can be loved and that He loves man. Very few Cree to this day have understood this element of charity. Paganism, deeply rooted in their hearts, ties them to the earth and fastens them to earthly needs. If they do not open themselves to this divine love sooner or later, they will lose even that gold nugget contained in the germ of paganism, without which the latter could not develop into a liberating love. Without divine love, civilization could become impoverishing and levelling for the Cree; plain materialism and a simple lie.

Here, then, was the message to his compatriots back home. This was his justification for expending himself on the handful of people that made up his precarious flock. This was his justification for being in Canada, even though he could not go back and claim that he had added one soul to the Christian Church: he had added a civilizing element to Cree culture, in the shape of Christian love.

Dimly he could see where the reality lay which he pursued. He saw the possibility of a genuine new creation, a Catholic Church whose rituals, theology and culture were drawn from Cree tradition, yet were profoundly Christian. As a movement in this direction, he decided to draw together a number of young Cree women, to develop a cadre of young religious based on Cree culture with Christian principles. Drawing upon the Kateri legend, he hoped eventually to train these young women to take over positions of leadership within the Church, perhaps even to train them to take over for the sisters in the residential schools. He brought together a group of these girls in Wabasca and began plans to try and organize the members into a prayer group with certain hours for prayers, and certain lessons in catechism and Church teachings. He also proposed a discipline involving walks through natural settings, with meditations based on flowers, shrubs, berries and wildlife. He eventually hoped to incorporate the idea of a *manitokan*, along with "stations" throughout the bush where ribbons could be tied as one completed one's meditation. He saw it as the basis for the natural growth of Christianity within the Cree Church. Unfortunately for his plans, another kind of natural process was taking place — two of the girls were pregnant. Faced with the horrendous task of talking the Church into recognizing the special place for Cree "natural marriage"[51] in the Church's life, Vandersteene abandoned the scheme. Not even a man of his idealism could seriously talk the bishop into a religious order with unwed mothers. But the name Kateri was to surface later in the saga of Edie Scott (see below, p. 243) and, additionally, in the founding of the Kateri School in Trout Lake.

Vandersteene shrugged off the setback. As a meditation group, he considered the idea successful; he would pick up the revised idea again while in Trout Lake. Quickly he finished his book and sent it off. He wanted it ready when he arrived in Flanders early in 1956.

If the confrontation with the Church over residential schools at Fort Vermilion had resulted in at least a partial victory, he was not quite ready for the Canadian government. Following the death of a delivering mother who could not be reached by the RCMP because of the time of year and the remoteness, government operatives imposed a move on the community. They would be moved north of the Peace River, to an area with plenty of good land for agriculture. There they would have new homes built for them. Fox Lake would be expanded to take all the families, and housing for the priest and sisters, along with a church, would be constructed. The Cree would be on the gravel road to Fort Vermilion, which could be reached by the police when necessary, and the Indians would have school and medical facilities available.

Not all Cree were convinced of the validity of this move. True, some of the families thought it better for their children to be near school; they would not have to send them away from home. True, medical and government services would be easier to obtain. And it had to be granted that the land had good agricultural potential. The majority agreed that it probably was a good idea.

Despite the fact that he no longer was directly involved in the mission, Vandersteene opposed it. The switch to agriculture was by no means sure — these were hunters and fishers. The road opened up white culture to Cree youth on an unprecedented scale. After all, a road that goes to the hospital also leads to the beer parlour. Government services were not so superlative that they were an essential requirement. The people had survived since the beginning of time in their settlement. Why should they be moved just for the benefits of whites? The move had grave implications for the culture of the settlement.[52]

Indian Affairs was adamant. They muttered darkly about the intrusion of the priest into government affairs, seeing Vandersteene's intercessions as a new kind of paternalism. The Church authorities quietly supported the government, and especially were convinced of the potential for turning the Cree into farmers. The move began late in 1955, just as Vandersteene was preparing to leave on his first furlough after serving for ten years. When he sailed off to Flanders not a few bureaucrats of several jurisdictions breathed a sigh of relief.

He was received with rejoicing. His favourite meat was prepared. At midnight, Vandersteene wanted potatoes in buttermilk. Trees gladly went off to find a farmer with buttermilk so they could be prepared. His family bathed in his tales of Canada, of the Cree, of his mature professional vision. He returned home in triumph. While making the rounds of family and friends, his reputation spread. The Oblates recognized a star when they had one, and arranged for him to work for their recruiting centre for six months. The man with the moccasins was sent everywhere: schools, churches, youth halls, seminaries — 61 lectures to 22,000 students alone, plus over 130 other appearances and talks. His book was translated into French and sold over 7,500 copies;[53] it was Belgium's best seller of the year. He fired the imagination of poets, students, clergy and ordinary believers, who saw in him the old, undiluted values of Catholicism. What a difference 10 years made!

His speeches were fascinating, evoking a world his listeners could only dream about. The stories, told with verve and lightheartedness, lifted the spirits, challenged the ideals. He worked hard, trying to galvanize the youth into a lifetime commitment to missions. One day he went to Brugge High School, and held the gang of restless young Flemings spellbound for an hour with his tales. Then he hit them: "If anyone here is no good, then he's good enough for Christ, he's good enough to work for Christ." The arrow sank deep into Paul Hernou. Paul dropped his defences. I'll follow Vandersteene, he decided. Vandersteene had made his first big convert.

Despite his success, his family knew all was not well. When he rolled out of bed in the morning, he hacked and coughed for 15 minutes before he came out of it. His conversation was filtered through chain-smoking. He wheezed after a tough night on the road. At times he looked pensive and withdrawn. He grew weary of the gruelling schedule, and took time off to paint some pictures to sell to raise money for the mission. But even this was not relaxing. He cranked out 100 in two weeks. They sold, despite their haste. Yet it all was so rushed, so frenetic. But, then, Flanders was rushed and frenetic. Everywhere, big money, materialism, fancy clothes and homes. There were moves to regularize Flemish language and literature in the same way as Dutch. The Ijzer monument was a holiday jaunt for so many young Flemish people; they had no idea of the blood that had been spilt there. Somehow, despite the adulation, this Flanders was no longer his Flanders, this no longer home. It brought shadows across his face.

Indeed, the more they praised his mission, the more he realized how little he belonged. He may have sensed they needed him to be in Canada for their own glory. Despite that, he met with groups of priests, talked pleasantly of the rigours of missions and admitted to the scourge of loneliness. Yet he praised the peace of God derived from a life in service to others, especially those in such need. He collected a suitcase full of books, poetry, philosophy, theology, art for those long nights in the missions. Despite the ministrations of his family, he longed for the tranquility of his Cree mission.

This was not all about a man itching to get back to work. He was also uneasy about the missions. Despite the incredible success of his book, he realized he had no real program to recontruct Cree missions. The Church, of which he was a faithful son, had very strong views about the stability of its liturgy. Changing liturgy, as he had discovered, could bring sharp rebukes from the archbishop. He also knew he could not do this alone; that if he was to propose radical changes such as he implied in *Wabasca*, he would need the support of other missionaries. His experience in the field regarding residential schools had not made him optimistic on that score.

Moreover, he had no real power within the Cree community itself. He had an extensive network of elders and believers, but he was still a novice in the Cree community. He knew his understanding of Cree religion was spotty. He had no authority within that tradition either. He could not institute reforms utilizing old Cree traditions without it, for he could easily be sabotaged by young radicals. Yet he had no clear idea of how he would go about gaining that authority. He was troubled by the impasse.

He found a way to give religious voice to his discomfort; a young woman religious was deeply touched by his message of commitment and lonely dedication, and besought him to write to her, drawing her deeper into the solitary piety that seemed to glow beneath the joviality and public persona. He agreed to lead her in a meditational correspondence, opening up an area of spiritual exploration and insight for both. This sister became Vandersteene's spiritual soulmate. She continues to this day insisting on her anonymity.

Yet he knew that the shadows in his life were larger than those across his face in Flanders. Like black clouds thundering across the Rockies, the news of his sled-wolves announced storms ahead: frantically searching for his scent on their food, and finding none, they refused to eat. Even the scent on Vandersteene's old gloves could only last so long. They turned away from all food, pined in the corner of the pen. Every human who came near was checked for that familiar smell, until even the energy to do that failed. Slowly death drew the life from them. Vandersteene, atuned to the nuances of the bush, pondered what that portended for the future.

Notes

1 Personal interview, 19 February 1979.
2 Ibid.
3 See Vandersteene to Routhier, 12 April 1948, MacLennan Archives, MacLennan, AB.
4 Omer Tanghe, *Leven en sterven in de missie der eenzamen* (Tielt en Amsterdam: Lannoo, 1978), p. 51; hereafter cited as *Leven*.
5 Ibid.
6 Personal interview, 19 February 1979.
7 Tanghe, *Leven*, p. 56.
8 Vandersteene's private notes.
9 Hernou interview, 24 August 1978.
10 Ibid.
11 Ibid.
12 Ibid.
13 Fr. Vantroys found another kind of silence unnerving. Cree are very sparse with positive comment about a priest's labour among them: "I guess the most difficult is that they give you no feedback. They seem like an untouched people. It is very seldom that they tell you something, something positive. It would be nice if they told you but they never do directly." Vandersteene appeared quite at home with silences, and, when training Hernou, insisted that he sit still and listen to the Cree for a long time before he spoke.
14 Fr. Roué interview, 22 June 1979.
15 Quoted in Jean-Paul Vantroys, *La Voix*, 35, 6 (September 1976).
16 Fr. Vantroys identifies this group as antagonistic to Vandersteene: "I don't think I ever heard an Indian say something against him. Those who said something against him were what I would call whitish.... They want to become white, they are ashamed of their language, they want to go to the big conference, they want to fly on the big jet to Ottawa, they belong to the new clan of Indians. They are the type of Indians I don't like; they don't like Fr. Vandersteene, because he stood for the old ways" (personal interview, 29 August 1978).
17 Fr. Roué interview, 22 June 1979.
18 Fr. Vantroys pointed out that these ideas are based upon Cree linguistic forms: "I think he got that idea from Cree culture, because there is a word *Iyiniw* which means mostly, or on the way to being Indian. There is the other word, just any kind of man,

you say *ayisiyiniw*, like a man. Then you have the word *Iyinisiwin* that means complete humanity and that means wisdom. So, on reflection, this looks like it comes from looking at the Cree language. He understood that the full Indian is a mature man and in that sense one should look for completion (among those in the Church)" (personal interview, 29 August 1978).

19 Wabasca means goose or duck down in Cree.

20 Letter to Routhier, 12 April 1948, from Wabasca.

21 At 37, Harold Cardinal was the youngest man ever to be head of the powerful Indian Association of Canada. Vandersteene eventually realized that, however much he distrusted the Cree politicians, there was something different about Harold Cardinal.

22 See Marie Cecilia Buehrle, *Kateri of the Mohawks* (Milwaukee: Bruce Publishing, 1954); and Daniel Sargent, *Catherine Tekakawitha* (Toronto: Longmans, Green, 1936).

23 See Fr. P. Hernou interview, 24 August 1978, and Vandersteene to Routhier, 28 January 1972.

24 Fr. Forget admitted that he had once arranged for students to come to Grouard school from the Yukon, an act that he described as "the greatest mistake I ever made in my life" (interview, 13 November 1978). This mixing of Beaver and Cree must have made Vandersteene livid, for it was, to him, the most unnatural arrangement imaginable; the Beaver and the Cree still remember the battles between each other over fur-trading areas.

25 This conversation is reconstructed from the recollections of Frs. Tessier, Forget, Fillion, Jean and Hernou.

26 Nabis Pierre Okemaw from Trout Lake reported that Vandersteene said he was "kicked out" of the residence. There is no confirmation of which view is correct.

27 Vantroys, *La Voix*, 35, 6 (September 1976): 151.

28 Personal interview, 16 July 1979.

29 Just how idyllic may be judged from Fr. Vantroys' comment about marriage among the flock: "In Little Red region, we had a stable situation marriage-wise. When I started, there were about 450 or 475 Indians and I don't think there were more than 2 or 3 couples who were irregular in their behaviour. The rest respected their marriages and partners."

30 R. Vandersteene, "Un art indien pour les Indiens," provided by Sister Bernadette of Jean D'Or Prairie from her personal papers, but without reference. It is from an unknown Oblate publication.

31 See citation in previous chapter (note 1), "Some Woodland Traditions and Legends," *WCJA*.

32 Quoted in Tanghe, *Leven*, p. 39.

33 At the time of this writing, Mary and Jesus are in Fox Lake Church, St. Joseph is in the Trout Lake cabin and Mary and Ste. Anne are in the Loon Lake Chapel. Apparently Fr. Vantroys, successor in Little Red, was restive in having Vandersteene's art around when he took over, and encouraged its being moved to other locales.

34 The Kratz story throws an intriguing sidelight on Vandersteene and the period. Hannah was a German physician and a Catholic who had married the Jewish Dr. Kratz and had moved to Jerusalem. According to Fr. Mariman, Kratz's conversion to Christianity in Jerusalem so angered his Jewish colleagues that the family had to flee to Italy just before the Arabs attacked Israel; they had connections in Rome, who arranged for them to immigrate to Canada. Unable to find a position in Montreal, Vandersteene suggested they move to Fort Vermilion. There are some charming stories of Vandersteene playing Santa Claus for the Kratz children.

35 In his letter to Routhier, Vandersteene does not paint a positive image of his views of the natives: "La famille du vieux est dans l'ignorance la plus brutale. . . . Ils ont encore les coeurs d'enfants" — but this would appear to be standard propaganda; he

soon changed that view and to the children became a doting uncle. He genuinely enjoyed children and never talked down to them, a point reiterated by several Cree.

36 A number of people noted this for me, but Sister Bernadette elucidated its meaning.

37 Mr. Mac McLean, a Cree from Saddle Lake, casually mentioned it in conversation, but he added with a laugh that there were likely a string of red-haired babies in the north! The context of his statement did not assure me of the validity of the remark, but I pursued it with many of his colleagues thereafter. Their comments are summed up by Sister Bernadette: "Fr. Vandersteene was sometimes a very opinionated man and he made enemies. It is not only possible but quite likely that someone started the rumour as a way of chastening him. No one among us who knew him ever believed it."

38 Canadians will be less inclined to believe this now, given the incredible revelations of sexual abuse and chicanery among Catholic clerics, most of which have been handled in court. It is necessary, I think, to be cautious about tarring all Catholic priests with one brush.

39 Vandersteene confided to a Flemish friend toward the end of his life that he had had two opportunities to scuttle his vows, one with a doctor and one with an Indian woman. With whom and where? There is nothing more than that.

40 Apparently Vandersteene wanted to build cabins at Little Red and bring the older students there for training under the jurisdiction of the elders.

41 Vandersteene to Routhier, 13 December 1954.

42 Routhier to Vandersteene, 28 December 1954.

43 Roué was to explain, in a voice given over to resignation: "Vandersteene was completely against the residential schools. Like it was one of the means of destroying the identity of the Indians, trying to make English out of them. In the beginning I did not agree with his view, that it was bad to have schools, that we should have left them to have their own way and exclude them from learning our language. There is a kind of weakness in his argument; he wanted to seclude them and keep them away, like in the book *Wabasca*. He wished to keep them, like in Trout Lake, away from any influence, and this is impossible. You just can't keep this from happening. It was evident that (white) civilization was coming in and someday the Indian would have to face that."

44 Oblate Fathers, *Residential Education for Indian Acculturation* (Ottawa: St. Paul's, 1958), p. 53.

45 See J. S. Frideres, "Education for Indians vs. Indian Education in Canada," *The Indian Historian*, 11, 1 (Winter 1978): 33. Note the lack of co-relation between Indian values and the Canadian school system (p. 34). Vandersteene was correct about the cultural lacunae, since native learning statistics are abyssmal in most categories (p. 33). Not all residential or church-related schools receive such massive condemnation, however, according to Thomas Lescelles' *Roman Catholic Residential Schools in British Columbia* (Vancouver: Order of OMI in BC, 1990), where he argues that many native parents are now asking for the residential schools to return (see pp. 100-104).

46 Sister Nancy came from the Hobbema reserve at Wetaskiwin, Alberta, and served in the Sisters of St. Joseph.

47 Tanghe, *Leven*, pp. 136-37.

48 E.F. Wilson (1844-1915) had earlier advocated both cultural synthesis and political autonomy in his mission life, but I have been unable to determine whether Vandersteene had read of his ideas. See David A. Nock, *A Victorian Missionary and Canadian Indian Policy: Cultural Synthesis vs. Cultural Replacement* (Waterloo, ON: Wilfrid Laurier University Press, 1988).

49 Vandersteene, *Wabasca*, p. 191.

50 See Werner Müller, *Die Religionen der Waldlandindianer Nordamerikas* (Berlin: Dieter Reimer, 1956), and Vandersteene, *Wabasca*, p. 192.

51 Vandersteene argued vigorously, at the unofficial level of course, that the Church should recognize natural Cree marriage, or "blanket" marriage, as the Cree sometimes called it. Basically this would accept that when a woman and man agreed that they were married (i.e., she joined him on his blanket) the Cree community recognized that as a permanent liaison. When the couple thus behaved married, and, after a suitable period remained together, then this was as permanent as marriage could be. Vandersteene wanted to confer on those who had such long-time relationships the Church's recognition, even as it was recognized in the community. His idea was to acknowledge that Cree culture was just as moral and lived by just as firm a rule as white society; he did not like the Church's constant condemnation of Cree couples not married in the Church as "living in sin."

52 A characteristic of Cree settlement life had been totally ignored, according to Fr. Hernou: "Look at the Fox Lake reserve now. The government brought together people from Little Red and Moose Lake and a few families from Fifth Meridian, and there were a few families living where Fox Lake is now. Well, the government thought it good to bring all them together around the mission, in a kind of compound. But all these families had their own leaders. Oh, a few were intermarried but really these families had their own leaders among themselves, they didn't like all being thrown in together. What is amazing in Fox Lake is that these different families are moving back to the corners of the reserve in family groups. When they do that there is less drinking."

53 See *La Voix*, 35, 6 (September 1976): 10.

Five

Intransigent Reality: Manitou's Land, Manitou's Children

> The people can tell when you're dewy-eyed about In-
> dians. . . . He was no romantic . . . he didn't say it was bet-
> ter to be a spruce than a poplar. . . . it was difficult for
> him. . . . nature is orderly, but somehow now the patterns
> have gone haywire.   — Johnsen Sewepagaham

Steentje left his home in Flanders in May of 1957 with a certain amount of trepidation about the future. Looking ahead, we can see that his life over the next eight years would change dramatically, and he must have had some premonition about it. He would get caught up in several processes over which he had no control and whose implications were far-reaching for him. Not the least was the aftermath of Vatican II. At the same time his status in the Cree community would be modified in a manner he could not have foreseen. That status change would also lead to a radical shift in his career, moving him away from his beloved missions and into a position of administration which seems the antithesis of his character. White encroachment, whether through oil or religion, pursued the Cree relentlessly. In some respects Manitou's land and Manitou's children would be ever more difficult, and he faced a reality that was ever more intransigent.

Vandersteene left Belgium without knowing where he would be placed. He knew that he could not go back to Little Red: the community had all been transferred to Fox Lake. There really was no place for him at Wabasca and Desmarais. So far as he knew, all the regular mission stations were filled with permanent missionaries and priests. Yet he was undaunted. He returned to campaign that he be sent to that group of people enshrined in his letter long ago to Routhier.

Notes to this chapter are on pp. 168-71.

Happily, while on his leave, things had changed in the Vicariate. The Hudson's Bay store had been closed in Trout Lake, along with the house of the manager. Fr. L.M. Quemeneur, the missionary at nearby St. Charles Point, suggested that the diocese purchase the buildings in order that a day school be established for the 30-40 children in the Trout Lake area. The Bay agreed to sell the property to the diocese. There had been an old missionary's house in the area and it could be pressed into service.

Another irony. He who railed against residential schools, and white education for Cree, flew into Trout Lake in July of 1957 to announce that a day school would be established, under his jurisdiction, provided approval could be received from provincial authorities. Thus Kateri School with Vandersteene as head came into being.

There were a number of reasons Vandersteene enthusiastically embraced the school. He was convinced that a more generous policy on Cree language could be established in an isolated environment. He had softened his stance somewhat, under the strong opposition of other brothers and sisters in the mission, especially those who were Canadian. This would also be his opportunity to introduce some Cree culture into the school program. It would also allow him the opportunity to use his knowledge of Cree to carry out a religious education program. Rather than have someone speaking in English to students, Vandersteene could now tailor a program of teaching based on an adaptation of Cree stories and legends. Moreover, sex education in schools, which was a controversial issue at the time could be handled by him, at least respecting Cree beliefs as much as possible. Since he knew the students personally, he also knew their foibles, and how far he could go with discipline. He once thrashed one Cardinal lad with the approbation of the parents. But finances were also a critical factor. While he had been resident in Desmarais/Wabasca, his support had come from the diocese, which underwrote his minor expenses. When his activity shifted to Fort Vermilion, and technically came under the Indian Residential School, his expenses were funded from the two levels of government for schools, that is, the salaries from the three sisters and the priest running the school were pooled and shared, allowing an allocation to be made. In addition, his work in Little Red had been supported by an allowance from the diocese. When he began the establishment of the Trout Lake school in 1957, he initially received funds from Demarais, plus a small allowance from the diocese. But those funds were very limited, and did not provide any capital for employment of the Cree in Trout Lake for odd jobs, or for any of the developments he wanted to pursue. Later, in 1961, when he was able to bring in teaching sisters to the Kateri School, their salaries, totalling $1,500 per month were split three ways. This allowed Vandersteene to provide some community support, as well as expend some funds for student assistance. The school's materials and costs were funded by the province. Hence the hard edge of funding served to ease his opposition to Indian schooling.

Realism was also a factor. While he generally disapproved of the academic structure of white education forced upon Indians, he was even less enthusiastic about people without sensitivity shouldering the task. Yet he acknowledged that the people wanted their children educated. His solution was that teachers sensitive to Cree ways should be doing it. He was unenthusiastic about religious education in Cree schools, obviously not because he opposed religion, but because those who taught it usually expressed it totally in white terms, ignoring those they were addressing. If a *moniyaw* (meaning paleface) had to teach religion, better that the *moniyaw* be someone who knew how to talk in Cree terms, that is, better it be he.

He set to work immediately, using materials from the old mission house to construct a new mission home and chapel along the lines of the one he had built in Little Red. Federal and provincial sources were tapped for grants to reconstruct the old store and turn it into a school, but provincial approval for the school had to get the authorization of the Alberta Department of Education, since the school came under provincial jurisdiction.

Special approval was necessary because Vandersteene was not trained as an educator. He did not have the required university courses to be granted a teaching certificate in the province. Even if he were able to get qualified teachers to come, the number of students would not justify the costs involved. From a cost effective standpoint, the children would be better transferred out to a residential school. This, of course, Vandersteene vigorously opposed. He offered to provide teaching sisters for the school, such as the Sisters of Providence who were teaching at Grouard, or the Soeurs de la Sagesse who were at Akitameg. The provincial curriculum, would, of course, be the basis for teaching.

On the surface, setting up anything in Trout Lake, let alone a school, might be seen as folly. About 300 km north of Slave Lake, its largest supply town, and buried in the centre of bush and water, it was served only by a monthly flight bringing mail and supplies, and by an emergency two-way radio. Just persuading career people to go there would be next to impossible. But Vandersteene saw the location as ideal. Finally, H. Swift, director of the Native Education Branch, agreed that "if anyone was foolish enough to try such a thing, I believe he deserves encouragement and the red tape should be dispensed with."[1] The school became operational as an Indian day school when a lay teacher, Mrs. Bernard from the Maritimes, arrived on 17 August 1961. Vandersteene now had his opportunity to develop a community-based educational system, in a relatively isolated environment, in a manner more in keeping with his principles of preserving Cree life.

During the interval, he set to work nurturing his little church, and journeying out to other outposts. Emilia Noskiye, one of the women who had been in his first Kateri Cree sisters experiment had moved to Chipewyan Lake, and he began to reconstruct a meditation group based around the original ideas, but with less concern for official status. Slowly he developed the study group. It was again unsuccessful, surviving only two years.

The Church went somewhat better. By his second year in Trout, he was able to write: "I'm beginning to have a small nucleus of faithful at weekly Mass and Communion; very small, but I hope, very firm. One day, God knows, it will explode. I nourish this nucleus as a mother feeds her babe."[2]

He recognized that it was impossible to deal only with the spiritual side of his parishioners; if they were without food, or were seriously ill, he could not stand by. Armed with his correspondence course from Chicago, he tended to the minor ills of the people. Before he left Flanders, he had arranged with his young convert Paul Hernou to have a collection taken to buy drugs for the mission. Paul sent these through the mails to Vandersteene.

The delight of his closely knit community bound him. He settled into its rhythms, the movement of seasons, the hardly discernible shifts of colour in the snow, the slow mellowing of age. He loved the Alberta north: the crunch of his boots on the snow in −40 weather; the dazzling brightness of a winter's sun that transformed every glance into an encounter with diamonds; the sour rot of an autumn day, with the geese fleeing to the south; that exquisite moment when the snow gives way in the spring and suddenly green sprouts everywhere. He embraced a country that tested fury upon its inhabitants and rewarded their mettle with occasional exuberance. Scurrying rabbits, bobbing ducks, solemn loons welcomed him to their domain. Alive as well to the whole range of the north's people, he rejoiced in their easy expression of natural life, and turned to his pen to celebrate the everyday-ness of the courtship and love he saw among his flock. So powerful was this aspect of his life to become that he eventually composed a poem, one of his first at Trout Lake, in praise of the naturalness of Cree sexuality and birth:

Love Game I

Unrest.

Young Cree woman
With distracted fingers
Swings hammock cradle
Half moon.

Then she is gone
Behind the blanket curtain
Cooing and caroling
Of spring starlings
In whispering rushes;
Through golden evening glow
Loud giggling loon
Comes and goes.

Mountain brook
Dashing and bumping
(her blood)
Rushing and splashing
Against bronze tainted
Stepping stones of laughter
On brink of waterfall
Suddenly so, after
Breathless fright.

Anguished groan rears
Whirlpool sucks in.

Sudden travail, strident
Stillness.
Drawn from the primeval depths
Weeps longdrawn plaint.

At forest end stirs not a sigh
The silent brook flows past
On moon reflecting lake, loon rocking
Spring starlings drowsing
In motionless rushes.

Through blanket curtain
Young Cree woman flitting

Starry-eyed
Red-hued bronze
Her cheek
Smiles at hanging cradle
(Half moon on her back)
Humming, sets the table
For her man.[3]

Trout Lake gave him the opportunity to use his skills in delivering babies. Several Sinclair children came into the world with his help, and his close ties with children became ever more precious and endearing.[4] While waiting for little Sophie Sinclair to be born in 1966, he penned possibly his first poem known to have been written in Cree about her birth. His Trout Lake children, he wrote back to Belgium, "were beautiful, with big black eyes and brilliant white teeth."[5] When, in 1961-62, a measles epidemic swept through Cree and Métis communities, Vandersteene turned with worried eye to his little "gems." He could not bear the possibility that they would be stricken and perhaps die, like the children he had so heartbreakingly recalled in *Wabasca*. He went to his knees. He beseeched the Virgin Mary that, if she would protect his little community, he would pledge his entire being to creating a grotto in her honour in Trout Lake, a magnificent garden full of flowers from all over the globe. When, after the scourge had passed and he had not lost one child, he fell to his knees once more in thanksgiving, and rising immediately began the task of bringing the Grotto of the Virgin in Trout Lake into existence. An immense undertaking, it required that he set up a greenhouse and trial beds for the plants that came from seeds he purchased from Africa, South America, Europe and the United States.[6] He called on his many contacts back in Flanders for this project, especially Willy, his brother, who was in the florist business: "Ah, he loved working in the ground, and he had an amazing fascination for plants. He wanted to know how we could get plants from Siberia, Africa and the Mediterranean, and he studied how to adapt them. He communicated with people in biology from here, and they sent him seeds for his experiments. He wrote to them about the behaviour of cactus from the Sahara in Alberta's climate."[7] It was a happy marriage of his piety and the abilities he had developed at his father's side in the nursery business. It was a warm and rewarding time in his life; when he left, there were 628 different plants in the grotto.

The rhythms of the isolated community appealed to him. He liked the serenity of the community in the evening, as the last rays of the sun lead the laughter of the children to silence, or the distant cry of the loon, and the whistle of the snow around the windows rooted his spirit. Without radio or television, he would slowly undertake his nightly oblations, then settle down in his old chair before the stove to read, often deeply engrossed until the purple of morning would send him to bed. All those marvels he had retrieved from Europe gradually piled up, with carefully underlined sections, or special notes in his scribbler. Tomes on Freud, Tillich and Teilhard de Chardin, volumes on Cézanne, and Picasso, biology, plant studies, history, music. They and the little mice scampering on his rafter built a restful but vibrantly spiritual life around him.

In this secure and pleasant environment, Vandersteene moved to become a Canadian citizen. He seldom discussed either the application or the ceremony awarding him his citizenship. Some colleagues did not believe he ever became "Canadian," and, indeed, Tanghe says he remained all his life a committed Fleming: "From the days of his youth until his death Rogier Vandersteene was an ardent Fleming."[8] Why, then, did he take out citizenship? It was not necessary.

There are, first of all, the reasons associated with being a missionary to a "foreign" country: people tend to regard long-term immigrants who never take out citizenship as a little disloyal. Second, he realized after his trip back to Flanders that his soul was no longer there. Whatever Flanders had been in his youth, it was no longer. Third, and perhaps most important, he recognized that he was "home," that these people were his people. It is reflected in the story of the elder who came to see him one day when his friend from Flanders was visiting. After the customary silence and a smoke, the conversation went like this:

> "Is that language you speak with this man the language of your tribe in Europe?"
> "Yes, grandfather."
> Silence.
> "You should not encourage him to stay too long."
> "Why, grandfather?"
> Silence.
> "You will feel sad about your tribe there. That is not your tribe now. This is your tribe."[9]

The "man of your tribe" was Fr. Omer Tanghe. Tanghe is head of an organization in Kortrijk that promotes Catholic missions. He has almost had a cottage industry in publishing materials on Vandersteene, including his biography on Vandersteene, which was book of the year in Belgium in 1978. To him belongs credit for much of the publicity generated about Steentje among the Flemings. Visits from Tanghe and another old friend, Fr. André Platteeuw, have influenced perceptions of the mission back home. In Platteeuw's case, he had first met Steentje in Waregem when Vandersteene was a teacher there, but they had been sent in different directions — André to the Flemish Church, Rogier to Canada. Despite the ten years they had been apart, they seemed to have many common bonds, and Steentje was as open, but perhaps a little wiser than before. Platteeuw's comment was: "Rogier was full of humour, which he used as a way of surviving. He was really a poet, and he showed me the beautiful side of his mission. I think the three weeks I spent with Rogier in Canada were the most wonderful of any in my life."[10] Platteeuw was the first close friend to visit Vandersteene in his home surroundings, and his views had a telling impact on family members and close friends. Paradoxically, visits from abroad were an activity that Steentje did everything he could to discourage.

During this time something occurred that was to charge Vandersteene with an almost remarkable enthusiasm: Vatican II. Many of the directions he took were framed by and formulated in accord with that extraordinary Council. Vandersteene particularly responded to the new directions in liturgy. As Josef Jungmann remarked, "It was in the provisions of the Constitution on the Sacred Liturgy more than anywhere else that the *aggiornamento* which John XXIII had demanded of the Council assumed visible and incisive forms."[11] Since he had long been actively involved in that movement, the liturgical revisions of Vatican II seemed deliberately designed for Vandersteene. The reform of the liturgy was to have far-reaching implications. Not only was sacrifice to be a central motif in the Eucharist, but the presence of Christ was to be perceived in the priest, the mass, the community and in the form of worship itself. Liturgy was itself seen to be a historically developing awareness of the presence of Christ.[12]

From the beginning, Vatican II took a flexible view about liturgical variations, affirming that the Church "respects and fosters the spiritual adornments and gifts of the various races and peoples" and allows for "legitimate variations and adaptations to different groups, regions and peoples, especially in mission lands."[13] Moreover, special modifications were to be allowed in "administration of the sacraments, processions, liturgical language, sacred music, and the arts." The use of the vernacular tongue was advocated, and lay members were to actively participate in the sacrament.[14] Although we have no written statement, Vandersteene must have been jubilant to read section 119 on the liturgy:

> In certain parts of the world, especially mission lands, there are peoples who have their own musical traditions, and these play a great part in their religious and social life. For this reason, due importance is to be

> attached to their music, and a suitable place is to be given to it, not only
> by way of forming their attitude toward religion, but also when there is
> question of adapting worship to their native genius. . . . therefore, when
> missionaries are being given training in music, every effort should be
> made to see that they become competent in promoting the traditional
> music of these peoples, both in schools and in sacred services, as far as
> may be practicable.[15]

The wide-ranging reforms of Vatican II appear to have acted like a burst dam on Vandersteene; he now set to work on several fronts to bring the spirit of the Council to bear on his mission. He realized that painting Cree pictures was a valuable tactic in making the Cree feel identified in the Church, but he knew he had to go beyond this. Even his creation of vestments with sewn-quill designs were only surface actions. He turned to ethnographic materials to help him. He searched the literature for old Cree religious stories, myths of creation, tales of Wisakaychak (a Cree trickster figure) and folk materials; he probed his fellow missionaries, and the elders he knew who trusted him, to gather Cree materials.

Vandersteene began a fundamental reinterpretation of the Bible: Cree materials functioned in the same way as Jewish stories in the Old Testament did to Christianity. If Christians could refer to the Genesis story, an essentially Jewish product, as inspired, why not the Cree stories for Cree? The Church had a whole oral tradition available for examination. Where the Bible spoke of the Lord as a shepherd, carrying the injured sheep home, he replaced that with the story of the sled dog that injured its foot and the driver carrying the dog home. Lying beside still waters is not a great idea among the Cree, because all water is cold, even in summer. Better to be sleeping in the sun with a nice breeze blowing, to keep the mosquitoes off. The pharisee and the publican became the white man and the Indian. The white man says: "Look at me Lord, I drive a good car, I have a nice home, my kids are clean, I have a good education, I don't drink like that Indian, dirty, drunk as a skunk." On the other hand, the Indian prayed." Lord, I'm a dirty Indian. I'm drunk, and I hit my wife and kids. I'm just a dirty Indian, forgive me Lord." When the New Testament speaks of the angel of the Lord coming and speaking to Mary, this becomes *powakan*, the helper/dream spirit. "The dream spirit takes the form of a lynx, a beaver or a wolf. When the spirit world speaks, it speaks through the vehicle of some form that we know. We know angels, they know spirit helpers."

Likewise he adopted some clearer principles on translation, especially on key terms. For example, he refused to use the English word God in any of his Cree discourses. He essentially banished the nondescript "Great Spirit," because it had no relevance to either English or Cree. Renditions of God were to be either Manitou, which refers to that mysterious reality behind all known things, or if the implication is the benevolent God, then he used Kisemanitou; if the concern was with a judgmental God, then he used Micimanitou. In other ways he insisted upon the use of Cree equivalents, even if conceptually they might not quite fit, because he held that language is the basis of belief and religion must be enshrined in its terms.

Vandersteene advocated an elaborate change in Catholic preaching. He argued that the truth-value in the parables of Jesus would never change, but the means of expressing them could and should. Otherwise, the meaning of some actions would be entirely lost, or worse still would distort the simple meaning. To those who objected that he was changing the words of Jesus he had one reply: The Apostles had more respect for the person of Jesus than they did for the exact words he said. He pointed out that many of the consecration formulae in the early church, said to have been given by Jesus, were changed according to the needs of the hearers and the development of the church. For example, no one "cursed a city" if their message was not received as Jesus was said to have instructed.[16] Where the New Testament speaks of Jesus' story of the master who went into a far country, and left his men with sewing and reaping, etc., none of which has any relevance to Cree, he reinterpreted the story in terms of the father who had to go on his traplines, and left his sons in charge of the camp: one had to feed the dogs, one had to carry the firewood, one had to bring the water. Since they never knew when father would return, they couldn't get lazy and not do the chores for fear that father would return. Parables, he held, were tools using what was about to reveal the mystery of God; they had to be adapted to the cultures in which they were given; they had to discard some of Jesus' wordings so that the people could get at the truth of His parable; they had to to be truthful to the spirit and style of Jesus' sayings, not to their content.[17]

Even so, conceptual differences played a role. He learned that white notions of half-truths or "white lies" had no place among his flock; he learned a priest could not fool with the underlying beliefs. He had to tell things exactly as they were:

> One time I baptized a little eight year old girl in Peerless Lake. I had baptized the father and another daughter the day before. Now the whole ceremony was in Latin, so I thought I would interpret to her before we started what we were about to do. "Now," I said, jokingly, "What we're going to do is chase Micimanitou out and put Kisemanitou in place." When she heard me say "Chase Micimanitou out," she fainted

dead away. When she came to, I said, "Oh, I'm sorry, I was just fib-bing."[18]

In Trout Lake, he began experimenting with Cree tunes and Cree drumming. That this should have only begun under Vandersteene is a remarkable testimony to how European the missionaries had re-mained, although the first missionaries to Canada, the Jesuits, had de-veloped Cree songs.[19] He wanted to move immediately into enshrining all aspects of worship in Cree culture, and music seemed to be the nat-ural direction to follow. He noted the Indian propensity to sing over and over a certain line of phrase, an important truth taught to him by old Edward in Peerless Lake:

> He gets up in the morning and he goes down to the lake shore, and he sings: "Ah, Ma-a-ni-tou," and then he says his prayers. Sometimes that's all he does, just sings "Ah Ma-a-ni-tou." And then he goes on his way. Sometimes I've been with him all day, and he will suddenly start to sing, "Ah Ma-a-ni-tou" over and over again. He doesn't need a lot of words like we do. Just one thought expresses it all. A Cree love song is just "I love you. I love you. I love you." Over and over again. Everything is built into it.[20]

When Sister Donna, a Sister of St. Chretienne, arrived to teach at the school, he enlisted her help in learning Cree songs, so that Christian beliefs could be sung to Cree tunes, using a drum. She was successful in transposing some songs into music to play on the organ. Vander-steene was later to learn that most of her material was derived from the so-called female song cycles. He realized he would need someone to do the same for male songs if the experiment were to become a suc-cess.[21] Vandersteene's influence turned the missionaries in the diocese in this direction, a direction described as the missionaries' "apostolic charge":

> "Indians love music very much, and several experiences have been re-ported where our [sic] Indians have come out of themselves immediate-ly, have sung and amused themselves in their own way and with what is proper. With these amicable encounters, these visits to their homes, it is possible to truly approach them and to win their affection and confi-dence."[22]

The "liturgical chant" as he called it, carries an important responsi-bility in the Christian congregation: he rejected both the notion of the chant as an "illustration beyond the text" and as "a holy noise." Rather it is that "one has a heart filled with mystery and one must express it in a manner beyond bare words." He noted that Cree are very reluctant to sing audibly, at least with the usual European Christian songs, so missionaries have despaired of using music as a necessary part of worship. Vandersteene disagreed. He held that Cree "sing silently with a heart overflowing and eyes wide open. They hear profoundly and they identify fully with what they hear." Moreover, Cree are not culturally disposed to singing all together, and some of those songs which have been translated for them might better be left "to die in peace," because they mean nothing in the thought world of the Cree.

His solution was to fashion a new kind of liturgical music for the Cree: "It is best to devise a long hymn in three parts (in a sense) and to sing nothing but that hymn during the mass (introit, gradual, post-communion) rather than sing three different hymns." Before Vatican II, the form of the service was entirely set by tradition, and in each of these moments of the mass, a psalm may well have been sung in Latin; the first to set the theme for the mass, the second to set the mood for reflection and the final to affirm the continuing presence of God after leaving His table. In post-Vatican II, each vernacular set its own structure, depending upon its cultural adaptation, which left Vandersteene pretty much on his own, because there were few Cree priests in Alberta. He translated the Greek of the "Lord have mercy on us" (*Kyrie eleison*) and suggested that they use tunes drawn from the tea dance. It was an immediate hit among the Cree. Sister Donna further took all the main parts of the mass, previously in Latin and now translated into Cree by Steentje, and set them to little tunes drawn from everyday Cree songs she had found musically easy. She then scripted the music in Western musical notation form for use with the organ, but with the expectation that the principal instrument would be the drum. The Cree in his mission were delighted.

For Vandersteene the factor that should remain constant in liturgical music is not the number of ideas that a song has in it, but the fact that it repeats certain fundamental ideas. This means that the song should have a basic catechetic ingredient. In this notion he was not far from the nature of Cree singing, that is, the music and song blend themselves into types for specific purposes. One can find the following "types" of songs among the Cree, even today: lullabyes, social songs, sweat songs, Thunderbird/grandmother/grandfather spirit songs, healing songs, warrior/other society songs, tea dance songs, and special occasion songs (gambling, honour and initiation songs). While they all are not universal among the northern Alberta Cree, they can be found among the Cree at large.[23] What is remarkable is that Vandersteene did not look to the drumming and song of the *wikokewin* for assistance in this process. He apparently never considered it.

In liturgical singing, as in all matters of Cree liturgy, Vandersteene emphasized the essential *kaseyitam* or the "singularity" of the Cree, a characteristic that has dimensions of the "lone wolf" in it; because of that cultural characteristic, he rejects the use of popular Christian phrases, like "Amen," "So be it," or even of the notation in the mass of "Be seated," a phrase which, when translated into Cree, borders on the obscene. They are corporate expressions that imply group submission to certain rules. Vandersteene believed that such protocols went against Cree culture, resulting in the people pulling back into passive resistance. On the same grounds he warned against the use of standard occasions of greeting, hello and goodbye, hand-shaking or even the "kiss of peace" that often were utilized in white services as a way to establish rapport and elevate the sense of congregational cohesion. None of these activities have any following in Cree culture and are rejected by them. Mindful that the *Constitution of the Sacred Liturgy*[24] set up the goal of "full active participation" by all members of the congregation, even to radical alteration if necessary to make the liturgy more acceptable, he argued for the use of Cree instruments, drums, and the adoption of Cree tunes and phrasings throughout.

Steentje suggested raising silence to a central position in the liturgy, because he insisted that silence was a medium through which Cree communed more effectively with their spiritual selves. In the same vein, he insisted that the "Our Father" be acculturated, being replaced by a liturgical chant of "Kisemanitou," with sheep beside still waters replaced by phrases more related to Cree lifestyle, such as a warm fire in a cabin during a snowstorm.[25]

With his innovations, his spiritual authority began spreading. People who heard of his translations of the parables, and his innovations in ritual indicated that they wanted him to come to their settlement to hold masses. In 1962 he began work on a series of sketches to use as visual aids in his sermons; these developed into carefully drawn pictures illustrating important aspects of Church doctrine — a catechism, so to speak, but with the drawings utilizing Cree scenery, local people and typical Cree life. They were widely copied within the diocese, and Sister Margaret Denis, of the Sisters of Service order, heard about them in Peace River. Thus began a partnership that ended a decade later with a catechism based on Vandersteene's drawings and text, and released as *Come Lord Jesus! The Story of the Church*, and since utilized across Canada.[26]

Under the impetus of such invitations and opportunities, Vandersteene widened the scope of people with whom he would share his ideas and his spiritual insights. He did not shy away from the widespread belief among Cree people in the validity of the dream. Visiting Emilia Noskiye in hospital in Edmonton, he listened as she related to him how, for two years, she had suffered from pains in her head, so much so that her eyes seemed slowly to be going blind. Before going, he rose, and gently placed his hand on her head, said a small prayer and left. Emilia settled down for the night. She continued: "I began to dream. As I dreamed, I saw Fr. Vandersteene enter the hospital room. He was dressed entirely in white. He spoke to me, as he came right up to my bed. Then he was gone. When I awoke the pain was gone and my eyesight was normal."[27] When she saw him the next time, she related the dream and the relief she now enjoyed. He laughed and allowed how it couldn't be him since he only wore baggy old green pants. But it is evident that Vandersteene was not laughing at the dream, per se. His mother had been a firm believer in the power of dreams, and Flemish folk belief accepts the importance of them. In *Wabasca*, he sketched the Cree justification for dream power:

> On His own part, God takes the intiative of entering into relationship with his people. He does this especially by means of dreams (*pawatam-yuwin*) which He sent to the wise men and which, very probably, He still sends at the present time. From these dreams come the first sacred songs — detailed narratives of the mystical experience of the visionary — which unfortunately have become partially unintelligible because of lack of precision due to too long an oral tradition. Thanks to these dreams, the knowledge of the medicinal properties of many tree roots, barks, leaves, and all sort of plants was revealed to them. Certain dreams have instigated prophesies and councils which were the origin of profound and radical conversions. The Cree is deeply convinced that God will nurture and protect His people, cure them and guide them, and fight on their side; for without God, His people would be unable to survive unharmed the incessant dangers with which the evil spirits worry them. The occult powers are so numerous that it is impossible for men to discover them all.[28]

Johnsen Sewepagaham, in fact, saw Vandersteene's acceptance of dreams and visions as proof of Steentje's being spiritually attuned to the Cree people. He recalled how the missionary had one time been trudging through a snowstorm with his dogteam, and he had become exceedingly tired, hungry and perhaps hypothermic. He sank down in the snow, wanted to give up, to die there in his tracks. Suddenly he heard his mother speak to him, telling him to get up on his feet and get going. He later admitted that if she had not spoken to him, he would have died. Both he and his Cree people firmly believed in the reality of that voice from beyond. Other dreams, as we shall see, would play a significant role later in his career.

Using his contacts from his previous movements through the region, he proceeded to build a network of people on whom he could rely, and to establish personal relationships with as many Cree as he could. He began to realize that the Cree people had a sense of identity that bridged their isolation, a sense that survived even in the most urban of environments. His trips around the mission stations were not then jaunts purely for Catholic religious reasons, that is, just to visit with a few close friends and to bring the mass to them. They also enabled him to come into contact with the whole range of feelings which encompassed the Cree life, and to embrace them. Sometimes these endeavours took both dangerous and humorous turns.

On one occasion Vandersteene left Wabasca to go by dogteam to Trout Lake. The wind was bitterly cold, but spring water had already begun flowing under the ice as he crossed the water. Suddenly he went down, only managing to keep from going under by pulling with all his might on the sleigh. He struggled to regain his position. He yelled to the dogs to move faster, but in so doing they pulled to the side, dumping him in a shallow rut filled with water. He realized he had only one hope, and grasping a rope from the sleigh, he pulled himself onto the load, and let the team have its head. He concentrated on trying to keep awake as the cold seeped into his feet and gradually numbed his body. He could not move, for the cold cemented his feet into clumps, and then froze them to the sleigh. Barely conscious when the team brought him into the yard, his parishioners recognized the yelp of his dogs and came to his rescue. They chopped him loose and gradually warmed him to prevent the freezing from doing too much damage.[29]

Of more happy note was the frying pan saga. With night coming on while on the trail, he happened upon a trapper's cabin, where he entered and spent the night. While unpacking to prepare some dinner, he discovered that he didn't have a frying pan with him, so he used the pan from the cabin. In the morning, he kept the frying pan from the hut for the remainder of this journey to Trout Lake, thinking that he would drop it back off when he returned to Wabasca. However, he changed his plans and did not return directly. He never did seem to get back to the cabin.

In the meantime the old trapper who had built the cabin on his traplines visited his lines and saw there was no frying pan. He knew full well that the only person who passed by here was the priest. He also knew that Vandersteene had a frying pan, since he had seen him on the trail once. About a year later, the old man went to see Vandersteene in Wabasca; the priest rushed out to greet him. He was really surprised how the old man was getting grey so quickly. Vandersteene said, "Boy, grandfather, you soon will have white hair!"

"No wonder about that," said the old man, "I have been thinking too much about how I would ask when I would be getting my frying pan back." They both roared. The old frying pan had linked them in a way Vandersteene could never have contrived.

Once while in Slave Lake, he came upon a young Cree from Wabasca, hopelessly drunk. Although he had no money, he asked the priest to help him go to Wabasca, so Vandersteene took him to a taxi, paid the $70 fare and sent him on his way. Later, when he was in Wabasca, the man had him over for dinner, but Vandersteene, now aware of how money structured the relationship between Indians and whites, made no mention of the fare or the event. White society would have felt the man should mention repayment of the money; Cree believe that when something is given it cannot be "paid" back—it is a gift from a brother. It was one of a series of occurrences that was to move him to view welfare in a negative light; eventually he would reject all forms of welfare for the Cree as being destructive of Cree identity structures, a rejection that gained him a certain right-wing reputation in both the larger white and Cree community.

He argued that since money handed out by welfare had no precedent in Cree culture, the money should be allocated the way traditional resources were when they were available—the community should share it. He viewed welfare as a way of forcing Cree to destroy their sense of personal identity, since the very notion of welfare put them in a subordinate relationship to white culture, a subordination built on the need to express gratitude. Continuously subjecting themselves to this humiliation, he argued, eroded the value in which they had been taught to hold their individual abilities and strengths. He openly opposed any form of welfare being introduced into Trout Lake. As a way of fending off its evil, he himself arranged to pay hunters and trappers to provide food for a school lunch program, using traditional foods. He thought many more programs like this could have been established if the authorities had cared about native lifestyle. Yet it was obvious that the people needed white food supplies. He could see that they could not all live on hunting and trapping, even if there were sufficient animals available. Some were unable to hunt or trap for health reasons, and without outside help, they would starve. He had to acknowledge that the Cree community was cohesive, but not to the point where someone checked for food at poorer homes regularly. He tried a number of schemes: grants from the government for feasibility studies on lumbering; setting up a small fishing-lure manufacturing group; studies on native plants and their use. So open was he to Cree initiatives that he sometimes set himself up for the greatest yarns.

When Paul Hernou was training with him after he arrived in 1966, he recalled how a young Cree came to Vandersteene, requesting $25 so he could purchase a dog for his team, so he could go trapping in the winter. Vandersteene gladly gave him the money. Next week another lad also came requesting $25 to buy a dog for his team. Vandersteene obliged. When a third young Cree came later in the week to borrow $25 for buying a dog, Paul wondered how this could be. In Flemish he asked Vandersteene how there could be so many dogs available for purchase. "Are you sure they are not selling the dog to each other?" he queried. Vandersteene asked the lad where he was buying the dog. The answer gave the game up. Vandersteene gave him the money, but told him he had already paid $75 for that dog. Later the lad told his buddies: "When they talk that strange language, we can go no further with that story." When Steentje left Trout Lake his accounting book indicated that people in the community owed him between $8,000 and $10,000.[30]

Vandersteene continued to attend and validate Cree traditional celebrations. He enjoyed round dances, those celebrations of the community after a marriage or other happy moment. He learned how to dance in true Cree fashion, and whenever he showed up, it was assured that he would take his turn shuffling delightedly around the floor. Continuing to embed himself in Cree life, he gladly attended Absalom Marrier's *wikokewin* in 1961. He enthusiastically participated in the pilgrimages to Lac Ste. Anne, that site of ancient sacredness to many tribes because of the healing properties of its waters, and transformed by the Church into a pilgrimage site to Mary's mother, Ste. Anne. It was a fruitful time for him to express his deep love for Flander's favourite, Mary and her mother.[31] The significance of this pilgrimage may also relate to what is known about the ancient Cree view of the location. This view takes two directions, one related to Ste. Anne as grandmother, one related to pilgrimage as a metaphor of Cree life. The sacred, healing nature of the waters comes about through the presence of a helping spirit, a grandmother spirit, associated with the location through dreams or vision quests. The grandmother spirit may be understood through the power of the female side of creation. In Cree conceptions, the female side is seen as equal in power to the male, since the female side is obviously equally embodied in the world around us, but it is not an absolute rendered in language in the way it is in French, for example.[32] A feature so fundamental as the female aspect of reality cannot just happen. It comes to be as an expression of the absolute and unseen reality that makes all things be. Besides coming to be as the females which we see in the animal and plant world, female power sometimes takes the form of spirit powers or mythic beings. As such they can appear to people in dreams and visions as helpers. What is now Lac Ste. Anne was, and perhaps still is to some tribes in the region, a grandmother helper-spirit place.[33]

The second point relates to pilgrimage as Cree life metaphor; pilgrimage means taking oneself out of the normal path and addressing oneself to special places of power. This has importance to the Cree because of the belief in continuous revelation, the belief that people are on a path and that sometimes there are deviations in the normal path that provide moments of high insight or significance. All these moments give the flavour of moving to new awarenesses in one's spiritual life. These moments need not take the form of visions or dreams, although they may. Anything that appears specially charged, or indicates special "luck" adds to the perception of relatedness with the spirit world, about which each such moment tells us a tiny bit more. Hence the notion of ongoing "power awakening" or "revelation" in Christian terms. Going on a pilgrimage to Lac Ste. Anne is, therefore, affording oneself the opportunity to encounter the grandmother spirit's beneficence. The result is that thousands of natives from Canada and the United States flock to its famous shores every year.

There is no solid evidence that he knew about these points, although it is certainly feasible. But whatever else it may have been, Vandersteene found the pilgrimage to Lac Ste. Anne a rich social occasion. His network of friends grew with his extrordinary conversational and religious skills. As Paul Gladue commented, "He talked *all* the time, so much so it was hard to get him to shut up. He came looking in everyone's tent for somebody to talk to and then he just talked and talked. He knew just about everybody, so he sure did lots of talking."[34]

It was during this early period at Trout Lake that something occurred that changed both his status and himself significantly. During his stint with Fr. Floc'h in Akitameg learning Cree, he had been shocked by the attitudes of the old priest toward traditional Cree practices. As his associate, Fr. Roué, long-time priest and teacher in the residential schools, noted:

> Some priests looked upon these ceremonies as something that was forbidden. I am sure they did it because they believed it was evil, whether they went to see them or not. I can understand why the Indians were a little reluctant to allow the priests to attend. You cannot say that this tradition should be completely eradicated. We see that truths were somehow or other transmitted by the old Indian ways.[35]

Old Jean-Baptiste, the Church's great early convert in Wabasca, had had a calumet, or medicine pipe and bundle, which had been ritually passed to him from his father. Medicine pipe bundles have a long and complicated history among native groups in North America. One scholar, Jordan Paper, has argued that ritual pipe-smoking is the most common form of religious practice among all native peoples.[36] Both stem and bowl have individual religious meanings, and pipes are so sacred that they are only passed on through proper ritual transfer. The songs representing the oral part of the pipe's ritual meaning are always part of the process during the transfer rituals. The smoke is held to be the vehicle which carries the earthly petitioner's message to the spirit world.

Fr. Floc'h had visited an old man one time and, during the course of the conversation, had argued with him about the validity of Cree traditions. Fr. Floc'h was opposed to the old man using the pipe in Cree rituals in the community, because he had become a Christian and was confirmed in the Church. In a decisive demonstration, he grabbed the pipe from the old man and snapped it in two.

Vandersteene was upset at the action. He returned later, asked the old man if he would lend him the pipe, and fixed it for him. Then he returned it and told the old man that he did not share his brother's view about traditional Cree practices. He did not broach the topic with Fr. Floc'h immediately, but later they had a heated discussion on the topic. They agreed to disagree. While Vandersteene was in Trout Lake, word reached him that old Mr. Alexandre Laboucan urgently wanted him to come. The message to his kin was clear. "I am dying. I do not believe my sons are worthy of this pipe. Vandersteene must receive this medicine pipe bundle.[37] Tell him to come." When they reminded him that Fr. Vandersteene was deep in the bush, and many days away, he remained adamant: "I will not die until Fr. Vandersteene comes here."

The message reached Vandersteene. He immediately set out with horses and on foot. For three days straight he travelled. Finally he arrived. The old man was overjoyed. He transferred the medicine pipe bundle to Vandersteene, saying pointedly, "I give you this pipe because my sons are not worthy of it. They have become like white men. You speak, you think and you live as we do. That is why I give you this pipe and medicine bundle; you are my son." To those around he turned and said, "He is your medicine man now." A short time later he died. Vandersteene was later to comment to Tanghe: "By receiving this calumet I have become a real Cree. You may have all I possess, because you are my friend and brother. But this pipe I cannot and may not give away or I would give up the union with my people. This would be suicide."[38]

Vandersteene returned to Trout Lake. If he did not know beforehand what this had done for him, he was soon to learn. The pipe bestowed immediate status on him, both within the Cree community and without. Among the Cree, the transfer of such a sacred item portended acceptance of the spiritual qualities and religious attitudes of Vandersteene by a recognized authority; one could be recognized by no higher power than an elder. He came to see that he was now within the traditional leadership structure, a structure that recognized each elder as having distinguished gifts for the community. The medicine pipe bundle made him a Cree elder.

Once recognized, immediately others began transferring to him other medicines. Norman Laboucane recognized his abilities with plants and healing, and transferred certain healing remedies to him. He explained at conference of nuns and priests:

> When Norman Laboucane made me a medicine man two years ago, by giving me 10 different kinds of Indian medicines, I paid him with tobacco. That is the acceptable way. A year before that he transferred two medicines to me. But I cannot say much about this. The group is a secret; it's called the "congregation" of the medicine men. Norman, I and a few others belong to this congregation of medicine men. I can't disclose the secret, even though I'm a "sorcerer" right now.[39]

Among the Oblates and his Catholic colleagues, the gift confirmed the extraordinary nature of Vandersteene's position as a missionary. Henceforth few would ever deign to differ with him about the Cree. At the same time, he became someone apart from the usual—here was a priest who somehow had entered that strange spiritual world of the medicine man. Vandersteene took on an aura all his own. Routhier acknowledged this with a very pointed statement: "Let's just say I left him very much to himself."

But the medicine pipe bundle imposed other differences upon him. He knew that not everybody would accept his new position, not the least of whom would be the old man's sons, who might have felt they had a prior claim. Even more, there were Cree who were "nationalist" about their artifacts, even if they didn't follow the old ways themselves. They resented the intrusion of Vandersteene into such an elite circle. It was a symbol of how rooted he now was among the Cree, a rootedness that none could deny. It was also a definitive mark of his Canadian psyche. He would never look back to Flanders in quite the same way again. At the same time, he would not look out on the larger Canadian society, and even to the larger Church that served it, as a critical part of his life, for he was now Cree. He was now a strange alien—not and yet Canadian, not and yet Flemish, not and yet Cree. It gave him a sense of strength.

Dimly he could see where the reality lay which he pursued. He now had the requisite credentials to rise above the limitations his predecessors had had. He would bring together leadership roles from two traditions and put them to service in a new kind of church. He saw the possibility of a genuine new creation, a Catholic church whose rituals, theology and culture were drawn from Cree tradition, yet were profoundly Christian. One night he dreamed that the Pope had come to his little mission, and had participated in celebrating Manitou's child with Manitou's people. It enlivened his resolve. It moved him to begin planning for a Cree church building in Trout Lake, with the style of a *mikiwap*. When he shared his vision with Routhier, the latter encouraged him to proceed, only to create a building large enough to hold a hundred people. Braced with his vision of the *wikokewin* as model, he set out to create a building worthy of the "Tent of the Ancestors." In *Pôle et Tropiques*, he wrote:

> Yonder, in the great tent of the Ancestors, I have made a marvellous discovery. I have assisted at a strange ceremony that fell into three parts. The first part was a sort of meditation: old legends of the Cree Indians were narrated. The story of Creation was told, more or less like the Bible, re-lived by the Cree Indians in song and dance. This happens in the presence of "past and future."
>
> In the presence of the past, because all the deceased are invited and are present in the form of dolls. Indeed, whenever anybody dies, a lock of hair of the dead person is put inside a doll. Some of the dolls have become quite bulky. They are sure to contain the hair of ancestors that died a very long time ago. As the "skin" of these dolls can easily be replaced when they are threadbare, the tribe can preserve them without much trouble for many centuries. Hence, through these dolls, the ancestors are symbolically present. In the presence of the future, too. The future is there in the person of the women who are carrying babies.
>
> In the second part of the ceremony an offering takes place. While the past is present in the form of dolls and the future in the presence of pregnant women, and whereas one has been meditating on Manitou's goodness, it is fit to offer Him a worthy sacrifice: meat that is consumed by fire.
>
> A third part introduces the rite of communion. Everyone present sits down in a circle and eats from that meat, after the "peace pipe" has gone round. Isn't that fantastic? Not one single Indian has heard the word of Christ: "When you bring your offering to the altar and you remember that somebody has something against you . . . go first and be reconciled with him." They have never heard this and yet

they experience that need far more strongly than we do. Being reconciled, they can now share the meat. When the love-feast is over, all remain seated, because the conversation, the dancing and the singing continues in earnest. And so this being together goes on until sunrise. The nocturnal ceremony ends with the dismissal, reminiscent in a way of our "Ite Missa Est." Suddenly the drums roll so vehemently that one's eardrums are in danger of breaking; shouts and howling are all around you and never seem to stop. In this way they send their dead away, back to their darkness. This moment is so lugubrious that children begin to cry.[40]

He was to remark that 15 years had gone by before he understood how this could be adapted to the Eucharist, so that he could explain the meaning of that rite to them; this seems excessive considering that he wrote in 1956 that he already saw the possibilities.[41] Later he was to tell Fr. Vantroys that he received the outline of the entire service in a dream.[42] Neverthless, he outlines how he will combine the two rituals when they consecrate the new church/ancestral structure during the consecration night.

Procession: 1. Elders (having at least one grandchild) with drums
2. Bishop
3. Vandersteene and Sisters

Consecration Ceremony: 1. Invocation of the Spirits
2. Elders, carrying bear fat, circle church
3. Bishop, carrying holy oil, circles church
4. Elders make ribbon offering to *manitokan* at altar (three different colours)
5. Bishop consecrates *manitokan*
6. Elders consecrate altar (bear fat)
7. Bishop consecrates altar (holy oil)

Offering: Presentation of offering to ministers

Invocation: 1. Elders stand and name all tribal members of honest memory
2. Entrance of the dancing dolls
3. Vandersteene invokes sainted Christians, St. Thérèse of Lisieux, the Virgin Mary, St. Catherine, Martyrs of Uganda
4. Elders invoke Christian saints
5. Bishop invokes French-Canadian Saints
6. Vandersteene invokes Charles the Good and St. Lutgard

Dance Ceremonial: 1. Elders
                      2. Bishop, with crosier
                      3. Fr. Provincial, carrying statue of Mary
                      4. Proceeds nine times around fires at altar

Texts/Scripture: 1. Elders, creation story
                    2. Vandersteene, Genesis, creation story
                    3. Epistle, with Our Lady brought to front
                    4. "Doll" of Jesus tied to Virgin Mary

Sacrifices: 1. Elders to altar with meat and water.
              2. Vandersteene to altar with "real" bread (not wafer)

Eucharist: 1. Traditional offertory, with explanations in Cree

Mass Prayers: 1. To unborn babies
                 2. To the dead, in form of dolls
                 3. For Pope, Bishop
                 4. Celebration of presence of Christ

Smoking of pipe: Passed to all (sign of peace).

Feast: All eat and drink to capacity.

Dismissal: 1. Strong address to ancestors: Return!
            2. Recession

This program of worship was to be followed twice a year, reminiscent of the tea dances spring and fall, although it would not contain the consecration elements of the altar and the building.

The church was to follow the Cree pattern of north-south direction. An elongated tipi, it was designed to use as few "outside" materials as possible, and to reflect as closely as it could the Cree values. The poles, resting in a pad of cement, were to remain open at the top so that the traditional pole shape of the tipi would be in evidence. At the south end he planned on placing a window formed from plexiglass of Jesus as an Indian, and of Mary as an Indian mother. The altar, a large stone, was to sit in front of the window, and the cross was to be replaced by a *manitokan*. Benches of local woods were to be placed in rows, leading to the north end of the building, where the door would be placed. The skylight roof was to be formed from opaque plastic, of the colour of finely scraped hides. The outside would be covered with heavy asphalt rolled roofing, and the upper part of the inside would be modelled from thin metal sheets. The inside walls would be of stripped and varnished spruce. Altogether, his plans were to have the church in operation as soon as possible, although he faced great difficulties in getting supplies. The easiest access was still flying in, but that was incredibly expensive. True to his convictions, Vandersteene wanted to have as much done as he could, because he knew his innovations had attracted attention in Ottawa, and the ferment arising out of Vatican II (1962-65) indicated changes were afoot. The authorities would be inquisitive. Perhaps his dream would come true quickly.

The problems he faced were considerable. He notes how he only started with a rake and some buckets. He hired local people to help, because he knew they needed extra work, and he had to make endless trips to bring in supplies; time dragged on, and, although he poured the floor in 1963, the building never seemed to be finished. He was somewhat disappointed with the response of his local parishioners: he had thought the project would galvanize their faith, contributing to a solidarity of spirit as he had back in Little Red. But they seemed preoccupied with other things, slow to react to the labour needs, and uncommitted to Vandersteene's timetable. Not even the unique design seemed to excite them.

At some point, he ceased work entirely; he realized he had made a mistake. While he never commented on this problem with his co-workers, Fr. Paul knew when he arrived in Trout Lake in 1966 that something was wrong with the building. In addition to some fundamental flaw, other functional problems became evident: water leaked from the roof, and cold seeped in through the walls, freezing and cracking materials inside. There was not sufficient money to start over. The project languished.

Part of the lack of response may have derived from the fact that he received word that his father was dying. The diocese gave him compassionate leave, and he flew back to Belgium. He called all the family home to Kortrijk for Christmas that year (1964), and in their presence administered the sacrament for the sick, in an adapted version of Dutch, another innovation for that time in church development. While his father lingered between life and death, Steentje turned to business — he painted 100 pictures and sold them for over 1,750 Belgian francs for his mission. His father died 13 January 1965, and Rogier was among the celebrants during the Requiem in the village church in Marke. Following the service, he assured his brothers and sisters: "Now I can quickly return to my Mission. Father is now with my dear mother. Now both of them will look after us from heaven." Despite the quarrel that he had had with his father about his choice of career, he admitted that they had come to a deeper appreciation of each other later.

> He had become my best friend. Originally he was very angry because I wanted to follow my vocation and enter the Oblate Order to

prepare for the missionary life. "That fool wants to go and live with the Eskimoes and the Indians," he had grumbled. . . . It took many months before he gave in. One day he suddenly came to the Oblate House in Waregem; he looked at me, fumbled in his pocket and took out his pocket watch. "For you," he said. This was the sign that he had surrendered and was willing to give me up to the missions. He remained many days in our monastery, in order to lay out the garden. When he went home he proudly told any visitor, while he pointed to a photograph with a bearded missionary's head: "My son Rogier. He is going to the North Pole as a missionary. A fine fellow."[43]

One wonders whether the grotto in Trout Lake was as much an offering to his father's spirit as in gratitude to Mary.

Another drain on his energy, and one more overwhelming, was his ongoing confrontation with government and bureaucracy. Throughout his entire career, he wrote countless letters to bureaucrats on behalf of his parishioners, but the period in Trout Lake was to be particularly intense. As a sample of the work he undertook in this area, and the repercussions, we will consider three events that came to a head during this period of his life.

In June 1961, Mary-Rose Gladue, a parishioner, was a tuberculosis patient at Camsell Hospital in Edmonton; while there she gave birth to a little girl, Dehlia. Because of a number of problems, including her inability to communicate in English, the baby was taken away. After being discharged, she returned to Trout Lake, without the baby. Vandersteene inquired about the child, and was very upset when she had no idea where they put the baby. He learned that she had signed papers which allowed the baby to be put up for adoption, even though she apparently did not know their purpose. Dehlia was adopted by a white family. Vandersteene was outraged, and began a letter campaign that involved a long and torturous route through the Camsell Hospital, the federal Department of Indian Affairs, Provincial Social Services and the Church. He finally had to threaten to take the case to the Supreme Court of Canada. After two years, little Dehlia was returned to her mother, now, of course, a complete stranger, and to Trout Lake, where everyone spoke Cree. The episode set Vandersteene's teeth on edge, and gave him a jaundiced view of government attitudes towards Indians, a perception shared by many others in the mission. There was some good in the episode, however; it cemented his relationship with Julian Gladue, the child's father, and made him the individual everyone called upon when they needed help. He remarked to a colleague that he spent most of the morning handling parishioner's correspondence to government offices.

The second event related to hunting and fishing regulations applied by the provincial government to native people. He discussed the issue with Rose Cardinal, who related the following:

> Life is pretty tough for the people in Trout Lake. They don't have much to survive on. Just dried meat, dried fish. The government said they can't hunt when they want, nor fish when they are hungry. They have to abide by the game warden's word. But they need to eat, so we had to devise some way of handling this. When the game wardens are coming in, they would call him on the wireless. They told him they were going to check on the fishing nets, to make sure they are legal and check to see if there is evidence of the Indians killing animals out of season. He knew the boys were going out hunting that day, so he told them, when you see a gas boat out on the lake, fire some shots up in the air. When the rangers came, he told them that the Indians in that vicinity will shoot white men found on their territory. They borrowed his boat anyway, and away they went. Before long they came back, saying "Yea, we heard shots up there so we thought we better turn back." They got in their car and beat it.[44]

The most bitter of his confrontations came with the proposal by the provincial government to build an all-weather road into Peerless and Trout Lakes. Vandersteene was elected by heads of the families to present their views to the panel who came in to the communities. Up until that time, there was an old wagon trail that curved and wriggled through the bush. It was totally unacceptable as a road for the oil rigs that were flooding into the area to take soundings for oil and gas. The government side, led by provincial officials in Regional Development, along with the federal Department of Indian Affairs, as well as the Indian Association of Alberta, came to hold hearings with the people about the proposal in 1962. Local Indian groups also sent observers.[45] The meeting was stormy.

The advantages of having a maintained road were made evident — ease of access to the outside world, quickness of response for emergency vehicles, connection to other Cree centres, development of a tourist industry and oil jobs. Vandersteene became visibly upset. Rising, he shook his fist at the presenters, and shouted that the Indians did not want white culture, they did not need the ease of access to alcohol, and they did not need oil companies crawling all over their land, killing the animals. He pointed out that what the people needed were programs developing hunting and trapping.[46] They were an independent and autonomous people who should be left alone. It was just for white man's benefit that they wanted the road to go in. Moreover, it was his view that the community could not take the quick development they were proposing, because it couldn't adapt that quickly. Besides, it would only be a while before whites would come in, buy up the shoreline and kick the Indians out of their own country. His face turned purple as he gesticulated heatedly.

Reports on the meeting hit the newspapers, and those representing the government said Vandersteene should have had no part in the meeting and that he was replacing the old paternalism of the Church with a paternalism to keep the Cree from developing. The provincial Indian newspaper, *The Native People*, castigated Vandersteene for "misrepresenting Indian beliefs" at the meeting.[47] Even moderate Indians were upset that all Cree should be regarded as hunters and trappers. Vandersteene wrote to his soulmate in Flanders:

> Trout Lake is constantly under seige and is constantly being fired at, from big as well as small, all sorts of canons and all sorts of armies. A band of trouble makers has tried to turn the whole issue upside down and has partially succeeded in doing so. The first results I have been able to prevent, thanks to God's Provision; but we have lost some and we have lost it forever: namely, the respect of most people for themselves. They have gone over into the attack with excitable words, radio reporters, newpaper reporters and even television personnel and cameras! ... about an insignificant little issue that had no significance for anyone with the exception perhaps of God, and that is not too obvious. They wanted to leave me outside the issue ... it is almost impossible because some of these people are honest. .... The question was that we have been accused of leading an inhuman existence and take pleasure in keeping the Indians ignorant and uneducated. My answer to them was that people here have made progress and that their sense of humour and their sense of well-being have not been lost in the process, and that making a great deal of noise does not necessarily indicate we are human ... I have been able to answer on television for at least twenty minutes. Since that time we have been left in peace from those quarters.[48]

Not for long, as it turned out. The government resolved to poll the people in the communities; the upshot was that the majority wanted the road. Indeed, it appeared that it was just the oldtimers and Vandersteene who wanted the road to stay as it was. The road was built.

The issue catapulted Trout Lake and Vandersteene into the country's attention; political pundits talked and wrote on all sides of the issue, radio talk shows discussed it, and even the American Indian Movement, a radical "red power" group from the United States, poked around. White liberals were awakened to this unique little community. One of the more attractive results was a National Film Board documentary, *The Cree of Trout Lake.*

Vandersteene may have felt that he had won a few scrimmages with the government over the issue, but he wasn't prepared for the religious fallout. What put him in deep despair was the devastation of his community brought on by his very defence of the Cree in the media. Sarcastically writing that

> "all sorts of Protestant sects and subsects" reacted to the existence of communities like Trout Lake, and rushed to convert it: Brrr! Brrr! Since then a chain reaction . . . one after another, it is enough to drive you nuts. Sometimes one with almost stupidly blinking eyes, sometimes two or three! Sometimes a group of four or more. They come from everywhere . . . only two people have been able to withstand this without swaying their faith: Pol Kruit and his wife Selapien.[49]

The "invasion" destroyed the unity of his little community for good. It was, in Fr. Roué's words, "Vandersteene's hour of darkness."

The impetus, ironically, came from Nabis Okemaw, one of his great heroes in *Wabasca.* The tortured path that eventually put them on opposite sides of the religious fence is difficult to trace. Vandersteene's mission diary mentions that Nabis came to him asking him to give him more financial assistance than others. Vandersteene asked why he should favour him over others, and Nabis suggested he should do so because he had been a good guide when Vandersteene had started out. Steentje questioned him carefully, and he felt Nabis was bargaining about something. He did nothing about favouring him with money. Soon after that, he heard of Okemaw linking up with the Jaycocks, who were currently holding religious meetings in Loon Lake. In 1966 the Christian and Missionary Alliance Church, under the leadership of Clarence Jaycocks, started services in Peerless Lake. The Jaycocks brothers, two Americans, originally from New York, had settled in Alberta several years before and had moved from native community to native community for 32 years, starting new churches. They bought the store in Peerless Lake, and began holding meetings on the weekends; they could provide some credit in the store and hence could attract some customers away from the store serving Trout Lake. In addition, the Cree enjoyed the country and western flavour of the music. Once they had the small church going in Peerless, they started to hold meetings in Trout Lake. Ruth Jaycocks sums up the attraction of their group to the Trout Lake people: "Well, a lot of them had their fill of drink, and they want to be delivered from it; and they have also had their fill of witchcraft, and they want to be delivered from that. You know, all they know is fear, and they don't feel they're going to heaven through it all, and they are tired of it."[50] Recalling their experience in Loon Lake, she noted that when they first arrived, the whole community was on a continuous binge. The congregation came on Sunday morning but they were all drunk, and Clarence had asked his wife, "Do you think there's any hope for this crowd?" Even the interpreter was drunk. Despite all that, the church grew and it now has an Indian pastor.

The Alliance made considerable inroads into Fr. Vandersteene's congregation. Vandersteene himself went to talk to Jaycocks; a heated discussion about the Bible and the Church ensued. As in most such encounters, nobody's mind was changed. Strangely, within a few months, the Alliance felt the same pangs as the Catholics, only this time it was done to them by the Pentecostals.[51]

The Pentecostals who came were independents of various convictions. They emphasized an emotional service, with much hand-clapping, singing and testimonies. In addition, many of them stressed healings and the extraordinary experience of "speaking in tongues." Fr. Jacques Johnson, from Grouard, intrigued by the influence the groups were having, attended one service and responded: "I went to Isadore LeBlanc's Pentecostal Church in High Level and actually saw a girl's leg lengthen. They held her legs out and I saw it visibly lengthen. I can't explain it, but it was an Indian girl. They seem to believe it happens. I'm not really sure where that fits in my theology!"[52]

Various preachers visited the area, holding tent campaigns in the summer, and attracting a wide spectrum of the population. The message against alcohol was always strongly stated, but instead of the process of sanctification offered by the Alliance, much greater emphasis was placed on the instantaneous "deliverance," a tactic that probably has some connections to Cree perceptions of spiritual power and special "luck." Ruth Jaycocks continues:

> I think the Indian people here and especially in Peerless Lake have a tendency to go for the spectacular, they've got to have a show. Where we have more trouble, is the Pentecostals seem to be a flash in the pan, I hate to say it, but it's the truth. They get the people all excited about religion, and then the novelty wears off. It's like a bubble that's burst.[53]

The bubble that burst left a real crater in the little community. Some of the very best people in Vandersteene's parish left to join either the Alliance or the Pentecostals. William Beaver, Louis Auger, Bernard and Harvey Houle all became ministers in one church or the other. While they were not all directly from Trout Lake, their influence was very much felt there. Most of Vandersteene's parishioners attended their services. In a letter to Routhier, dated 17 January 1968, he summed up the "loss": in Peerless Lake, 2 boys and 14 girls, in Trout Lake, 12 Catholics have left, of which 9 have left the Church, the remainder having moved to other parishes. Of those remaining four couples and a single lady were "loyal," while six single people and two couples "had been seriously tempted." He adds that there are two men who would not have anything to do with any religion. In a small community, the impact was immediate: Just what do you share with those who have "gone over"?

He explained his strategy to Routhier. He had asked the people at church the first Sunday after the preachers' arrival and the children at school (during religious education) what Mr. Donald Yellowknee had told them: phrases like "that bad old church" and "I stopped praying with the devil" surfaced. The following Sunday, he announced that he had the intention of separating those who were faithful and those who were affected by "l'esprit pentecostal." At school he announced to the children that those who had abandoned the Church should not be allowed to take communion during the coming Christmas season. The third Sunday he had asked those who were frequenting the Pentecostal services to tell him privately (none did) and during religious education, he had told them that he intended to refuse those who were Pentecostals communion even if he had to do it publicly. The fourth Sunday was Christmas, and, in place of the traditional midnight mass in the Church, he had sought approval from the sisters and his visitors (Frs. Tessier and Vantroys) to have invitations from individual families for masses to be held at their homes. He was overwhelmed with the congregation's response ("Presque incroyable!" he wrote) and so Christmas masses were held entirely by invitation to private homes. This left the task of inviting people in the congregation's hands.[54] He apparently never told Routhier about the special form of Christmas Sunday service.

During the three weeks leading up to Christmas, Vandersteene attempted several forms of damage control: one was through sermons. He reminded them of St. Paul's condemnation of those who could not discern the Body of Christ; he urged people to decide which pants they wanted to wear, and to keep them on. Even with such plain language, the defections continued.[55] Vandersteene decided to call a halt to people who were moving back and forth. He elected to give an Advent service in his own little chapel, using the *wikokewin* invitation formula, that is, a private conversation and invitation some time ahead of the service. Some people learned that they had not been invited, and came to him to complain. Then he addressed the issue of the Alliance church, and would give them an invitation. Those who did not ask, he considered had "gone over."

Those who vacillated did so for important reasons. Some felt a perceived benefit from their Catholic roots. For some, it was the issue of missing "God's bread." The mass, and the rituals attached to it, represented something magical, symbolized in the notion that they were receiving God in the wafer. Not participating in that left them somehow empty. Others heard of circumstances they wanted no part of: a Pentecostal woman in Fort Chipewyan was converted, and then her child died. The minister said they would stay and pray for the child to be raised from the dead, even though the child had been embalmed. After two days, the RCMP informed her that if the child was not buried by the next day, they would seize the body. The minister just dug a hole, said a few words over the child and buried it. The mother was beside herself because none of the elaborate rites of the Catholic Church were performed; she was deeply depressed because she believed her child would go to hell.

For many of the Cree, the rites of the Church may be lacking in some respects, but they provided deep solace at death. In addition, more than one thought they had to remain Catholic because the family allowance was paid after a child was baptized in the Church; they apparently considered that the money would be cut off if membership ceased. A few went and remained sceptical: Johnny Cardinal wondered, "Why would this preacher, who runs this store, preach to us on Sunday that the end of the world is coming in a week or so, and then turn around and make a big wholesale order for his store?" Vandersteene appreciated the scepticism, but most of all he did not want people to be two-faced about their commitments. If Vandersteene and Jaycocks agreed on one thing, it was the damage that welfare was doing to the Cree people. Both argued vigorously that all the programs of Canada Manpower, Canada Works, student training programs, etc. were creating a dependence among the people that would have far-reaching consequences. But Vandersteene had to face his own quandary over distribution of charity given from outside for the community. A parishioner came and insisted that any charity that came should only be given to Catholics. For example, every year funds came in for special gifts for the people from churches, and Catholic and charitable organizations sent boxes of clothes. In addition, Vandersteene had funds from several sources, including the diocese, to help with projects, such as grubstakes for trappers. The temptation was evident.

Vandersteene, and his successor Paul, refused to apply the "membership" yardstick — boxes and funds were equitably given, regardless of the religion of the family.

The attempt at broadmindedness did have its glitches. One man came and asked Fr. Paul if it would make a difference whether he was Catholic or not in receiving outside gifts. When Paul reiterated the policy, the man turned and said, "Good! Then I'm going to join the Pentecostals!"

Vandersteene went through several personal phases in confronting the onslaught. He initially was very angry, and confided to associates that he was sick of the "battle with the sects." At the annual meeting of the diocesan missionaries he confided to Fr. Roué that he was very discouraged by what had happened, and fumed, "That's it, I'm really going to resign that post. It's just a disaster! I've only a few families left." But then he would remember the gentle words of old Julian Gladue: "Look at this picture when you first came here," said the old member, pointing to a snapshot pinned to the wall of his cabin. "Three people! Even with those who have gone, you still have more than that. Don't worry about it so much." Later he was to acknowledge that perhaps the Catholic Church and he himself might have to take some blame: "Perhaps this indicates the superficiality of our previous preachings and of their belief."[56] It was from this crisis that his notion of remnant was born, an insight that would have far-reaching implications for his views on a Cree Church.

Vandersteene knew he was no match for the Protestants on alcohol; Steentje liked his beer, and even made some from potatoes one year.[57] He couldn't see how he could attack that problem with any kind of religious authority. Besides he had to accept that some of the converts had quit drinking completely. That may have taken the edge off his anger. Even Jaycocks was to find Vandersteene mellowing after a year or two, especially with the ecumenical thrust of Vatican II.

But Vandersteene was hard-headed in some things. He initially had lost no time in trying to deal with the split within the community and had come up against the message of his old friend Nabis:

> Fr. Vandersteene, unlike the Alliance and Pentecostals, never said this was a sin. In the Bible it says some things are sins, but Fr. Vandersteene never said that. And he was doing things that were here before the missionaries, and they said these were wicked, right from the devil. The main problem was Fr. Vandersteene never said what a person should or should not do. They said you should not drink, and other things.[58]

Vandersteene never talked to Nabis again.

Into this maelstrom came another shadow of the past. Although it wasn't the Pope, special Vatican envoy Cardinal Pignedoli was visiting Canada. He wanted to celebrate the mass with this controversial and dynamic priest in his mission. He wanted to see this phenomenon for himself. The Cardinal and Archbishop Routhier arrived in an airplane. His Excellency wanted to say the mass and have Vandersteene translate it into Cree. "Oh, no!" said the peppery priest, "You have it all wrong. Here the vernacular language is Cree. I'll say the Mass, you can concelebrate it with me." Cardinal Pignedoli deferred. Routhier was not pleased. He knew that the Alliance were just up the road talking to some of the families of Trout Lake in English. Vandersteene persisted with a "normal" Cree service, that is, he preached for over three-quarters of an hour. The Cardinal shifted about, said his rosary, read his book.

Later, Vandersteene's parishioners queried him about the strange behaviour of the Cardinal. Hadn't he warned them to put their rosaries away during the sermon? Didn't he know he was not to do all those things during mass? Vandersteene supposed that he came from far away and didn't know how we had to act in church in Canada. For his part, the good Cardinal growled to Routhier that Vandersteene shouldn't do all those things during the mass unless he had permission, like lifting the host way above his head in a kind of a salute to the sky, a motif adopted from the pipe presentation rituals, or singing Lord have mercy in Cree with drum accompaniment. Routhier assured Cardinal Pignedoli that Steentje had his permission. Of course Rome had not yet given its approval. The Cardinal shrugged it off.

If troubles were piling up in the mission station, another aspect of his life seemed to be blossoming: the lecture circuit. Already he had organized retreats for the sisters working in native situations, slowly encouraging and teaching them about Cree life. His reputation spread east to Ottawa, south to Edmonton and Calgary and north to Yellowknife. He had invitations from schools, educational boards, government agencies and universities to share his point of view.

The Bishop decided by the summer of 1968 that Paul was sufficiently conversant in Cree to handle Trout Lake, and so he proposed that Vandersteene slowly disengage himself from Trout Lake to head up a special team overseeing changes to liturgy, theology and organization for the mission churches. That would allow him to be a resource person for the whole mission organization. Making his headquarters first at St. Bruno's mission on 30 September 1968, Vandersteene made the final move to an office in the "cathedral" complex, as he called it, at Grouard on 21 October 1969. In anticipation of his administrative position, he was elected to the Provincial's Council of the Oblates in 1968, and he began the process of organizing a Presbytery Council on Missions. It was a move into troubled waters, and Vandersteene knew it. He wrote to the Flemish religious: "A strange case! Almost nowhere was there a pure missionary work, evangelical work, done in the past, a lot of social work and now that the social aspect of this work is going by the wayside (to the state) many missionaries are standing looking past their noses, not knowing what to do."[59] He looked out his window in Grouard into a vacuum, without bush, without birds, without children's laughter. It was painful. But at least he could teach a little Cree in Slave Lake to keep in touch,[60] and he now had a car to get him around. He wrote to his friend that living in Grouard and travelling so widely had made him aware of how much of a Cree he had become, "I had become half native." He arranged for his friend, Dr. William Krynen, to prescribe him some relaxants for his stomach. The stress of travel and deadlines replaced Trout's easy life of children, mice and his beloved grotto.

Steentje was clear what he wanted for the missions:

> We are bound to fail if our chief preoccupation as missionaries is to set up structures (and usually Western structures). For this is a strange body. You have to bring the Spirit of Jesus to life in their own Cree life. From within their own contemplative life, let them think about God, the Friend of Man, the great Manitou who came to us in Christ, in order to help us live in faith in the One Spirit.[61]

He also knew the history of missions, the legacy of "acculturation" that still hung around in his colleagues' minds, and the continuing bad press the Church was getting over residential schools. His instincts led him to set the problem in its largest context, the development of the Church out of its European matrix. At some point the Church itself had gone wrong. He began linking together insights and positions he had taken. He believed that old notions of adapting to the aboriginals would no longer work. Language skills, applying superficial Christianizing elements in Cree churches and even the transformation of the visible symbols in Cree churches was not going to effect what was needed. The reality was more intransigent. The Cree conceptual system did not respond to some of the fundamental ways which the Church used to present its message. Seldom had he seen much evidence of piety toward Christ among the Cree. He found sympathy with Jesus, and they responded to the use of Manitou. But Manitou was a special sense of nature present all around, and did not involve the same notions which Europeans found conceptually embodied in God. He knew the negative view that many missionaries had of medicine men, and he also knew that those he had contact with believed their skills came from God. Somehow he had to bring aboriginal ideas about prophecy to the consciousness of the Church; he also had to get his colleagues to understand the meanings in the ceremonial pipe and the other Cree rituals. Some way had to be found to value Cree myths and stories, because, without those, Cree cultural identity could not be tapped. The Church had to look closely at Cree life, to accept Cree marriages and leadership as valid if it ever was to build a Cree Church. In order to do that, he realized he had to get a feel for the larger Church to determine where it would stand in his struggle.

His initial reaction to the latter was not positive. He attended a conference of nuns and priests in Edmonton, and his comments indicate that his view was that the larger Church is in some difficulty:

> The priests form a very good and laudable group, but the sisters, though of good will, were often of extreme views in all directions. Some are still frightened or scared of people and there are already others who have replaced God by mankind. Some are lost in the new youth movement and others who swear against it. All these things are suspended in mid-air and none of them could find good footing. Most, however, were healthy women, seeking and finding. I have learned a great deal not so much from the lesson (i.e., conference) itself but through the study of this group of earnest and sometimes unbalanced but good people. Of course during such a meeting one only meets the best, but always hears of the others. Here also are priests who are dropping out of the ministry, sisters are leaving the cloisters . . . and among many who still remain there is a light-hearted sort of misplaced praise for all that concerns the church, vows, prayer, etc.[62]

At the end of his first year, however, he felt somewhat better. On 14 January 1970 he wrote to the religious: "I think that it is a much more inspiring and encouraging job when seen in its entirety. We should not see all things so black!" For the next three years, he threw himself into mapping out a mission strategy that would incorporate his insights.

Vandersteene's mature analysis began by viewing what the Church had done in North America. As early as 1965, he was warning his colleagues: "Don't read any more of those American Indian books, and put away all those mission books that tell you how to convert the Indian."[63] He saw that, while the Church undoubtedly had been a strong force for good, some very destructive effects came about because of her presence. This was so because the Church had not seen herself only as an instrument of evangelism, but also one of civilization:

> Churches were not only becoming power structures, they were also part
> of a colonizing heavier structure. In Europe religious division followed
> the cracks of state borders in a development not of conviction but of con-
> venience. Nationality and religion were officially one, persecution was a
> state affair, conversion was treason, state, language and religion spread
> together and grew powerful or weak together.... Most missionaries
> who came ... were inhibited by that view.[64]

The school was a perfect tool for this kind of church, since it provided a
means for both conversion and civilization. Yet that very development
of "civilization" encouraged the coming of whites, who, as bearers of
this favoured civilization, consistently pushed the Indians to the
periphery of the community, and, in some cases, of the Church's concern. The Church became "pawns in a game," eventually looking upon
a few hours of catechism during school hours as an achievement, when
it was, in fact, "pathetic." Moreover, the Church became, sometimes
unwittingly, the tool for all kinds of European destruction, treaties
which split communities between treaty and non-treaty, language
which deliberately undermined confidence in the traditional tongues,
lifestyle that favoured the swelling ranks of technically trained whites,
and schools by enforcing and maintaining government policy for the
funding involved. The mission church, with her focus on the local
people, gave way to "national" concerns, of a church with a "national"
message. The Indian became the "neglected" minority. The missionary
became the purveyor of "inflationary Christianity," concerned with
numbers of souls converted, of natives in residential schools, of cathe-
drals and churches built, all legacies of a European value system. It was
part of the European organizational process to impose a nature on the
local church.

Yet it was this underlying "cultural" assumption in the way the
Church developed that was clearly wrong, because, he wrote,

> Christianity can never identify itself with any human society, social
> structure, form of government, establishment, form of charity, evo-
> lution or revolution: it is a divine power for all of them, changing
> from the inside all them.... Christianity needs a pre-existing cul-
> ture; it is a yeast, not a culture in itself.

Strangely, the mission-cum-school community did aid the life of
many natives, introducing incentive, hygiene, cleanliness, management and the religious atmosphere of European village life centred on
the Church. It provided the impetus for a group of young natives to
turn their critical abilities back onto the Church itself and bring the
Church to see her own folly. It gave many the skill to reject the form of
the Church presented and to look for another vision, without the Euro-

pean overlay. They have helped her see that the Church's present task is to go back to her true roots, to pursue her original goal of trying to work out Jesus' words within aboriginal traditions: "I come not to destroy but to fulfill," that is, to bring the message of love present in Christ to Cree life.

Steentje saw the Church, indeed all major religions, in a state of contention between two forces, a state he called "ferment":

> All the great religions are involved in this ferment, in a constant struggle between magic and religion . . . magic in "seeing, possessing and dominating," and religion in "believing, hoping and loving." Aboriginal people all over the world were taught to trade one magic for another, charms became scripture, incantations became readings from the Bible, guardian spirits became angels. New laws are laid down, no meat on Friday, no work on Sunday, no smoking, no drinking, no eating of blood, all new taboos replacing old taboos that often had no reason and may only be a nuisance.

None of them were or are rooted in aboriginal life. Now the Church must turn to the task of bringing aboriginal traditions to fulfillment, to live with Christ in the ferment.

This was the philosophic underpinning of Vandersteene's message. It became the justification for the re-evaluation of Cree tradition in Alberta, and it was the justification for rebuilding aboriginal traditions across Canada. In bringing this vision to play in his district, he first produced a small children's catechism. Entitled *La catechèse des enfants Indiens*, it was not a general catechism for natives, as the title suggests; rather it was exclusively a Cree document. This Cree character reflects his assumption that the Church must first be a local church, built upon the local culture, before it can become anything universal. Thus he defines as religious in Cree life the *wikokewin*, the *meskisimowin*, the *astotuwin*, dreams, prayers and offerings, white magic, the *powakan*, conjurations, sorceries and projected powers, some dreams, some prayers and some offerings.[65] All of these were found interwoven, and were seldom in a pure state, although there are people who are purely of each type. The same bifurcation he sees in religious beings, where he notes Kisemanitou is religious, whereas *manitowok* are magical power spirits. All of these ideas, however, should be used as the basis for explaining what the Church means by its various beliefs; for example, the sacrament of confirmation can be explained best by considering the initiation rites of the Cree. The young man is encouraged to go on a fast, and to have a dream that will introduce his totem or *powakan* to him. With that dream, he ceases to be a child and becomes a young man capable of transmitting life to his people. Similarly, the young woman, at the onset of menstruation, learns the meaning of life and death, the notion that in her body, life can be given and, at the same time, life requires the regular shedding of her blood (in menstruation) and, finally, the taking of her body in death. Regardless of which initiation rite is used for explication, each recognizes the continuing presence of the initiation's outcome, as totem, or as expression of life.

The Eucharist is best explained with the notion of sacrifice. According to Vandersteene, Cree enshrine the notion of sacrifice in two important aspects of their culture: in the hunt when, with the death of the animal, a sacrifice is made. On the one hand, a portion of the animal is given to the fire as an offering to the animal's spirit, who gave this creature for the community, and, on the other, in the *wikokewin* rite, where a portion of the food is fed to the fire as an offering to the ancestors present, followed by the general participation in eating by all those present. The symbolism of the sacrificial lamb is best explicated by the story of the Bear, who gave himself that the people could eat.[66] The model for this use of the Cree stories is the Jewish Scripture, which has furnished the Church with many of its main analogies. Cree stories function in the same way and should find their way into Cree understanding of Christ by the same means.

The values which the Church looks to can best be created through the elders,[67] those who express notions of a "sober and stable life," Cree youth learn these values primarily through existential means, that is, in the experience of life through interaction with the elders. The elders show patience and wisdom when dealing with the young, and see their role as being primarily a model for the youth. Values derived from the hunt or as a warrior were originally those defining the youth, and they continue to do so in some sense, even though the importance of these roles have declined or been abandoned. Morals and taboos were passed on through the family, which is the basic structural unit recognized in Cree culture.

It is at this point that Vandersteene opts for the notion of a base community, a concept first developed in the Church in South America, and central to liberation theology.[68] This community is not a "pure" Cree community; he assumes that the missionary will be part of the environment, but instead of the missionary defining the cultural life of the community, the people will do so. Food, clothes, buildings, accoutrements of civilization (running water), modes of thinking must all conform to the community's vision. The missionary must become dependent upon the people and subsume his/her culture to that of the community, acting as a yeast. Working out of their language, and drawing upon their culture, the message of the Church is brought to those who are attracted. This suggests that the missionary acts as a ferment in the community to bring about the development of the Church, not a vehicle for overwhelming the culture in place. Indeed, he says pointedly that "the local church will not be seen in the first place as a Canadian Church (or part of it) but as a local church. Canadian standards will not be necessarily the local standards."[69]

Steentje was thoroughly aware that in most Cree communities this base community was fundamentally splintered, culturally and religiously. He was also aware that there were simply not enough missionaries to be present in all communities. Therefore he proposed the idea of a remnant. This notion arose first from the destruction of his community church in Trout Lake, which left him with only a handful of people. Originally it was his idea that there was a juxaposition between the elder/remnant leadership, that is, the aged leaders from each community who had stood the test of time, and represented the traditional wisdom and leadership, should be those who fit best this description. But his experience with Nabis and others had apparently changed that. He writes:

> We must try to discover a nucleus of Christianity, a truly religious nucleus: those who are truly Christian, that will demand in some places one year, in other places more than one year. It all depends how deep missionary fervour has penetrated. This second phase will especially be a time of the bringing of the word in catechism and liturgy of a purer and more intensive nature. We will see who drifts to the top under the influence of this more intensive and purified evangelization.[70]

He was convinced that the remnant must be taught to understand the passion of Christ, because that commitment to sacrifice was the example for all Christian leaders. He stressed the use of the Cree word *tutakawiyak*, which means to be treated exactly like, that is, the leaders will be not only persecuted, they will be treated exactly like Christ. Thus the remnant must be fully aware of the spiritual nature of the enterprise. At the same time, he emphasized Cree parables, the vexatious temptations of Christ which were open to all leaders, and the beatitude of the Father, who, he affirms "est une maman! Ma maman, mais mieux encore." They must be taught that Cree culture was given for Cree people, white for white and that Cree cultural concepts, like the belief that remembering a spirit/ancestor makes that one actually present must be valued as a way for the remnant to carry on without the white missionaries. He advocated the identifying and selecting of these two or three people from each community who would head up this remnant, providing a nucleus around which both the Church and the community could achieve some sense of wholeness and blessing. These leaders, a "council of elders," would be brought together for intensive training during the summer, so that the meaning of the Church could be developed from within their consciousness. In this manner, a truly Cree-based church would arise to enrich the larger Church and Canadian society as a whole. This is the message he trundled from group to group, "from one end of Cree country to the other . . . about the same distance as Spain to Moscow."

Vandersteene used the annual general meetings of the Missionary Association as the main launching pad for his ideas. He knew how radical many of his ideas were; he would begin his sessions with a characteristic "Well, this is going to be a surprise and shock to you. You'll be surprised with the teaching I'm going to suggest today!" For conservatives among the missionaries (unfortunately for Steentje, *not* rare among them) his ideas were so far out that they were incomprehensible. They wondered among themselves how he could get away with all these ideas surely not condoned by Rome; even Vandersteene recognized the huge change it would make among the missionaries, and he privately acknowledged that some would never accept the liberation theology implied. At one session he brought out his pipe, and bringing them all, missionaries, priests and sisters into a circle on the floor, he explained to them the significance of the pipe, and proceeded with a pipe ceremony. It was the first pipe many had seen outside a museum. They smoked it with fascination, and, for some, clearly raised eyebrows. Stubbornly he plodded forward.

Living in Grouard allowed him the benefit of learning what was going on in the Cree community at large, and he came more and more under the influence of the Cardinals in Sucker Creek. Harold had slowly turned toward traditional Cree practices, both as a reaction to white political power, and as a means to learn the deeper meanings of Cree culture. On one occasion, Harold was about to smoke his calumet when Vandersteene arrived. He joined in the ritual smoke, and then agreed that he would attend a sweat-lodge ceremony after Sunday mass. Harold's parents were conscious of the criticism in the community of their son's "pagan" leanings, and, when she thought her son was out of hearing range, Rose Cardinal asked Steentje his opinion of the direction in which he was going. Vandersteene assured her that all religions come from the same source, and that each interpreted their understanding of God through their cultural system. He pointed out that any representation of Jesus as blond-haired and blue-eyed was purely cultural, and that there is nothing that says that, if an Indian wishes to see an angel in the form of a bear or a moose, that it is less valid than the way the Church has seen angels or beings of God. "Therefore the ceremonies that we have had are equally valid, the only difference being that we bring in the message of Christ." Moreover, he insisted that whites had been wrong to impose their way of praying upon the Indian people, and, indeed, "attending your ceremonies is just as valid as attending mass."

Harold had been listening. His reflection on what Vandersteene had said is a measure of their mutual respect:

> I was very pleased with the way that he handled the question. Not only did I admire the intellectual integrity of his position, but I appreciated that he removed the doubts for my parents' minds about what I was doing. To top things off, after the mass was over, he came out and participated in the sweat with us. If there ever was any needs that my parents had in order to stand up to the criticims, he gave them the strength to say that what we were doing was not wrong.[71]

As part of his work among the Cree, he had, for several years, attended John Snow's Native Ecumenical Conference on the Stoney reserve west of Calgary. In 1970, the meeting was held at the Crow reservation in Montana. Out of that conference came an official call to Christian institutions that reflected Vandersteene's most recent views. Section four states: "We petition denominational authorities to permit those who work among Indian groups the freedom to use native languages, traditions, dances, legends and their own ancient religions as instruments of the Christian life."[72] He returned confident that he was on the right track.

Periodically, he returned to Trout Lake. Under Fr. Paul Hernou the church had regained some of its lost members, and, in July of 1970 he could report that almost all Catholic families were in mass. Slowly he started again on the tipi church, saying that "Already I have finished the first lead glass window and I have placed it. It is a lead glass window of plastic ground glass and plastic and fibreglass with plastic. It is a great success and it glows with Flemish colours: gold and brown on a multicoloured background."[73]

His travel was extensive, because education, government and church leaders were relying on his views for the development of positions on native culture in Canada. It took its toll. Sitting at a desk or in a plane or car undermined his usual activity established in the mission. His legs began to give him problems, and that only made him more sedentary. He grew heavy and overweight. He did little in the way of exercise. Colleagues and friends nagged him to go to the doctor for a checkup.

Perhaps hovering in the back of his mind was the claim he had once made to Fr. Vantroys: "I pray to God every morning that I am never posted among white people, because it would be very hard to return to the Indians afterwards," because here he was becoming the darling of the white establishment, and that's not what he had been called to do. Would his body ever support his return to the mission? In an ominous note of 3 March 1970 he wrote to his Flemish religious:

> So far as my health is concerned . . . my heart . . . a little pain now and again especially when I work hurriedly. I just have to make an attempt to control myself. And I am also going outside more to exercise! I think it will pass and if it does not pass it will pass anyway. . . . We should not make a great drama out of this! Pray for me. As long as our Lord wants to, I will do my best. You should do the same. I bless you.[74]

Those Cree close to him admired his work on their behalf, and worried about his health. They replaced, "he who speaks good Cree" with another name: *Ka Miyohtwat*, literally 'the good man' but usually translated as "The little man with the big heart." But his heart did not find his work prospering. By 1972, he wrote, "My work here consists of inspiring the missionaries: but with most I am banging my head against a brick wall. And my head is starting to hurt, so is my heart." For most, his insistence on living like the Cree was folly. Even those who shared the concern for Indians, like Fr. Vantroys, would not accept his requirement that he move out of his comfortable home on the mission to share in a shack like his parishioners. Vandersteene's response was forthright: "You're just too lazy!" — but it was never said with rancour, and, anyway his colleagues were now used to seeing him as an idealist. They continually referred to him as "prophet Vandersteene," a designation that he resented as a way of ignoring what he was trying to do. The silent resistance of the Church was slowly grinding him down.

His letters to his Flemish soulmate were fewer and fewer. Finally, in his last letter before he informs her that he is on his way home, he writes: "I do not think there will be a great number of visits after the one next year because I will be 55 and I think I will be starting to think about retirement. . . . I wish you much courage. Life is like the muddy road from Trout Lake to Red Earth."[75] Nobody could get up that muddy road without having a full head of steam and tire chains.

Notes

1 *La Voix*, 35, 6 (September 1976): 147.

2 Ibid.

3 Tanghe, *Leven*, pp. 93-94.

4 Dr. Mary Jackson who lived and served the northern communities for 30 years, could hardly believe this when she read it in an earlier paper, since native men have nothing to do with child-bearing activities, and it is usually left up to an elderly lady of the community. The answer may be that he did not carry out that activity in the Fort Vermilion, Fox Lake and Jean D'Or areas, that is, in areas to which she would have had access. But several sources, including native women, have confirmed that he did act as midwife on several occasions in Trout Lake.

5 To Willy Vandersteene, June 1963.

6 Dr. J.B. Woods, the physician who served the region by air from Peace River for over a decade, considered Vandersteene a first-class horticulturalist. He himself took him plants and shrubs. He was particularly impressed in the way he employed the Cree in his enterprises: they mixed his own soil from peat moss, dirt and fertilizer, which they had collected and for which he paid them (personal interview, 29 August 1979).

7 Willy commented on this side of Vandersteene: "When you saw Rogier, he looked so ordinary, so humble, but he had a brilliant scientific mind. He could find the smallest plant. He saw natural order in everything, which was a kind of reflection of God. I believe he was a kind of natural mystic" (personal interview, 1987).

8 Tanghe, *Leven*, pp. 119-26, chap. 8.

9 Recounted by Fr. Paul Hernou, personal interview, 24 August, 1978.

10 Personal interview, 10 July 1985.

11 See Josef Andreas Jungmann, "Constitution on the Sacred Liturgy," in Herbert Vorgrimler, ed., *Commentary on the Documents of Vatican II*, translated by L. Adolphus, K. Smyth and R. Strachan (New York: Herder and Herder; Dorval-Montreal: Palm Publishers, 1969), Vol. 1, p. 1.

12 Walter M. Abbott, S.J., ed., *The Documents of Vatican II* (New York: Guild Press, 1966), p. 590. For general discussion of this topic, and Belgian contributions to the Belgian liturgical renewal, precursor to Vatican II's liturgical reforms, see Louis Bouyer, *Liturgical Piety* (Notre Dame, IN: University of Notre Dame Press, 1954).

13 Ibid., p. 151.

14 Ibid., pp. 156, 162.

15 Ibid., pp. 172-73.

16 Luke 9:5.

17 From a lecture given at a retreat 20 February 1975.

18 Retreat tapes, "Among the Cree," given to Daughters of Wisdom, Red Deer, 10 May 1965; hereafter cited as "ATC."

19 Eastern Cree had a hymn book, admittedly just a translation of the hymns and psalms of the Church, but, nevertheless far ahead of this, published by the Catholic Church in 1883. Vandersteene comments on the Jesuits' attitude to the Hurons several times in his speeches and writings.

20 Vandersteene, "ATC."

21 This material comes from a presentation entitled "Le chant et la musique," probably presented in 1969-70 at a diocesan conference. From Vandersteene's notes to the conference.

22 *La Voix*, 23 (January 1964).

23 These are just songs I have encountered in various locales, and at various times; this is not the result of systematic study. Obviously there are many other kinds of songs. One has the distinct impression that Vandersteene realized there was a whole area for exploration but he had neither the tools nor, perhaps, the inclination. We can say he had barely scratched the surface.

24 I am indebted to my friend Fr. Jack Dolan of St. Thomas University for assistance with these references.

25 Vandersteene, "Le chant et la musique," pp. 6-8.

26 Rogier Vandersteene, O.M.I., in collaboration with Margaret Denis, S.O.S., *Come Lord Jesus! The Story of the Church* (Ottawa: Canadian Catholic Conference, 1973). The contact may have arisen from Fr. Henri Goudreault at St. Paul University in Ottawa, who invited Vandersteene for lectures there.

27 Related by Fr. Hernou, 24 August 1978.

28 See Vandersteene, *Wabasca*, p. 61.

29 Related by Fr. Hernou, 24 August 1978, but based on stories commonly heard among the Cree. The following two stories are also from Fr. Hernou.

30 Fr. Vantroys outlines the problem this way: "Indians are just becoming little whites. They come around and say, 'Look, Father, so and so will give me five dollars an hour for some job, while you only give us five dollars for a job.' They refuse to see that it is coming out of Vandersteene's own pocket, or, at least, that most of the work had to be voluntary because of lack of funds."

31 It is easy to argue that Vandersteene participated in this out of a Flemish background. After all Ijzer was a pilgrimage he made every year he returned home, and shrines to Mary dot Flanders' roads. But there are more specifically Cree interpretations of the Lac Ste. Anne phenomenon, which have arisen out of my conversations among the Cree elders concerning the spiritual quest or the pilgrimage journey itself. I have no idea how much of that Vandersteene ascribed to, since it is not found in any of his notes.

32 Cree identifies animate and inanimate, absolute or relative as structures in its linguistic divisions. Theologically, Cree recognizes Micimanitou and Kisemanitou as permanently good or bad in power. Neither are associated absolutely with either the earth or sky, so, for example, sky-father and earth-mother cannot apply. Gender is name-specific, meaning that gender resides in the word as assumed, i.e., female, *iskwew*, bitch, *kiskonak*. See Joel Sherzer, "Areal Linguistics in North America," in Thomas A. Sebock, ed., *Current Trends in Linguistics* (The Hague: Mouton, 1973), pp. 749-95; and Brian Craik, "The Animate in Cree Languages and Ideology," in William Cowan, ed., *Papers of the 13th Algonquian Conference* (Ottawa: Carleton University Press, 1982), pp. 31-32.

33 This perhaps explains why some elders/tribes find the term "mother earth" meaningful, while others do not. Those without this reference to a "grandmother" place have, perhaps, a more subtle feeling for the sacredness of the land, but not necessarily any universal "feminine" embodiment in earth. See Maureen Korp, "Before Mother Earth: The Amerindian Earth Mound," *Studies in Religion/Sciences Religieuses*, 19, 1 (1990): 17-25.

34 Personal interview, Paul Gladue (Julian's son), 23 June 1979.

35 Personal interview, Fr. Roué, 22 June 1979.

36 Jordan Paper, *Offering Smoke: The Sacred Pipe and Native American Religion* (Edmonton: University of Alberta Press, 1988).

37 Medicine pipe bundles incorporate objects associated with visions together into one bundle, including feathers, bones and other gifts from the spirit helper, as well as songs and rituals and the pipe itself. The entire bundle becomes symbolic of religious and medicinal power. See Earle H. Waugh and K.D. Prithipaul, eds., *Native Religious Traditions* (Waterloo, ON: Wilfrid Laurier University Press, 1979), esp. pp. 3 and 197.

38 Tanghe, *Leven*, p. 69.

39 Vandersteene, "ATC."

40 *Pôle et Tropiques: Revue apostolique des missionnaires Oblats de Marie Immaculée* (Gemmenich, Belgium) (January 1977): 26.

41 Vandersteene, *Wabasca*, p. 191.

42 Vantroys interview, 4 July 1979.

43 Tanghe, *Leven*, p. 30.
44 Rose Cardinal interview, 22 June 1979. Vandersteene delighted in needling game wardens, including setting them up to look stupid, as he once did with ducks' legs sticking out of straw. The warden grabbed them for evidence . . . there was no body attached. Paul Gladue noted: "The last ten years has killed the hunter culture here, and the white man has to be largely responsible for that."
45 Clara Yellowknee's comments are found in Appendix 2, p. 312.
46 On several occasions Vandersteene assailed both levels of government for developing programs that had nothing to do with who the Cree were, rather than what whites *thought* the Cree should be. For example, he could not see why industries like farming or gold could be subsidized, while trapping and hunting could not.
47 Arnold Strynadka, *The Native People* (October 1971), p. 16, col. 2. Vandersteene wrote back to Strynadka on 16 November 1971, saying that many young native people seem to reverse the issue of being Cree and white, that is, they ask whether one can be white and Cree, the point being that they have already given up the ship if they are that far along. He then adds that he would not write about Indian affairs again: "I know when I am not welcome." It would appear that Vandersteene was wounded by the change of misrepresentation, especially since he had been a student of myths, legends and native stories. Roy Piepenberg, executive member of the Indian Association of Alberta, said Vandersteene's paternalism was to protect Cree, rather than in the past when the Church just decided what was good for them. He could not comment on whether Vandersteene wanted a bicultural, bilingual situation for Cree, or something more permanently "Cree" (personal interview, 5 May 1979).
48 Vandersteene, *Wanneer gij*, dated 21 March 1967, pp. 13-15.
49 Ibid., p. 14.
50 Ruth Jaycocks interview, 30 June 1979.
51 As Ruth Jaycocks was to admit in the interview.
52 Fr. Jacques Johnson, Director of Missions at the time of this research, 29 June 1979. He also had negative views about native medicine, especially the belief that someone can put a hex on you. He had an experience of one young man who apparently suffered a great deal because he believed someone had cursed him. Johnson's prayer of exorcism brought him much relief. If Vandersteene was aware of the evils of bad medicine, he says nothing of it in his writings.
53 Ruth Jaycocks interview, 30 June 1979.
54 Vandersteene to Routhier from Slave Lake, 17 January 1968. He also includes a note on his invitations and activities: "To Whitehorse, Yukon 14-15 February, a seminar on 'Positive and Constructive Public Welfare' for the provincial Bureau of Public Health in Athabasca later in the month, and supervising the retreat of Fr. Vantroys."
55 Commenting on this period in Vandersteene's career, Dr. Woods of Grouard pointed to the liveliness of the Alliance and Pentecostals compared to the "staid old Catholic ritual."
56 To Sister Gloria Bernard, 20 August 1967.
57 His relatives said he liked all kinds of drinks: wine, beer, cognac, whiskey, so they could see how he would have a tough time making a pronouncement about alcohol. He was apparently far more circumspect in Canada.
58 Nabis Okemaw, 27 June 1979, Peerless Lake.
59 Vandersteene, *Wanneer gij*, p. 23.
60 R. Sinclair hired him to teach introductory Cree in Slave Lake and noted that his Cree was somewhat different than that known in his area. In addition, Slave Lake may be said to serve as a dividing line between the two dialects of Cree, although this has to be taken in a very relative sense.
61 Tanghe, *Leven*, p. 39.
62 Vandersteene, *Wanneer gij*, p. 35.

63 Vandersteene, "ATC." All following quotations are culled from the six tapes. I appreciate Fr. Jacques Johnson making these available to me. I have been unable to determine how many of these ideas are original. Theodore F. Zuern, S.J., published "Indians Must Be Indians," *The Catholic Digest* (April 1969), pp. 76-80, containing many of the same ideas, apparently developed from his seven-year stint among the urban Indians of Rapid City, Iowa.

64 I have been unable to trace the precise influences on his thought expressed here. It is clear that the ideas are not new, they are part of the rhetoric behind liberation theology. It is possible that he had read R. Hernegger, *Macht Ohne Auftrag? Die Entsehung des Staats- und Volkskirche* (Freiburg: Olten, 1963), where it states explicitly, "The religion that marked the West was not properly the Christian message" (p. 431), and had similar sentiments.

65 R. Vandersteene, *La catechèse des enfants Indiens*, dup. copy (Grouard: N.p., n.d).

66 See below, p. 189.

67 In 1974, Fr. Nicolas Roué gave a report on his study of the Indian diaconate program; strangely, the justification for the urgency of the program was not Cree-based, but church-based: "I say *yes*, this makes it an urgent necessity. Let us face the facts: the number of priests and sisters is going down, and this trend is not going to change. One of the duties of the Mission is to prepare a native clergy to eventually take over from the Missionary from abroad and assume the responsibility of the local Church." And on this Fr. Eugene Hillman, S.J., comments: "Churches which fail or refuse to find ways of becoming self-reliant in this matter of personnel for the pastoral ministry will simply die out. Now it is a question of indigenization or of death" ("The Formation of Lay Deacons," photocopied handout).

68 See Leonardo Boff, *Church: Charism and Power* (New York: Crossroad, 1985), especially his chap. 10: "Underlying Ecclesiologies of the Base Ecclesial Communities." Note his bibliography for further reading.

69 Letter to the Missionary Congress, dated 20 May 1970. It is interesting to see the role of the official organization in this scenario — the Bishop is "part and head of the local church." He could not have thought that through very carefully. In one presentation, he says: "By our presence here we are attached to the archdiocese of Grouard and are under the jurisdiction of the Archbishop. Our group of missionaries enjoys a great autonomy in the exercise of our pastorate. Our relations with Monseignor [sic] Routhier OMI were good. He was comprehensive [sic] and manifested an interest in our work. His annual visit was very cordial. From the point of view of contact with the order, he was very supple." Since this is a meeting of the missionaries, one wonders if there was a touch of damning with faint praise present.

70 Vandersteene, *Wanneer gij*, pp. 39-40.

71 Personal interview, Harold Cardinal, 26 June 1979, at Assumption. On the other hand, Vandersteene wrote to his Flemish soulmate that he had stopped to visit some young Indians in Sucker Creek who were returning to pagan religion and no longer worshipping the "real" God (Vandersteene, *Wanneer gij*, pp. 17-18). It appears he was not too sure that he could talk frankly with her about his views on Cree religion.

72 Reported by C.S. Price and quoted in Paul B. Steinmetz, S.J., *Pipe, Bible and Peyote among the Oglala Sioux: A Study in Religious Identity* (Knoxville: University of Tennessee Press, 1990), p. 109.

73 Fr. Hernou interview, 27 August 1978.

74 Vandersteene, *Wanneer gij*, p. 99.

75 Ibid., p. 59.

Six

The Great Mystery: Visible and Touchable in Art

> In many ways art is similar to religion. Its development consists not in new discoveries which invalidate the old truths (as is obviously the case with science). Its development relies on sudden illuminations like lightning, in which explosions burst in the sky like fireworks . . . this illumination shows with blinding light new perspectives, new truths, which are at once basically nothing but the organic development of earlier wisdom.
> — Wassily Kandinsky, *The Spiritual in Art*

On the surface it would appear that Vandersteene's artistic output was very much the servant of his mission — his first serious artistic canvases were created to reflect biblical and doctrinal themes in his work in the mission of Wabasca, and throughout his career his religious context dictated both the quantity and type of production. A number of his associates, however, stressed that he was more an artist than anything else; close friends like Platteeuw insisted on his essentially artistic vision in trying for an understanding of his lifework. More than one regarded his mind as far more in tune with the artist than the theologian.

This poses some rather difficult problems. First, we have no complete record of his artistic production because it is spread over three continents (North America, Europe and Africa) and some of it has disappeared, as works of lesser artists are wont to do.

All his first Canadian art work is in Fox Lake, stored there from Little Red. Some of his work would appear to have been almost created on the spot; his "cartoon-type" work in the catechism comes to mind, because it uses a very primitive style. But we know his better work is more complicated than that, since we have his sketchbooks. Some of his ideas were in his sketchbook for 15 years before they appeared as

---

Notes to this chapter are on pp. 195-96.

paintings. Yet even his paintings have an immediacy, which seems to suggest that a painting simmered for many years, sometimes through many years of suffering and growth, and then sprang fully to life. In fact, the best glimpse of his artistic corpus is through these small loose-leaf binders, over a dozen of them, which gather both religious and secular themes together side by side. Many of his paintings were only available to me through these sketchbooks.

No one would claim that Vandersteene developed a new artistic language; he drew heavily upon the artistic traditions of Belgium, and more particularly Flemish art, for his inspiration. Neither his time nor activity allowed him the leisure to actively turn his observations into paintings, but judging by what colleagues say, and what we have in his sketchbooks, his ability to see the world in artistic ways was considerable. If not original, he has been very much inspired by the Cree social relationships, both in terms of subject matter, and in terms of characterization. Very few of his paintings deal with natural scenes exclusively. These factors indicate an additional problem: he does not fit into the genre of so-called Indian art. His works cannot, then, be easily compared with others of a type that draws its power from aboriginal sources.

Moreover, very little of his work shows sympathy for the abstract, a style very much in vogue among professional artists in western Canada. A few pieces of wood sculpture are abstract, and several line drawings, but purely abstract paintings are not found. In addition, only rarely does one find non-figural themes among his corpus. In a major way, he drew his topics from the people and the spaces of northern Alberta. He is the first missionary among the aboriginals in Alberta to do so; among the few mission painters, Vandersteene may be the most important that Canada has produced.[1]

Still, what has to be determined is how much his artistic activity shaped his vision. There is an astonishing amount of craftsmanship and styles among his artistic output. He painted in oils, acrylics and watercolours; he also coloured with pencils and pen and ink. He did sculpting, mostly with natural shapes and materials, like tree roots. He did stained glasswork, woodcut etchings, garden design and drafting. Among the works which he left are houses, churches, including the tipi church at Trout Lake and several greenhouses; among his crafts were floral design for moosehair tufting, scores of uniquely crafted and beautifully painted fishing lures and handmade woodcut Christmas cards. He had great skill in gardening and had plants from all over the world arranged aesthetically in his grotto. His collection of cactii was impressive, and early in his career he had toyed with plant grafting and development, especially with an eye to encouraging aboriginal plant wisdom and craft; aspects of this interest show up in his art. He apparently never took up photography, although many of his sketches have almost a photographic quality to them. His line drawings, often used for illustrating lessons to his flock, were dramatic and poignant, many times reflecting some particular Cree person he was trying to influence. His sense of nature was heavily influenced by aboriginal notions that human life was part of a natural order, but he also shares a strong Flemish nature-mysticism. Thus, like his early artistic bent in seminary, his interests and talents were eclectic, and he interweaves all of them without apparent rhyme, reason or conflict.

During the years when he acted as director of missions and laboured to develop a Cree Church, he painted no new canvases. Indeed, if we were to count his truly artistic canvases, we would not be speaking of more than 30 for his lifetime, not a prolific quantity, given the quickness with which he sometimes worked.[2] Besides, allowance has to be made for the time spent on one of the last and, for him, most important creations: the book of catechism. He hand-drew all the major display cards for all the published copies of the text, a chore that had to be started over when a flood destroyed the masters in the basement. The publishers required over a hundred of these drawings. At the same time he enjoyed drawing and sketching secular topics: he has a whole series on the positions which rabbits take when caught in a snare. How much weight should be given to these facts in the measurement of his life?

The Shape of a Synoptic Artistic Language

It is evident that Vandersteene never thought his art was a distinctive and perhaps contradictory aspect of his life. As we have seen, he began painting seriously as part of a young artists' group with his associates while he was at the Oblate school. He had not painted much before that. It was an expression born out of his experience in the cloisters, and it seemed to remain a language with the deepest religious roots.

The relationship between religious/metaphysical perceptions and art has long intrigued thinkers and writers. Artistic expression has often derived its inspiration and economic support from religion, and the relationship between cultural artifacts and art make the relationship complex and multidimensional. There are some who would argue that all true art, despite its subject matter, is religious, while others regard art as solely functional.

A number of writers and thinkers reject the need for such an explicit religious artistic language. They argue that art itself has religious meanings. Two such writers are Heidegger and his student Martin. Heidegger once called the artist the "Shepherd of Being," and, in his analysis of Van Gogh's painting of shoes, had argued:

> The painting is of a pair of peasant's shoes — and nothing else. Just a pair of shoes; yet around and through them emerges the world in which the peasant traces his furrows, watches patiently for the wheat to bloom, or trudges tiredly at evening back from the fields. The cycles of time — Spring, Summer, Autumn, Winter — enfold these simple boots, as presence, emerges through the painting of the shoes; yet in such a way that it enfolds them in their concrete thingness — just a pair of shoes, and nothing else — as the simple, serviceable gear that they are.[3]

It goes without saying that Vandersteene was much closer in his understanding of art to Heidegger than to those who regard art as a pure aesthetic expression devoid of metaphysical content. A contemporary exponent of Heideggerian aesthetics, F.D. Martin, suggests that "a participative experience" engages the artist in the reality around him. As Martin sees it, the artist must allow the reality encountered to force itself upon him/her, in two kinds of creativity, the receptive and the constructive. In the former, the artist must "let Being be," while in the latter, Being is unveiled to others through the artistic creation. Martin's use of capitals indicates that he thinks there is one objective reality which engages the attention and relates directly to the artist. Thus Martin asserts:

> Art is a gift of Being. That is why art, despite its autonomy, has always served as the principal sacred bridge — although, admittedly, very narrowly framed in the Puritan tradition — to the religious experience, and continues to do so even in these apparently post-religious times. . . . To be is to participate, to be creatively absorbed with the presence of Being, and then we may be at one with sun and stone, as Nabokov writes somewhere. And then the corroding acids of technology can be contained and even functions may partake of the beauty of being. Every object and event, no matter how mundane, is potentially sacramental.[4]

The close relationship of art and religion is borne out in the controversial practise of French Dominican Marie-Allain Couturier who insisted that "It is safer to turn to geniuses without faith than to believers without talent"; so saying he hired sceptics like Matisse, Braque, Chagall, to paint for the Church he was building in the French Alps. Couturier firmly believed that "all great art is spiritual since the genius of the artist lies in the depths, the secret inner being from whence faith also springs."[5]

Others argue that whatever the culture from which it derives, a great work of art is a potential *source* of spiritual insight, falling short of words in the power of syllogistic argument and even to the ability to suggest the content of the imagination's inward eye, but far superior in the evocative power to haunt and illuminate. Thus Wassily Kandinsky,[6] the pioneer of abstract painting at the turn of the century, spoke of art as *resembling* religion in taking what is known and transforming it, showing it "in new perspectives and in a blinding light." In Kandinsky's view, both art and religion have the ability to reconstitute the artifacts of culture in new and powerful ways, even if they do not bring any new ingredients to the culture. It is the breakthrough which configures both art and religion.

Obviously Vandersteene would have difficulty with this notion, because he insisted on the historical uniqueness of Christ, and the transformation that He brought to the world. The issue of Christian exclusivism would seem to militate against unifying the artistic and religious experiences along Kandinsky's lines. Thus even if such an analysis locates the springs of art and religion together, it cannot account for the specific themes and directions a religious art itself takes. That requires a direction within the religious culture of the time that cannot appeal to a general notion of "being" as its basis. Hence, some kind of Christian theory of artistic consciousness would seem necessary.

As one might expect, the theoretical picture is complicated. John McManners points to the new situation facing the understanding of art today; it is the problematic of finding a true public language for the pious individual's vision:

> Instead of the collaboration of many craftsmen in a masterpiece (like a cathedral) which is understandable by everybody, the most characteristic manifestation of spirituality in art today is the "testimony," the individual artist witnessing to his view of the universe in his total *oeuvre*. But we lack a common artistic form applicable to public worship and private meditation.[7]

One individual who has tried to grapple with a Christian "theology of art" is Urs Von Balthasar, a Dutch Jesuit who has been writing about aesthetics for many years. The first volume of his most influential work has now been translated into English and is entitled *The Glory of the Lord; A Theological Aesthetics: Seeing the Form*.[8] It has had considerable impact on the Catholic interpretation of the aesthetic experience.[9] His work was published at the time of Vandersteene's sojourn in seminary and may well have been discussed in his circle of artistic friends. Fr. Paul Hernou, Vandersteene's protégé and successor, directly links Vandersteene to Von Balthasar's work; Vandersteene had his books in his library. Despite the fact that I have not found explicit reference to Von

Balthasar in any of Vandersteene's published work, there is good evidence that he accepted many of his ideas.

Von Balthasar argues that God reveals himself in the aesthetic expression itself *and* in the sense of splendour that we encounter in various types of beauty. He holds that God is present in every example of beauty, and that this beauty allows us to perceive something beyond the external appearance. The perception we have is mediated through the particular exemplum of beauty, but it is grounded in the promise of a real "encounter with Being," as we have seen in Heidegger. Thus every example of beauty mediates God for us.

Moreover, Von Balthasar insists that there is delivered, along with the particular expression of beauty, a certain entrancement and rapture. He states this to be an *"eros*-love," a notion which he acknowledges comes from the early Christian mystic and theologian Dionysius the Areopagite.[10] Dionysius had insisted that God was drawn out of himself in the world, and at the same time He had inspired humans to be transported out of themselves toward Him. Von Balthasar quotes a long passage from the early theologian, ending with this claim: "Both to possess eros and to love erotically belong to everything Good and Beautiful, and eros has its primal roots in the Beautiful and the Good: eros exists and comes into being only through the Beautiful and the Good."[11] Hence his theology of aesthetics is based upon an engagement of the human in objects of beauty because they are expressions of the being of God. It is precisely because we participate in the world with passion and are "caught up" in interacting with it that Von Balthasar can insist that God is both object of this eros and the one who causes this eros to be part of our lives to begin with.

It follows from this that every truly beautiful expression is a "genuine self-representation, a genuine unfolding of himself in the worldly stuff of nature, man, and history," an event that he calls an "appearance" or an "epiphany."[12] It is not the multiple variety of images around us that are significant; they are merely the form through which the artist expresses the encounter with Being. Jesus Christ is but the most supreme form of this revealing nature of God.

This view fits quite well with Vandersteene's work. One particular aspect of Von Balthasar's corpus has merit from Steentje's point of view: the attempt to create is an attempt to "say something" about that which engages one. Thus North American aboriginal culture is not fundamentally different from European culture. Both are ways of engaging with that Being which is held to lie behind the myriad forms in the world. Aboriginal perceptions of reality have as much viability as European, native religious symbols have potentially as much significance as Christian. Yet for both Vandersteene and Von Balthasar, Christ remains the most epiphanic of all forms. Vandersteene notes: "Only Christianity sees the Great Mystery as present and attainable, visible and touchable, because it not only believes in Death and Resurrection but also in Incarnation: What you do to others you do to me."[13]

Hence the use of aboriginal imagery, at least in some sense, reflects the *presence* Vandersteene sees in all religious forms. This justifies the exploration of the reality of the world through that imagery. But Vandersteene cannot bring himself to see, as does Von Balthasar, that it is the *image* of Christ which is superior to Indian images. Steentje affirms that it is the fact that the mystery becomes human that makes the difference. He would argue against those who think his interpretation of God is so much "ghost in the machine." For him, Christ's life is guarantor of God's presence. Shunting deconstructionists aside, Vandersteene holds that their derision is scuttled by the historical Jesus. What was before hidden in images, now can be seen and felt.

It would seem to follow from this that native imagery would always be an inferior system in either writer for understanding the divine. Vandersteene does not hold this, however, because he affirms that Christ only adds new and vital concepts to human understanding, He does not modify the basic truth of God being present in native culture. Speaking about the side effects of Christianity on the native, Vandersteene said: "Christianity never has [had] the call to crush, smash or smother [culture] but to penetrate, heal, invigorate and fertilize the already *pre-existing presence of God* with the contact of Christ who is love, light and the true Way."[14]

There are, thus, areas in which Vandersteene appears to be far more hesitant in the application of Von Balthasar's theory, for the latter would insist that Christ is the crowning expression of God in culture, whereas Vandersteene would insist that Christ's incarnation is a mode of human expression superior to all others. The historical Christ is a necessary one. It would be difficult to see how Vandersteene can give any more than provisional validity to native imagery if it did not express Christ-type values. It is perhaps this deep problematic that motivated his constant search for an artistic language to capture aboriginal truths. In an earlier work, I indicated how this search led him from the application and modification of an Eastern Christian iconography through to the radical appropriation of the bear on the cross;[15] yet none of these images seem to have risen above McManners' plaint noted above. The Cree Church has not adopted his imagery.

McManners also sees three overriding themes in Christian art: triumph, friendship and sorrow. The first developed quickly after

Plate 1

Plate 2

Plate 3

Plate 4

Plate 5

Plate 6

Plate 7

Plate 9

Plate 8

Plate 10

Plate 11

Plate 12

Plate 13

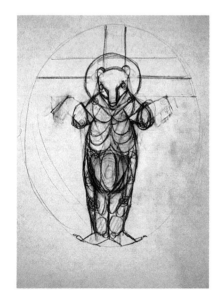

Plate 14

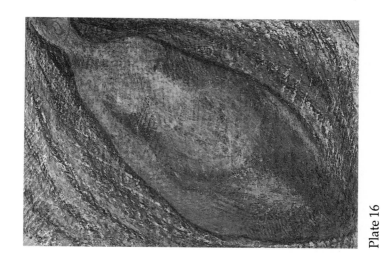

Plate 16

Plate 15

Plate 19

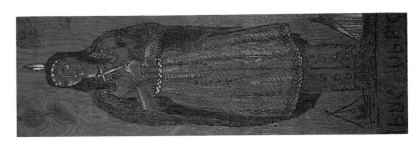

Plate 18

Plate 17

Plate 21

Plate 20

Plate 23

Plate 22

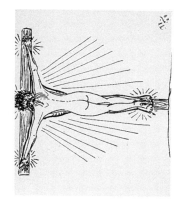

Plate 26

Plate 25

Plate 24

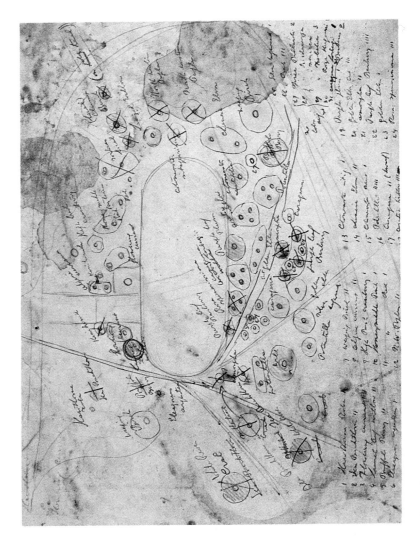

Plate 27

Constantine accepted Christianity and made it his state religion. The grandeur and regality of Christ's position in the hierarchy of God was replicated in the popular vision of the Byzantine court. The result was an art that was rich and sumptuous, centred on the splendours of heaven and the transcendent dimension. At the end of the medieval period, a shift began as Christian society moved away from the monarchical. With the twelfth and early thirteenth centuries came a reaffirmation of the common Jesus, the friend of sinners and ordinary people. The harbinger of this notion is Abelard's theory of the atonement, which stresses that when we see Christ's passionate and suffering love for us, the experience triggers the awakening of our love for Him. Jesus' family life, the madonna and child, the infancy stories of Jesus and other humanizing themes inspired the patrons, and, armed with the wealth of the Church and its rich patrons, the art of the Church moved in a new direction, a direction McManners calls "reversion to tenderness, to the magic spring time of the sacred story."[16]

The third motivator was sorrow, a multifaceted concept that drew inspiration from a disparate range of people in Jesus' experience: the tragedy of such a good-looking blond-headed young man stumbling beneath the load, the agony of a mother dealing with the senselessness of her son's death, the distraught disciples slinking away in fear and self-loathing. Where the Renaissance artist could not bring himself to paint the gruesomeness of Christ's death, he could turn the environment into a fear-ridden and hellish place. The clouds roiled and darkened, rain and misery poured around the Saviour and his few anguished followers. What seems peculiar is that Vandersteene's art reflects all three themes, but with interpretations of each that might differ from the normal meaning of those descriptors.

Flemish Influences: Impressionism, Expressionism, Avant-garde

"Roger used to talk to me with expert knowledge about the Masters of the Flemish school. Indeed, in my modest opinion, his paintings seem to be inspired by that school: liveliness of colour, attention to the the concrete details of daily life." So said his friend Tanghe. In fact there is good evidence to see Vandersteene's work within even narrower Flemish contexts, that is, those related to local painters, such as Notebaert from Zweregem and Staf Stientjes from Tiegem and Stefaan Van Gheluwe from Kortrijk. Certainly these were his earliest influences. One of his closest friends was Frans Claerhout, who became a painter/ priest in South Africa.

As a youth he became involved with a group of painters at St. Martens Latem, a small village in a pastoral setting not far from Marke. St. Martens Latem became the focal point for a community of Flemish artists shortly after the turn of the century. Independent-minded and even iconoclastic, they concentrated on the artists known as the symbolists.[17] The symbolists disregarded the disjunction between the normal colour and shape of the symmetry expected by their viewers in the symbolists' representation of nature, and nature itself. Thus a tree in a painting can have more significance as an expression of fertility or as a bucolic environment than as a plant. Moreover, the symbolists would not agree with McManners that the split between private and public worlds in the representation of piety was so absolute; symbolists held that the private language of the artist could appeal directly to the viewers and give a message even if the viewers could not articulate exactly why they saw something significant. The painting made the artist's language public and appealed, even if the public did not know why. So powerful were such presentations that old or partially concealed symbols could have a total impact and could give powerful messages, and the "hiddenness" of the shape could even make it more powerful. This is why the elements in a work of art may be quite different than the sum of a painting and seeing something familiar can send one off on a visual journey to find something else. The eye is captured by details never noticed in the total impact.

Gustaaf van de Woestijne (1881-1947) was an important representative of this early period and a dynamic and spiritual symbolist in the first group of Latem painters. These artists came under the spell of the Flemish primitivists and the homespun but brilliant Pieter Breughel. De Woestijne had an early impact on Vandersteene, who took up his Flemish primitivist ideology. Some of his paintings during seminary show strong influences of this ideology, and it had an impact on his first works in Canada, as is evident in Plate 1.

Primitivism hoped to reduce the exuberance of the natural order to its most essential ingredients, as if the artist were distilling and conveying to the viewer the quintessential reality, shorn of all extraneous details. But, as we know, under the guise of reducing, the primitivist did not distill nature, but effectively created another form of nature. This form of nature was reduced in complexity, yet packed with emotions because it purged the vision of all those myriad details that softened the starkness of nature's essence. For the layperson, what was being painted could still be recognized as a familiar "object," but the message of the painting was remarkably different than the natural form. This strange new kind of realism was the style that Vandersteene and his colleagues had experimented with in seminary.

It was, of course, but a step for the artistic community to create a nature that never existed — a "natural" order that might represent what the artist thought summed up the meaning of nature. Expressionism became the artistic form that moved in that direction. Vincent Van Gogh from nearby Holland used paint in a "thick, palette-knife" style as a way of delivering an emotional message, which, at the time, seemed to reflect a world foreign and mysterious. It is significant that Steentje adapted this style for a painting of the Cree woman removing frozen mukluks (Plate 1). There are several canvases of similar style, all of them found in Flemish homes. None of his work destined for Canadian viewers utilizes this style.

Flemish primitivism also raises the question of nature mysticism. Several of Vandersteene's friends and relatives, especially in Europe, regarded him as a nature mystic. Vandersteene is actually connected in two ways to this tradition, through Flanders and through Germany. Both have an artistic dimension.

We mentioned earlier the significance of Albert Servaes.[18] Servaes belonged to two traditions, both the impressionist and the expressionist, and believed strongly in the evocative power of painting. Vandersteene encountered Servaes first when he went with his group from the Oblate college to paint with him, and a number of his later paintings reflect Servaes' striking religious mysticism. Thus Servaes painted a Christ who was emaciated and gaunt, reflecting a human who had suffered so much that the physical body was almost translucent. Some evidence of this influence is preserved in Plate 8, entitled *St. Julia*. In addition, Vandersteene was strongly influenced by Servaes' Virgin Mary / female form mysticism, as we shall see below. But there are also some residual strains of impressionism, as can be seen in his *Landscape* (Plate 2).

Impressionist paintings were a delight to look at; their airy, light, joyful canvases celebrated the colour and vividness of the world. Sandy beaches, expansive seas, a kind and benevolent nature. Vandersteene's earliest paintings in Little Red River have an idyllic quality derived from this impressionistic vision, although they also have elements of primitivism. In reference to one of them (Plate 3) Fr. Vantroys commented:

> I clearly recall how he had, during May of 1952 painted in Fort Vermilion a scenery of the Little Red River ... including real Indian figures. Rogier took two to three days to complete this painting. Many times I stopped before this scenery marvelling at the exactness with which he reproduced with a few strokes the likeness of a particular Indian's normal attitude.[19]

This painting probably represents Vandersteene's attempt to adopt the visually delightful style which he associated with a simpler artistic moment in Europe. In actuality, the attempt to create such a moment was already past, even for Gustaaf De Smet (1877-1943), who, while an expressionist, nevertheless looked for an uncomplicated, calm moment as an ideal. Vandersteene almost mimics De Smet with his Cree *Virgin and Child* (Plate 4), because the virgin has the same sense of peace and serenity to be found in De Smet's *Dorpsvrouw*, a painting of a matronly woman with closed eyes.

The horrors of the First World War brought a denouement to the history of impressionism. Out of that experience poured forth the ugliness of the times, and, along with it, the attempt to mount the violent mood and tame it sufficiently for the artists' brush to capture. At the same time, nationalist Flanders artists began depicting Flemish themes and concerns so that the expressionism that developed was distinctively their own. James Ensor, who painted Christ on the cross in the midst of a contemporary Belgian fair, stresses the incongruence and satire of this new movement. It uses a visionary landscape and a surrealism to depict a world that is somehow a little bizarre. Vandersteene retains the contemporary setting, but drops the surrealism: he sets Mary and Jesus in the midst of a powwow (Plate 5). The Cree would see the humour in the painting, especially since Vandersteene painted real people into the work (several of them not members or "unbelievers"); some other Canadians would view the possibility of Mary and Jesus at such an event with derision and sarcasm, a response not unlike the response Ensor's painting originally elicited in Belgium. Both paintings emphasize the immediacy and social fabric of belief, a theme that Vandersteene was to emphasize over and over again in many aspects of his work.

Constant Permeke (1886-1952), was one of the greatest of the European expressionists and a towering figure in modern graphic art. Permeke had a cosmic feeling for his subjects, lifting them to the monumental. Nature flows like a common thread through all aspects of life, birth, life, death, so the joy of being is just in the existing, and in the staggering belief that the ordinary person has profound signficance. Vandersteene paints this monumental sense into the *Portrait* (Plate 6). Permeke often has moody, almost primal colours, a concept replicated in the *Annuciation* (Plate 7) but found in greater force in other paintings not represented here.

The paintings of Edgard Tytgat (1879-1957), are full of significant details, even if the subject matter is quite ordinary. He often uses women as the central symbolic figure, and juxtaposes light and dark figures to provide a symmetry. Contrastive backgrounds are found in his work. Frequently images seem to float. As we have seen, some of his paintings on the wall at Wabasca are reminiscent of this style (Plate 3).

If the context in which Vandersteene first encountered expressionism was Flanders, his sense of natural mysticism very much reflects the German natural mystics of Die Brücke.[20] Just about all the elements singled out by Émile Nolde and applied to Ludwig Meidner could be slightly altered and applied to Vandersteene: "For him, the Bible and his personal relationship with the idea of Christ were closely linked with childhood memories and his feelings for the North German landscape. He was a pantheist, and the smallest corner of nature for him was filled with the glory of God." Alter pantheism to natural theism and change Bible to Church and you have Vandersteene.[21] "His desire for a new faith, independent of churches and inspired by a deep involvement with life, close contact with Nature, belief in the importance of direct and unself-conscious emotion and honest approach to the business of painting are characteristic of the entire expressionist movement."[22] Once more there are resonances with Vandersteene. From the perspective of his art, then, Steentje was far more influenced by the intuitive mysticism of nature than by Nazi politics, which certainly came much later in his development. This throws a different light on the interpretation of this aspect of his life, since we know that Vandersteene's interest in expressionism was already in place from his early years in the seminary.

One other aspect of his artistic creativity must have come from Germany: his woodcuts. Die Brücke, and particularly Kirchner, experimented with the woodcut as early as 1913. Vandersteene adopted this form for many of his personal cards and Christmas greetings (Plate 9), obviously because he could personalize the colours, but also because he enjoyed the crafting of wood necessary to produce the print. He was also using the natural to craft the supernatural.

Interestingly, Vandersteene painted few Canadian landscapes, in and for themselves. He did not appear to be influenced by the Canadian mania for wilderness scenes which Canadians covet for their living room walls. Landscape only becomes a factor against which a particular event or moment is painted. He does have some drawings and mythological sketches which involve stylized locales (Plate 10) but neither forest, winter weather, nor water were of interest to him. Indeed, without his care and concern for cactii and the plants of the grotto, we would be hard pressed to prove his natural mysticism. His paintings are directed otherwise. After the series of paintings at Wabasca, the natural world's backdrop passes out of his art. Perhaps he did not regard *that* landscape as formidable and threatening, as landscapes tended to be under the hand of the expressionist.

It is evident that Steentje did not continue his engagement with movements in Belgian art after he moved to Canada. There are no canvases that draw us to consider Brusselmans, for example, with his almost brick-like solid figures, and his reduction of art to an essential, clear mass. Brusselmans' search is like the physicist's, a search for the basic unit of the cosmos that can then be replicated over and over to determine why we are the way we are. As with individual persons, there is mood and tone to the way these are arranged, a certain synthesis that has uniqueness, but is still only a replication of a basic unit. The closest that Vandersteene comes to this vision are his stained-glass windows at Trout Lake (Plate 11).

One individual who does not seem to be represented in the Vandersteene corpus is Jos Speybrouck, from Kortrijk (1891-1956), who must have been known to him. Like Vandersteene he was an idealistic proponent of the Flemish movement, and like Vandersteene, he was a creative phenomenon: he wrote, painted, drafted and composed poetry. Also like Vandersteene, he was inspired by Albrecht Rodenbach, for whose book *Gudrun*[23] he designed the prints. Politically, Speybrouck was not aligned to Flemish nationalism but he often identified with the movement through his art. He has one very famous cartoon-style poster, "Move aside, Flanders is here" that became the rallying cry of a whole generation of young nationalists. His style was much copied in student papers such as *De Blauwvoet* of the Catholic Flemish Student Union in Leuven. His work was effective in bringing ordinary Flemish citizens into the movement, even if they did not join the organization. Later, however, he retreated into a pietist longing for brotherly unity. Perhaps the reason Vandersteene was not attracted to him was that Speybrouck had already shifted away from his nationalist themes when Steentje moved to Canada, and he died before Vandersteene returned. Certainly his lack of commitment to the independence movement would have been cause for Vandersteene to be cool towards him. At any rate, none of his themes or styles appear in Vandersteene's work.

The Several Centres of the Sacred

A. Creating a Cree Christian Imagery

St. Joseph and the Child. Vandersteene began by adapting the icon as a religious form to express Cree truth. Plate 12 is a conventional iconic piece, originally painted for the altar in Little Red River, and now at the church in Fox Lake. Why would he move outside Catholic tradition to the Eastern Church for a meaningful artistic form?

One answer might be that even at this early date he realized that the Catholic symbol system did not speak in a language which Cree could understand. Perhaps it was the implied literalness in Catholic imagery that posed a problem. Perhaps it was that Cree imbue forms with reality in a different manner. But it might be that the icon in its Eastern context plays its most critical role during worship. The presence of the saints within the church and on the iconostasis "creates" heaven within the building, transforming the space into a sacred place conducive to worship. As the ritual is enacted, the worshipper is symbolically transformed into the presence of the saints and God. Moreover, a special relationship obtains between the worshipper and the icon, as Burckhardt asserts: "The icon penetrates the bodily consciousness of the man and the man as it were projects himself into the image. Having found in himself that of which the image is an expression, he transmits back to it a subtle power which then shines forth on others."[24] For the Cree worshippers, Vandersteene is signalling that their close family relationships are reflected in the life of Jesus and his earthly father. Even as they hover protectingly over their young, even so does God hold them. The grandfather image is a powerful one among traditional Cree, and associating St. Joseph with that image opens up for the Cree worshipper the nuances derived from their ancient beliefs. Steentje "Indianizes" the image in a very simplistic manner, by dressing him in traditional Cree clothes. He also retains the simple aboriginal house in the background, thus placing the encounter with the Cree worshipper within an environment familiar and accepting. In that sense, Vandersteene has de-Europeanized the entire icon, retaining only the pose, the style and the demeanour as essential. St. Joseph retains his Christian halo, however, and, in the manner of most icons, is portrayed as thin and gaunt.

From this icon, we are able to detect that Vandersteene was casting widely for a vehicle by which to express his belief that Christianity could live within the simple lifestyle of the Cree, yet could shine through that simplicity in true religious form. He gives the image great strength and character, tenderness and spirituality. There is a sense of dignity that relates to his growing appreciation of the depth of native culture, and a sense of tranquility which he felt to live at the heart of native life. There is none of the tragedy and social dislocation usually cited about native life, and no trauma such as he witnessed in his time in Fort Vermilion, when he rebelled against the residential system. Simplicity was not poverty, and it had its own luminiscent expression, as

the heavily grained wood testifies. The painting is almost totally ab-
stracted from the life the Cree person was more and more to encounter.
As such it uses the iconic structure to eliminate the contemporary and
to hark back to a time idealized, perhaps, by both Steentje and his older
converts. It is this image that he may have most successfully conveyed:
Christianity is associated with the old, old ways and can express those
values effectively.

It is important to note what he did not do. He did not utilize the image of the shaman, traditionally the most holy figure in the aboriginal
sacred world. Nor did he experiment with the famous x-ray or the spiritual "zones" style which is a favourite motif among native artists. In
this style, figures are reduced to skeletons and colours depict the spiritual zones within the skeletal frame. Such a reduction is associated
with the spiritual power of the shaman when he is given a gift by a
spirit helper. The impression is then that Vandersteene wished to relate
to the everyday Cree lifestyle and situation, but he did not want to
wander into more expressive areas of Cree religion. Perhaps at this
time he had no notion of their significance. For our purposes, however,
it is of great import that the figure remains rooted very much in traditional Christian iconography.

The Good Samaritan. Vandersteene used art as a means of teaching;
most of what has been preserved functioned either as props for his sermons or as illustrations of biblical scenes which captured the mood of
the passage. Plate 15's line drawing is one of the latter. It probably belongs to the period of his life when he resided in Trout Lake and periodically visited the other communities either by plane or horse-drawn
wagon (1957-68). It demonstrates the great flexibility in style which has
been noted earlier, yet it is a powerful illustration of several contemporary truths. If the natural environment in the previous painting is
friendly and simple, in this picture it is sinister and threatening. The
tree serves as a counterpoint to the figures and appears to be flailing at
them like a possessed witch. The struggle to stand is evident in both
figures, and the poise and dignity is lost in the wrestling. There is no
benign presence here and, even if the purposes differ markedly from
the former picture, there is no evident religious character to the picture.
If God is present here, He cannot be seen in the figures.

This sketch belongs to the period when Vandersteene had to defend
the isolation of Trout Lake against the government; it was the period of
the challenge of the Alliance and Pentecostals; it was a time when he
had to cope with the defection of his old friend Okemaw and the criticism of his isolated vision of the Cree by urban Cree and government
officials. He objected to the Church's traditional role of mediator be-

tween the desires of the white bureacracy and the aboriginals. As we have seen, he felt the Church was abandoning its stand on the side of the bush Cree. The complexity of the issues and the debate within and without the Church was exhausting. This sketch belongs to those years.

It should not surprise us that the victim in the good Samaritan is muscular and appears to be capable of taking care of himself. If Vandersteene ever viewed the aboriginals as little children needing help, as had prevailed in *Wabasca*, by this period of his life he thought them to be buffeted by forces beyond the control of even the most robust. In this period, he set the aboriginal within the vortex of state and ecclesiastical power:

> Even if, at first, all the churches made use of the native tongues, they never really tried to assimilate Indian culture, except the Jesuits in New France (i.e., Huron Mass and liturgy). Most believed Indian culture to be barbarical [sic]. True, Bible, prayer books, religious instructions and newsheets were printed in all major Indian languages, and people taught to read them . . . but only for the time being . . . until the poor savage would be civilized enough to read French or English. Churches were not only becoming power structures, they were also part of a colonializing heavier structure.[25]

These are the views of the mature and battle-scarred Vandersteene. We can see now why this drawing is expressed the way it is: The Good Samaritan, metaphor for the missionary, struggles valiantly to help, but the situation almost forces him out of the picture. The aboriginal, though strong physically, is nonetheless victimized by a terror-filled world that offers no sustenance from within it. The Good Samaritan is underdeveloped and nebulous. He is pushed to the margins. The stark quality of the black and white drawing only accentuates the sinister nature of the moment, and there seems to be no saving grace even if the drawing is to illustrate the famous assistance given. In many ways, then, this picture presents a far more sophisticated view of the aboriginal and his situation.

The clothing is as nearly contemporary as it can be; there are no moccasins or native bead-work coats. There is nothing essentially aboriginal about the picture; there is no facile reference to native environment nor dress. The image could be of any person. The victim seems to struggle with his helper even while he tries to gain his feet. His aim is strong and clenched, but it has no object against which to strike. Even the Good Samaritan seems to be working at cross-purposes with the victim. The effort appears to be in vain and, without the rest of the story, this image leaves one very depressed and helpless.

While the drawing may be interpreted as a metaphor of Vandersteene's own inner struggle, the fact that it was used in a teaching situation indicates that it was drawn for his parishioners. The realities of the political and religious world put both the victim and his would-be saviour into a moment of mutual participation, but there is no mark of superiority or power in the Good Samaritan. This probably represents his notion of the yeast of the Church: "The History of Christianity is the story of that yeast, raising different cultures, [then] disappearing in[to] them until they are one bread. . . . When Christianity is at its yeasting stage it seems small, irrelevant, finished. But it is a leaven, light and sensitive, joyful, free and very alive."[26]

Thus, even within the despair of the Good Samaritan, Vandersteene sees the moment of caring as revelatory of the Church's true role. The story of the Good Samaritan is radically altered by the picture; help may never come for either the victim or his helper, but they have shared a special moment together.

Mother and Child. May may be Mary's month in Flanders, but Vandersteene made it December in Canada. As we have noted, he habitually made his own Christmas cards from a woodcut by pressing copies on coloured paper; often the Virgin and Child adorn them. Many of these were originally sketched in his 12 sketchbooks, from which they turned up in sermon illustrations or on cards. This line drawing (Plate 13) never made it onto a card, but I have chosen it because it signifies another dimension of his personality. Those who have viewed his entire corpus are unanimous in declaring that he had a very sensitive eye for the female form. We will deal further with this issue in the next section. Here it is only necessary to examine how this fits with his perceptions of aboriginal belief.

The Cree have a special place in their hearts for the "naturalness" of motherhood; religiously, this is expressed in stories about ancestral women who perform heroic deeds, and provide the children for the world. Later, it would supply the Cree with the spiritual grounding for their attention to Mary and other biblical women. We have seen how missionaries imported a marble Ste. Anne and set her up at a spot on Lac Ste. Anne where aboriginal peoples traditionally went for healing, and devotion to the healing waters of the grandmother spirit now blends with devotion to the tender and gracious help accorded to the believers from Ste. Anne.

Cree women have no problem understanding how Vandersteene came to have such a sense of a pregnant woman's body: he was a midwife. This drawing encapsulates his vision of the sensuousness and vitality of Cree women, and links it with the underlying fertility motifs present in aboriginal belief. A similar notion undergirds Flemish perceptions of Mary. Hence Mary is either associated with the generalized fertility of the earth, or with a deeper strain of European earth-mother consciousness. Either way, the star joyously celebrates. When this drawing is compared with earlier images in his career, where many times both male and female cannot be distinguished and the sexual dimension of bodies are understated, the contrast is remarkable. There do not appear to be any overt "spiritual" qualities expressed here. Rather, the warmth of the shape and the security afforded the baby in the great arms suggests both peace and vigour.

The Bear Crucified. This drawing represents the movement Vandersteene has made in his understanding of the Church. Here is the light from "the great mystery" breaking through in aboriginal images. Towards the end of his life, Steentje moved away from adapting Christian images for the Cree; rather, he began to choose Cree images through which to explore the meaning of Christianity. Probably one of the most powerful is one close to the end of his life, the bear.

Unfortunately we have only this sketch left of his idea (Plate 14). He had planned on producing a statue of the bear on the cross for the Trout Lake Church. Failing that, he wanted to carve the bear on the cross onto the chalice. He never had time. This is the rough outline of his conception. His movement in this direction is both sensitive and inspiring.

The bear occupies a powerful and dominant position within northern peoples' traditions. Cults of the bear are known throughout northern Canada, in Alaska, across Siberia and into Japan.[27] Even among people who do not normally eat bear, important myths are found. Vandersteene had learned of the bear from the teaching sessions provided by a number of elders. He also read the German scholar Werner Müller's 1956 work *Die Religionen der Waldlandindianer Nordamerikas* in which a significant section (pp. 291-95) deals with the bear.[28] But more importantly for Steentje, myths of the bear were heard in all the settlements with which he dealt: he noted that he had heard the following legend in Wabasca, Trout Lake, Little Red River, Saddle Lake and Fort Chipewyan.[29]

> BEAR came to earth one day and saw a berry-picking Cree woman. It was in the fall. He took her as his wife. They had two children: a boy and a girl. The boy and the girl were BEAR-CHILDREN. They had their father's and their mother's natures. They could appear as bear or as man.

> When the children had already grown, a famine broke out in the land of the Cree and people were starving.
> BIG BEAR told his wife, "Why should your family die? We have plenty of food. Send for them." So the BEAR-CHILDREN went to tell their grandparents. They came with the whole family. When BEAR saw them coming, He went out to receive them and told them: "Shoot me and eat my body so you will never starve again."

This is Vandersteene's use of the myth. He saw it as a prefigured expression of the sacrifice of Jesus. It is a novel idea to homologize Jesus and the bear, but it is common lore among the Cree that the bear, once killed and suspended, looks very much like a man. Vandersteene built upon this theme. In Garden River he had even instituted placing bear fat on the altar table during the mass.

Vandersteene's picture illustrates a perception of great insight and sensitivity, but it may well be a vision that was doomed. Apart from the fewer and fewer bear found in the region, is the relative paucity of information about the story among the Cree population at large. The story of the significance of the bear may rest only with the higher echelon of the medicine man. Without widespread knowledge of the story, it is difficult to see how it could support the meanings Vandersteene saw in it. The image has not inspired aboriginal artists to represent it as it appears here.

B. *Mary/Cree Woman/Mother/Female*

Vandersteene's meditation on the female form in his art[30] is extensive; female figures, studies, and presence dominates his sketch books. They are a central feature in a well over half his art. His friends and family give a wide variety of reasons for this fact, and they all reflect something about the creative Steentje. Fr. Baratto, his colleague and fellow-missionary, argues that his paintings and drawings of women derive from his appreciation of the character of Cree women:

> Vandersteene's drawings of Indian women are very sensitive. The women appear as very resilient. They look simple, but there is a history behind them. One might judge them too quickly; in fact, every line has a meaning. Sometimes his paintings represented living people. For example, he drew faces of people going to see the baby Jesus who never went to church. He knew about the moccasin telegraph. He knew it would get the message out to the individuals.[31]

His brother Eric, though not as close to Rogier as others, nevertheless had the impression from him that he enjoyed painting women because of their connection to Flemish popular mysticism about the Virgin Mary. Eric explicitly linked sexuality and painting: "I don't think there is any doubt that Roger received some kind of sexual release through painting women; since they were forbidden to him, this was his way of encountering them." The artist Willem was far more explicit:

> He has greatly attracted to the Holy Mother; maybe she even was a surrogate wife for him. Mystical relations were very important when I was in the convent. When you see these great men who sing about the Holy Mother, they are so inspired. I believe mystics all have this feel for female form. He had a very deep appreciation of the woman. She is an expression of cosmic reality. His understanding comes at a deeper level than just an encounter with one woman.[32] I believe you can transform sexual drive into great spiritual power. Most men like Vandersteene are both man and woman, a complete human. You must understand that he was an artist. What we create is a world, meaning, reality. That's it. We cannot live without this imagination.[33]

For Mieke Vandersteene, Willy's wife, there just was no doubt. Vandersteene related to the real flesh and blood woman. It was not imagination. The fascination for women came out of his inner being:

> This is a real, sexual woman [Plate 16]. This is not "holy" stuff. This is a celebration of women's sexuality, perhaps even a sexual body as you find in Neolithic statues. Roger loved every woman from the youngest to oldest, because he had a love for their *natural* being. He also was attractive *to* women.[34]

His work reflects first of all the varying moods he saw in the Virgin Mary and her Child. They encompass everything from traditional obedience in the *Annunciation* in a Cree setting (Plate 7), to stained-glass Cree *Virgin and Child* (Plate 17), to iconic *Mother and Child* (Plate 18), to artistic piece with local faces (Plate 19), to fertility figure *Madonna and Child* (Plate 13), to symbolic *Holy Family* (Plate 20),[35] to stylized woodcut Christmas scene (Plate 9). His depictions of women likewise show a sensitivity to several levels of mood and character: meditative (Plates 10, 21), strength (Plate 22), nurturing (Plate 13), introspection (Plate 23) and wisdom/self-conscious reserve (Plate 25). Others not represented here include an almost Buddhist image of a pure female form rising from a flower, a tender moment between two pregnant nudes, a cubist line drawing of a pregnant nude, and the closest we have to a Canadian aboriginal artistic study in a modified x-ray style. His studies of the martyr-saints, including *St. Julia* (Plate 8) depict gruesome and gaunt figures, in this case, with little resemblance of the rotund nudes mentioned earlier. There is great tenderness and closeness (and, interestingly, equality) between Adam and Eve in his mythological paintings and there is genuine sensuousness in the paintings that might be considered non-religious (e.g., Plates 23, 16). Certainly there is little of the femme fatale present here, with its emphasis on the esoteric reaches of Neoplatonic philosophy, its negative mystique usually associated with the occult, or, for that matter, the Neo-Catholicism that purified the Virgin of her female attributes. All his works portray a personal and emotional engagement with the female body and present an insight into the human life of the female quite fresh and remarkable.

C. *The Natural/Spiritual Order*

His friend Tanghe recounts: "I remember one day that he looked up at the grey sky and said: 'Beautiful! beautiful! The world is sometimes somber and black, but whenever God's white light only just touches this world, then she becomes gray, a very beautiful gray.' "[36]

As Vandersteene matured he developed more and more in sympathy with Cree conceptions of the enlivened character of the natural world. He accepted that there were many pockets of power in the world, that there were gifted people who were that way for no apparent reason, and that there were ritualized ways of relating to the plant and animal worlds. As we have seen, he expressed this at one level in the notion of adopting Cree culture as the basis for interpreting Christianity; at another it required that something "fit" its environment. Thus, creating a proper architectural style for the Cree Church in Trout Lake was as necessary as speaking Cree. That which fit culturally was acceptable, that which did not had to be abandoned. A grotto fit because it was designed purely around the growing of natural plants, admittedly with a design, but with due care for the place of each contiguous to its neighbours. Both the grotto and the church fit Trout Lake, and visitors revel in the sense of place; there is a peace and tranquility that is only partially evident in the organizational drawing of the grotto (Plate 27). Like defining the aesthetic, the dimensions of this fit are difficult to articulate.

Another level of the meaning of natural is added by his work with plants, and particularly cactii. There is no doubt that Vandersteene had a certain affinity for this plant. He literally admired the prickly exterior but soft and juicy interior. He often spoke of his own parallel nature. Moreover, he drew sketches of cactii, drawing from the visual experience he had from raising over 100 different kinds of them. He kept an accurate record of every type of flower, where the original plant had been obtained (he had cactii from several places in the world, including the United States, Africa and Europe) and how it fared in Alberta. He loved cactus flowers so much that for Christmas he would design a cactus Christmas card for all his friends. Those who received the pretty woodcut, with the baby in a papoose rising from its centre, knew they had received something very special. At his wake, the Cree, mindful of his love, placed a pot of cactus flowers in his arms.

This is a completely different sense of the natural or "valuing the land" than we find in many natural mystics. It is different than we find in his poems (see, for example, *Love Game I* above, pp. 130-31). In this mysticism, the land is loved for its gifts, for the sudden delights its animals and plants afford. This is a spiritually selective natural mysticism, one born out of a keen observation of the moods and movements in the natural world and expressed as: "That deeply serious aspect of life which can often be experienced in depth, though perhaps looking trite, sometimes even verging on the ridiculous."[37] His sketches of snared rabbits reflect their evident struggle and torment; but he saw this same struggle and torment in Christ (Plate 24). This is a naturalism that never reveals all its secrets; it often has to be taken as it comes to awareness (Plate 15).

D. Illustrationism

While his art may interest us more than other aspects of his career, Steentje's greatest religious-art production was the teaching book *Come Lord Jesus!* Plainly, for most aboriginal believers across the land, the images that Vandersteene created for catechism and teaching sessions are far more alive than the paintings we have been dwelling upon. It is ironic, then, that his illustrations should be the most publicized aspect of his career.

His illustrationism did not begin with that book, but really derives from his first encounter with the Cree people and his attempt to pictorially present Christian stories. Wabasca's church, that now serves as a school, still has his frescoes on the walls with scenes from both the Old and New Testaments; here are figures of men, animals and landscapes drawn from the surrounding environment. This is his way of saying that God is present here, even if the Book comes from half a world away. These are his first steps to illuminate Cree life with Christian images "Cree-ized."

The same motifs are at work in *Come Lord Jesus!* He deliberately draws house and buildings familiar to the reserve. The priest may be featured in several of them, but it is really the local social situation that frames the whole. People make up the vision he presents.

One of the more spectacular images in his book is that of the nude woman crucified with Jesus face to face (Plate 26). More than one of his colleagues thinks this image is too complicated for the ordinary believer, let alone for the aboriginal who has none of the sophisticated background necessary to interpret it. In reality, the conception does not really originate with Vandersteene. It appears that he adapted it from a poem written by Catherine de Hueck Doherty, a Russian woman who had emigrated to Canada after a turbulent life as a refugee from the October revolution. Once settled in Canada, Doherty decided to dedicate her life to the poor and the destitute in the slums of the big cities. In 1947 she founded Madonna House in Combermere, a village several hours north of Toronto, and men and women joined her religious society. Around the mid-1960s she wrote a poem entitled *What Is a Nun?*[38] Part of it read:

> A nun is a woman
> Hanging on the other
> Side of his cross
> knowing that it becomes
> His marriage bed with her
> The moment she asks
> "To be lifted up" with him.

It is obviously a fascinating mix of "bride of Christ" conceptions with very concrete sexual overtones. One suspects the Cree understood very well what he was trying to say. It is perhaps worth mentioning that a sculpture of a woman on the cross (without Jesus) created a storm of controversy in Toronto several years ago. The clergyman insisted that it represented the fact that women had been crucified in many cultures, and that the image did what it should do . . . jar people.[39] It is unlikely that Vandersteene would have intended to jar his Cree friends. But viewing the pieces of his artistic portfolio here, and knowing something of his personality, it would seem that he may not have been adverse to doing that to the rest of us.

Obviously something very powerful moved him to create this art. Perhaps it was a world he felt compelled to create. It is easier to understand the motto first enunciated when he was in school in 1935: painting is a mirror in which the human is God. But it is no easier to understand Vandersteene's religious world. Creating a "world" like God, whether on canvas or in institutional formation, is at cross-purposes with his belief that the historical framework, or culture, we are born into is God's long-term activity. Would the same thing be accomplished if one didn't paint, and didn't build churches? Lodging somewhere in his inner self were eddies of doubt along with the chutes of faith. His poetry, personal as it is, helps to uncover those currents.

Notes

1 The Jesuits were the first to use sketches and paintings for religious purposes.
2 This does not include the 100 paintings he was said to have dashed off to raise money for his mission in Belgium. I am referring to those paintings which he seriously created for display in churches or as permanent gifts for friends and family.
3 William Barrett, "Art and Being," in Sidney Hook, ed., *Art and Philosophy: A Symposium* (New York: New York University Press, 1966), p. 172.
4 F.D. Martin, "The Aesthetic in Religious Experience," *Religious Studies*, 4, 1 (October 1968): 20.
5 Quoted in John McManners, ed., *The Oxford Illustrated History of Christianity* (Oxford: Oxford University Press, 1990), p. 13.
6 Wassily Kandinsky is regarded as one of the founders of abstract art. One of his most influential books was *Über das Geistige in der Kunst*, translated as *The Spiritual in Art*, a version of the Salier translation with F. Golffring, M. Harrison and F. Ostertag (New York: Witenborg, Schultz, 1947).
7 McManners, *Oxford Illustrated History*, p. 11.
8 Hans Urs Von Balthasar, *The Glory of the Lord: A Theological Aesthetics*, Vol. 1: *Seeing the Form*, translated by E. Leiva-Merkakis (Edinburgh: T. & T. Clark, 1982).
9 See, for example, reviews of *The Glory of the Lord* in the following: Frank B. Brown, *The Journal of Religion*, 65 (October 1985): 563-65; John MacQuarrie, *King's Theological Review*, 7 (Autumn 1984): 57-58; Edward T. Oakes, *America*, 149 (31 December 1983): 436-37, and T.F. O'Meara, *Theological Studies*, 45 (June 1984): 365-67.
10 Von Balthasar, *The Glory of the Lord*, p. 122.
11 Ibid.
12 Ibid., p. 124.
13 Drawn from his lecture notes, used at a missionary conference during his Grouard period, i.e., 1968-73. Cited as "Notes" here, pp. 13-14.
14 "Notes," p. 2 (italics mine).
15 See Earle H. Waugh, "Vandersteene's Art: Christian Interaction with Cree Culture," *Proceedings of the Fort Chipewyan and Fort Vermilion Bicentennial Conference* (Edmonton: Boreal Institute for Northern Studies, 1990), pp. 118-27.
16 McManners, *Oxford Illustrated History*, p. 14.
17 See Chapter One for a further discussion of the symbolist school.
18 See Chapter One above, p. 16.
19 Fr. Vantroys, *La Voix*, 35, 6 (September 1976): 150.
20 "Die Brücke" was the name of a rebel group of German artists, of which Emile Nolde (1867-1956) was a member, generally held to be in the vanguard of expressionism. They used masses of pigments without subjecting themselves to structural contours. See Frederick Hartt, *Art: A History of Painting, Sculpture, Architecture*, 2 vols. (New York: Harry N. Abrams, 1976), Vol. 2, pp. 390-91.
21 Whitford, *Expressionism*, p. 135-36.
22 Ibid., p. 147.
23 Vandersteene wrote to his Flemish soulmate: "As far as we are concerned, we live by the word of Rodenbach; we remember *Gudrun*: Even the chosen few will tumble to earth while trying to ascend" (Vandersteene, *Wanneer gij*, p. 21).
24 Titus Burckhardt, *Sacred Art in East and West* (London: Perennial Books, 1967), pp. 117-18.
25 "Notes," p. 11.
26 Ibid., p. 12.
27 Mircea Eliade, *Shamanism and the Archaic Technques of Ecstasy* (New York: Bollingen, 1968), p. 458, and bibliography in n. 122.

28 Werner Müller, *Die Religionen der Waldlandindianer Nordamerikas* (Berlin: Dietrich Reimer, 1956), pp. 291-95.

29 He notes this in an undated photocopied handout from a teaching session, found among his personal effects.

30 I can find no evidence that he read any of the feminist criticism of patriarchal art. It was not, I think, until the 1970s that this process began, and then it was only among very specialized circles. For examples of this criticism, see Gisela Ecker, ed., *Feminist Aesthetics*, translated by Harriet Andersen (Boston: Beacon Press, 1985); and Griselda Pollock, *Vision and Difference: Femininity, Feminism and the Histories of Art* (New York: Routledge, 1988).

31 Fr. V. Baratto, personal interview, 27 June 1979.

32 This is in reference to the possibility that he had an affair with a Cree woman (Laughing Waters) in Little Red River.

33 Willem Vermandere, personal interview, 11 July 1987.

34 Mietje Vandersteene, personal interview, 12 July 1987.

35 One could argue that the idyllic scenarios were *social* scenes; that for Steentje, what was critical about Cree life was its social "family" fabric. Family, of course, in Cree communities does not always mean marriage in the Church's sense.

36 Tanghe, *Leven*, p. 140.

37 Ibid., p. 40.

38 Omer Tanghe, *As I Have Loved You: The Life of Catherine de Hueck Doherty* (Dublin: Veritas Publications, 1988), p. 51; originally published in Flemish in Belgium in 1985.

39 The congregation belonged to the United Church of Canada (Bloor Street United) and the clergyman, Rev. Clifford Elliot, said the sculpture was placed there for the Easter season (*Edmonton Journal*, Saturday, 9 June 1979, Religion Section).

Seven

Sojourn Charts: Poetry in Serenity and Flux

> The world hangs loosely on its hinges. . . .
> — Vandersteene, *Wanneer gij*, p. 117

Vandersteene is a Christian poet. Still, he unites several other strands in his poetry that make it both rich and complex. Sometimes these strands are inner-generated and sublime; at other times they are as concrete as the snow and rocks. There is no doubt how he measured his poetry—it was intensely personal. It was shared only with close associates and intimates. It was always written in Flemish, with the exception of a few pieces in Cree. It was, however, always meant for a reader. All recipients understood that it came out of a deeply private encounter. It was an activity of his solitude; selections from his letters to his soulmate in Flanders, while late in his life, nevertheless encapsulate its nature:

> I go around a lot by car, and after most of the visits and journeys, I have to fight despondency . . . you have seen through me with those poems. They generally represent the fruits of a battle . . . pray for me often. . . . all that trouble with the car has one big advantage (perhaps even more than one); I generally write my poems there; I am usually full of inspiration then. Then I can also pray and there is peace and quiet around me. This also helps me to carry on; it helps me greatly. You realize anew how every trial has another side, like a medal. . . . Sometimes it means rephrasing and copying . . . in a way it is a healing medicine to send those poems . . . so the fight is fought . . . often in the Toyota and in prayer and in poetry.[1]

None of it was made and then thrown away, with the exception, perhaps, of pieces that would betray emotions that reflection dictated it unwise to convey.[2] His poetry required work, struggle, trial and error, change, modification and rejections. He could write a poem at least

---

Notes to this chapter are on pp. 219-20.

half a dozen different ways before fixing it by making two copies, one of which went into a file. Clearly he felt something important was in these poems, or they would not have been accorded such treatment.

Although Tanghe says Steentje wrote poetry from the time of his novitiate, *Levensvervulling*, the title given to the published collection of his poetry, includes only three pieces written before he came to Canada, one in 1940 and two in 1942. He would have been at Waregem and about to take his first vows. All three are explictly religious.[3] If there are poems of other intent during his early years, they are now scattered. Thus poetry *from the beginning* was an expression apparently suited for religious reflection and contemplation.

The private and religious nature of his poetry makes them a particularly rewarding area for examining the influences and the issues that shaped his life. It is little wonder, then, that there has been considerable controversy over their publication.

In his will, Vandersteene specified that all his writings in Flemish were to become the possession of the Flemish Province of the Oblates of Mary Immaculate or of his brother Wilfried. The original concern of the Flemish Oblates was to collect them, explain sections unclear for the reader, and generally to edit them with purposes congruent with Oblate self-understanding. Steentje's poetry languished in the face of the Province's lack of finding someone capable of handling the task. Meanwhile, Tanghe agitated for the poems to be released and published, drawing upon Vandersteene's letter to the nun in Flanders to whom Steentje had sent many poems:

> Please give the poems to Omer Tanghe if he wishes to copy them . . . perhaps they will be more legible. But before he publishes them or even makes a selection from it [sic] I would like to see the proofs. . . . I have no objections to it . . . if it brings joy to someone. . . . After all we no longer are ourselves neither in body nor in soul once we follow Christ . . . sometimes others know this a lot better than us [sic].[4]

Fr. Hernou, known as Maskwa (Bear) among the Cree, the executor of the will, sent copies of the poems to the Flemish Oblates and to the family. Family members first decided they would edit them. Who would do it raised issues about special relationships, and controversy flared. Jos, who had been in Canada when he died, and had taken upon himself to preserve Rogier's memorabilia, finally won the day. The choice was not without dissent.

When suggestions were made that the corpus be translated, it seemed evident that Jos' interpretations would not do, primarily because he showed little sensitivity to the Indians, referring to them as savages, etc. and once again something had to be done. Finally the family agreed to refer the corpus to Gabrielle Demedts, who was a recognized poet in Flanders and a relative of Steentje's old Belgian friend André Demedts, with whom he went to school. She chose the most important poems from among those available, and these were published, along with a Foreword by Omer Tanghe, as *Levensvervulling*, in Roeselare in 1979.

Poetry as Journey to a Familiar Cultural Homeland

The easiest and in some ways most natural position to take about Steentje's poetic corpus is to regard it as his way of maintaining a lifeline — and perhaps his lifeblood — to an essentially traditional Flemish homeland. God, nature, life, love, landscape, work all fall within the clearly demarcated boundaries of a core of nationalist and religious writers. Such an analysis has the advantage that his poetic ancestors are well known and studied, and we have already surveyed the ample evidence of his ties to the homeland. But his poetry was too personal, and, in some ways, too religious to be facilely assigned just to "Flanders" writers. In fact, there is a specific character even to that influence.

It is tempting to believe that Vandersteene regarded himself as walking in Gezelle's footsteps. Even if that is an exaggeration, Guido Gezelle without doubt cast a long shadow in Steentje's life and poetry. Indeed, it is remarkable how many characteristics they shared. There have been very few leaders in the church who were both priest and poet, so these clerics are united in a rare form of expression. But even more: both their fathers were horticulturalists, both intensely loved the natural beauty of the Flanders countryside, both chafed under the early school life and its restrictions, both openly chose the priesthood even though there were good reasons why they should not have gone that way, both had an inherent craving for freedom, and both had serious conflicts with Church policy. Despite this, both were totally committed to the Church, submitting to its control. Both, too, had folk followers, with Gezelle becoming famous, among other things, for his poetry about cigar traders and subsequently having a cigar named after him, while Vandersteene attracted more than local Catholic interest, as is evident from Tanghe's many works and the popular folk song based on his life.

Such similarities mask a deeper relatedness. Both were deeply Flemish nationalists, but at a different time and place; each celebrated the common folk with relish and delight: Vandersteene, the Cree, Gezelle, the Flemish. Quite evidently, both were saturated with mystical perceptions of God, life and nature that can only be described as profound. Both, too, held fervent allegiance to liturgical forms. Both wrote with strong impressionist leanings.

Vandersteene quoted Gezelle often when speaking with the Flemish; he appears several times in his letters to his soulmate. Some poems, like the fragment quoted at the beginning, resemble in theme some of Gezelle's work.[5] It is speculation, because there is nothing in the sources to indicate the influence, but Gezelle had been enthralled with aboriginal culture, and translated Longfellow's *Hiawatha's Song*, and it is possible Vandersteene's own interests had been piqued by Gezelle's translation of the tale. Certainly Steentje would have chafed at the implications of some literary clubs, like The New Youth, who joke about the "old guys" — Gezelle, Verschaeve and Rodenbach.[6] He took offence at such slights and confided to relatives and friends that it made him feel out of sync with Flanders.

Despite these evident connections, we should not ignore the time difference, and the very real fact that Vandersteene had a markedly different experience than Gezelle. This is reflected in the central focus of the poetry: Vandersteene's work is primarily the occasion for religious meditation. Three deviations from this spring to mind, although there may be others: *Nachtkoor* (*Night Chorus*), *Avond* (*Evening*) and *Liefdespel* (*Love Game I*, see above, pp. 130-31);[7] no explicit religious language is present, as demonstrated in the following:

> *Evening*
>
> Fir tree flames
> Ablaze
> Twilight glowing.
>
> Horizon's smoky light
> Waters afire:
> I wade through stars.
>
> Day and wind lie down
> Sounds of the night
> Not yet awoken.
>
> The universe bubbles up
> From the nightingale
> In me.

True, the drama spreading around him here provokes an awareness of the depths, "the universe," which might, in another context be "God," but he retains all natural symbols in his attempt to explain the source of his inspiration. Indeed, what it portends is what many another writer has done: the muse, in the familiar form of a nightingale, begins to sing in poetry.[8]

Despite the just claim that Vandersteene loved Flanders only slightly less than the Cree, the claim is not reflected in his poetry, his most personal testimony. In his whole poetic corpus, including poems not included in the collection, I can find only one poem addressed specifically to Flanders: *Maartmorgen* (*March Morning*), dated 8 March 1975.[9] Certainly there are no poems addressed to such cultural artifacts as the Leie River or the golden spurs, as one finds in Gezelle.[10] Steentje, however, has poems to the Peace and Wabasca Rivers, both important in his life in the missions.[11]

Steentje does follow the well-known technique of Gezelle's in utilizing the natural world as a frame and occasion to encounter Christian truth. An example of this in Gezelle is *Ik mis u* (*I Miss You*):[12]

Attractive Lure

Baited spoon
Swims an eel and dives,
Rises hips swaying
Playful and alluring.

Flashes
Past glistening flag
Dead frightened fish.

Baited spoon
Water's harlequin
Maimed and mauled
Fisher of men.

17 September 1975

Certainly the most erotic of this genre is his *Love Game II*, which comes out of his early experience in Trout Lake and demonstrates his awareness of the powerful sexual emotions that attract people. The bid to have God violate him is a concept unfamiliar, and possibly unpalatable, to many readers, but the language is well known in mystical circles:

Love Game II

For me the game was a game
For you it was seriousness

I know it now: too late:
Like a fool I played with fire!
The blowtorch flame of your love
Has scorched my entrails.

Enough, O God, it is enough!
Why always wanting
To go to extremes?
Oh God, You know no measure!
The gift horn of your fullness
Remains a thorn inside me!

Your fullness empties me
Your abundance
Wakes unsated hunger.
For whoever once tested
The ecstasy of your compelling love
Is ever filled with keen nostalgia.

I am before You, God
Parrying but naked
In fear of what's to come
And anguish that it might not come;
Half willing, half vanquished
O God, my God, come violate my heart!

The notion that immense spiritual lessons are to be found in the behaviour of lovers is a theme that he never again explores, but it is reflective of his "natural" perspective that is also represented in the female body found in his art. There, the sexual theme appears to be that the female form is the natural one to represent the fullness of spiritual fertility; here he anticipates as a woman lover the slaking of his thirst by God.

Given his devotion to Flemish culture, it would not be surprising to find that several nationalist writers had played a role in his creativity, and, indeed, we know this to be the case from his own hand. For the nationalist trait, we need look no further than Albrecht Rodenbach (1856-80). Steentje never tired of quoting Rodenbach, especially from *Gudrun*:"If even the chosen ones fall down in increasing numbers, the Church itself will still be reborn in steadfastness."[13] Rodenbach had been a student at the seminary at Roeselare, where he had come under the influence of Gezelle's confidant and follower, the priest-poet Hugo Verriest (1840-1923), an ardent Flemish nationalist. Rodenbach would make the same objection to his superiors which Vandersteene did for the Cree children — that people should be allowed to speak their own tongue during recreation periods — and with the same result. "No!" Rodenbach rebelled. He organized youth movements and Flemish student newspapers. His poems and songs ignited the youth, and he had natural leadership skills. His epic work, *Gudrun*, was set in the third century in "ancient Belgium," and the beautiful maiden, Gudrun, was captured by the Romans. Greatly in danger of being destroyed, she was gallantly rescued by her Flemish lovers and, like Flanders, was saved. A clever blend of mythic formulas, folklore, goddess worship and Catholic tradition, it was extremely popular among Flemish nationalists. It became part of the literary base upon which the Young Flemings movement was built. Although he died in his twenties, Rodenbach took on heroic proportions among the militants.[14] He was one of Vandersteene's idols. Steentje's early poem on death might have arisen from Rodenbach's meditation on the same theme.[15]

In his book, Tanghe mentions the writer Felix Timmermans.[16] Timmermans' work on the journal of literary humour *Pallieter* established the author as a major force abroad;[17] yet it was his feel for the so-called rural novel which stressed the homespun values of the old farm and its fertile soil, the laid-back character and the simple lifestyle. Light-hearted and jovial, Timmermans represented something of the salt-of-the-earth Flemish citizen, establishing the conception of the solidness and stability of rural Flanders. If Vandersteene transplanted one idea to Canada, it was that. Isolated "bush" communities constituted the Cree's greatest gift to the country. But he never explicitly celebrated that feature in his poetry. The closest we get to the "natural" community is the aboriginal family, enshrined in *Liefdespel*[18] (quoted in its entirety above, pp. 130-31, as *Love Game I*).

> Through blanket curtain
> Young Cree woman flitting
> Starry-eyed
> Red-hued bronze
> Her cheek
> Smiles at hanging cradle
> (Half moon on her back)
> Humming, sets the table
> For her man.

This formulation of a primal community, and especially the emphasis on the good, solid, irreducible character of the *folk* has much in common with many writers and painters — from the artist Pieter Breughel to the dynamic young writers associated with the periodical *Van Nu en Straks* (usually translated as *From Now On*) and the Dutch literary movement, the Nieuwe Gids.[19] The author who gave definitive form to this rich folk reality, however, was Stijn Streuvels (1871-1969), a master of prose, who turned the West Flemish landscape into his microcosm. Greshoff signals the critical stance of this writer:

> In Streuvels' world nature, as well as man, seems to be above normal in every movement; every gesture is supernormal, every character seems to have a different reason for existence than does mundane man. Personages of such unusual tendencies, and deeds of such unusual dimensions are beyond the idea of time. In Streuvels' work, therefore, the past and the future have no role.[20]

As we have seen, Vandersteene regarded the Cree community in a similar vein, and his *Love Game I* represents the idealization. But he was not concerned to glorify this natural environment; like Streuvels, he wanted only to affirm that the world of meaning found in the rich Flemish folk culture presented a world worth exploring and raising to cosmic status. The closest Vandersteene came to creating as powerful and significant a work as *Langs de Wegen*[21] was the story about the Cree he sketched in *Wabasca*. Despite that fact, this poem conveys the same thematic signature.

It is tempting to see Vandersteene's use of poetry solely as a teaching tool, a means to pass on some message of the inner life. This is especially true of the poems he sent to his soulmate in Flanders:[22]

> *Growth*
>
> compulsion
> and surrender
> resignation
> becomes urgency
> as the horizon
> germinates
> forgotten joy
> renewed

This kind of autobiographical poem, since it is deliberately sent to inspire, is reminiscent of Karel van de Woestijne's (1878-1929)[23] symbolical autobiography, which purports to see in his life larger lessons for his fellow Flemings; some might also see the vitalist tradition in Steentje's contemporary René Verbeeck (1904-). One does not find in Steentje's poetry a heightened sense of personal estrangement from God, although there are tenors of Augustinian angst in his writings. However, what pain there is comes from openness before God; indeed the openness to God prevents the frozenness of a lost relationship:[24]

Naked Before God

Naked by the fire that day
knew I, my God
that if I were not so before You
after every battle won or lost
the sweat of angst and labour
frozen between flesh and spirit
my heart would chill.

Hence, even though he praised Cyriel Verschaeve,[25] whose poems and plays encode the passion and anxiety of an Augustine, the vast majority of Vandersteene's poems do not reveal a man with a troubled spiritual soul. If anything, his religious life is closer to the high idealism of August Vermeylen, an idealism that was founded upon an ability to analyze the most tortured life and understand the ways of God. This is best exemplified in his meditation on being a missionary:

The Missionary[26]

Sometimes I wanted
To feel safe
And sheltered
Like the husky
Who presses his cold muzzle
Into the warm hollow
Of his master's hand.
But You have driven me on
Towards the fog banks
Over the lake
Towards the black horizon
Of the forests
To promise to blowing snowdrift
The miracle of life
To frozen winter branches
The trembling of leaves
To the advent of autumn
Announce the summer days.
Lord, in the hollow of Your hand,
I would like to shelter now;
But to bear fruit
You have strewn me out again. . . .

Finally, some influence might be traced as far back as Jan Van Ruysbroeck (d. 1381). This was a writer of the people, who tried to use the language of the masses to foster in them a deeper, more meditative life. The Prior of Groenendael, as he was identified, believed in bringing laymen into touch with the deepest of Catholic mysteries, and encouraged a kind of natural mysticism for them.[27] In one of his earliest pieces in Canada, *Evening Prayer by the Campfire*,[28] Steentje catches this same theme, and enunciates a profound sense of presence within the Canadian wilderness.

The Poem as Parable

Vandersteene finds the poem an ideal form for exploring both religious and natural meaning in his own discovery of its truths. He tells his soulmate:

> The work that we have to do here won't run away either, and sometimes it is like the little birds in the nest: all day long their little gaping mouths are asking for more and chirp to show the urgency, and the poor devils, who have laid the eggs are eaten up in the process. That is another parable! I have always enjoyed using parables, that is at least one small point in which I seem to resemble the Lord, and probably for the same reasons . . . they speak out and they cover up, they open and they close, they give inner vision and exceptional appearance; initiates understand and others cannot take offence. Since I have translated the readings for the Mass into the Cree language, I have an ever stronger preference for parables.[29]

Some of his poems are self-consciously parabolic, as in his *Easter Communion*:[30]

> Paschal mystery
> The Lord risen and glorified
> Went through death with me
> In the breaking of this bread.
>
> And I decaying and distraught
> In eating of this Bread
> Am already risen and glorified.
> Easter mystery.

Here, he meditates on two senses of tranformed body: how he as priest crucifies the Lord anew at each mass, while his own natural disintegration in time is offset by the presence of the Eternal in him. This he, himself, explains: "We carry *within ourselves* the answer to all that tragic search, that dissolute, chaotic, neurotic, exhausting fussing on the spot: the Paschal mystery is alive in us. It is *with* and *from* that Paschal Mystery that we should go to the people."[31]

A more sophisticated parable obtains in his *Northern Night*:[32]

> summer night
> in which evening glow
> flows into morning red
>
> God's love blooms
> tense awareness
> of day and sun
>
> on smouldering horizon
> at once hidden and revealed
> anguish subsides.

In northern Alberta in the summertime, it is possible to read the newspaper outdoors at 2 a.m in the morning because the sun never sets. At the darkest moment there is but a red glow at the horizon, a moment he describes tellingly as "smouldering." The poem is written, however, in the full heat of battle with his cancer, indeed, was written about a month before his death. The resurrecting sun brought a message of peace to his fear that he might nod some night and never rise. Reading the meanings of the northern night brought peace and calm to his fearful soul, and the natural environment provided a parable from which he drew renewal of spirit. Yet the smouldering indicates that the parable is not closure, for there is a "tense awareness" that the day and sun will come, with its heat and oppressiveness, a point made ominous by the fact that anguish just subsides, it does not abandon him.

The most powerful writings relate to the journey within. It is here that Vandersteene demonstrates a highly refined technique, and provides us a window to his most sensitive emotions. In these poems, there is such a tight weave between the tone and emotion, the titling and the text, the positive and the negative, that it is worth examining this sojourn in greater depth. The occasion for our selection is that his poem was included in the letter to his soulmate dated 15 November 1975, just before he decided "to go to the garage to have a complete checkup of a few parts." Because sound patterns are important, both Flemish and English will be provided:

> *Angstavond*
>
> te laten zakken om te sterven
> zo moe ben ik

doch vreemde
en toch vertrouwde wil
dwingt mij tot schouwen

'k heb maar de kop
te laten vallen om dood te zijn
en om te leven 't hoofd te buigen
hoe dun is 't vlies
tussen hemel en hel
vanavond . . .

Evening of Terror

I am so tired
I only have to drop my head a little
to die

however a strange
and yet familiar will
forces me to watch

I only have to drop my head
to be dead
and to nod my head to life

how thin is the membrane
between heaven and hell
tonight. . . .

The poem falls naturally into two parts, signalled by the personal pro-
noun, a factor underlined by a special meaning of the personal. The
poem brings together existentialist resonances, human fatigue, night
and death, all of which add their own peculiar nuances to its meaning.
The title, *Angstavond*, signals instantly an existentialist piece of writing
popular during and immediately after the Second World War in
Europe and associated with Camus and Sartre (it did not become popular in North America until the hippie generation of the 1960s and
1970s). Since the notion does not appear in his earlier poems, this provides one concrete proof that North American culture *was* having an
impact on him, in spite of his Flemish-centrism. Existentialism was a
philosophy that rejected traditional ways of understanding human existence and replaced it with conceptions deriving from human experience; writers like Camus and Sartre were the popularizers of the view,
and philosophers like Heidegger etched the spectre of the human-

standing-before-death as the generator of values. Most existentialists, with the exception of Kierkegaard, were atheists, however, so Vandersteene's appropriation of the motif is significant.

Fatigue was a theme which Vandersteene probed in several of his poems. In his *Evening Prayer by the Campfire*, the fatigue is physical, deriving from his difficult and exhausting journey by dogsled through the bush. Without "one part of my body without pain," he struggles to find the energy even to mentally move through the rosary. He cannot. But then he contemplates that the movement of the day has been a rosary, that the fatigue itself is a paean to the Blessed Virgin. So the states of his body become offerings of praise and petitions presented to the Higher Being. He has no need to ritualize them conventionally; they have already been received and answered with the peace in his heart. In this poem, the very movement to bow would be a ritual acceptance of death. It is no longer a matter of whether prayers will be offered and how. It is a matter of whether, by one submissive move of his head, he will step from the human into the divine realm. This is fatigue beyond the energy of life. This is a fatigue of the soul. He desperately holds to this side of the membrane, but he knows that the least motion of eagerness for that world would cast free his body. Such fatigue of the human condition is a profound existential experience.

Evening and night play an important role in Steentje's poetry. Some of his most significant pieces identify that time specifically. Part of the reason for this is that that time is slow coming in northern Alberta — sunsets take quite some time in the spring and summer — indeed, may never come. On the other hand, darkness comes early, falling quickly and darkly in winter. It stretches on and on, and for the insomniac like Vandersteene, the morning light may never seem to come. All of his evening pieces are cosmic; they introduce another dimension into meaning, urging another dimension upon the experience. In this poem, the title and the last word form dark bookends for the progressive lowering of his human soul — he trudges half-heartedly to the cavern of his own death, and peers curiously at the phenomenon of watching himself die. Night is not then totally dark, for it opens his eyes to the precarious state in which his life sits, and by doing so suspends him before his own denouement. Night thus becomes a timeless moment in which he grasps the relatedness of his being to the beyond, and, almost as curious fact, characterizes the split not as between life and death but between heaven and hell.

But night leads irrevocably to death in the poem. The angst he faces comes about because his fatigue has left nothing between him and his own death but the drop of his head. Yet even this introduces him to something fascinating, that "strange yet familiar will," which apparently grasps him by the hair and thrusts him toward the scene: Look how close you are to the abyss. What will is this? What weird force makes one look at one's own tenacious grasp in the face of death? Drawing from existentialist philosophy, being-before-death is the last stand of the human before nothingness. Vandersteene will not move that far. His being before death can only be conceived as being before the choice of heaven or hell, as if to deliberately lower his head is to commit suicide and thus bar himself from heaven forever. The will to stand and look is once more an ethical choice, a choosing to do what is right from his deep faith and religious commitment. Even for the merest human acceptance, expressed in the gentlest shaking of the head, he will assert that he will not give up his life to his own will. Like Christ, it must be taken by God, not bought with human coin. Easy death is the defeat of the true human, who will not force the issue even with the drop of a head.

The word pattern of the poem underlines this sombre existential event, and tonal pattern linkages confirm the critical moment: from *sterven* (die), to *shouwen* (watch or survey), to *buigen* (bend or bow), the words form a series of funerary images: at death, one watches the deceased as never before, and the presence of death makes the dead into a figure larger than ordinary life. At death, one bows, either in respect or in contemplation. *Vlies* brings into relief the life cycle, for the membrane is that which held the baby in place just before it broke to usher the child into life. His use of *hoofd*, "drop," in this context, connects with the "dropping" at childbirth, recalls his labours as midwife and bares one of the most touching and paradigmatic experiences humans can have: witnessing the birth of a child. Its use here sets the whole meditation into a natural life event, posing the soul-rending problem of human responsibility in entering into the next world. Moreover, the "oo" of *hoofd* and *dood* cultivates the sound of "o" throughout, emphasizing the awe of the experience, sonally linked by the *-vond* of the title and the *-vond* of the last word, "tonight." Even in English the same motif can been grasped through the infinitive "to" and the decisive sound of "only" and "tonight." Perhaps the formation of the sound is metaphorically anchored in birthing imagery, and Vandersteene is now ready to face the next birth he will have, that of heaven.

In earlier poems, the fatigue and tentativeness brought about the upthrust of faith: God, or Mary, or Jesus sprang up in the innermost being to provide the raison d'être for confidence. This does not happen here. Is this then a poem of suicide? Did Vandersteene feel that his lifestyle and decisions had brought him to the point of breaking into the next life? Did he believe that at some point his hold on this world would be so tenuous that he might just bow his head and embrace death? Had he arrived at that supreme human moment when the will to hold back the next world is no longer worth the effort? Or is he saying to the keeper of the moment of birth, no, not now? Can Vandersteene tell the Creator when his time is fulfilled? Perhaps. In that case, Vandersteene is both body giving birth, and child being born. He is woman in the throes of labour reserving resources for the supreme moment; he is man transfixed by a strange distance from the parameters of the occasion; he is a child reluctant to break the membrane into a new world. Is this poem, then, a dramatic interweaving of existentialism, Christian consciousness and life-cycle mysticism, or is it only an embodiment of a profound world-weariness in the face of premonitions of death?

The Cancer Poems

That the first assumption would seem to have more weight can be drawn not just from this poem, but from a series of poems which I have called the cancer poems. These are poems written while he confronted the spectre of cancer. These poems intensify and increase the impact of the earlier writings and are marked by an emotional density and tension. Some are taut. Some reflect nibbling fear. Some highlight the suspense that humans face when a life-threatening disease threatens. There are moments of barely missed betrayal. Above all, and in common with all his poems, there is the whisper of another dimension, sometimes expressed in dread, sometimes in acceptance and faith. Among several, the following two poems reflect some of the complexity of his emotions:

Cancer I

The doctor was still saying something. . . .
Curtains are pulled open,
The ward, the window, the sun . . .
The buzzing of the city . . .
Nothing has changed
Cancer
I push away the horror
Manfully
A draught of sour wine
Does not dull the knowledge
At once

Of being not merely mortal
But moribund . . .

I have looked death
In the eyes
And saw emptiness;
Have entered
Behind closing eyelids:
In past grown dim
A fading play of shadows
And in the sockets of the eye
God is too far or too bright
Three days of hell.

The past telescopes
Behind my back
One plain space without perspective.
Bound tightly
And turned to what is coming
Blindfolded
I await powerless
God's knockout . . .

Untie the blindfold —
Believe:
What hits me
Has no face:
Emmanuel
Who rages in my lungs
Of whom I preached
That He was love
Lighten the pressure
Which still blurs my sight;
In my wandering spirit,
Spirit of Jesus,
Liberate the faith that
Penetrates undimmed.
I followed Him
A Simon of Cyrene.
What am I still doing
With this cross
Ages ago already
Past Calvary's top He climbed.

Friend, sharer of my secret
Follow Me . . .

We have become used to the road
In us the goal grew blurred
Calvary's other side
Is strange to me
It hardly charms me.

Yet I break the threads
Of the familiar
To find the unbeholden
That I, — through not understanding — now trust.

Surrender
Desolate resignation
Into your hands I commend my spirit,
Father,
Urgently but without joy . . .

A child's dream vocation
A smile, a word, open arms
To the poor the outgoing gesture
The Oblate's cross rather than merry eyes

To the old land the new message
Always and again
Woven through with the old mystery
But never completed in one piece
Everything remains unfinished
Word and deed have gone
Threads on full bobbins are broken
A frayed dream
Rolls across the warp of weaver's loom.

Father, Your Glory
Still ever comes as a defeat;
The seed must die,
For the sake of Your Kingdom
Your will be done. . . .

29 February 1976

Reflections

I will not betray the love
That forces me to plead
This also is surrender:
Your will be done

My God, so undeserved are your graces
And in and round me love sings out:
"You are each other's gift"
Your will be done

                              5 July 1976

Steentje had an artist's soul. Art and especially poetry gave him a language. He liked quoting Gezelle's image of the beetle, not, I think, because the beetle was all that significant, but because he thought the act of living was the creation's praise to God: "For those who have ears and eyes, every living thing has a living language and they all have the same message to offer: they say what the little water beetle in Gezelle's poem said and wrote (I write and I write and rewrite again the most holy names of God").[33] Thus, when he came face to face with the potentially destructive disease, he lapsed into that language most responsive to his inner being.

It is instructive that he still sent these poems to his friend in Flanders. Inevitably, they were accompanied by meditations, sermonizing even, which set the context for their being read. For example, accompanying his first poem was his comment on Easter, a comment quite traditional in its understanding:[34]

> We are the living reaffirmation of Christ, the Living Eucharist, the Eternal Thank-you of mankind; like a mother fed by the flesh and blood of her Christ is full to bursting with milk for the people. . . . Happy Easter and Happy Pentecost.
>   We have therefore to go into the depths, to live on a deeper level, to believe more deeply, to trust more deeply and to love more deeply: God is not in the tumult but in the strong silence in the peace of Jesus, who remains peace even in the roaring and folly of war.

Thus his cancer poems try to chronicle his inner states because he believes they are important for the readers to know: they can measure their own emotional reactions to terror and trouble by charting their journey against his emotional map. Like signposts on the road, we follow his directions: "I push the horror away," "not merely mortal but moribund," "three days of hell," "I await powerless God's knockout,"

"What hits me has no face," "liberate the faith," "I break the threads of the familiar," all these mark the thrashing of the tortured soul, finally caught in its own mortality. Then he resigns, "urgently but without joy," bitter because away back there he had chosen the arms of the Oblate cross rather than the arms of his own children by which his Flemish brethren measure surely their immortality, and all the unfinished work haunts him. Finally he lapses into his most precious helper, the natural metaphor — his seed shall die, in order for another World to come.

If we return for a moment to the contiguity between Gezelle and Vandersteene, there is a deep sense of failure at not having replicated themselves *in the Church's vineyards*. Gezelle had a crisis of confidence when his favourite student Van Oye did not return to his tutelage but instead left the seminary and went into medical school. It mattered little that Eugene's father put a great deal of pressure upon him to do so. For Gezelle, he lost more than a student. He failed as a pastor to sculpt the priesthood so surely in the young man's mind that he would not be dissuaded by an insistent father. But even more, Van Oye's leaving destroyed the priest's plans for a Flemish school of poet-priests. Van Nuis claims he never recovered from this.[35] Similarly, it weighed heavily on Steentje that he had not achieved anything: He had not seen a Cree Church born, he had not persuaded anyone from his family to join him in the mission field, he could not count on the Cree to be steadfast Catholics; he had only one convert to mission work of substance, Maskwa, and he did not have the capabilities of a Van Oye. In any case one convert was all he had for a whole life of labour. He had seen no possible fulfillment of the hope for a young Indian who would carry the Church to victory; indeed, he had seen one leave. He had not completed the one project so near to his heart, the Trout Lake church. It is likely that Vandersteene's assignment to Fox Lake, Jean D'Or and Garden River constituted the breaking point for his idealism. He never quite recovered.[36] He moved more and more into poetry. *Cancer I* shows that it is the one form through which he could measure and interpret his life, and it bears the whole brunt of it. He does not, for example, use painting to the same end.

His *Reflections* is a much more balanced Christian understanding: His life has been a gift of God's love, even as those he has lived with have been gifts to him. Can one fault the gift-giver? God's overriding will must be done.

Is this the last statement of Vandersteene? Like other critical points, we do not know. Dr. Krynen believed that this is much too acquiescent for Vandersteene. He recalls reading a poem that virtually cursed God for letting him come to this point. It was not a gracious going into that great night. But it is not part of his poetic holdings, nor is it to be found in his letters and other writings. Yet even if it were to be found, would it change who Vandersteene was for us? His cancer poems are highly edited meditations whose powers were ultimately strong enough to carry the intensity that his life demanded of them; they are the most personal public measure we have of his inner life. Steentje may have cursed God. He may well have cursed himself. The distance between his inner self and the great mystery was so close that, in some moods, he perceived them to be the same. Having chosen a life subservient to a power beyond, he would not betray that lifelong commitment by begging for some other history. I think *Reflections* is the best map of his journey we are likely to get.

The Poetic Sojourn in Retrospective

Vandersteene's poetry may be very personal, but it also is very much part of larger movements in Flanders and Canada. Despite the traditional priestly range of his educational opportunities, he must have come under the spell of non-Church writers, like Paul van Ostaijen (1896-1928), who belonged to the young Flemish literati impressed with German expressionism, and had a connection with the Dutch writer Nijhoff and the famous modernist group De Stijl. In fact, Steentje's poems, for all their traditionalist themes, reflect very modern theoretical perspectives. For example, Vandersteene is not at all maudlin about "nature," He does not glorify it, nor "worship" it like the romantics. Like his attitude to the Cree, Vandersteene is clear-eyed about what nature is. It is part of a reality that he must navigate. Above all this applies to his own "inner nature." Several remarkable passages demonstrate the thoroughly modern technique of objectifying his own inner states through the sensitive "lego-ing" of words. This suggests that words have colour, texture and quality which, when brought together in poetry, construct an impact, a power quite separate from what the writer may have intended. Once built, the poem is on its own. Its force grows out of history in the world of experience it encounters among its readers. A.L. Sotemann deftly sums up the new energy unleashed among us in the modern world: "Ever since the disappearance of the great philosophies and the great religions, there has been only art to show us a reality above this world and its mundane nature. Consequently, writing becomes a form of positive mysticism."[37]

Nature does not exist as a scientific cause-and-effect structure, but as a means of sorting through a range of relationships that need placing and evaluating. Thus "God" could be seen as quite "natural" to someone as a tree, who then places God in the network of "facts" from which one has constructed a reality. Contrariwise, nature is given, in a neutral manner, and only amazing distortion would allow one to declare it, as Plato did, as inferior, or worse still, as the Manicheans, the embodiment of evil.

In Vandersteene's poetry, nature tends to the beautiful. He is very much Belgian when he embraces a nature that is gift. Canadian views of nature are much less sanguine. The geopiety at the heart of Canadian writing does not worship at an altar of a warm and gentle countryside, but in an unforgiving atmosphere that is as capable of destroying as of loving.[38] There are moments when Vandersteene hints at this. In *Evening Prayer by the Campfire*, the sinister is not far off: the forest that stands "still and cold like a black ring wall," his feet bruised, his body paining, and "My face is mauled by the wind" as he pauses to "hail snow too deep and hail biting wind." In *The Missionary*, God drives him "towards the fog banks," "towards the black horizon / Of the forests" to press his message on a "blowing snowdrift." Alienation from this nature abounds in Canadian writing. Vandersteene only hints at this: in *Prayer*, he whimpers, "I'm ever more alone / In this sudden night / Oh! stay with me / Till all is consummated."[39] He writes to his soulmate that "The world hangs loosely upon its hinges," while the aboriginals he serves are blowing wherever they are buffeted. Things seem out of sync. Thus, while the overriding pressure in his writing is the natural mysticism of a lyrical Flemish environment, his personal experience has brought him face to face with a tougher version. They sit side by side in his poetry.

Finally, Vandersteene faces a reality that his Christian vision often provides with markers. But not always. Riding through a chaos in which nothing makes sense, propelled into a maelstrom of charges and counter-charges, pulled by several loyalties and opinions, Steentje panics. Where in all this madness, is God? In a profound plea, he begs God to come out from behind his own constructions and reassure him of His presence. He never receives an answer:[40]

> *Call to God*
>
> In the summer heat
> And winter cold
> I have
> With child-like eyes
> Searched for You
> And found You not.
> A trace of You! But You?!

In my own heart
I've tracked You
There where You dwell
As I am taught;
I caught a glimpse of You. But You?

In line and verse and paint
I grasped for You
And did not catch You.
A trace of You! But You?!
Yet You were in my head and hands
And in my striving
My urge towards You.

With Your own word
As fingertips
I have kneaded souls
And with Your chisel
I hewed them
But in the work of art
I recognised You not.
A trace of You! But You?!

Yet it was You
Who sent me out
To proclaim the word
That wakes an echo
Towards You!

You who are everywhere,
And always,
And in all
Where are You now?

27 February 1974

There were some experiences that broke all the bounds, some sojourns that had no fixed route, and some worlds that had no charts at all. His poetry is the only form he knows to encounter their reality.

Notes

1 Vandersteene, *Wanneer gij*, pp. 39, 65, 68.
2 Some associates, including Dr. Krynen, said they had seen poetry that raised serious doubts about God's existence. I have not found them.
3 They are entitled, *Magnificat*, *Lenten Oath* and *Death*.
4 Vandersteene, *Wanneer gij*, p. 77.
5 See, for example, "Eer ge ooit het oordeel vellen komt," in Guido Gezelle, *Laatste Verzen* (Amsterdam: L.J. Veen, 1903), p. 7.
6 Michel van der Plas, Dutch author and poet, wrote a study of his life entitled *Mijnheer Gezelle*, which was awarded a prize in 1991 by the Flemish newspaper, *De Standaard*. In a statement in that newpaper of 26 October 1991 (section 4), it is reported that the book had sold 15,000 copies, but less than half were sold in Belgium, an interesting fact which would seem to indicate that books about him sell better in Holland than in Flanders.
7 The first was written in June 1974, and is quoted at the heading of Chapter One; the other two were written during the spring and early summer of 1973, one in Kuurne, Belgium. See Roger Vandersteene, *Levensvervulling*, edited by Gabrielle Demedts (Roeselare: Hernieuwen-Uitgaven pvba, 1979), p. 28-31.
8 This poem has some superficial similarities to Gezelle's *Dien Avond en Die Roze* (*This Evening and This Rose*), in *Anthologie de la poésie Neerlandaise*, translated by Maurice Carème (Bruxelles: Asedi, 1967), p. 3, since both are dedicated to someone very close (Steentje's to Wilfried, his brother, Gezelle's to his friend Eugene Van Oye). But Gezelle's is very pointedly addressed to "you," whereas there is nothing in Vandersteene's of that personal equivalence.
9 Vandersteene, *Levensvervulling*, pp. 55-60.
10 Gezelle, *De Leie*, *Groeninge'ns Grootheid of De Slag van de Gulden Spooren*, in *Laatste*, pp. 81-82; 21-27.
11 See Vandersteene, *Levensvervulling*, pp. 21 and 22.
12 Written to Van Oye in celebration of their last communion together. It is often interpreted as a love poem. See Hermine J. Van Nuis, *Guido Gezelle: Flemish Poet-Priest* (New York: Greenwood Press, 1981), p. 50, *Leven*. Compare with Gezelle, *Excelsior*, in *Laatste*, pp. 44-45. *Attractive Lure* is found in Tanghe, *Leven*, p. 104.
13 Vandersteene, *Wanneer gij*, p. 30.
14 See Jan Greshoff, "Belgian Literature in the Dutch Language," in Jan-Albert Goris, ed., *Belgium* (Berkeley: University of California Press, 1946), pp. 286-300.
15 See above for *Dood*; compare *Macte Animo*, in *Anthologie*, p. 31.
16 See Tanghe, *Leven*, p. 36.
17 For example, Sertorius says that Timmermans was the first living Fleming known in Germany (Lili Sertorius, *Literarisches Scaffen und Volkstum in Flandern* [Berlin: Verlag "Das Deutsche Volk," 1932], p. 94). The book also presents a helpful analysis of other writers and painters of interest to Vandersteene, especially as they bear on the folk tradition.
18 Vandersteene, *Levensvervulling*, pp. 28-31.
19 André De Ridder, *Anthologie des écrivains flamands contemporains* (Paris: Champion, 1926), and André De Ridder, *La Littérature flamande contemporaine (1890-1923)* (Paris: Champion, 1923), are excellent surveys for the years formative for Vandersteene.
20 Gershoff, "Belgian Literature," p. 294.
21 Stijn Streuvels, *Langs de Wegen* (*Along the Roads*), translated by Edward Crankshaw (Boston, MA: Twayne Publishers, 1975).
22 Dated 17 June 1976 (Vandersteene, *Wanneer gij*, p. 123).
23 We have earlier met his brother Gustaaf who was a painter connected to the Latem school. Karel was born in Gent and was both a poet and a writer. He was associated with the "Nu en Straks" movement.

24 Dated 21 August 1974, unpublished.

25 The poetry of Verschaeve became part of the Flemish political scene when a verse was used as the town oath by a Flemish burgomaster. The verse is: "Glorious land in mourning / Beloved in distress, / Again be great and free. / For we are true to thee, / Oh Flanders, to the death," said to have been sworn in at Denderleeuw in July 1926 (see S.B. Clough, *A History of the Flemish Movement in Belgium* [New York: R.R. Smith, 1930], p. 231).

26 Given to Tanghe when he was home during the illness and death of his father (Tanghe, *Leven*, p. 108).

27 See Reinder P. Meijer, *Literature of the Low Countries* (The Hague: Martinus Nijhoff, 1978), p. 108. A fuller account of his mystical ideology is found below in the "Theoretical Epilogue," pp. 292ff.

28 The poem is found on pp. 115-17. See Vandersteene, *Levensvervulling*, pp. 17-20.

29 Vandersteene, *Wanneer gij*, p. 40.

30 Dated April 1974 (Tanghe, *Leven*, p. 109). The theme reflects the poetic orientation of Anton Van Wilderode, who wrote after the war but who was a traditionalist; Steentje's soulmate once sent him the entire collected works of the writer, according to a note in his letters to her (Vandersteene, *Wanneer gij*, p. 77).

31 Ibid., p. 41.

32 Vandersteene, *Levensvervulling*, p. 81.

33 See Vandersteene, *Wanneer gij*, p. 42.

34 Ibid., p. 40.

35 Van Nuis, *Guido Gezelle*, p. 38.

36 It is quite remarkable that Gezelle had the same thing happen to him when he was transferred to Brugge to work with English-speaking students. This cut him off from his Flemish associates and inspiration. It left him bereft, according to Van Nuis, *Guido Gezelle*, p. 39.

37 A.L. Sotemann, "Martinus Nijhoff's Poetry in Its European Context," in Francis Bulhof, ed., *Nijhoff, Van Ostaijen, "De Stijl": Modernism in the Netherlands and Belgium in the First Quarter of the 20th Century* (The Hague: Martinus Nijhoff, 1976), p. 108.

38 See below, Chapter Ten, for a discussion of the "alien land" in Canadian literature.

39 Tanghe, *Leven*, p. 81.

40 Ibid., pp. 102-103.

Eight

Wrestling the Spirits: Powagan, Beethoven, Cancer

> What you heard in the night was not a rifle shot: it was
> the sound of the voice of Kisemanitou, calling our little
> sister home.   — Vandersteene, sermon at funeral, 1974

The Crucial Years

V andersteene's move to the diocesan level had a profound effect on
his perspective; he encountered a much larger world in several
respects. The years of change began, not with his initial movement into
the Church's administrative branch, although doubtless that had its
impact. It came with a closer relationship with elders, medicine men
and native thinkers who were part of a wider spectrum of religious ferment on the Canadian scene. Because he travelled widely across Canada, he experienced first-hand the aboriginalization movement that
was percolating beneath the surface and which took many forms: aboriginal activism on political issues, the growth of tribal institutions
(some of them quite wealthy), the expansion of pan-Indian spirituality,
native art for the Canadian and international public, and Indian environmental consciousness. It ended with the voice of Kisemanitou calling him. They were only six years, 1970-76. A short time, really, in the
span of his 56 years; but Steentje wrestled with several weighty spirits.
They were not peaceful encounters.

His frame of mind is best symbolized by his cars. Until he headed
up the diocesan missionary team's rewrite of mission activity, he had
never owned a car. If he had to go anywhere, he flew, hiring little
planes or drawing on the flights by government officials, physicians
and oil company explorers. Sometimes he took the wagon or dogsled.
The sled he used less and less because it just was no longer practical in

---

Notes to this chapter are on pp. 260-62.

an Alberta that was pouring money into roads. The diocese bought him a used Toyota. A symbiotic relationship developed between Steentje and his car. With vast distances to travel, at least when compared with Flanders, where you could drive across the whole country in three hours, the car became a measure of his ability to conquer the country. Skidding into snowbanks, weathering blistering summer heat, cajoling and cursing the old Toyota became so much part of his persona, that, as we have seen, he wrote poems in his cars. He wrote poems about his cars. It was, one suspects, Vandersteene's late engagement with a male rite de passage in Canada.

There were practical rewards for this freedom to roam: one was music. Not just any music, Beethoven. For hours on the road, over and over the little tapes wound a magical spell. This is not poetic on my part; in 1976 Jos sat amazed as they fled Edmonton International Airport: his brother, tough Canadian missionary, sobbed openly as the Ninth flooded over him. He abandoned his soul to the strength and nuance of that great symphony. Is this something Flemish? The Flemish knew why he loved Beethoven, but I can only regard the evidence as anecdotal: his brother Wilfried fingered Beethoven's structure — formed, but free. But more, "Beethoven's music allowed him to defend himself against his fears."

The use of Beethoven in this manner apparently was a Vandersteene family trait. Willem Vermandere, Flemish sculptor and writer of a popular ballad celebrating Vandersteene, said Beethoven is the music of the solitary Flemish. In moments of isolation Beethoven stirs the Flanders soul in ways like no other classical musician. A tone of the eternal soil.

Another practical reward: linkage with new forms of aboriginal development. After moving to Grouard in 1969, he increased his contacts with Frank and Harold Cardinal, and with the elders around Fort Chipweyan and Hobbema. He realized that his vision of Cree identity had been too narrowly drawn.[1] He also realized that the tiny mission of Trout Lake, his creation and ideal, was scarcely a microcosm of Cree existence. There were movements afoot that had not touched the lifestyle of his little brothers and sisters, dear as they were to him. Indeed, Trout Lake was a world apart, unique.

His travels took him to the Yukon, to Toronto, to the MacKenzie Delta, to the Blackfoot, to Ottawa. In this vast land, he began to see larger patterns of aboriginal belief. His encounters with elders opened his eyes to deeper notions of aboriginal people: he encountered many different kinds of elders, some whose nativeness was reflective of what he felt were Christian values. His old argument was perhaps to be drawn differently: where it had been if God could be a Jew, there was no reason why God couldn't be Cree, now he shifted to the generic "Indian." Manifestly not the same, at least as far as the Church was concerned, he drew the line now as white/Indian in a way he had not before. Now the problems his little flock had in Trout Lake were only signs of a deeper problematic.

He had stressed the notion of the Cree family, and argued for the validity of Cree living patterns, sometimes unblessed by the Church, but for all that still formally recognized and adhered to by the committed. As he saw it, with divorce running rampant among Canadian Catholics, he saw no benefit in insisting that Cree commitments outside the Church were any less viable than those within. To get to the idea of the real presence in the family, he went back to Jewish scriptures to the notion of the passover meal. There the extended family gathered to celebrate their common roots and common religious meanings. Jesus validated this perception of family by elevating it to the level of rite, an elevation that Catholics revered and enshrined in the mass. He had seen this reflection of the family of God in the Cree community, and, of more religious embodiment, in the *wikokewin* rituals.

He met some elders who spoke of the Creator giving not only the land but an attitude towards the land. These elders talked with a kind of "Sermon on the Mount" idealism. He also discovered that they not only *told* but *created* stories of the Wisakaychak type, using them to give insights into the moral nature of the universe. Parables. Amazing, since this was an old tool of Jesus and the Christian preacher. Again he saw common patterns across tribal and cultural divisions: it was not direct moralizing, but storytelling providing gentle guidance on those issues touching the ambiguous. Steentje learned the power of the prophetic word, not from Christian prophets, but from aboriginal. It was a style he relished and utilized because it fit so well with his own modus operandi.

He learned of the meaning of power associated with his medicine man status: that the power was given by Manitou (i.e., both Kisemanitou and Micimanitou), but that its use was to be determined by the holder. So long as the holder determined that its benefits would be good, and had a fidelity to the beneficial ideology of Manitou's power, medicine blessed the people. But if the holder determined to punish with his power, Manitou did not prevent him. The temptation to subvert the positive purpose of medicine for personal gain was always present. The medicine man is in a constant dialogue with his own intentions. Vandersteene came to understand the temptations of Jesus this way. Jesus was not tempted because he was a man who had to overcome temptation. He was tempted because he had all the power and could have forced people to do as he directed. This is why traditional medicine was so feared: if the medicine man determined that you were flaunting the rules or breaking taboos, or being disrespectful of the powers, he could use the medicine against you. Inexplicable bad luck or illness almost always had this meaning. Bad medicine stories also became part of his understanding: A hunter who shot at a moose 100 yds away, and missed, then picked up the fur-bearing bullet[2] — someone has poisoned my hunting he reasoned. He heard stories of medicine battles between families over who had the most powerful medicine, so he could see how, for example, some Cree trembled at accepting a Christian priest-cum-Cree medicine man.

He also discovered the notion of reconciliation within Cree tradition and saw it painted across the aboriginal consciousness. Cree did not talk about relationships with God. They were not theological like whites, with their easy reference to God as if they had an airy familiarity with the Creator. That would be audacious, and reserved solely for the most powerful. Cree saw the best way of talking about the forgiveness of God, and indeed of the love of God, was to speak first of all through communal relationships. Talking about an abstract God and being forgiven by Him strains belief if you are sitting beside someone you hate. When a community has been restored to health, then the presence of Manitou is acknowledged. Being reconciled with an estranged brother, or forgiving a wounding sister is the earmark of Manitou-consciousness.

He found this to be why elders refused to speak of punishment for a crime in terms of an "abstract" jail term, for that only further alienates. Justice was best done in terms of reconciling the individual with the community. Crime, insofar as it existed, was not crime against another person, but crime towards the matrix from which all came. It was crime against Manitou, in the shape of this offended individual and this, one's own community.

He realized that the medicine man had played a beneficial role in traditional society by virtue of the very ambiguity of his power. The individual who committed an offence could have the powers of the spirit world descend upon him. Part of the strategy of control was the very silence the medicine man maintained about his knowledge of spirit powers.

There were other patterns that Vandersteene believed reflected trans-tribal consciousness. Wherever he went in Canada he heard of the bear, and its power. He realized that some symbols in Cree tradition were rooted in a larger aboriginal system, a system that he saw arising out of appropriation across cultural lines of meaningful signs. Like the power of the cross, the bear had the ability to leap cultural solidarities and unite people on a larger level. He understood also the idea of progressive discovery, of learning as an ongoing aspect of revelation. He could see the advantages of this notion of revelation, so clearly articulated in dream spirits or spiritual encounters with the spirit world throughout life. He also began to see the conflict with his own beliefs.

It was no secret how widespread the aboriginal belief in dreams was found to be. He himself knew the power of dreams. His Flemish soul believed in them firmly. Dreams were a language in which the sacred world spoke. They were not to be shared. They were teachings, and could only be discussed with an elder who was skilled in interpreting their meaning. He knew the significance, then, when the Cree came to him and told him a dream. He developed his own priestly ideology for dreams: they were a spiritual force akin to confession.

All the while, he listened carefully to Harold Cardinal, aboriginal activist and now his friend. He often attended smokes, and sometimes participated in sweats. He picked up the dynamic that was developing in Canada over First Nation rights, and he did not hesitate to appear at radical American Indian Movement meetings. It gave him great satisfaction to hear a comment made at a Red Power meeting at Sturgeon Lake. There were both old and young people at the meeting. Everyone became silent when he came in, and several young people resented that he showed up. The leaders of the old people shut them up by saying, "What do you have to complain about? He's redder than you are!"

Harold Cardinal, stressed from his role as head of the Indian Association of Canada, and exhausted from writing his last book, needed complete bed rest. While he did not have a nervous breakdown, he was extremely fatigued. The doctors put him in the hospital in Edmonton. Vandersteene drove all the way from Grouard to Edmonton, and he obtained his room number from information. But when he went to his room, a nurse barred his way. "No! No visitors are allowed. Mr. Cardinal needs his rest."

Steentje remonstrated with her. "But I came all the way from Grouard to see my brother. It's really too bad. . . ." Harold recognized his voice from outside the door and he rang the bell. "That man outside my door has to come in. That's my brother."

It is during this time that he was creating and refining his catechism. We have seen the significance of his art for this project. But the figure of Jesus is scarcely sexual. If he was a man, there is no evidence of it in the nudes. Why? Was this just sensitivity to Cree norms of public nudity?

Perhaps. But he was, in fact, intrigued by stories of androgyny among the Indians. From Fr. Mariman he learned of the strange belief among some that Adam had suckled Eve, because, unlike the Jewish/Christian story, she did not come "mature." She had to be nurtured to adulthood. Moreover, among the Dene, he had heard there was the story of a man whose wife had died in childbirth and he had developed breasts with milk to suckle their baby. Vandersteene remarked that the notion was also found among the French, for a trumpeter in the army of Napoleon grew milk-laden breasts to nurse a baby whose mother had died. The non-sexual appearance of Jesus is in direct contrast with female representation, which in the catechism is explicit and even shocking. Indian androgyny may provide the explanation for this phenomenon.

It is not too much to expect that Steentje had another book planned, but the nature of this book is starkly non-religious, judging by the outline he left.[3] The story apparently was to be illustrated with reference to over 50 people whom Vandersteene listed, who represented various aspects of this sad tale. At one level, it was evidently designed to answer those who had criticized his stance on the Trout Lake road, but it was also designed to tell the true story of the road through Sturgeon Lake reserve, an area to which he had seldom travelled.

The contrast with *Wabasca* could hardly be greater. This is a book of tragedy, but it is really the story of how very well-meaning people destroyed aboriginal life. It addresses the ethical underpinnings of Canadian development, critiquing it through the tragedy of what it had visited upon the aboriginal people. Entitled *And They Made Roads*, this book probed the cultural injustice which Indians faced when they had dealings with white society. It is a moral tale.

Its hero is old Okemaw, whose life is examined through four different phases of national development. The first sketches the pre-contact state, characterized by a nomadic hunting/fishing/trapping lifestyle; the next stage is the coming of the company store and the fur demand, which built an international trade on the hunting/trapping skill of the Indians and depended upon their transportation network to stock the international fur market. Once those workers had been incorporated into that system, and they had diversified their talents in response to the economy, they then lost the skill to hunt and trap. The store became the hunting ground, providing continuous sustenance and further involving the Indian in a structure over which others had control. Reliance on the local store undermined independence in food supply. Livelihood was no longer skill- or labour-based.

"Charity" ushered in the third phase: the rise of the mission. From Vandersteene's perspective, this was not a purely religious activity. It was a competition between various factions of Christianity, leading to a corruption of the mission process into statistics: Children were "bought" for the Church rolls, through the institution of charity, or through appropriation of government largesse. The Church hoped to create a second-generation organization that would ignore the shallow motives behind the "conversions" — a "buying children to create children" program. This is Vandersteene's most visceral condemnation of the Church mission program.

The fourth stage was the gradual takeover by white government through the Church's officials and schools. Eventually the aboriginals were weakened by the process, and the foreigners were able to split their power through agreements and treaties, and to push them back onto unproductive land, or onto reserves whose animal base was too small or fragile to sustain their hunting traditions. Without the means to be traditional, Indians had to adopt white labour patterns.

In the meantime, white society was moving away from a labour-based economy, long the only means that the aboriginal had of participating in white society, towards an acquisition culture. In this culture, one does not need to work but only needs to collect riches. The sale of natural resources displaces both aboriginal and his food animals.

Despite what governments and white institutions said, whites had no intention of adjusting to "Indian" needs; they really just set the aboriginal up to integrate or die. Stereotypically, white society, including the sisters and priests of the missions, regarded aboriginals generally as beneath respect, their inclinations towards hunting/trapping lifestyle perceived as hopelessly out of date. The symbol of this attitude was in the treatment of the children, who were forcibly removed from their environment and put into the artificial environment of residential schools. Any reference to their traditional lifestyle or identity was systematically and universally undermined. Language and customs were regarded as irrelevant, even damaging to their assimilation, despite the plain evidence of sophisticated languages of obvious depth and achievement. When assimilation seemed to be slow, this became an excuse for further white inroads into native life, such as white school systems, white housing projects, white purchase of Indian land to "help them out." From the white viewpoint, the aboriginal was in the way.

The people themselves, on the other hand, had few options; they used anti-social behaviour as the only way of coping with a continuous negative image. They gravitated easily to the underbelly of white society and used the language of the environment: alcohol, drugs and prostitution. An "Indian" became a scandal. Whites had the publican they wanted. The degradation was complete.

This moral tale is woven around the experience of the people of Sturgeon Lake. They had horses on the reserve, and a trail that served the horses as a road. Whites came to live around the reserve, and built a school for their children. They bought a school bus, but they did not want to drive around the reserve, and they appealed to the government to arrange with the Indians to upgrade the trail into a road. The Indians did not want the road through their reserve, since they did not want or need the access it implied. The Church covertly agreed with the whites, and helped to undermine Indian resistance. The government made short-term promises of employment to the people and they succumbed to the combined pressures.

The promise of jobs died quickly. The road construction used few if any Indians because they were "unskilled and unreliable." But the road was built, and since it was fairly primitive, being narrow and muddy, the Indians adjusted to its presence. But such a road did not satify the whites. The government, at the insistence of the white settlers, pushed Indians to accept a major highway. The missionaries agreed, because they wanted the freedom to get to town. They wanted ease of access to white culture. The highway is built and carried more traffic than school buses; the highway became a thoroughfare for semis and truckers, cross-country tourists and travellers. The tranquillity of the reserve had given way to the roar of bulldozers and trucks.

The road was too dangerous for the Indians to use with their horses, so they were forced to drive their teams in the ditch. Children and animals were not safe on reserve land because of the road. Since the road cut the reserve in half, animals did not have free rein, rodents came in, and the traditional food-base animals retreated away from the reserve, destroying the Indian's independent supply. Girls hitchhiked to town, and got involved in white culture; young males bought old cars and went to town to seek odd jobs and entertainment. They were attracted by the consumerism of the white culture, and rebelled against their own. But they were unskilled and they ended up full of despair at the treatment they received and the lack of opportunity. The centre of reserve culture slipped away from its traditions towards the town, fed by the easy money of welfare.

Meanwhile, the sense of isolation and community that sustained the values has been undermined, and, along with it that precious sense of protection that came with reserve life. The ecosystem was dramatically changed; it was no longer Indian. The elder crushed.

There is nothing terribly new about this moral tale. It has been repli-cated in dozens of studies and chronicled *ad nauseam* across Canada. Nor is the Church spared in the critique. What is remarkable is that Vandersteene thought it had to be told again.

Despite that fact that his dramatic sketch could be enlivened with his rich larder of stories, the end result has a "just so" quality to it. Both whites and Indians appear to be one-dimensional. The significance of this book is not really the tragedy Steentje wants to bring to print, but the absence of any theological language. This is a book about power and powerlessness.

In his starkest terms, Steentje holds that there is no appreciable dif-ference between the government and the Church as institutions: they are both expressions of white culture. Gone are the rehearsals of ele-mental sin and its effect on all people; absent are the great clashes of aboriginal and white values. A simple road becomes the tool of a civili-zation's destruction, because those who have power cannot see the ef-fect of their power on those who don't have it.

This book has the shape of the liberation movement, just beginning to be felt in Canada. Evidently Vandersteene no longer thought the Cree could resist the onslaught, unlike the Trout Lake case (see above, pp. 157ff.) where they could have just said no to the road. But he recog-nized that this was not the whole truth. He conceded that being alienated from the larger Canadian culture was not the way that most aboriginals wanted to live. At a fundamental level, Cree and First Na-tions people are part of Canada, indeed, have always been Canadian and *cannot* be shut off from it. Nothing in Cree tradition could justify an isolationist stance, despite what the white man had said about the reserves. Nor is there anything essentially malicious in white culture per se, even with the role that it has played in bringing about the de-mise of Sturgeon Lake. It just cannot see. The tragedy for Vandersteene is that white culture cannot see the value of aboriginal culture, and takes no steps to ensure its survival, *when that culture is an essential part of the country in which they all live and of which they all are children.* This is a religious message of a much more fundamental kind.

God and the Church: Scorched Entrails

One day after Vandersteene had given one of his unique and impas-sioned conference presentations, Archbishop Routhier pressed his hand. "Fine job, Vandersteene, tough but true." Then with his back a little straighter and his tone a little less jolly, he added: "No doubt about it. You're a true Fleming. The Flemings stand with their feet in the mud, but their heads reach to the stars."[4] It was meant as a compliment, but the ethnic undertow reflects some of the spirits unleashed by his reforms: Steentje was less than enthusiastic about his Canadian confrères. For one thing, he thought them illdisposed to the loneliness of the missions. After all, he pointed out, the diocese had had three very talented young priests, but they transferred out or quit. He was right, but the context was larger; the Church across Canada was reeling under defections. Nuns and priests were leaving their orders, either for secular activities or to marry. The priests he met at conferences were pleasant enough, but he was not impressed with their depth. A number of the sisters he saw as lurching from one vision of the Church to another, and he told his soulmate in Flanders that their return from summer holidays was always hectic. They brought back ideas that had no viability in their task at the missions.

He did not make light of the agony of being a lonely priest in a remote mission. He knew the taste of abandonment. With an ironic chuckle he told the story of the old priest in Pelly Bay in the Arctic; a southern Canadian, he was assigned to the mission and was absolutely bored. He devised one way of maintaining his sanity, he carried stones from a pile on one side of his house to a pile on the other. The stone pile moved back and forth for years just because he needed something to keep himself occupied. Steentje knew this bone-shattering, maddening experience. But he felt that he, and others like him, had learned to fill their lives with God. When his friend Omer Tanghe asked him, "What do you do, when the temperature is 50 below?" he answered without reflection,

> Then I remain around my log cabin and busy myself with chopping wood or other manual work. I study or I write. I model with plastic clay, I paint or I think. But we bush missionaries spend a lot of time in prayer in our cabin. You have to learn to fill your aloneness and solitude with God Himself. That is why we have the Blessed Sacrament in our cabin. You will notice this in every Mission. Behind a curtain in the living room we keep the Eucharist. Without Jesus we could not stick it. But this solitude with Him, I could not do without it any more.[5]

Which is to say that a number of Canadian missionaries had problems because they had never learned the value of solitude as meditation. But there was more to it than that: he genuinely felt that serving aboriginals in Canada was an activity that the Europeans could do better, because the Canadians were somehow in competition with the aboriginals for the land, a competition at the heart of the Canadian white's psyche. Possessing the land meant contradictory things for whites and Indians (a common idea that runs through much aboriginal/white debate). European priests did not have the same legacy.

They had no need to possess the land. Therefore they were free to love the Cree as people. He commented that the Flemish and the Cree people were very much alike. The Roman armies came and tried to conquer them, but the Flemish people, like the Cree, were a muskeg people, living in the marshes. Rome could not do anything with them. Such successes in the face of overwhelming odds drove their independence very deep. Cree, he held, had the same quality.

He bristled when his fellow-missionaries openly criticized the Indians for their "moral lapses," or their "lack of discipline." If there was one thing that made him angry, it was criticism of the Cree — he would rage on and on about it. While on furlough, he would recreate his sessions with his colleagues in Canada, and as Willem put it, "he was very hard against his own fellow Belgians, against his own fellow missionaries. He even had the sisters in tears. But he never said one bad word against the Indians." It was precisely this lack of objectivity that undermined his effectiveness in promoting a new kind of mission evangelism because whites wouldn't listen when the Cree were beyond critique. Fr. Platteeuw, his old school chum, summed it up well: "He loved them, like a man loves his wife; he was intelligent, bright, and critical, but when it came to the Cree people, he couldn't judge them, because he loved them. He resigned himself to seeing the Cree as his 'Flemish' people."

His fellow-missionaries loved the Church, but they weren't about to adopt Steentje's dream without revision. His "flawless" Cree were not the Cree they had to deal with day in and day out; his monolithic Cree character was a fiction. To argue so created a sizeable credibility gap with some priests.

Fr. Joseph Jean from Desmarais disagreed fundamentally with him. There was no possible way of bringing together traditional Cree ways and modern life. They were completely incompatible. Aboriginals had to cope with modern life, frustrations and all, just like all of us. Steentje's ideas of aboriginals pitted against a ravenous white mass was just too grandiose to take. His ideas were plagued with Canadian scepticism.

Some were willing to concede that the Cree had a certain character, but they were more persuaded to couch their rejection in terms of temperament: Fr. Virgilio Baratto, who was in Cadotte Lake and then was transferred to St. Charles Point mission, near Trout Lake said:

> Father Vandersteene was against everything that brings constriction. In this, he is very much like the Cree. They are upset with rules and restrictions. No matter how many times you teach them rules of hockey or baseball, they break them. I think he came to Canada to be free of rules.

He left residential school and went into bush because he was like that. He basically had the soul of an artist.[6]

Artists, of course, had not built the Church. They were necessary, but their perception of reality is guilded. Dogma and liturgical reform had never been formulated that way in the history of the Church, and it could not be constructed that way now.

Vandersteene faced a slowly rising tide of opposition. At first it was oblique comments about Trout Lake and its insular life, sweetened with pleasant smiles and gentle ribbing: "You have a beautiful life, in that place. No worries. You don't have a great deal to do there. You don't have to work hard to sustain your lifestyle. What, four of you for so few Catholics! There is no sense in studying Cree because the Indians will all be speaking English soon. That's a *real* mission. You do an awful lot for *those* Cree people." These were barely veiled insinuations that Trout Lake was quite different from the missions others faced, with the unstated premise that perhaps Trout Lake since the Pentecostals was not all that ideal a place to utilize as an example to build an entire church upon.

The Bishop saw the slow erosion of his glorious vision of a Cree Church, and blamed it, too conveniently, on his lack of management skills: "I don't think administration was in him at all." Perhaps not, but there were rumours that the Bishop was basically opposed to all that "old stuff," meaning the use of the *wikokewin* as model for his masses. He didn't like the pipe-smoking and Indian ceremonies. Steentje's supporters rallied around him, and placated their disappointment with the belief that his notions of church were too far ahead of his colleagues. Those with more distance, including some Cree elders, wondered aloud whether he, too, would have to leave the Church to form his version of the authentic Cree Church.

At issue were two very different views of a liberated Cree Church. The priest and sisters of the diocese stepped aside to watch a battle between two titans: Vandersteene and Lamothe on this one. Lamothe was a Métis, who had become a priest in the early 1960s. His star rose rapidly among missionaries, because here, for the first time, was a partly Cree brother who brought with him a thorough background in aboriginal affairs. He was clever. Moreover, he had a good theological mind. Here was a priest from "the other side." The battle was joined on the economic basis of liberation theology.

Lamothe said that any reform of the Church among the Cree had to involve fundamental economic reform. The Church could not hope to win the Cree unless it took a rigid stand against the way Canadian society cut up the money pie. Everywhere across the country, despite the wealth pouring in on all sides, the Indians were a deprived people. The resources went for bigger and better widgets for the whites and the few favoured Indian bands, while the vast majority of aboriginals were living far below the poverty line. No reform would take place, and neither Cree nor any other aboriginal group would listen to the Church until it put itself in jeopardy with its well-heeled friends and fought for equality.

Pointing to the Church in South America that had dared to stand with the aboriginals against Rome and the barons of the establishment, he argued that was the only vision of the Church that would activate a crushed and subdued people. The dream he nurtured was that of a risen Christ, breaking the bonds of the believers and transforming their lives into creative children of God.

He trained a withering eye on Vandersteene's reforms. He thought the Flemish missionary's adaptation of *wikokewin* was robbing the museum. The Church couldn't become Cree just by adapting something that had already lost its power. Lamothe accepted that liturgical and conceptual reform was necessary, but unlike Vandersteene, he could not see grounding that reform in a suffering Saviour ideology. He and his people had suffered and suffered. They wanted no more of it. They wanted liberation.

He thought Vandersteene's perception of the Cree as hunters and trappers was wishful thinking. He pointed to the great masses of Cree who were abandoning the reserves to flock to the cities. This was not a group of people pining for the forests. These were real people desperately trying to participate in the larger Canadian community. Lamothe had strong allies; Routhier, for one, agreed that it was hard to worry about religion if the people were starving.

The conflict had deep theological roots. As a group the missionaries could not solve the duality implicit in these views. At a basic level, the views were not exclusive, neither one nor the other. But the group as a whole did not want to do the hard work to solve the issues. For his part, Vandersteene did not recognize until it was too late that his rigidity had driven the team apart. His was a "stay the course" theme. To his soulmate he wrote: "Other missionaries are completely preoccupied with development; they see all and everyone in socio-economic terms and forget man — the real living man right before their noses. This socio-economic approach is cheap, it pleases the 'apostle' and it saves him the trouble to be human with people, the pain and the labour and also the joy. They continue to be superficial."[7] So the issue became one of nuance between the "prophet" Vandersteene and the "apostle" Lamothe. The group dithered. Lamothe was dismayed. He saw little hope of real reform in the Church. He became involved with a woman, and walked away from the Church.

Somewhere in the welter of claims was Vandersteene's unwavering attitude. For within the diocese there were conflicts over loyalty to theological models. Steentje would not compromise. His own commitments to the meaning of Christ and of God could not be reconciled with another. For that reason, Vandersteene could not embrace the liberationist Christ. For that reason, too, he could not accept the ecstatic Pentecostals. Ground zero: the love of Christ burned with pain. He had penned it to God in Trout Lake:

> For me the game was a game
> For you it was seriousness
> I know it now, too late;
> Like a fool I played with fire!
> The blowtorch flame of your love
> Has scorched my entrails.
> Enough, O God, it is enough![8]

Vandersteene could not and would not leave the Church. He would not take the step which Lamothe insisted was the mark of conviction — if the Church will not reform according to your plan, leave. But Steentje would not give up his vision of a Church reformed around his Cree assumptions, despite the strong current of resistance running through his colleagues. He proposed an idea of native leaders, drawn from the best Catholics of the Cree communities. He wanted to train Cree men in their own community for the priesthood. He might have looked to one or two men as possible candidates to ordain in their own community, like Julian Gladue of Trout Lake or Jimmy Blessie of Garden River. He would have felt they were his equal. But he knew it would never be accepted by Rome, let alone in Grouard, Alberta. But Rome *did* accept the idea of a local deacon presiding over mass on Sunday. The missionaries voted to send a fact-finding group to explore the idea as it was developing in other areas. It was not headed up by Vandersteene.

Meanwhile he continued to develop the essentials of a Cree liturgy. He presented some hymns in Cree to the annual missionary conference, and immediately had those who thought the whole exercise was a lost cause, because in every one of the missions Canadian culture was overrunning Cree culture, especially the Cree language. At the same time he knew that, even Garden River (which was in some ways the most traditional of all posts under his jurisdiction) had little commitment to maintaining an entirely Cree environment. This factor was confirmed by a government study for the Northlands School Division Study, which reported in 1973:

> No significant interest was found at the local level in developing native cultural programs. The Study group concluded that there is no strong demand for Cree in the schools insofar as the people are concerned. They do not want something different from what is available to other Alberta children.[9]

He stuck to his guns. Fidelity to the Cree was foundational: "Yes, we know white culture is coming. Then all this work will have been useless. But, at least we will have done it. We will have shown these people that we respect them, that we respect their culture, even if it is lost to the eyes of the world. We have to show them that it is not lost in the eyes of the believer, and it is not lost in the eyes of God."[10]

But his bravado failed him when he was alone. Touring around to the missions in his old Toyota, he drummed up support among the dispirited troops, then "I drive around a great deal and after most of the visits and travels, I combat disillusionment." As an antidote, he grew cactii "those little rascals are tough and they are prickly . . . that's their beauty."[11] So after kicking against the pricks, he drives home to embrace the prickles.

Return to Flanders: The Calm before the Storm

His letters home indicated that he missed Flanders far more in the last 10 years of his life than in his first missionary years. He noted that he was closer to 60 than 50, and he recalled old Fr. Peel from Brugge, whose philosophy of life proved quite accurate: 20 years of growth, 20 years of bloom, and 20 years of neither this nor that, then the rest "Oohh my neck, Ouch my bum." So it was with some anticipation that he left for home on furlough, early in 1973. Yet the moment he arrived home, it was almost as if there was no place in the world like the Vicariate of Grouard. Anaïs and her husband were straightforward people, quite capable of talking rationally about the problems and possibilities of the aboriginals, especially since Canada's aboriginals were receiving a great deal of press in Europe. While he spoke often of his missions, he seldom said anything about Indian rights or land claims. He told them he wasn't interested in politics in Canada. His range of views included the Pentecostals and the sects destroying his mission, and he was particularly vehement about the sectarians using the sweat lodge as a drawing card for their religion. He talked a great deal about adapting the liturgy to the Cree language and culture.

On his home turf, he spoke vigorously against the Protestant groups that were destroying his churches, and he argued just as forcefully that the Cree should be left alone. But when challenged with, "Well, why are you there then?" he affirmed that he was sensitive to their culture, and sought to preserve their identity. Bringing them Catholic faith was akin to their traditions, while Protestant religion was not. Those who did not have stars in their eyes over the local hero returned home could only marvel at his intolerance.

· For most, these were only small blemishes on a sterling character. With his calling-card moccasins and unruly white hair, he had entered into the folk culture of Flanders. Everywhere he went he faced the spotlight. He went on national TV, and declared prophetically, "I'm going there to die," but no one regarded it as more than an expression of his dedication. Churches and schools once more embraced him as a favoured son, and he basked in the public display of affection. Later he would feel a little sheepish about this adulation, but then, he realized that Flanders needed him for its own reasons.

On 15 July 1973, he accompanied his friend Omer Tanghe to a missionary rally at his church, and the old idealism shone through. Taking a small notebook from his pocket, he ripped a page from from it and with a flourish, said, "For you. Hot from the oven."[12]

The Missionary

Sometimes I wanted
To feel safe
And sheltered
Like the husky
Who presses his cold muzzle
Into the warm hollow
Of his master's hand.
But You have driven me on
Towards the fog banks
Over the lake
Towards the black horizon
Of the forests
To promise to blowing snowdrift
The miracle of life
To frozen winter branches
The trembling of leaves
To the advent of autumn
Announce the summer days.
Lord, in the hollow of Your hand,

> I would like to shelter now;
> But to bear fruit
> You have strewn me out again. . . .

Despite the universal accolades, his return saddened him. He came back looking for the solace of his mother's church and country, perhaps as a way to regain her comfort for a soul besotted with a vision that kept retreating. Instead, he felt disjointed in Flanders. Some of his closest friends had become wealthy. When they invited him over, it was with feigned delight, of a hospitality stilted and forced. After these sessions he would recall nostalgically that once upon a time, they had gathered around the kitchen table with a cup of coffee, laughing and joking. Now when they invited him, they had a formal dinner, served in the dining room with expensive wine and polite conversation. Roger remarked that Flanders had lost its soul. Perhaps he failed to see that he was no longer Steentje, but a kind of national treasure. For those who knew what was going on around him, they saw that he took his fellow Flemings back to a simpler time, to the roots of Flemish goodness. But he was more an oddity than anything.

Students listened in fascinated silence to his wondrous tales of dog-sleds and cold nights and Indians in the midst of the bush, but when it was all done, not one stepped forward to take the offer to stand in his place. Not even the youths of his own family would opt for his lifestyle. After an evening of confronting this passiveness, he would return home despondent, "If I lived here, I would never go to church," he muttered. But then, almost in contrition, he would add, "I would not leave the Church. We have a contract to make the Church better, because it is dangerous to go outside the Church. But the Church can be very wrong." He visited with old friends, and late into the night, another side of Vandersteene emerged, a man goaded on several sides. None would encounter that side of Steentje more poignantly than Willem Vermandere.

Willem Vermandere is a Flemish artist and folk singer of considerable fame, who has performed in various cities in Europe and Africa. He had first seen Vandersteene when Willem had been in the Oblate school and Roger came to talk to the students about Indian life. In 1964 he saw him again and heard fantastic tales about the Indians. Now Roger seemed more preoccupied, more serious, more withdrawn.

> The last time I saw him was in 1973, when he came to the concert hall where I was singing; he came to my home afterwards. He told me he believed what the Indians told him, that life's journey is just like a trip down a great river. We're all on the river in a small boat, while the currents swirl and twist. There is no need to worry if the boat turns side-

ways, or bobs about. The trip down the river is a journey to understanding. After every crisis, comes an important understanding. Hence there
were no accidents or crises, there were just occasions for understanding.
At the end of the river, you will have the understanding to enter the
great sea of the dead, the eternal ocean.[13]

When Vandersteene saw him in 1973 chaos abounded. The world was
just plain crazy. All the money, all the things. For what purpose? Were
the people happier? No! They were miserable. For him, the Cree represented an alternative, another way to live. He genuinely believed that
the simple lifestyle of the Cree should be adapted by others. Being in
touch with that great natural understanding was more important than
wealth.

For Willem, the change was profound. When Vandersteene started
out in Canada, he was just the man with the beard. But at the end, he
was the man of Manitou. Willem saw Vandersteene as a kind of parable of human life. Like everyman, with aging, Steentje gradually closed
the windows. With age, he possessed nothing, because, in his culture, it
was all passed to children or grandchildren, except that Steentje had
neither. Willem saw him replicating a famous case in Flanders of an
old man, whose wife had died, and because he had no children he
resigned himself to dying. He just set fire to his old house, dying in the
conflagration. Willem believed that Roger felt the Flemish need to
leave children. He had none. That increased his pessimism. He had to
believe that things had not been in vain. He had to exhaust his meaning in Canada. Willem believed that what he found in Canada was a
deeper form of mysticism.

Steentje was very conscious of the need for family unity, but in 1973
he realized that he was a failure in the task at maintaining that unity.
When he left the first time, he had made no attempt to keep in touch, to
make a difference with the family. He knew the family had lost its centre with the death of their mother, and had looked to him as the replacement. He ducked the issue. When he returned they still wanted
him. They fought over where he would stay, whom he would see. This
furlough he wanted to stay with Anaïs in the home where his father
had died, but some of the others were not happy about that and complained constantly to him.

Whatever his own wishes, he was the ideological centre of the family — each needed him for different reasons. He had to face their contentions and claims, some of them very strange. Johan related how,
during serious personal and health problems, Roger had counselled
him. As a way of drawing him away from his difficulties, Steentje had
tried to involve him in an international discussion on a topic they both

loved: plants. Steentje sent him over 150 pictures of flowers and plants taken in and around Trout Lake, and they had communicated regularly about cactii. On a previous visit, Johan had asked Roger for a piece of one of his cactii, and they both rejoiced at how well it was now doing. It was like a symbol of their mutual connection.

Before Vandersteene returned home in 1973, Johan had had a serious car accident; Steentje visited him often in his convalescence and they became very close. But with others, he was a complete failure. Eric, for example, could not reach him. Others too. They could rehearse their problems to him, but, somehow, he could not hear them. They seemed to slide by him. Eric said it quite flatly, "He just couldn't see your problems. When you had troubles, you couldn't go to Roger; he couldn't help you. He was a fanatic and couldn't understand the problems of ordinary people. He only wanted one thing ... to get away from Belgium to get on with dying with his Indians."

Roger to Eric: "When you look back 30 years from now, you will have something to remember, like the children. I will have nothing." It was a mixed message. On the one hand, he wanted them to put their problems in context: "Don't complain so much, at least you are going to leave with more than I am." On the other he was addressing a wisp of decay at his core — he left no one after him, either in the field or at home. None of his many nieces or nephews cared to give their lives to the Church.[14]

Either by design or by habit, he tried to convey the foreignness of his life. A concrete example was the baptism. He was to baptize the last child of his brothers and sisters, the daughter of Mietje and Pol Dewaegheneire. He insisted that they sit quietly in the garden where the baptism was to take place until the "spirit" was ready. They waited for over an hour before he started the ceremony, and then he dragged it on for another hour, almost as if he wanted to recreate Cree time for them in the middle of Kortrijk. Perhaps he was. This last child was very special to Roger. At a moment of depression he remarked to Mietje on the loneliness he suffered. The cruelty of his life was having no confidant, no one close to share the anguish and the joy. Commenting on the fact that people come to him with problems, he said, "Sometimes I feel like I'm a garbage can. The problem is I have nowhere to put mine." Mietje remarked that this was not the Roger of yesteryears. Here was a vulnerability always before kept under wraps.

Increasingly he turned to mystical themes. Wilfried, although not now a Catholic, spent hours with him, exploring what he believed. Steentje had come to the mature belief that God was present in the cosmos, that you could feel Him in the natural order of the universe. He stated quite firmly: "I found God in the first ten years of my mission in Alberta. Now that I am there, I will stay." Whenever he had to speak at church, they always asked him, "How many converts have you made?" He would never give them a figure. His friends and church members couldn't understand why he would waste his time going back without making converts. "Oh," said Roger, "there was a very big convert to God — me. There, I felt His breath. There I felt Him within me. When He came to me, then I could speak about Him."[15] Such "locational" encounters with God reflects a strong native religious centre, and testifies to a dramatic modification of his theological views. Nature has a role in the experiencing of God.

When he left Canada, he was filled with foreboding about where he would be when he came back. There was certainly no guarantee he would still be heading up the team for the Cree missions. He was not sure where he would like to go, Trout probably, but Maskwa needed more work on his Cree, and Trout was the best place for that. He talked it over with the Bishop, who promised him that no transfer would be made until he returned. Then, while he was away, he received a letter saying he was being transferred to Fox Lake. So much for promises.

A few nights before he left Flanders, he visited with Johan. The cactus had grown well and was incredibly large now, but there was something very eerie about it. They noticed that when Roger was ill, the flower drooped, and when he felt better the flower revived. Both were firmly convinced of some deep connection between the plant and Roger. They wondered at this, and had no explanation for it. "We talked quietly about death that day. I knew he was very sick. I told him, 'Roger, you will go back to your Indians and you will die there.' 'Yes,' he said, 'I know.' Just before he left, he said to me: 'Johan, before I die, I will give you a sign.'"[16]

When he returned from Flanders he had $5,000 from his family for another Toyota. He didn't know whether he would need it or not.

The New-Old Mission: You Can't Go Home

He was not happy about being transferred to the triple missions of Fox Lake, Jean D'Or and Garden River; they were strung out east of High Level, and were often difficult to get to. The Bishop had his reasons: Fr. Roué wanted to transfer, because he was quite ill. Fr. Lamothe had left the priesthood to marry. Fr. Tessier, who was 64, and priest at Grouard, died just before Fr. Fournier, aged 46, priest at Faust, passed away. With a paucity of staff, if you transfer one, you transfer them all.

Steentje was upset. He wrote to his friend, Omer: "We, who are already short of manpower, have only six priests left who speak Cree. One sometimes asks oneself what is God's purpose in all this, for it is certain He has a purpose. We are short of people and yet, He comes and takes away from the few we have got . . . perhaps before long we will have to review and revise our whole approach to the Mission."[17]

Despite the rationale, Vandersteene was hurt by the transfer. Perhaps he had hoped to continue his administrative work. Perhaps he thought his work as a resource person was worth more than that for which he was given credit. His letter to the Bishop agreeing to "take a stroll in Jean D'Or" only hid the disjunction he felt.

On 4 December 1973 Vandersteene resigned from the pastoral team, filled up his car with what he could take from Grouard, mourned quietly over his cactii that had missed his tender care and were now wilted or dead, and departed for the north. En route, he swung into Falher to see Fr. Bélanger, the Provincial, and to leave him his will: "I hereby leave to Mr. Harold Cardinal, Sherwood Park, Alta. my ceremonial pipe and sacred herbs. If it is still in my possession at death. This was my most precious gift from the Cree people. I want to return it to my people so that they may remember me. Signed this day, Nov. 3, 1973, Grouard, Alberta." The execution of the will he left in the loyal hands of his friend and colleague, Maskwa. He pointed the nose of the car towards High Level.

He was under no illusion about these missions. They sat in grievous social and cultural situations:

> The district here is not as beautiful as some of the other mission posts and the whole village is ugly and dirty . . . a sweeping together under pressure of the government without cohesion and without inspiration. Jean D'Or is even worse. Reserves. The ugliness slowly seems to be rubbing off on the Indians. . . . They are becoming sad sacks and some even ugly brutes.[18]

Despite the fact that these three villages had people from his beloved Little Red River, there was no rhyme or reason to the groupings. The people were out of touch with themselves. He did not like the change in the people. Nor did he like moving from one mission to another, in a constant shifting from one mass to another in a hectic rotation of travel. "You can't transplant an old tree too often," he noted to his Cree friends.

He met again people whom he had known 20 years ago in Little Red, and they weren't the same people. Their thinking was completely different. Some people had not at all developed as he had hoped. He spoke of a woman he had known in Little Red. She had changed so dramatically, he could not comprehend her. Now all she wanted was money. "You can't go home," he sighed to Maskwa.

Once again the Cree taught him a lesson: A white man must every-day earn anew his place in an aboriginal community. When he was young, he had the stamina to face that. Musing alone among people indifferent, he kept calling for that strength deep within. Some days he did not have it. Retreating to his house, he played Beethoven incessant-ly, even when the Cree visited. Sullenly "looking for a sort of inner unity, a continual deeper line in my life,"[19] he slowly nursed a few cac-tii along, collected samples of medicine plants, sought out diamond willows and added to his collection of rocks and fossils.

His return to Jean D'Or broke any romanticism he may have ever had. Death stalked the place. New Year's Eve. What does one do when there is not much to do? One visits. The rounds started early, with cups of tea and then cups of liquor. Moving from house to house, in a cele-bration to mark the end and the beginning. Someone was playing with a gun, it went off, and hit an eight-year-old girl in the abdomen. No nurses, no doctor, no police, no priest and over 100 km to get help in Fort Vermilion. The little girl reassured her family that she was only going to be with Kisemanitou. She recounted the priest's words: Kisemanitou was coming for each of us in our time. She was dead within two hours.

Steentje arrived the next morning from Fox Lake to help the little community cope with the agony. Many years before he had spoken critically of Cree wailing practices, of bands of mourners moving from one house to the next in a ritual wail after a burial. Inevitably they began drinking. He deflected them away from this practice by asking each to come forward at the funeral service and to touch her: "Take a good look at her, so you will remember what she looks like, because at the resurrection of the dead, you'll meet her again. Look really closely, because in heaven she's all grown up now. Ask her to pray for you and promise her you'll come to where she is, so you can be together." Then he had told them to go home and celebrate, because Kisemanitou had taken one of his children to himself, and she was really happy. The wailing and drinking had eased off. Once again he spoke reassuringly to the parents.

But even his closest adherents must have wondered at his comment in the funeral sermon: "What you heard in the night was not a rifle shot: it was the sound of the voice of Kisemanitou, calling our little sister home. She was ripe and she fell in the hands of Kisemanitou like a fruit that is ripe. She died with the faith of a wise old woman."[20]

The dream of a Cree Church germinated in smaller ways; pleased with the artistic talents of a number of the children in Jean D'Or, he sought to foster their creativity. He went to school to show how he created his images, and marvelled in the enthusiasm and vivacity of the young artists. Around the country, native art had become extremely popular: Norval Morriseau, Eddie Cobinese, Bill Reid, a half dozen others were incredibly successful. Inuit art from Baker Lake co-operatives and other Arctic centres was the toast of southern collectors. New aboriginal artists were breaking into the field every day, and he pointed the Cree children with pride to the impressive achievements of these native artists. The children responded warmly.

To celebrate this artistic trend, he and the sisters combined to present a plaque every year for the best artist in the school. The prize, called the Vandersteene Art Prize, was instituted in the spring of 1974 and first offered in November for the most outstanding artistic talent. Thereafter, the prize was awarded every year, with Vandersteene acting as adjudicator. Steentje revelled in the art.

Nor had his old idea of a spiritual sisterhood disappeared. Edie Scott was one of Madonna House's successes. Steentje had come upon Scott, a woman of Cree blood who had been taken into the house from tragic circumstances. Early in her life she had been married to a white man, who had beaten and later abandoned her. Penniless, deserted and heart-sick, she slipped into the slum subculture of Toronto. An attractive woman with characteristic black braids and high cheekbones, she had for years eked out an existence within the poverty of Canada's largest city. Finally members of Madonna House found her. She turned inward as a way of coping with the agony of her life, and resolved to give herself over to a life of spiritual meditation and prayer.

Vandersteene was convinced that from such witnesses by Cree people, a genuine Cree spirituality could gradually take shape. He encouraged Madonna House to send her to the Cree diocese of Northern Alberta, as one means to develop the spiritual depth of the Cree people. She was assigned to the Grouard Mission.

The move was not a success. The nuns and priests were not sympathetic to someone who had to be supported while contributing nothing to the social benefit of the community. She did not speak Cree, so she was not accepted by the Cree community. Nor had she any standing within the local Métis community. She felt isolated and rejected by those who should have appreciated the benefits of a Cree contemplative in their midst. She returned to the Madonna House, dejected and dispirited.

Vandersteene wrote to lessen her alienation and to encourage her:

Ours is the peace of Christ. Nobody can take this peace away from us, neither failure nor success. What is failure and what is success after the Easter feast? Because He was crucified, God has glorified Him. . . . His cross is His glory. Live and re-live this Paschal Mystery always in your life.[21]

But even Vandersteene accepted that something concrete would have to be done to integrate her into the community. He proposed that he write her a course in Cree language, so that she could properly communicate not only with her people, but with her own inner self:

I would like you to look at your study of the Cree language not so much as a way to chat with the Indians or to get to know certain things about them, but much rather as a way to enrich yourself through contact with the Cree culture, and in order to give everything that you posssess to each other, and to share with each other. The Cree language, better than any other language, can express what is going on in your heart, your soul and your body. I hope you will become enthusiastic about your language and your people, as I have become when I began to understand the Cree.[22]

He encouraged her to come back to the diocese, but instead of being left in Grouard, he suggested that she be brought closer to him so that he could supervise her meditations more effectively. Out of Peace River, not far from the pilgrimage centre of Eleske, where an annual pilgrimage to the Virgin Mary was held, they constructed a little house for her. She shifted from this accommodation to Garden River on occasion, until floods washed away her house, and they built something higher and closer to the Eleske shrine.

Vandersteene struggled with the Cree course, and by the early 1970s he had completed the main part of the correspondence course for Edie. He acknowledged that it took him a long time to do it because he had no desire to do linguistic work. What he did finish, however, constituted some 450 pages of dictionary and explanation. He never felt that he had completed the project. But it seemed formidable to Edie, who struggled with it for many years.

The stay in Jean D'Or brought him into close proximation with sisters who were his supporters for the Cree Church. Shifts had taken place among the sisters: Sister Gloria, a devotee of Vandersteene, and Sister Jean, did not want to teach any more in Trout Lake, and finally, Sister Gloria went to teach at Jean D'Or. At Trout Lake, the sisters had been replaced by four teachers for the Northland School division that had taken over the school.

Despite the group of positive sisters around, he sometimes showed an almost fanatical discipline. Every year, during summer, the sisters set up their tipi outdoors, to take advantage of the pleasant, cool life-style of that kind of dwelling, and, at the same time, to follow the lead of the little Cree flock. He objected vociferously to the sisters in Jean D'Or mowing down the tall grass in a nearby open spot because within it were wild rose brushes among the grasses. When they complained that the roses tore their legs within the tipi if they did not do so, he dismissed their reasoning: "But you plant flowers around your trailer and you don't cut them down. Why cut down the roses that have always grown where they are?"

Nor would he allow anyone to cut the lawn. He was biting in his criticism of the sisters for trying to make their home look "civilized and suburban" by cutting the grass. For his part, he would not tolerate anyone bringing a mower near his house. The grass grew wild. Nor did his influence stop at the borders of his mission. He only allowed the lawn to be cut in one place: in front of the grotto in Trout Lake. Eyebrows went up over that. Only the Virgin Mary should have the grass cut.

On 20 December 1974 he went to Garden River, where he was called out because one of his parishioners was drunk and beating up his wife; when he arrived the belligerent was in bed, the rifle set aside and the children safely stowed at a neighbour's. This was only the fourth or fifth time in 29 years that he had been called for a domestic conflict, he wrote in a letter to Flanders, and he marvelled at this fact. Indeed, he recounts that he has only been hit twice in such disputes.

A day later he had to leave to hold mass in Jean D'Or on the 23rd, and then on to midnight mass in Fox Lake on the 24th. Despite the terrible roads that sometimes left him skidding into the ditch, he liked being in the car: "This is usually where I make most of my poems, and I am chuck [*sic*] full of inspiration. That is where I can pray, it is peaceful and silent around me. So the battles are fought . . . quite often in the Toyota and in prayer, and in poems."[23]

At one point in 1974, when he spelled off Maskwa at Trout Lake, he had time to ponder his years as head of the missions, and he examined again his earlier contentions about the international nature of the team: Flemish, French and Canadian. He came to the conclusion that this diversity should be considered as a source of enrichment, a sign of the nature of the genuine Church, rather than a hindrance as he had once perceived it. Indeed, he began to argue that such diversity had been God's strategy of evangelism right from the beginning for the Church. Once he dispelled his incorrect division between those more capable

(Europeans) and the less (Canadians), a number of things fell into place: The incomprehensions sometimes encountered were far more due to the educational differences or diverse work experiences than anything else. He concluded that he had been wrong—nationality really did not influence the team that much. Vandersteene was mellowing. It was the first major sign of an attempt at reconciliation with those who took a different tack than he.

Moreover, he realized that he had broken a fundamental rule of leadership: you can go no faster than your flock. Fr. René Bélanger, the Oblate Provincial, sketched his shift: His fellow priests and missionaries were not just being difficult. They would be ready to move, but it would take time. He wanted to get them to think together about the problems of the missions and he wanted and needed to get everyone to change their attitudes to missions. These revisions were based on a holistic approach to evangelization, where everyone in the diocese had to be an evangelist. As a consequence, he decided that he could not go so fast in his own mind until everyone had caught up. The shift came because he was working more on his own attitude towards his confrères, rather than focussing on the ideals of his missiology. After 1974, he had more care and concern for them.

Still, reading his comments to his soulmate in Flanders, there was a strain in him that would not mellow. Gazing at the muddy, swollen porridge that the Peace River was in spring of 1975, he mused about politics in the Church:

> The current washes all the dirt before everyone's noses. There is a lot of backbiting and insufficient amount of reasoning from scriptures ... or prayer. But that is how people are, not too susceptibile for simplicity: Blessed are the poor in spirit and heart, for they shall see God! But most of them will not see God but only themselves. This is also true in the religious state. The pure of heart, that do not fabricate or work in politics, will never constitute a majority. But God continues to write straight on crooked lines.[24]

For years, Steentje had a special relationship with his young brother Jos, for whom he was godfather at his christening. For years, too, Jos wanted to come to Canada. As the stories multiplied about Vandersteene's almost legendary missions back in Flanders, Jos pressed him for an invitation. Earlier in the year, Trees and her husband had visited, apparently with the approval of Steentje, and Jos wrote to him early in November, reminding him that he had ties not grounded upon money but spirit and he wanted to see him. Vandersteene wrote back to delay his trip a little because of his workload. But the letter confirmed his fears: The message about his personal well-being carried back by his sister must have been bad. This realization seemed to have pushed him to listen more closely to the groans of his body.

So immediately after, he decided he had to go to a doctor. His complaint was general more than specific. He never really felt good. No matter how much Alka Seltzer he had, his stomach always seemed to be upset. Regardless of what he ate, he always had cramps, undistinguishing little nudges and pains in his intestines, pressure around his heart. Worse still, morning came too soon. A long car ride, a trip through a blizzard, left him exhausted for days, and once he got down, it took forever to get back up to speed. Colds came easily and left reluctantly. Many things he used to do without question, he simply could no longer do.

Until now, he had put this down to the ravages of age. But he knew this was false pretence. He was, after all, much younger than some priests and missionaries. But he no longer had the will to propel himself out of a chair to do some of the things he dearly loved doing, like walking by the river and looking for diamond willow, or searching the bush for new plants. Even now his current reading love, cheap novels, sat undisturbed by his chair.

Adopting the genial view of humouring his body like his old Toyota, he told his friends that he needed to go into the garage to have a complete checkup of a few parts. Judging by the times he had delivered the Toyota over to the mechanic, he said, he reckoned it was time to hit the human mechanic. But alone, without the cloak of humour, fear gnawed at him.

Evening of Fear

I am so tired
I only have to drop my head a little
to die.

However a strange
and yet familiar will
forces me to watch.

I only have to drop my head
to be dead
and to nod my head to live.

How thin is the membrane
between heaven and hell
tonight.[25]

Even so, he told everybody he was waiting to go to the garage until January.

Body Blow: Cancer

He didn't make it. Early in December, he went to see his old friend Bill Krynen. Dr. Krynen was Dutch, so they shared a common language. He was a generation younger, and educated in an entirely different environment. Krynen liked Vandersteene — a touch on the eccentric side, although he liked his native intelligence and lack of stuffiness. When Steentje came back from Krynen's office, with the opinion of both the doctor and his colleague to get to Edmonton as quickly as possible, he seemed to know the jig was up. "I'm in a hurry to leave," he joked with forced ease. Not Jean D'Or. Not Canada. Not the Church. Life.

On 3 January 1976, he wrote to Omer Tanghe:

> For your New Year, as well as for my Christmas present, this little note, like a child's pants ... short and dirty. Between two hospital sessions, I am writing a few letters ... and the news I am sending round is not too good. I have just come back from the Charles Camsell Hospital in Edmonton, where after more than 3 weeks of tests, they have discovered a cancerous tumour in the top of my left lung. They cannot cut it out. At first they wanted to let it shrivel up, and send me home around the 10th or the 15th of January, to await the inevitable. Then everybody at once began to pray for my recovery. I was totally shaken and cannot understand it even now.[26]

Over the next two months he wrestled with the spirits, with God, with his wounded pride, with his unfinished business. Jos wrote to him to say he was coming, whether he agreed to it or not. Steentje could only think of trying to keep up his spirits in front of his hero-worshipping brother. He asked him to please delay until after his treatments. It was in poetry that he poured out his soul, and it is in poetry that we really fathom his agony. He wrestles with God.[27]

As every man under the death sentence, Steentje twisted and turned. He pleaded for his friends in Brugge, his family and associates in Kortrijk to raid heaven with their prayers. His soulmate journeyed to Lourdes. Desperately he looked for a way out. A second chance.

> Yes there was one. Another doctor in Edmonton said he would take a second look, another evaluation. Early in March, he was buoyed, first by the tremendous outpouring of prayer support for him all around the diocese and abroad, and second by the results of the second evaluation. Still firmly committed to God, he raised his faith to acknowledge the uncharted river of His will: "I still am, but the old will to live asserted itself

again. I see clearly that one has to have tried everything (as Jesus did) before one is sure of God's will; and that one has to avoid the danger of seeing sloth, discouragement or letting oneself go, as surrender to God's will. So, as you see, the river is full of whirlpools, even up to the last turning. A little cross for you, my brother. Roger."[28]

He began radiation therapy. Dismissed from the Camsell on 12 February, he was sent home to rest until his return for further radiation on the 26th. The news was good. "The doctor and my present doctor believe in a possible cure." The bags of letters from around the country and abroad affirm that not only had cobalt been bombing, his friends had also been strafing heaven. In an Easter meditation he wrote: "It is the same in spring. When all the snow has gone, it still takes weeks before the first green shoots appear. And thus we live in parables all our lives." Bombs and shoots.

Spring. He returned to Trout Lake to visit his beloved garden, and commune with the new life bursting about the forest. He loves those little kids. Grabs them around their lithe arms and wrestles them down to the barely dry greening lawn. The cool sweet smell of rotting leaves left over from fall's demise, the heady chirp of baby birds, the orchestration of frogs, warmed him to life.

He prodded Maskwa to bestir himself and go with him to the forest. Disappointment:

My dunky brother does not want to accompany me and is rather fed up with it. The Word of Jesus frequently comes to mind: the spirit is willing (and sensitive) but the flesh is weak (and does not improve any). I sometimes try to imagine how sad it is for those who are doing nothing but aging slowly: a slow death. But even for ourselves it is the same, after all faith does not change the facts. The only thing is that we know that it is not winter that comes but a very real summer . . . And forever.[29]

The breath of death forced him to confront some of the strong stands he had taken; he warmed to some of his former parishioners in Trout Lake who had gone the Pentecostal way, and he eventually realized that he had no inside view on God's plans. Here he was dying, and he had no idea what God was doing with him. If the Holy Church could not be all things to all people, maybe there was a larger view of the Church. Reconcilitation began and, by the summer, he no longer resented the Pentecostals.

Mindful of how much he had despised head counts, he nevertheless tallied up the work for the 1974-76 period. They would have made his friends back home in Kortrijk happy: In Jean D'Or, he had 42 baptisms, 2 marriages and 4 funerals. In Fox Lake he had 124 baptisms, 8 marriages and 17 funerals. All this in addition to his conferences and visit-

ing assignments. Not bad for someone who found it difficult to moti-
vate himself out of a chair. He took down his old friend St. Augustine,
turned to his *Confessions*, and slowly began working his way through
their familiar pages.

But the greatest move was towards the medicine men. Joseph
Nanooch of Fox Lake, with whom he had had some estrangement, was
his first contact. He talked to the new Archbishop Legaré, who gave
him permission to consult with medicine men. Nanooch treated him
with a ground powder, described as elements from a meteorite. He
also sought out Paddle Prairie's Dick Alook.

Alook, who had a unique diagnostic process, saw Vandersteene in
the early spring of 1976. Alook realized the cancer was very bad. His
diagnosis was based upon signs that appear on the back of an individual's neck. These signs determine how many treatments the patient
will require. Level one required strict treatment, two was critical and
required complete bedrest. Three was life-threatening; according to
Alook, the illness was in his arteries, had affected the lungs and perhaps even his heart. On occasion, level three paralyzed the patient.
Four was beyond help. "When I saw Vandersteene," he said, "he was
at level three. It was a difficult case to deal with." Vandersteene, who
found it problematic to get to Paddle Prairie, never came to see him
again.

Wayne Harries, a medicine man from Wyoming came to Jean D'Or,
and Vandersteene consulted with him. He verified the diagnosis and
the treatments he had been using. Dan Supernault, medicine man from
Pouce Coupe, BC, happened to visit Fort Vermilion and he, too, had
treated Vandersteene for cancer with the same kind of powder. The
only significant difference was the frequency and water mix. Although
he saw him only once, Supernault felt the radioactive powder had
worked effectively with the other medicines he had received.

All three treated him for reaction to the radium treatment at the hospital and from the medicines they gave him. Joseph insisted that he
had to give up work: his comment was, "In my view he was cured of
his cancer. That's not what killed him. But a sick person like him
should keep quiet for quite a while, perhaps even for a few years, and
not run around like he was a young man of thirty. He didn't give his
medicines a chance. He didn't seem to realize what he was doing."

July 1975. His brother Jos was coming, along with a friend. While he
waited, he captured the radium therapy in his own personal net:

Struggle

A new doctor smiles
Advises radium —

Heaven is stormed
Drum fire
To whoever knocks
Door will be opened
Even at depth of night

Barrage of twenty days
Beats back malady
The doctor smiles.
No longer are you
Moribund.

I celebrate —
I thank
Says Father Provincial.

12 July 1976

He didn't believe it. On the way home, he dropped a photo off at Fr. Provincial — for his obituary. Left alone by the vacationing sisters, he abandoned the tipi, drove to Fox Lake and escaped to the basement of his house. He wrote to the Flemish soulmate:

Yesterday was the Flemish national holiday and, of course, I did not forget. It was also the 33rd anniversary of my initiation into the priesthood . . . my how time flies! I have celebrated these two great events alone and with a great deal of sweat (I walked around alone in Jean D'Or and I walked from here to the airport) and I spent it in the coolness of the basement of the mission house at Fox Lake by celebrating a mass by myself, with a half glass of Missal wine and a cigar (and a number of pipes) and many, many memories.[30]

Afterwards he slipped over to chat with Johnsen Sewepagaham, son of the grand old man Jean-Baptiste, who had meant so much to him. He seemed resigned. He said: "I have had a long life and I'm satisfied. I notice my friends from school are passing away. I won't be around too much longer."

At the end of the week, he left to go to the pilgrimage at Eleske. All the missionaries would be there. Edie Scott. Archbishop Legaré. Fr. Provincial. Jimmy Blessie. The Blessed Mother.

In a moment of prayer, bewildered by his apparent lack of progress under the best doctors and best medicine men in the West, and ravaged by another severe cold, he beseeched his Oblate founder Eugène de Mazenod to bring his case to God:

> You wept.
> Because you had no more sons to send,
> So now you send me
> Ever ready to serve.
> I speak their language, as they say,
> To the heart of the people.
> Alas, this sickness binds me.
> I leave the job unfinished
> No one comes to relieve me.
> In the name of the Churches of the Cree,
> In Jesus' name,
> Say but a word of mediation.
> Father, did you hear from Father Eugène?[31]

Bizarre Denouement

Steentje wrote to Jos to come ahead. They were to proceed immediately from Edmonton to Trout Lake, so Jos could take pictures of the place that was hailed abroad as idyllic. Then north to Eleske for the pilgrimage, then on to the three northern missions. Better than two thousand km, and then back south. He wrote a brief note to his soulmate: All the visitors so far had gone well and by August they would all be gone. He seemed to breathe a sigh of relief.

When he arrived in Edmonton International Airport on 20 July, Jos wanted to call his wife to let her know that he had arrived. Vandersteene objected, it was too expensive, it was too difficult to get Belgium, you had to collect a lot of coins. Finally Steentje agreed to ask somebody how to find out how much it cost to call Belgium, and they referred him to the long-distance operator, who informed him that the price was $9.10. Then they went around to everyone trying to get coins for the phone call. He finally had to acknowledge that he never called Belgium.

Jos was mystified by this. Steentje had talked of how difficult it was to call from his missions, especially from Trout Lake during the days of the radio phone. But everywhere else there seemed to be no difficulty in calling anywhere in the world. Later Jos ruminated on this: "It was almost as if he did not want people to know how easy it was to contact him; it was almost as if he wanted to isolate himself." Finally Rogier made the phone call, saying, "Fine. *I* will call the most beautiful flower in Belgium!"

That done, Jos suggested they have a beer before they set out. Vandersteene said that was impossible: "Oh, no! You can't do that here! You can't drink beer at the airport." Jos didn't believe him, for right in front of them was a bar, wide open with customers drinking.

Almost immediately he wished he hadn't insisted. Steentje had five bottles of Heineken beer, and was feeling extremely relaxed when they finally hit the road. Jos was frantic with his driving: "Take care! I've got four children and a wife!" But Vandersteene was in heaven. He turned on his tape of Beethoven and wept and wept as they caromed along. His unwilling passenger rejoiced privately when they reached the highway north of St. Albert. At least they had less of a chance of hitting someone. To this day Jos does not know why Vandersteene did what he did next. Jos's itinerary had been set before he left Flanders. Vandersteene had written to him about that. First to Trout Lake to take photos of the mission, then north to the pilgrimage at Eleske and then on to Fox Lake. When he arrived, Vandersteene abruptly announced that all plans were changed. He indicated that they must leave immediately for the north. Jos knew that a pilgrimage was coming up at Eleske, but it would not yet be started. There was no explanation. Along the way, Vandersteene insisted that he buy lots of film, especially 8mm film for his camera, only to discover that the heat had affected the camera, and it would not work. Jos suggested they not worry about the camera, but get it fixed in High Level. Once again, Vandersteene refused. By this time they were in Peace River, and Steentje insisted that they turn right around and drive back to Edmonton to get it fixed. Another long day's drive. After spending two extra days, they started north. They spent an eventful but ordinary few days driving between Eleske, Fox Lake, Jean D'Or and Garden River.

Jimmy Blessie recounted how Vandersteene made a point of talking about the missions, and how he couldn't be a priest anymore. This was regarded as peculiar by everyone around, but then they did not always know what Vandersteene was talking about. "You are the oldest one of all the old guys," he said. Jimmy could not see the relevance of his comments.

While at Jean D'Or, he felt very much weaker, and the cough he developed from the cold rainy weather at Eleske had gone deeper into his chest. Krynen did not like what he saw. He told Vandersteene to return as quickly as possible to the hospital in Edmonton, preferably immediately by air. Vandersteene pleaded that his brother was doing all the driving and that he would have nothing to do but sit. The doctor relented, but told him not to turn off and go to Trout Lake — he was to go directly to the hospital.

The next three days were bizarre. Instructions to Jos were precise: he must be ready to leave at eight in the morning, yet Steentje only got around to leaving at 11, "Indian time," he said. They arrived in High Level about 4 p.m. and went to the rectory. "Have you eaten"? asked the father. "Oh, yes," lied Steentje. The father served some coffee and cookies, and that had been the first they had eaten since breakfast. "Because," he told Jos, "Four o'clock is too early to eat, we have to get to Falher." At Falher, the Father asked "Would you like to eat"? "Oh no," said Vandersteene, "It's too late!" It was seven o'clock.

The next morning they left with only coffee to go to MacLennan to the Archbishop's house. He was not there, so they pressed on to Grouard. The Father was not home.

"Roger, this is too much! I have to eat. I have driven over 2000k without food. You said once that you have to eat in Canada when you can because you never know what will happen. Let's go to a restaurant. I will pay. Just let's get something to eat!"

"No! We will eat in Slave Lake!"

They arrived in Slave Lake. Fr. Alain Gendre was out. Vandersteene relented, but just. They went to a restaurant and Steentje gave him two minutes to eat. Two minutes. He himself did not eat. When they returned to find the Father still absent, Jos insisted, since the door was open, that they go in and wait for him. "After all, we're not thieves, Roger!" Vandersteene was livid with anger.

Jos, upset by Steentje's attitude, and blindingly tired, went out, crawled in the car and lapsed into a dead sleep. Several hours later, he awoke to Roger shaking him.

"Hurry, you're going to take the plane to Trout Lake."

"But I don't want to go to Trout Lake, I want to stay with you!" Jos retorted.

"You did not come here to do what you want. I will tell you what to do and you will do it or you will never see Trout Lake!" Eyes flaming, face flushed and violet, Steentje seemed out of his head. Jos was beside himself. Hoping that the priest could help Vandersteene calm down, he went to search out Fr. Gendre. Despite the pleas of Fr. Gendre, Steentje remainded adamant. He prepared to leave.

"I returned to his room and opened the door just before I got in the car. I will never forget his eyes. They were cold and very hard. I turned and left for Trout Lake. That's the last I saw him alive."[32]

Manitou's Shot

All the missionaries knew of his condition; they knew he had chronic bronchitis, made more difficult by an asthmatic condition and smoking. But they all believed that he was in remission from the cancer. He seemed to be coping with it all quite well. Gendre and Vandersteene talked until midnight, when he went to bed. As usual, coughing racked his body. But then he started gasping, clutching his chest, trying to get his breath. Between gasps, he told Gendre that sometimes his asthma took his breath away, until finally he had to lapse into a kind of unconsciousness. Then the regular patterns of his breathing took over. But he didn't seem to be coming out of this coughing fit. When Fr. Gendre went in, he was on his knees by the foot of the bed, gasping for breath.

Johan picks up the story:

> The night he died, I saw everything. I saw him in that little room in Slave Lake. There was another man there, but it was a priest. I knew it was not Jos. He looked at me and said, "Please help me. I am dying."
> Then the gasping stopped. He slumped.

Quietly Johan recalls the moment: "I knew Roger was dead before we received the news. The flower split wide open on the cactus plant. I knew he was gone."[33]

Fr. Gendre struggled to place him on the bed, then rushed to call the ambulance. There was no stir. When they wheeled him away, everybody knew he was dead. Manitou's shot had been quick and accurate.

The Conflicts of Death

Then began the great debate: What had killed Rogier Vandersteene? He would have found it all very silly. It was his time. God called him. But there are others who think that God's timing is not always so easily detected. How far will we follow the threads?

Maskwa and the medicine men are quite convinced that he did not die from cancer, but from a heart attack brought on by overexertion. He was a very ill man, who should have been sent to recuperate in completely relaxing circumstances, according to his physician. A man hounded by his family responsibilities, but who had no idea how to relate to them as family, as symbolized by the disaster of Jos's trip. An immigrant who measured Canada by the Flanders of his youth, was alienated from both and threw himself at God as a means of escape. A visionary whose life was so inextricably bound to the Cree and the Church that he spent himself trying to reconcile them. A medicine man who knew when the spirits were calling him, and who hiked down life's path so forcefully that he walked right through onto the spirit side. These "reasons" for death are not neutral; even if medically he died from a heart attack, that will not constitute the reason. The complex of attitudes and affirmations that surrounded Vandersteene in life, surround him in death. Steentje died as much by the way he handled his life as the way he handled his cancer.

Maskwa, who was driving through the area the day after his death, learned from René Bélanger that he was executor of the will, and that he had *not* received Vandersteene's calumet. It hit him hard.[34] Nevertheless, he turned to the tasks that had to be done. He tallied Steentje's personal wealth: two wallets, one with $25 and two credit cards. In the other he had a $10 bill with a note attached: "An apple for thirst" — that is, hedge against being caught without money. The little man with the big heart had $1,185.45 in his chequing account, plus a cheque among his personal effects for $600 from his sister Anaïs. And a rapidly aging Toyota. Not much for a man whose impact was felt on two continents.

As in life, so in death. Maskwa and Jos dropped in on the Cardinals, then quickly moved to the Archbishop's at MacLennan. The Church swung its ritual apparatus into place. The main funeral service would be held in Girouxville, with internment in the great Oblate cemetery. But the preliminary service would be in Grouard, where the Cree would participate. But how? And who?

No church ritual would define the final moment of a great leader and chief like Vandersteene. Jos returned from Trout Lake immediately, took Steentje's car, and he and Maskwa drove to Frank Cardinal's place in Sucker Creek. Then they moved on to Falher, to read the will. Maskwa telephoned Harold, and told him about the gift of the calumet. He asked if Harold would come to Grouard to accept the pipe. Harold agreed. The tone of the Grouard service was set: it would be the Cree service.

The Cree affirmed that they would give Vandersteene a chief's burial. Following embalming, he would be brought to Grouard, where three days and two nights would be spent in a full Cree wake, with attendants and drumming and plenty of time for the spirit world to welcome a new chief on the path of the other world. There would be time for the women to make him a new pair of specially sewn moccasins for his trip on the long road to the Ancestors' house, as well as a stole of moosehide beautifully decorated with beadwork.

The leaders of the Indians were Frank Cardinal, Harold Cardinal, Peter Ochiese, Donald Cardinal and Martha Champion. Peter Ochiese, traditional medicine man and chief, wanted Cree ceremonial prominent in the service. He would only enter the Church when they showed him Vandersteene's medicine pipe and bag, and he insisted on seeing Vandersteene's pipe before it was given to Harold. For his part, Ochiese affirmed that his participation would only be among the chiefs.

Accompanied by Cree headdress, official Cree clothing, drumming and Cree singing chosen for its honouring qualities, the Indian service was conducted in Cree, with Fr. Roué and Maskwa heading the Church's contingent. Archbishop Legaré gave a short eulogy. But it was the transfer of the medicine pipe and bag that was the highlight of the service. Presented by Maskwa to Harold Cardinal,[35] it was a moving moment for the Cree. Harold reflected on the gift:

> For our people, there is no gift more valuable than the pipe Father left us. For you to perhaps understand the importance of our pipe, it would be like taking the host and chalice away from you and leaving you without a way of speaking to your Creator. For our people, the pipe serves as our way of talking to our creator. Our elders believe that your way, your truth, your knowledge is valid. But so is ours. Our people believe that someday in the future, if we all try to do the will of our Father, our people will understand each other's prayers more clearly. I want to say thank you to my brother, who left us this pipe, who left us these gifts. I am sure he is with our Father where he will make good intercession on our behalf. We are still our Father's children and we want to continue to be our Father's children. We are coming to our Father's house from our brother's house so that we can discover the meaning of our sorrows, and discover the meaning of our land. We ask our brother to bring this message to our father on our behalf. We ask our brother to ask our Father to bless all people today, throughout this land.[36]

Later on the CBC, Canada's national television, Harold underlined the personal appreciation of Vandersteene: "This was the only white man that I am able to call my brother, yet no one knows him. He is a priest called Vandersteene."

The next day, 11 August, at 10:30 a.m., a second Eucharistic celebration took place in the Church of Our Lourdes in Girouxville, celebrated by Archbishop Henri Legaré together with 30 priests. There, too, was the Oblates' cemetery. Jimmy Blessie, one of the "elders" from Garden River, spoke on behalf of the Cree people. At the end of mass, Maskwa and Jos Vandersteene sang together a Flemish hymn to the Virgin Mary, "Love Gave You a Thousand Names."

There were 14 fellow missionaries present, plus the Provincial of the Oblates, Fr. René Bélanger, and Archbishop Legaré of the Vicariate of Grouard-MacLennan. The eulogy, read by Archbishop Legaré, stressed Vandersteene's prophetic character and his vision of the Cree Church. Amid the solemn pomp of the cathedral, the Church bade adieu to one of its celebrated sons, and then laid him beneath the welcoming soil of Alberta's great north.

Half the world away, in the village of Marke, Belgium, they were remembering too. From the Flemish eulogy by Omer Tanghe:

> And in the role of the great Oblate pioneers of the high north, your name will have a great place. You wrote to us "What I will do upstairs, in the silence over there? I won't do a thing. I will not sing. His arms are strong and pure. I will only be happy over there." Occasionally, from the happy hunting ground, think of us, watch over us.[37]

Aftermath

The hole left by Vandersteene's death was beyond measure from the Church's perspective. An excellent Cree-speaker, he had carried the Cree Church on his shoulders for so long that, with his death, the whole structure seemed about ready to collapse. Most critical were the issues of servicing the three northern communities. There was only one individual with the youth and stamina able to handle the travel in serving all these posts, Vandersteene's understudy, Maskwa. Bélanger met with Fr. Paul, and they worked out a schedule of flights into and out of the northern communities, so he could provide services at least twice a month at each of the missions. It would be a peripatetic ministry, but until the Church had a deacon program functioning (which would shift responsibility of mass to selected elders) it would have to do.

Maskwa, as executor, had to turn his attention to the many artifacts of Steentje's life: cactii and fossils, books and studies, sermons and poems, medicines and diamond willows, paintings and mail. He turned first to the mail, 70 letters from people around the globe and across Canada, well-wishers, petitioners, government agencies, Church officials. That was the easy part. Then he had to deal with Vandersteene's oeuvre.

He had no idea what to do with the various medicines which Vandersteene had in his possession. In Fox Lake Steentje was compiling information on dandelions, strawberry roots, and other native medicines and their uses and purposes. Various medicine men would come to his house, asking if Vandersteene had herbs or roots. Steentje, of course, had never discussed his medicines with Fr. Paul. Maskwa recalls one such occurrence.

> The medicine man from Wabasca, Sylvester Auger, he came to Trout Lake and dropped by my house. He said that he required some heart medicine for a lady, but he had forgotten to bring the root.

"Wait a minute grandfather, maybe I can help you. Fr. Vandersteene
left this root."
"That's just what I need. Can I have some of it?"
"Sure, take it."
"Oh no, I won't take it all, just what I need."

Also, in the grotto, there were several medicinal plants, and the
medicine man asked permission to cut some because he needed them
for healing purposes. Taking the medicine required special prayers and
offerings, so he thanked Kisemanitou for the gift of so rare a plant.
Placing tobacco at the root, he thanked Kisemanitou for Fr. Vandersteene, who had found it somewhere and put it right in the garden for
when it was needed. He put the tobacco by the plant and prayed
toward the roots. He thanked God for Fr. Vandersteene bringing the
plant to that place. Then he gave the long prayer of thanks which
opens the Catholic service.[38]

Then there were all those who wanted mementoes of Steentje: Jos,
who wanted everything he could get his hands on of Rogier's for a proposed display-museum in Flanders, colleagues who wanted paintings,
books or fossils, family who wanted souvenirs, the Oblate archive for
his papers and letters. Everyone seemed to want something permanent
to keep Vandersteene around. But of all the artifacts, the poems were
the most difficult, and, as we have indicated, the most contentious.

There was another legacy. The Trout Lake church. There it sat,
unfinished. Maskwa was taunted by it every time he saw it. But he had
no idea what had to be done with it. Maskwa had a bone to pick with
Steentje — What did he want done with the church?

The Cree conception of the other world features a parallel world to
this, much grander and more extensive, but still intimately related to
this one. Maskwa knew that at special times and in special ways you
could talk to people on the other side. He also knew that nobody really
died in traditional Cree culture, they just walked through to the other
side, where they roamed about as if protected by a one-way glass.

The key to communication with the people on the other side is the
mind; through the mind, one can fix an individual who has passed into
the other side into an image, and this image becomes the connector
with the spirit. Memory is a central feature of this process. Vandersteene himself had taught Maskwa about communication with the
other side. For example he had affirmed that speaking with one's spirit
person always has to be in the language of one's grandmother. Hence
communication Cree-style, with Vandersteene required speaking
Flemish for Maskwa.

So a few days after he died, I was thinking about him and the Church. I was in Trout Lake on a Sunday night. I told Vandersteene that if he wanted me to finish the Church in Trout Lake, he would have to tell me what was wrong with it. Monday morning I went to Fox Lake; it was the first time I had been in Fox Lake since his death. On my desk was a paper describing the smoking of the ceremonial pipe. The elders all sit with their backs to the north. That was it! The *direction* was the mistake. Vandersteene had not paid enough attention to the *wikokewin* tent. The spirits always entered from the south. He had placed the door to the north. The window would have to be taken out and changed to the other end of the building. The door would have to be on the south end. Once I knew the problem, I talked to Peter Ochiese and Henry Paul, and they confirmed the mistake.[39]

At least now he knew what had to be done.

The next day he went to Garden River. From the time Vandersteene had died, Jimmy Blessie had been haunted by Vandersteene's cryptic sayings. He rolled them over and over in his mind. Then he saw what Vandersteene was talking about. Steentje was asking Jimmy to help in the Church, to take over from him. The next day, Fr. Paul asked him to relate the story.

Maskwa was firm about what happened next: "When I asked the congregation to pray for Fr. Vandersteene, and that Jimmy would be blessed here, both Jimmy and I received a message from Fr. Vandersteene. Jimmy has been more the leader of the congregation since."[40] Like the information about a spirit helper, however, this message was not made public.

One thing had yet to be done. Vandersteene had to be welcomed into the family of the Ancestors, and there was only one way to do that — a *wikokewin*. The largest *wikokewin* was held in Sucker Creek on 2 October 1976 by Frank and Harold Cardinal. It had six fires and over 200 people. Henry Paul from the Alexander reserve and Peter Ochiese from the Ochiese reserve were the chief elders. Peter's son sang for the first time in honour of Vandersteene, and he smoked the pipe three times. He told Vandersteene, present in the doll-effigy that "Even though I don't know you, I am thankful to you because on this occasion. It is the first time I am able to sing." This was followed by two smaller *wikokewin*; Fox Lake held the ceremony under Joseph Nanooch. There was another one given by Pierre Laboucan. Medicine man, elder and chief, Vandersteene was now duly in place on the other side.

Other kinds of establishments blossomed with recognitions: Despite their differences, the government of Alberta, in recognition of Vandersteene's impact on the peoples of northern Alberta, officially renamed the former Island Lake as Vandersteene Lake, while the city of Kortrijk,

Belgium named a street after him. What would have pleased him most of all, his friend Willem penned a ballad in his honour. It became the folk song of the year in 1976.

In the skein of life, there is sometimes the madness to pull at a protruding thread; seven years earlier he had complained "my heart . . . a little pain now and then. . . ." Just what kind of pain had that been?

Notes

1 Vandersteene speculated in his conversations about the origins of the Cree. He attached some significance to the black spot which he said was found on the buttocks of a newborn Cree child. He believed this meant that they had some connection with the Mongolian people. He may have been aware of Fr. Petito, who was an Oblate among the Inuit before he returned to France at age 33. He had learned several languages, written several books. He thought Inuit and Jews were related because they both practised circumcision. Fr. Mariman suggested he was influenced early on by a little monograph entitled "Are They Israelites?" perhaps a British-Israel tract.
2 The point is that the bullet had hit the animal, but bad medicine prevented it from killing the prey.
3 It is in manuscript form among his papers in Girouxville.
4 Tanghe, *Leven*, p. 96.
5 Ibid., p. 90.
6 Fr. V. Baratto, personal interview, 27 June 1979.
7 Vandersteene, *Wanneer gij*, p. 54.
8 *Love Game II*, quoted above, pp. 201-202, in Tanghe, *Leven*, p. 35.
9 See R.J. Carney, D. Evasiuk and W.H. Swift, *Report of the Northland School Division Study Group* (Edmonton, 1975), p. 33.
10 Mission notes, from letter to fellow missionaries, 20 May 1970.
11 Vandersteene, *Wanneer gij*, p. 55.
12 Tanghe, *Leven*, p. 109.
13 Willem Vermandere, personal interview, 11 July 1987.
14 Eric Vandersteene, personal interview, 10 July 1987.
15 Pol Dewaegheneire, personal interview, 10 July 1987.
16 This story could not be verified, and was received by some of the members of the family with scepticism.
17 Tanghe, *Leven*, p. 25.
18 Vandersteene, *Wanneer gij*, p. 83.
19 Ibid.
20 Vandersteene, sermon for funeral, 1974.
21 Vandersteene, *Wanneer gij*, pp. 96-97.
22 Ibid., p. 96.
23 Ibid., p. 88.
24 Ibid., p. 91.
25 Ibid., p. 101.
26 Tanghe, *Leven*, p. 22.
27 See, for example, his *Cancer* poem, above, pp. 211-13 (Vandersteene, *Levensvervulling*, pp. 75-77).
28 Tanghe, *Leven*, p. 22.
29 Vandersteene, *Wanneer gij*, p. 97.
30 Ibid., p. 93.
31 Tanghe, *Leven*, pp. 116-17.
32 Jos Vandersteene, personal interview, 11 July 1987.

33 Johan Vandersteene, personal interview, 10 July 1987.
34 Maskwa had hoped beyond all hope that Vandersteene would pass the calumet to him as his "heir apparent"; he knew nothing of the pipe going to Harold until he talked to Bélanger before the Cree service. He later learned that Frank had had a dream about Harold which he had shared with Vandersteene, which evidently pointed to Harold as a gifted Cree spiritual practitioner. I think this dream sealed the fate of the pipe.
35 Lamothe said one could view the gift of the calumet to Harold in two ways: a mistake or a wish. If Vandersteene saw Harold as a hope for a Cree Church, that was surely mistaken, for when Steentje returned from abroad, Harold was already beyond the Church. If it was a recognition of a hope that Harold had the talents, capacity, ability to be a strong leader, and the pipe was to impress him to continue, then it is a wish. A wish for the Cree people. Maskwa thought it was both a recognition of the Cree people and an expression of appreciation to Harold. The family of the original owner had their own views, primarily that it should have returned to the family.
36 Tapes from funeral service at Grouard, 10 August 1976.
37 Eulogy text courtesy of Omer Tanghe.
38 Maskwa asked what the plant was for, but the medicine man deferred until he had been given a gift of tobacco. The plant was muskrat root, which, if chewed, had a terrible taste, but would treat a sore throat and laryngitis. By the next day, the voice would be restored (Fr. Hernou, personal interview, 24 August 1978). Maskwa contends that Vandersteene knew what the problem was with the church, but that he did not think the direction would be of such importance, given the layout of the land (ibid.).
39 Ibid.
40 Fr. Hernou, personal interview, 26 August 1978.

Nine

Beyond the Dissonance: Legacy of a Quest

> You who are everywhere,
> And always,
> And in all
> Where are You now?
> — R. Vandersteene, *Call to God*

Does a career in a religious organization indicate religiosity? Does convention and tradition entirely constitute religious experience? We cannot, I think, encounter Rogier Vandersteene's life without seriously reconsidering the way we conceptualize religion. Perhaps Steentje reflects a new feature in religion today: patterns of religiosity lie as much without the tradition as within. Yet it is also probably true that Vandersteene would have not engaged "the without" had it not been for "the within."

Still, a life is never consciously lived in such bifurcation. Nor was Vandersteene's. We have to try to see the patterns that undergirded his activity and probe the themes that retained their power throughout his too-short existence. Thus, this chapter will deal primarily with the patterns that provide some measure of intregation to his life. When that is complete, we can then come to some tentative conclusions concerning his legacy.

Integrative Patterns in Vandersteene's Life and Career

For the Vandersteene persona, the patterns merge and diverge in response to various crises and possibilities in his life; overall they function in the same manner as the primary colours of our Cree metaphor of Chapter Two. These colours change and metamorphose under the trauma of shifting events, yet their contribution to the whole is unmistakeable. The primary patterns are five: the quest, the calling, the

---

Notes to this chapter are on pp. 289-91.

"apocalyptic" God, living death and the "other." All of these can be understood as interactive in that they reflect several levels of meaning: in some the personal dominates, in others the national, or the social. Yet they all co-exist in this fascinating life. It is to their analysis that we turn now.

The Quest and Its Perception

Vandersteene, right from early age, seemed to be searching for a reality beyond that laid out in his humble origins. His giving of himself to the priesthood, his move to the Oblates, his missionary idealism, and his almost fanatical commitment to the Cree missions indicate an individual dedicated to a vision not clearly defined but profound in meaning. This quest moved him beyond the standards Canadian missionaries usually applied to their commitments, into a personal rapprochement with the spirit world of Cree tradition. The catholicity he pursued was a religion that united Cree tradition and Catholicism at a level beyond that proposed by earlier missionaries, and constituted a dramatic revision of current Catholic ritual. The quest led him into new forms of religious expression identified here as interstitial, that is, constructed on continuing Catholic principles but incorporating essentially new interpretive dimensions from Cree in such a manner as to constitute a new reality.

The pursuit of this reality forced him to encounter religion in quite different forms. Early in my study of Vandersteene I searched among his writings for the mandatory theological style so associated with the intellectual tradition in Catholicism. I did not find it. There were no long letters of theological speculation. There were no complex analyses of Catholic doctrine or Church dogma. There were, indeed, few discussions of contemporary theological writers. Exegesis, homily, exhortation, yes. But disquisitions associated with theology, no. Given the environment of his training, I found this to be unusual. For some, this may seem unbelievable.

That is not to say that Vandersteene had not thought through some of the Church's primary problems, as we have seen. He seemed very much aware of Church regulations and their theoretical basis. He knew, for example, the limits to which he could go in modifying the mass in pre-Vatican II days. He knew very well the Church's reasons for these limits. He could rehearse with his colleagues the latest theological ideas, and he often did. *But he never seems to have held that the solution to the Church's problems was a revised theology of the conventional sort.* He was not an advocate for a radical liberation theology for the Cree.

Rather, he took a much more pragmatic view of the issues involved. To put it another way, the sights and the sounds of the mission field were determinative for his "theology," not the other way around. Consequently, there is something very situation-oriented about his approach.

Vandersteene thought that religion was carried first and foremost among the Cree by an immediacy quite distinctive from Euro-Catholicism. What was needed was a vehicle to communicate with this immediacy. He began, then, to look around him and probe what Cree life valued. He saw the significance of people, each other, relatives, old folk, family. They spent hours talking, communing, interacting. They knew instinctively from the glint of an eye or the tilt of the head whether all was well or not. The incredible depth of meaning resident in the ordinary discourse of the Cree underlined that everyday life, with its small triumphs and sorrows, was where people found reality.

He was saying something very significant when, on Belgian national television, he reported that he had been the only convert during his first years in Canada. In effect, he learned to "see" and to "hear" in a different manner. His paintings show that he "saw" the Cree, not as noble but vanquished "Indians" of European construction, but as humorous, pleasant, salt-of-the-earth inhabitants of a world of their own, with a value system that was simple, practical, restrained, joyous.

He lived so long among the Cree that he realized that there was a *quality* in ordinary life that quite escaped the European. He concluded that the only way of speaking that language was to adapt European modes unsung by the theologians: painting, poetry and music. Here was a language that spoke volumes just by non-verbal expression, in an intuitive manner consonant with the way Cree experienced life. A gentle breeze set the willow leaves waving, making the whole environment alive and vigorous; a visit from a friend, with scarcely a word spoken, when life had dealt a cruel blow. It gave a quality of caring to existence. These he tried to recreate in his canvases, in his poetry and in his liturgical modifications. Thus, the only way he knew to respond to Cree reality was to translate it into artistic discourse.

He learned to "hear" differently. No anthropologist spent long complex days among the Cree trying to reconstruct the nuances of the drum. But Vandersteene sensed its immediate importance. The muffled, incessant cadence drew no complex studies by enthusiastic ethnomusicologists, but Vandersteene understood that it shaped the sonal world, not just of the tiny village during powwows, but of the rhythms of the spirit world. While it may not appear profound, *the same drumbeat measures the steps of the spirit world as marks off the movements of humans*. Nothing else can be said to have the same importance, from the perspectives of spirit vision to the abilities of the ancestral dancers. How could he translate this highly textured "language" to Euro-Canadian Catholicism?

Of course, Vandersteene only slowly altered his consciousness. He did not move from European patterns of thought and awareness to Cree overnight. Yet by the time he moved to Trout Lake, he surely had moved beyond conventional communications. His near-death on the trail when his mother's voice brought him back shows that his antennae had been altered. Like the Cree, he heard spirit voices, comprehended the meaning of "luck" and looked carefully at how his inner self was shaped as much by a chance meeting or a storm as by ideas. His poetry indicates that he had undergone a transformation that comes from "experiencing" like an old Cree.

He was virtually forced into the artistic environment, since nothing, save rituals, seemed to have equivalent meanings across the two cultures. He had only one alternative: to live his life within an artist's framework, to comprehend his own life through the intuitions of hue and tone. Once he did that, the world of the Cree swung into place in his mental makeup. It became foundational for a reinterpretation of the meaning of life, not only for himself as priest among the Cree, but as a human being entranced by the life of another. When he did so, he realized that such a viewpoint set up and fed into the possibility of his leadership as both Catholic priest and Cree chief.

The Calling: Dynamics of Leadership

There can be no doubt that Vandersteene, from the time of his early youth, knew his capabilities of leadership. There never seemed to be a moment when he did not know and respect his burden of leading people. This was evident from his mother's knee.

He had, however, no way of knowing just what the leadership would entail. He did not see it in the eyes of his father. Nor could he discover it in the local priests of the parish. It appears that he found it in the great heroes of Flemish tradition, in their poetry, valours and tragedies, that is, in the imaginative world created around legendary figures.

By rooting his leadership models in the creative imagination of the past, Vandersteene opened himslf to a leadership role that could break with traditional norms; without that potential, he could never have comprehended the roles he would bring together, that is, "sorcerer" and priest/prophet. By virtue of being free from the constraints of bureaucratic governance, he could deviate from norms for a higher good. Still, he very early smarted from the problematic of being in both worlds. They were not on the same wavelength; the lyrics were completely dissonant.

Vandersteene adhered to the belief that fundamental tensions had to be endured and overcome by someone who grasped the deepest strands of both European and Cree culture. Thus he held that he would succeed when he brought together leadership models from both the Church and the Cree. His joining of these two is all the more remarkable because he had the mind of an idealist and tended to see things without shades of gray. Thus, part of him could have had an acceptable career just by being a conventional priest. But he was too much of a rebel against the status quo for that. He instinctively felt that the two modes of leadership were essential for him to accomplish his calling. The resulting dynamic — that of problematic tensions and higher resolution — was a continuing pattern throughout his life.

The tension of trying to reach a people who put the world together in a way that was not part of his operating procedures brought him constantly up against his own religious conceptions. He personally subjected himself to the most caustic of the differences, because he had an amazing confidence that God would integrate them through his experience. Whether this vision is held to be of shamanic or Christian origin may not be immediately obvious, but it is clear that Vandersteene thought that suffering constant personal reversals was necessary for transformation. Hence, the personal encounter with a different religious ecology was an absolutely necessary prolegomenon to integration and resolution.

This plan of action highlights two Cree conceptions: the processes of confrontation and resolution are basic to Cree specialist traditions. On the one hand, the Cree spiritual person endlessly probes the spirit world for signs. On the other, processes of forming one's inner being require encounters with spirit helpers — implying modification of personality. Insofar as these constitute a fundamental unifying characteristic of Vandersteene's leadership, they indicate his replication of Cree religious traditions. The way this pattern shifts can be gleaned from the two poles of leadership: sorcerer and priest/prophet.

Christ's Sorcerer. There is an identifiable progression in Vandersteene's awareness of leadership roles. We begin with the Cree, because the lines of change can be easily calibrated: he moves from foreigner to medicine man through successive stages of experience. The first stage of Vandersteene's attempts to encounter Cree leadership was through his work in language; he found genuine sustenance and insights in the Cree language. His section on *ocitaw*,[1] and his appreciation for the flexibility and growth possibilities in Cree, demonstrate how critical his commitment to this was. Language is one of the foundational pillars of being "at home." Here was one tension he faced and resolved.

There then followed in succession social interactions, signalled by his participation in Cree eating and smoking patterns, adaptation of visiting rituals,[2] and modes of living (shacks and tipis instead of "houses"), and then the deepening of the process through personal involvement, attending dances and rituals. It is the latter that became the point of launch into the inner world of the Cree, and led to his first encounter with the realities of Cree spirituality, the world of the *wikokewin*. As he indicates in *Wabasca*, this encounter was the basis of much of his later liturgical speculation. He could clearly see the roles which the "priests" of the *wikokewin* played, and they paralleled his own. At the same time, he realized that these roles were not conveyed by an organization, but arose out of the gifts from beyond to the community.

Status conferred by gifts required community acknowledgement, and that demanded a membership not easily won. That is why the most important encounter with the Cree came with the transfer to him of the calumet, and his subsequent reception of Cree medicines. Here was genuine community acceptance and recognition. Vandersteene recognized the responsibility of being an elder and medicine man, but he also saw *he was free to use the powers for promoting his own ends, viz., for the Church.*

Had he done so, this would have made Vandersteene's ethics functional, even manipulative. Cree traditionally recognized this as a natural possibility for those receiving power: the spirits gave power, the sorcerer decides how to use it. No such charge was ever levelled at him, by friend or enemy. That he refused to use the powers bequeathed to him directly for purposes of developing his own church is a measure of Vandersteene's honesty. He held himself to be a Cree and his responsibility to his Cree people would not allow him to utilize the symbols of traditional religion for the Church's benefit. He also believed this manipulative ethic to be part of the Church's unfortunate history in Canada. He saw a more profound way.

The paths he was trodding can be seen beneath the surface. By becoming a member of the fraternity of medicine men and healers, Vandersteene was initiated into the Cree way of healing, with its attendant divisions of labour and its reliance on "ways of seeing" not available to ordinary people. It was in this context that his dream world became more significant. Instead of insight as the basis for modification of ritual forms, which he described in his book, he now acknowledged that it was a dream that introduced him to this new way of looking at the mass; the Flemish folk tradition of dream significance was bolstered by his Cree experience and elevated to the position of revealing truths. Even the encounter with ancestor spirits in dreams was replicated in his life when he was said to have appeared at Emilia Noskiye's hospital bed to heal. Because he was now a power figure, people could bring their dreams to him and he could help them find their meaning, and his parishioners could dream about him coming to minister to them. Through the dream world, Vandersteene himself moved into, and became for others, part of the traditional vehicle by which the sacred communicates with humans.

Once he matured, there was no doubt about his powers. People told stories of him singing and bringing rain, of recognizing what was going to happen, of having insight into what people were doing. His extraordinary experiences were the stuff of counting coup (aboriginal community celebration of heroic feats) and were accorded the spirit-gifted-elder status.

Vandersteene never tells us what he thinks of these "Cree" experiences, although in true Cree fashion he belittled his apparent successes. Despite this, he must have taken them as validators for the position he had taken. These small victories along the way, and the resolutions they brought, were read as signposts toward the final resolution that would bring about the Cree Church. This was God's path.

His own roots validated the adaptations to Cree ontology that he was undergoing. He saw traditional folk traditions among the Flemish people present and activated in his life among the Cree, so a deep part of his being suddenly meshed with Cree traditions. He felt that there was a more profound wisdom at the base of both of these ancient peoples and he had access to it.

The many small victories propelled him even deeper into the meaning of Cree leadership. Since that leadership was supple and elastic, and depended upon the particular situation requiring someone's gifts, one could not speak with absolute conviction about a leader's "characteristics." We do know that Cree held that their specialists of the sacred needed extraordinary skills.

Mitew, sorcerer, was the way Vandersteene described himself for his Catholic colleagues, but his use of that term was technically improper. Rather, Steentje was the owner of a pipe/medicine bundle. As we have seen, that should be designated as *maskikiwiyiniwiw*, or one with doctoring abilities. Vandersteene knew very well the technical use of these terms, since they appear correctly in his Cree course. At the same time, Vandersteene was regarded by some of the Cree to have prophetic abilities, abilities identified in Cree as *okiskiwahikew* or *okakeskihkemow*. Thus, if we follow Cree etymology, it would seem that, in practice, Vandersteene combined two types of leadership, one based on owner-ship of medicines and the other based on a recognized public gift of wisdom to foresee events and to guide the Cree accordingly.

Thus, by any measure, the abilities which Vandersteene brought to the task placed him well up in the Cree hierarchy. The medicine man, operating out of a sense of disability, is held to be compensated by the spirits for the burden of medicines which he owns. The seer, deriving authority from insight and wisdom, charts the paths and leads the people into the future. Both are intimately connected to the well-being of the Cree people, and both imply abilities to "read" the symptoms, make diagnoses and prescribe responses. These are the accoutrements of the great spiritual chiefs.

These are tasks beyond the normal ability of the ordinary Cree (to say nothing of the ordinary missionary). The mode of operation may be public, and require payment, but the knowledge possessed is pri-vate, even secret. Communication with the spirits is always secret and individual, depending upon the life experience/ordeals of the leader, so only mature people are able to shoulder the responsibility. Such reponsibility is enormous in traditional Cree religious circles, because good and evil sit side by side in the world and manifestations of both are expected.

The successful religious specialists will use all his/her skills to offset evil and promote good. Since power continually waxes and wanes, the power of evil and the power of good are constantly shifting relative to each other and to humans; that pattern depends greatly on the moral rectitude of the people as a whole. Bad acts impact upon the collective rectitude, disturbing the balance of good and evil that reside in a stable state of reciprocity. Both the medicine man and the seer are committed to well-being, because that is the state indicating balance. Both must be able to deal with the continual shifting going on and give *direction for the coming to be*.[3] As Mary Douglas has maintained,[4] leaders who work with this perception of reality rely upon ritual form to provide the lan-guage and the logic for bringing about the most sacred of ends: the re-establishment of balance. It is with the restoration of well-being that the skills of the leaders are recognized and praised, and their powers evident.

We are now in a position to evaluate the nature of Vandersteene's "sorcerer" leadership. The traditional Cree powers he gained were considerable, for they gave him the confidence to pursue his vision of a Christian Cree liturgical form, a form which immediately brought resistance from some of his fellow priests.[5] He recognized the state of flux in which the Cree lived, and intuited that the Cree nation was seriously off balance. This did not daunt him, however, for he conceived of himself as having the power and authority to bring about a religious restoration.[6]

From the standpoint of Vandersteene's Christian concerns, there was a weakness to the Cree system: such a leader operated entirely on his/her own. In order to comprehend some of his reactions we must be aware that possessing spirit power of this type was highly valued by him as a gift from God, but that its price within traditional Cree society was loneliness and difference. It is an irony to be savoured. The more Cree Steentje became, the more distant he became from the ordinary Cree person.

A Catholic Prophet. From the Church's side, he possessed a clear conception of the distinction between the role of the laity and the priesthood. He never had much sympathy for those priests and nuns who wanted to leave the Church to marry. He adhered very strongly to the special kind of discipline that the Church imposed upon him, even resisting the intrusion of members of his family into his work with the wall of remoteness. It is the very depth of such commitment that argues against his affair with Laughing Waters, even if it is evident that he had very strong emotional ties with her. His role in encouraging and inspiring his Flemish soulmate is another measure of the distinctiveness of his view of priesthood.

The mettle of his priestly commitments are best measured by his idols — Eugène de Mazenod, the father of the Oblates, whose ability to work within the system to bring about his goals inspired Vandersteene to do the same in Canada, and Fr. Damian, who gave himself to the lepers with such abandon that he condemned himself to death. Nor should we leave aside the religious heroes of Flemish nationalism, Frs. Verschaeve and Gezelle, to name only two. Together these people became Christian "helper spirits" who imprinted upon his soul a distinctive leadership style, a leadership among the Catholic missionaries that was never doubted, at least in most areas.

The language used to solidify this image is significant, for it gives Steentje a distinctive signature among the priests. Archbishop Legaré regarded him as a *prophet*, as did his associate Fr. Vantroys (a label Vandersteene emphatically rejected).[7] All admitted that he was a gifted linguist, far beyond the norm in their community. Fr. Camillo thought he was "crazy," a characteristic that he thought most missionaries shared, because of the tremendous commitment with few tangible results. Sister Bernadette regarded him as a very special person, whose memory lingered with them far beyond the usual. Maskwa thought him so much enculturated that he even thought like the Cree. Even those with reservations about him or his reforms had to admit that he was a dynamic leader thoroughly convinced of his calling. Those aspects of his character, like his belligerence, stubbornness and romanticism were all seen as part of an individual with extraordinary abilities. Vandersteene thus brought together in himself abilities and skills that made him above the ordinary in the priesthood.

We are now in a position to comprehend the significance of the merger of Cree and Catholic leadership models. It was his quest, his extraordinary religious vision, that tied the two leadership systems together. Even when people who knew him could not agree on what was extraordinary, they were united on that principle. Second, they agreed that Vandersteene stood for change, for a new form of Cree-Christian relationship. Most church-related authorities accepted that things would never be the same and that change was necessary if the Church were to survive among the Cree, but they had absolutely no idea about how that should be done. Vandersteene had a clear, principled plan. Among sympathetic Catholic colleagues, he was able to locate, negotiate and come to rest in a cohesive world with the Cree in which they, themselves, could vicariously participate.

Most Cree recognized that the old traditions of hunting and trapping were dying, that the old ways were undergoing profound modification, but they had no idea of how to accommodate the changes. Becoming white seemed the only, and yet despised, way. To the Cree, here was a man who moved beyond that polarity. He was able to hold the dysfunctional state of being white and Indian together; indeed, he seemed to thrive on the tensions and incompatibilities between the two.[8]

The move to hold these together, however, reveals something about his perception of his own power; he could, for example, manipulate the ingredients of ritual to provide the formula for true divine encounter. Power was available, it just had to be accessed in ways that appealed to the Cree. Catholicism was about the encounter with spiritual power, and any form that allowed the people to access it was legitimate.

It should be noted that Vandersteene's vision of his own authority in this area devalues the traditional view of liturgy in one way, that is, that abiding ritual forms could not be manipulated for anyone's purposes. At the same time, it reflects the traditional notion of the clergy in the Church having responsibility to bringing God to the masses. Some may have designated this power as prophetic in the Christian sense, but he really brought together both Cree medicine man/seer, with Christian priest/prophet in a dynamic manner.

In a sense, then, Vandersteene internalized the process for both groups by acknowledging the dissonance of the two systems, but then pressing on towards a new religious integration. For both groups he affirmed a basic assumption: that all true change was religiously imbued and religiously driven. From both his traditions, therefore, the legitimacy of his liturgical reforms revolved around whether or not his leadership could resolve the fundamental tensions between Cree religion and Christianity. From that singular position, Vandersteene believed he had not finished his task. Therefore he had failed. He was correct.

The "Apocalyptic" God

Towards the end of his career, Vandersteene lived in a world with whose nature he felt increasingly out of touch. The dissonance was so great that he constructed techniques to distance it, controlling its din by a natural and private liturgy of life mediated by a return to the music of his Flemish character, the soothing strains of Beethoven. It is tempting to think that this state of affairs was generated by the deterioration of his health. In my view, this explanation is not satisfactory. Such a view disregards the sense of doom generated by the world wars that resided furtively and potently within his consciousness. A more critical case can be made that he harboured throughout his life a particularly powerful sense of the apocalyptic.

Vandersteene's conception of the apocalyptic derives in part from the history and cultural experience of the Flemish people. It is evident that he imported great dollops of the "marginalized" and "other" arising out of his Flemish background. Indeed, he believed that he could better minister to the Cree because of his background. He saw the Cree and aboriginals in general as increasingly tragic figures, much the same as the great Flemish people of the past had been (and in some ways, still were). A significant portion of his lifework was spent trying to stem the tide that seemed to be washing over these suppressed people. He felt very personally the marginalization of the Cree; it was but a step, then, for him to see his life-meaning completely synchronized with Cree experience.

Still it was not the tensions of difference between whites and Cree that brought him the most pain. *It was that he was not able to exercise even minimal control over the dissonance within his own life.* It forced him to continually evaluate where he was going and what he was doing. He always seemed to be in transition. He was in the process of another review when his health heightened the urgency. Still, even with the significance of this personal anguish, it is not going too far to say that his own apocalypse underlined the reality of a larger catastrophe.

Career failure might just be battles lost, with the war yet to be fought and won. But when the battles were set aside because he had to wrestle with his own mortality this triggered a critical probe of the very basis of his faith. For Vandersteene the personal search for God in the midst of suffering was the natural outcome of trying to cope with his own meaning when the carefully crafted understanding of leadership we have just evaluated seemed to be coming unravelled. It inevitably led him to larger issues, such as the very nature of the Christian God.

The first element in the search was related to the health of the missions and the second to the collapse of his initiative to found a true Cree Church. Why would God prepare him with the accoutrements of both Cree and Catholic power only to destroy him?

Thus, a key element in his constant struggle towards the end of his life was his last mission field, the Peace River missions. Instead of a dynamic Cree Church, he nursed along a mission of abysmal proportions. His work consisted of dashing from one locale to the next, ministering to a group of people who had not progressed since his early days among them. Unhappy with the dismal prospects of spending the rest of his career in these grubby missions, with their poverty, lack of traditional Cree identity and the dominance of alcoholism, he began searching for an inner light, some indication from God that the vision he had had was not an illusion. At the same time, he was acutely conscious that his own grand plans had marginalized him among the authorities and among some of his colleagues. There would be no massive movement toward developing an indigenous Cree Church as Vandersteene had fervently hoped.

At a deeper level, with the death and departure of several priests, his spiritual persona could not make sense of God wiping out most of the prime labourers in the Cree vineyard. This seemed to up the ante considerably. What possible purpose could be served by leaving the mission bereft? God Himself seemed to be mowing down those who represented the last hope for a Cree Church — those missionaries who spoke Cree. The sinister disease wracking his lungs was but a physical expression of a more profound ailment. It is one thing when your colleagues throw roadblocks in your way. It is quite another when God seems to be deliberately sabotaging your best plans for His glory. Why was God killing his initiatives and why was He now killing him? In his darkest hour he would have felt kindred to Nietzsche: "Everything in the hero's sphere turns to tragedy."[9] Vandersteene could not comprehend a God who appeared to have complicity in the coming apocalypse.

It is in his poetry that we find the central focus for his bewilderment: God Himself. God, the foundation of the Western world's religious consciousness, and the very centre of his life, seemed to have vanished. His inner stance is best represented in his great crisis poem, *Call to God*.

> In the summer heat
> And winter cold
> I have
> With child-like eyes
> Searched for You
> And found You not.
> A trace of You! But You?!
>
> In my own heart
> I've tracked You
> There where You dwell
> As I am taught;
> I caught a glimpse of You. But You?
>
> In line and verse and paint
> I grasped for You
> And did not catch You.
> A trace of You! But You?!
> Yet You were in my head and hands
> And in my striving
> My urge towards You.
>
> With Your own word
> As fingertips
> I have kneaded souls
> And with Your chisel
> I hewed them
> But in the work of art
> I recognised You not.
> A trace of You! But You?!
>
> Yet it was You
> Who sent me out
> To proclaim the Word
> That wakes an echo
> Towards You!
>
> You who are everywhere,
> And always,
> And in all
> Where are You now?

Written early in 1974, the year after his return from his last furlough, the dark night of his soul brought him to the very edge of unbelief.

This was the final arpeggio in the cacophony. Job cried out, and he received an answer. Why not him? His whirlwind movements at the end of his life betray a man desperate to keep some semblence of direction, even when he did not understand God's purposes. His experience seemed resistant to the familiar comfort of logic. Like something out of Wisakaychak's tales, the ways of God seemed chaotic, quite beyond fathoming. There was no deciphering God's meaning. If a man dedicated his every ability to God, trusting that God would sensibily utilize those talents, what conclusion can be drawn when that God seems bent on destroying what they have together constructed? Where was faith to find its moorings during the ensuing chaos? In the act of faith alone? What kind of faith operated during an apocalypse?

At various points, hopeful that others could help with the answer, Vandersteene looked outward toward the greater Canadian religious institutions. He turned back with disillusionment. Instead of a church pulling great minds to its work, it was drained by the hemorrhage of disloyalty among Catholic clerics. Canadian clergy evinced little concern for the burdens of the aboriginal churches. To make matters worse, even his own family were exemplars of this infectious secularism; none followed him to the mission field, despite his pleas. In sum, his personal traumas could not be assuaged through reliance on Catholic society, whether in Canada or in Flanders.

As for the triumph of secularism in Canada, the cost was more than the failure to realize a universal Christian culture: it was also the social toll secularism required. The most challenging period of his life came when Albertan society was the most affluent, at the end of a period of sustained financial growth in the province, during which money flowed freely, and Alberta espoused a vigorous materialist lifestyle. Nothing happening made any sense. Surrounded by Cree youth madly abandoning their traditions and racing pell-mell after the materialism of their white compatriots, Steentje could not reconcile God's benevolence with this destruction. Not only had Cree youth abandoned their traditions, but they had almost panicked to fill the void with the most pathetic ingredients of modern life:

> We can compare the modern Indian with the modern youth of the West. They seem to depend on each other a great deal. As well, "civilization" is beating a path to their door, with all its problems, especially seen in susceptible primitive cultures. And now, there is a radio in three places, T.V. in two, state schools, roads, fractioning between old and young, materialism, etc. . . . There is no way to handle it, as you know.[10]

At the heart of the situation was the "colonial" vision of the white Euro-Canadian, a "seeing" based upon a reductionist attitude toward Indian culture and religion:

> But sometimes, we saw a thing (from another culture) and we hid behind a set of symbols in our heads and instead of saying, "The set of symbols that others have, there's truth in there," no, we went on with our own symbol and we smashed theirs. When we smashed the symbol, we smashed what was inside too, in this case, the practice of the Indian religion. Now we can't find anything among young Indians, because we disregarded the bases of his [sic] life. For their sense of wrong-doing, even their sense of what was fun, differed from ours. Now they just don't believe in anything.[11]

Yet that tragedy had many sides to it, and Vandersteene recognized that such activity was costly for more than the aboriginals, it was costly for Canada's soul, costly for the church, and costly for all those who participated in the smashing — it left them all bereft of moral authority.[12]

Yet it was the church which possessed a greater ache. Vandersteene argued that the evidences of moral loss were found everywhere in the Canadian religious establishment. For example, not a single Alberta missionary studied Cree chant despite the absolutely central importance of music and song in native culture.[13] The most glaringly strange things were done — training indigenous priests in Toronto or Ottawa, when they should have been trained in the bush where their people lived. Moreover, even though the Church knew for years that it should indigenize, that did not happen, in part because of its commitment to an unwieldy bureaucracy:

> The liturgy should have been changed, the Our Father, and the official prayers, and other aspects should have been changed but, of course, nobody did it. Church bureaucracy from Europe stood in the way. In the olden days, you had to contact all the bishops. Then there's the diversity of the Cree: They go on down from Calgary, there are even some in the US, they go way up to the east in Quebec, on both sides of border. Some are in Ontario, even Newfoundland. Really, we would have had to get the whole of Canada and probably the United States together just to change the Hail Mary.[14]

True, the dominant attitude was less virulent in the Church. Yet that institution brought its own colonialism to interactions with aboriginal cultures, predisposed to the construction of a particular type of church, with certain European expectations required, dictated by a certain Euro-value system: "It was degrees of being bad that we were looking for, not being good."[15] It certainly did not take into consideration *their* normative value system.

Wherever he turned in the Church, then, he saw the tragedy of God's people committed to Cree souls, but constructing organizations consciously or unconsciously designed to eradicate them as distinctive children of God. The taste of gall rose in the throats of both peoples.

The loss of moral rectitude about the Cree, however, did not ultimately rest upon the Church: it fell upon Canadians as a whole. The destructive attitude worked two ways. It fomented a clash that weakened the Cree: "As soon as they had contact with our civilization they just went all to pieces. I never saw dirty shacks like that until I saw that place. Shacks held together with cardboard.... It's terrible. You don't see that in the bush." From the point of view of the Cree the rejection of a valid place for Cree culture denied them the pride of their own cultural achievements. Vandersteene made much of the fact that a sophisticated language of widespread use in Canada before the Europeans came was systematically undermined, and the whole cultural matrix that sustained it was not even recognized as inherently valuable, despite its importance in the early days of exploration and discovery. He lamented now that even some Cree had capitulated to this attitude on language.

Of the same magnitude was the moral blight it generated on the souls of other Canadians: the material destruction meted out upon those who lived and thrived in Canada before the whites came spoke volumes about the moral blindness of whites. They, in effect, eliminated the Cree as people from whom they could learn what living in Canada might mean. The sense of moral "superiority" dashed the possibility of encountering the insights of a religion that had been generated out of the Canadian experience. Such results were the ultimate cost of colonialism — the reduction of the Cree community to the savage, while white Canadians stood condemned by their complicity in the process. No wonder whites were stymied by the crime of aboriginal youth — the whites had no finger left to point. There was no way out of the impasse. Canadians now faced an apocalypse of their own construction.

It would be easy to just ignore the thrust of his argument, and to deny the logic of his prophetic vision. Vandersteene regarded the problem as a personal one, for he, himself was part of this system in some way. Did he not become a Canadian, thus allying himself with the forces of destruction? How could he not stand condemned at his own bar?

Vandersteene felt that tension very deeply, and I believe it drove him ever deeper in his attempt to bring together the European and the Cree within himself. His response was, so to speak, to try to vicariously live a life that crossed over into the Cree to prove that Euro-Canadians can become one with the Cree. There was a different kind of being that could be developed which would allow the two separate realities of Cree and white to live together integratively. He literally spent his life in staving off the end results of the apocalypse. He committed the most personal of his resources to bringing together the two cultural traditions that had only experienced physical and moral destruction in their contiguity.

Despite this, it should be noted that at the heart of his solution was a profoundly felt conviction that the Cree would survive as a distinctive people. Even when he pushed his logic of Euro-Canadian destruction ruthlessly, as he often did when addressing his own colleagues in the Church, he could not bring himself to accept its predicted result. Perhaps it was his love of the Cree people, but even in his darkest mood he could not believe that the apocalypse would end in their complete destruction. The attitudes of colonialism would be blunted on two simple truths: aboriginals were here to stay, and aboriginals will retain their identity because they are *of* this country.

Vandersteene rejected assimilation. The Cree will be "absorbed." The distinction is important. His view was based on his belief that the Cree will retain a separate identity, even if they adopted majority language and cultural patterns. Like the Flemish people in the Roman empire, they might be swamped, but they will not be overcome.

His solution was also related to the notion that aboriginals are *ur-Canadian*, and integration will require "engagement" with them by the whites, *if the whites are to become part of the country.* He seemed to look to a day when the European element of whites would be subjected to the discipline of the land, opening the way for Cree "absorption" into a larger, genuinely Canadian culture:

> One day, some day, they will all be absorbed. All our role is now is to make the absorption as smooth as can be. He's still a perfect Indian boy even if he doesn't know a word of Cree. Yet, he's still a functioning Indian in mentality and that's what makes it possible to engage him in his difference . . . he still won't be a white guy in school. He may change languages in the next generation but he's still an Indian in his soul.[16]

Vandersteene's task was to blaze a trail, presumably because he saw what was necessary for both whites and Cree. His social mission was in some respects greater than his religious mission, but the results of his attempt to test his thesis within the Church were surely a measure of its possibilities in larger Canadian society. It failed. His failure is, from that perspective, a Canadian tragedy.

Living Death: Christ-Metaphor

We have seen how much of Vandersteene's piety was formed around the mass and the continuous death and resurrection of Christ in the liturgy, indeed, so much so that a Christ-metaphor appears to be operative. There are some very significant factors in this regard. What is striking is that brokenness, sacrifice and death were continuous companions from the time of his birth, and judging by his poems and letters, played an important role in his self-interpretation. We know that his frailty at birth motivated his being dedicated to Mary. He was constantly reminded of his tenuous life by the blue he wore, the death and destruction of war around him, and his illness in school that required him to stay home for a year and cost the family dearly for gold shots. His earliest published poem of 4 October 1940 portrays him as a bird caught in God's net, breaking his wings and smashing his beak.[17] Two year later, as he was entering orders, he wrote:[18]

> ### Death
>
> O when I die
> like a panther's
> will be my jubilant leap,
> unable to miss its prey,
> for thus fiercely
> that fiercely have I desired You.
>
> 9 May 1942

Yet neither in his letters nor his poems does one encounter an individual cowering from fear. Vandersteene felt angst but he did not fear death. He felt himself to have experienced the brokenness of Christ, through the pains and tribulations of life, so that the news of the murder of his fellow Belgian for his faith in Africa elicited no remorse, but celebration. In short, brokenness, sacrifice and death are but a preface to a God-charged life; he never abandoned the notion that death is a moment to leap towards God.

His favourite pilgrimage was to the site of much sacrifice and death — to Ijzer, a trek that he made on every anniversary he was in Flanders and which he remembered every year when he was abroad. Sacrifice or tragedy marked the lives of all his nationalist heroes. The journey to his life career in Canada was interrupted by the death of his mother, and he had to deal with the symbolic "death" of family solidarity, caused in large part by his departure. On several occasions he nearly died while on the trail in the midst of a snowstorm. His earliest stay in Canada was marred by ill health, and he felt he owed his life to the Sewepagaham family who nursed him back to health again. Throughout his many letters to his Flemish soulmate, he has countless urgings concerning death. This is one meditation on Easter:

> Happy Easter to you! Easter is a feast that lasts all through the year, and all through life. It is our life! It begins with the lasting remembrance of Him who died and who is alive and who comes to us as bread and wine; then we go out to others in the same manner. For the commandment of Love is the last commandment for those who follow him: "each of you, as I you, and fully as I do. . . ." Then comes the phase of being devoured, and being like Him, eaten up. It is a horrid spectacle: "You shall weep and lament, moan and groan, and go to pieces under it. . . ." But they will enjoy it in a superficial and selfish way; they will be given new life by it. Then comes the burial, the oblivion, the loneliness, the descent to hell, the constraint, the darkness and also the disquiet of those who sealed the tomb. And then follows the explosion of light and joy: We carry within ourselves and each Christian carries within himself, but we carry it more deeply and more strongly that Easter . . . that being eternally slaughtered and eaten up, and just because of that we are the continuing life that remains. We are the living affirmation of Christ, the living Eucharist, the eternal thank-you of mankind; like a mother fed by the flesh and blood of her Christ is full to bursting with milk for the people. . . . Happy Easter and Happy Pentecost.[19]

A few months before his death, he faced his own living death. Then, feeling burdened by himself, he articulated a breaking free of himself in order to live until he dies:[20]

Danger

Sympathy
imprisons me
intensely conscious of myself
I feel each pain and discomfort
and taste my dying.

Seated at table
across from myself
as guest
I have neither smile nor appetite
I lay in bed with myself
and cannot sleep.

> I must break out of myself
> and through the encirclement
> if I wish to live till I die!

3 April 1976

There are those who will see in Vandersteene's experience a life shot through with sacrifice and death; it is striking how like the Eliadean pattern of shamanism this death-consciousness appears. One major difference remains, however: the shaman undergoes processes of death in order to be a channel for healing and well-being among the people. He does not see his physical death as contributing to that gift. Vandersteene does. The meaning of Christ was written in the life-processes of his being. There is something of this mythic dimension in Vandersteene's death. Even as his life ebbed away, he figuratively fed himself to his religious task. Thus in the Cree story of the self-sacrificing bear do we find a Christ-metaphor of deep significance to Vandersteene; it was a powerful vision of death in life.[21]

It is likely that this Christ-metaphor served as the driving force behind his priesthood. It is a forceful image of the purpose of life, not particularly attractive to ordinary mortals, but nevertheless powerful and all-embracing for Steentje. Emulating Christ did not just mean acting morally, living faithfully or thinking rationally — it meant giving over to the disintegration of his being daily, so that he could be transformed into the presence of the sacred in the world.[22]

The Struggle with the "Other"

The final essential feature of Vandersteene's vision is in encountering the "other." It, too, was at the heart of his mission. How can one engage the other in meaningful ways? Is my knowledge of the other's motivations anything other than a construct? Steentje himself had alerted us to the problem when he confessed that, even after all those years among the Cree, he was still an outsider and a stranger. The hermeneutical problem is not one of trying and rejecting various methods in getting to know the other. The essential issue is that we have no direct way of engaging *being*, that is that central core of the object about which we wish to *know*. Who are you? is not a plea for information, but an attempt to engage the reality of the other.

Contemporary writers like Ricoeur, Taylor, Gadamer[23] and Geertz accept that there can be no absolute in determining the meaning of an object, because everything we know rests in a social substrate. That substrate is constantly reconstituting and reinterpreting our social life, and therefore our common life together. It follows that any means we use in describing the other falls immediately upon itself: it wants to make the other into *something*, usually so we can exercise control over it. As Bernstein puts it, "It is extremely easy to pay lip service to recognizing and respecting plurality, difference and otherness, but perhaps nothing is more difficult to achieve in practice — and such an achievement is always temporary and fragile. It is self-deceptive illusion to think that the 'other' can always be heard in friendly dialogue."[24]

It is an issue that every immigrant to Canada faces at some level. Vandersteene calls into question a facile notion of the other, such as is usually found in multicultural discussions. He felt very deeply his own problematic of the immigrant in Canada.[25] Canada's policy of multiculturalism is generally regarded as a political doctrine to offset criticism of the bilingualism in recognition of the francophone role in Canada.[26] On the one hand, Vandersteene is indicative of the lengths to which immigrants will go to come to terms with the culture in place in this part of the world, indeed, to become part of it. It is a factor seldom broached in Canadian discussions of the value of immigrants. On the other hand, that Vandersteene should detect the essential weakness of "belonging" by the various elements of Canadian society indicates that the "other" has many unexamined sides to it.

Judging from Vandersteene's views, the really serious business of engaging the other in Canadian society has not yet taken place. It is indicative of the problem that the only conscious division within Canadian culture, characterized as "two solitudes," is that of the English- and French-speaking people.[27] The phrase is still held to be the essence of Canadian culture, even as the nation wrestles with another potential breakup.

Yet, for Steentje, the most identifiable multicultural other in Canada is neither the immigrant nor the French but the aboriginal. That other will remain regardless of any national fracturing. Disenfranchised more than any other group, the aboriginal nevertheless has prior claim to the land and to the structures of the mind moulded by the Canadian ecology. As we have seen, Vandersteene at various points argues that until white Canadians engage the reality expressed by aboriginals, those Canadians will not themselves be part of the Canadian environment.

Vandersteene believed that recognizing aboriginal spirituality is thus essential for the growth of the Canadian identity, because it constitutes a primordial mode through which the truth of Canada came to be expressed. Such a view opens up the possibility of understanding "Canadian" in a manner not based on facile multiculturalism, but on a profound sharing of a primary vision of the Canadian reality. For Vandersteene, then, the otherness of the aboriginal is an opportunity for other Canadians to engage Canada's collective psychological/mythic history.

Moreover, he believes that that engagement is the morally right thing to do, because white Canadians will remain in a moral wilderness until it is done. It is God's pattern for coming to terms with the other. Only when that occurs can Canada be constituted by people who are all truly Canadian. Until that time, all Canadians, native or white, will be challenged deep within their moral being, for neither can claim to be Canadian while rejecting the other which forms part of their collective identity.

Vandersteene clearly believes the initiative must be taken by Canadian whites in this integrative process, for ultimately he enslaved himself to its moral views. Here is a sensitive vision of Canadian identity that may have greater import than his personal quest to find the Cree ritual reflecting Christian sacrificial conceptions.

Critical Evaluation of His Legacy

We know that several famous personages have attempted to integrate Christianity and tribal traditions, including Black Elk[28] and the Jesuit Paul B. Steinmetz, who was also accepted as a holy man by the Sioux and who promoted an integrationist religion which he identified as Ecumenicism II in his book *Pipe, Bible, and Peyote among the Oglala Lakota* (begun *c*. 1970). It consists primarily of the integration of the Sacred Pipe and Christ.[29] I have no evidence that Vandersteene knew the latter, although it is possible he had read the former. It is also possible but unlikely that he had read W.E.H. Stanner's study on sacramentalism among the Australian aborigines before he began formulating his own views.[30] Assuming that he had not come in contact with these works (they were not in his extensive library), Vandersteene's formula for integration places him among the most creative missionary minds of his time, even if one does not agree with Maskwa that he is "ahead of his time."

Early in the book, we noted the impact of reformist liturgical movements on Vandersteene.[31] It is less clear how much he would have agreed with Karrer that the mass was an act of thanksgiving and praise to God, and not the repetition of Christ's sacrifice. From his own comments and meditations, including those we have quoted above, he would have rejected them. He did, however, strongly support another aspect of that movement, and that is the "Real Presence" of Christ in the Eucharist, and of course, he fully backed the aggiornamento movement insofar as it stressed the primacy of the mass in local languages and cultures. From the perspective of that movement, Vandersteene was only carrying out the original vision of the movement within his own mission to the Cree.

We have seen that Vandersteene saw in the *wikokewin* the Cree equivalent of the mass. By using the ritual elements of this ceremonial visitation he believed he could contruct a genuine Cree liturgy with explanations and rationales derived from the celebration of the dead. In the *wikokewin* model, we have Vandersteene's richest involvement in Cree liturgical life.

Critics who think he dwelt on Cree forms considered as "old things" must admit that he only stressed those elements he still saw as powerful among the Cree. He did not jump to utilize old forms purely for their traditional significance. This was an encounter with the other governed by the practicality of what was significant on the ground. This stands against his former colleague Art Lamothe's view that to "try to preserve a ceremony like the *wikokewin* beyond its natural life is not a legitimate apostolic expression." Vandersteene would have said it is very much alive, a position more consonant with the facts.

Still, even of the *wikokewin* he could not have been said to have been a traditionalist. His *Wabasca* demonstrates that his analysis of the rite is dominated by Christian notions of Christ as offering, while the rite was originally designed to ritually honor and place the spirits of the dead among the non-human persons of the other side. Rituals of eating were subordinated to peripheral meanings, to the affirmation of community solidarity with those beyond, while the drumming, dancing and offering to the spirits were ultimately constructed to put the spirit world in debt to the living and thus curry their favour to continue to provide for the community's needs. Vandersteene's structural adaptation of *wikokewin* indicates that he was trying to capture the essence of the total experience (i.e., encounter with the spirit world) by stressing key elements. He obviously believed that the key elements of the ritual provided for the portability of its power.

Once more it seems certain that this was not just appropriation for the facile goal of making the mass Cree; what is implicit in his designation of the *wikokewin* as sacrifice is the claim that the ritual must overcome a fundamental tension, the feeling of separateness from the ancestral spirits that were the source of the community's survival in both worlds. Here was a primordial chasm between the living and the dead; the rite must integrate two incompatible realms of existence. *Not yet being an ancestor imposes a suffering upon all Cree people*. They are cut off from the reality of the community's true being, and must now ritually call those non-human persons to "pity" them. Something must be done to interlock the two realms, those who walk on other side and those who walk on this side. The answer as to how this can come about is ritual: the liturgy imposes a debt on the sacred powers. The grandfathers are called to account because of a basic belief, reciprocity. Conferring honour, according status, acknowledgment must be reciprocated with sustenance and help.

The rituals themselves are less important than bringing about the interrelationship of the two worlds. Realizing the reciprocity and acting upon it was the main goal, and Steentje believed that if the liturgy encapsulated the necessary encounter, then an authentic Cree liturgy was born. Vandersteene never believed the *wikokewin* to be item by item the same as the Christian mass, despite the criticism of Fr. Baratto (see Appendix 2, p. 320). That would have made Cree liturgy only different in name. It was, rather, that the rhythmic movement of separation and integration was felt in the new form, thus accommodating the basic ritual power of the original Cree ceremony. The reformed liturgy of Vandersteene saw itself as a process by which the separated human and divine integrated, just as life provided the processes by which the essential sacred qualities called Kisemanitou and Micimanitou were assimilated, so his liturgy was really based on Cree philosophy rather than the *wikokewin* itself.

Despite his knowledge of Cree tradition, it has to be noted that what he stressed was quite selective. His concern for Cree ritual had little or no reference to thirst dances or vision quests, both of which may have been waning in the region, particularly the latter, but which we know were classically part of the Cree complex. He must have been familiar with both of these elements, yet they play no role in his public expression of the genuine Cree liturgy.

He shows no concern for the Shaking-Tent rite, at least in his writings and speeches, indicating that he had no intention of exploring all the older forms of Cree spirituality that had been, at one time, in place in his community. Nor do we have sources indicating he was aware of the controversy as to whether the *wikokewin* was part of "original" Cree ceremonial, or whether it was introduced at the time that ghost dance religion was sweeping North American tribes.[32] If the *wikokewin* was even influenced by that movement, and he was aware of it, did he then disregard the problem because that would have weakened his belief in it being part of original Cree culture?

In contrast to his extensive work on the *wikokewin*, he made no attempt to adapt vision-quest ideology into his understanding of Cree psychology; he apparently did not engage in discussion with people who had had such an experience and could have talked knowledgeably about it to him. We have only one report of such an engagement, hardly up to his usual careful level of study.[33]

More seriously, at least for the Church, why did he not develop a full-blown Cree theology? Initially this was a puzzle to me because he obviously had the resources to reinterpret the Church's message, and follow in the pathway of liberation theology around the world. After all, his colleagues in South America had made impressive gains for their people by writing such works. Yet, there is no evidence that he tried to do this.

As we have noted earlier, he may not have done this because he realized how hopeless this was from a Cree standpoint. Cree had given priority to *encounters* with sacred as the means to building selfhood, that is, had set up a *process* for developing *ocitaw*. That process is deemed lifelong, without any underlying personhood to constitute it. Moreover, the Cree did not have a concordance of spirit helpers with culturally defined characteristics, and he had no oral collections of spirit-helper experiences that could provide the basis for the requisite translation *because Cree could not (and would not) betray their experiences by making them public. Making encounters with sacred powers public was to de-sacralize them.* No Cree with any appreciation of his experience would think of such a thing.

Moreover, personal experience such as was rendered into text by the Christian mystics had no place among the Cree because Cree could not believe that something so sacred should be or could be publically verbalized, that is, committed to writing. The closest Cree come to an explication of generalized personal experience is in the allegorical stories of the trickster figure, Wisakaychak, and the characteristics enshrined in them are purposely kept very fluid.

Without a resident "self," what can God redeem? Historically Christian theology had privileged the Greek concept of the soul as an essence, a generalized pattern of selfhood, created in its basic structure right from the beginning of its existence. Salvation could be achieved because God could cancel the basic flaw in each soul through Christ's sacrifice, and grant eternal life to the essence of the person — the soul. If we accept that traditional theology was heavily committed to Greek notions of the self, it is evident that no traditional theological view could prevail if he were to be true to Cree traditions.

Can one then have a Cree Church without a theology? The tensions between the two traditions appear to militate against any easy compromise. Vandersteene never broaches this topic. It is not likely he could have seriously conceived it. Were he to have done so, he would have had to collapse the distinction between church and nation, since Cree had no conception of an institution mediating between them and the sacred.

Thus Vandersteene's vision of the Cree Church had an inherent weakness because the core Cree identity could not be martialled in the service of the Church's traditional theological requirements. Steentje was confined by his own theological foundations when he came to formulate Cree ritual based upon Cree selfhood. At an intellectual level, at least, the failure arises because of the essential difference between the European and Cree systems of understanding religious meaning. There can be no translatability when no medium can be agreed upon.

At the end of his career he seemed to affirm an essentially pragmatic approach, perhaps believing that a theological requirement was an essentially European requirement. He spent much of his time and effort in adapting the pipe, drum and Cree song into his services. In one respect, the last aspects of his work were more central than the earlier: traditional Cree believed that drumming and song is the sacred language of the heart, since no true ceremonial can take place without them. In some ways it is more constitutive of the sacred in Cree rituals than rites like *wikokewin*. Once the pipe was given to him, he incorporated the pipe into the mass too: where Cree refused to give anyone the kiss of peace as called for in the Euro-Canadian mass, the calumet could provide a meaningful Cree alternative. Smoking the pipe together was, at least on one level, the acceptance of peace between brethren, and was a vehicle communicating solidarity to the spirit world. Clearly he realized how critical pipe rituals were in traditional Cree life.

His use of the pipe in the mass as an equivalent to the kiss of peace suggests that he believed the prime Cree meaning of the pipe itself to be promotion of peace; in fact, however, that meaning is decidedly pan-Indian, and perhaps of recent construction.[34] Certainly it is not traditional in Cree religion. Indeed, Harold Cardinal emphasizes that all of Steentje's reforms must be examined in that light:

> In the North American context, there is a movement that is comprised of young people from many tribes pursuing intertribal religion. For example, you have Sioux coming into Alberta to talk to the old Cree people to get the perspectives of traditional Indian religion. You have Cree that go to the Arapaho in Wyoming. Generally, throughout North America, this movement has been underway for the last ten or fifteen years. There are a lot of others, some college-educated, who are just like these young people. They are basically travelling to get a better understanding of their roots and an understanding of their religion and different ceremonies. Eventually, they go back to their homes and to their own communities. I think now its probably moving into another phase . . . between the Indians of the two Americas. Father Vandersteene had very much in

common with that movement whether or not the two are synonymous or not.[35]

Since Vandersteene was unable to sell his *wikokewin* reform to the Church, the interstitial religion he proposed did not survive his death. Various aspects of his reforms continue to have an impact, such as the the mass utilizing Cree metaphors, the catechism and the use of drumming and Cree song, but these additions can hardly be seen as radical or as essential as his adaptation of the ghost dance rite. The diocese is continuing to develop lay members to take leadership roles in the Church. But the noble sentiments of a genuine Cree Church, founded upon a ritual encounter with Cree ancestors, has found no lasting expression. Perhaps it was a vision more suited to the Cree of 1760s than of the 1960s — a model of adaptation that accepts equality between religions — a quest more suited for a minority church of the first century, than a twentieth-century European worldwide religio-cultural authority.

At the end of his life, then, Vandersteene's ideas were reduced to a syncreticism of a type the Church has often advocated, that is, without a radical Cree reformulation of the meaning of the Eucharist. Thus died a noble experiment in interstitial religion, and one of the most important legacies of interreligious encounter in Canada in this century.

Notes

1 See Roger Vandersteene, "Some Woodland Cree Traditions and Legends," excerpted from *Wabasca* and translated by T. Habgood in *WCJA*, 1, 1 (1969): 41ff.

2 It was while developing such aspects that he became involved with Laughing Waters. I do not think there is enough evidence to prove that he had an "affair," but I do think he was very close, both emotionally and physically, to her. I suspect that his ill health was connected with the issue.

3 Donald Handelman considers this situation as "in process" in his analysis of the ritual clown. I can find no evidence of ritual clowns among these Cree. See "Ritual Clown: Attributes and Affinities," *Anthropos: International Review of Ethnology and Linguistics*, 76 (1981): 321f. Vandersteene liked to present himself as a clown, acting somewhat like a loony uncle with the Cree children. He even has a sketch of himself as a clown. But he was not known for public behaviour that was strange (at least from the Cree side). Rather they regarded him as having *bonhomie*.

4 Mary Douglas, *Purity and Danger: An Analysis of Concepts of Pollution and Taboo* (London: Routledge & Kegan Paul, 1980), p. 63.

5 See Appendix 2, pp. 315-16 and 320, for Art Lamothe's and Fr. Baratto's comments.

6 It is well to recognize, however, that for the traditional Cree the only personage accorded this privilege was the trickster figure Wisakaychak, or perhaps a rare shaman-chief. Very often, the behaviour of such extraordinary leaders was held to be bizarre, or even clownlike, and most people regarded such people as socially eccentric and spiritually beyond their ken. Thus, on the basis of the perception of Vandersteene among the Cree, he partook of a leadership quality that not only warranted the Cree burying him as a chief, but in certain respects as a shaman as well.

7 Fr. Vantroys has some valid reasons why Vandersteene rejected the designation, see Vantroys, Appendix 2, p. 319.

8 Something of this is present in Archbishop Routhier's comments, where he compares Steentje to Lacombe, calling him a "roamer," that is, more Indian than white. See Appendix 2, pp. 319-20.

9 Friedrich Nietzsche, *Beyond Good and Evil*, translated by Walter Kaufmann (New York: Vintage Books, 1966), p. 90.

10 With the Cree the notion of the overpowering nature of the European and its ubiquitous presence is a common theme in liberationist theologies, an ideology whose roots owe much to Marx and later Michel Foucault. For an outline of the latter's views and a recent critique see Nancy Fraser, *Unruly Practices: Power, Discourse and Gender in Contemporary Social Theory* (Minneapolis: University of Minnesota Press, 1989), especially "Foucault on Modern Power," chap. 1, pp. 17-34.

11 The idea of culture as symbol system is most commonly associated with the writings of Clifford Geertz (see Clifford Geertz, ed., *Myth, Symbol and Culture* [New York: Norton, 1974]).

12 An interesting co-relation with this idea is found in Malek Bennabi, *Vocation de l'Islam* (Paris: Seuil, 1954); in English, *Islam in History and Society* (Chicago: Kazi Publications, 1988). Colonialism "kills the colonized materially and the colonizer morally" (p. 111).

13 Not quite true. See James Evans, *Cree Syllabic Hymn Book: Norway House* (1841; reprint, Toronto: Bibliographical Society of Canada, 1954).

14 Vandersteene, "ATC."

15 Ibid.

16 Vandersteene is making a distinction between absorption and assimilation, as this quotation shows. He probably ended up thinking that aboriginals would never ever assimilate, but that they would be absorbed into a larger society. His views mirror A. Irving Hallowell's on the psychological centre of Lakota identity: "a persistent core of psychological constellations, aboriginal in nature ... is clearly discernible through all levels of acculturation yet studied. For this reason all the Ojibwa referred to are still Indians in a psychological sense, whatever clothes they wear, whatever their occupation, whether they speak English or not, and regardless of race mixture. While culturally speaking, they appear more and more like whites at 'higher' levels of acculturation, there is no evidence at all for a basic psychological shift in a parallel direction" ("Ojibwa Personality and Acculturation," *Selected Papers of the XXIXth International Congress of Americanists*, edited by Sol Tax, vol. 29, no. 2 [Chicago: University of Chicago Press, 1954], p. 112).

17 Vandersteene, *Levensvervulling*, p. 12.

18 Ibid., p. 14.

19 Vandersteene, *Wanneer gij*, p. 26.

20 Vandersteene, *Levensvervulling*, p. 78.

21 See above, pp. 189-90.

22 Had Vandersteene been willing to do it, he could have explored the various meanings of the trickster figure Wisakaychak, where he would have found an alternative language of life and death. In these stories, the sacred is deliberately unknowable, weird, strange. That is because no net of words or rational structure could catch the meaning. There can be no theology in the Euro-Canadian sense because human logic fails before its presence. Words, a mere human invention, collapse in the encounter with the Cree sacred. Only by Vandersteene venturing into alternatives to his Christocentric piety could he have found another route to solve that issue. It is a measure of how great the distance is between Western religious tradition and its God who speaks in literate form, accommodating Himself to a Book (the ultimate expression in Islam), and Cree tradition with fluid oral tales and encounter ceremonial forms, that the one way we have come to appreciate native truth is through art.

23 See, for example, Hans-Georg Gadamer, *Truth and Method* (New York: Seabury Press, 1975); Paul Ricoeur, *The Conflict of Interpretation*, edited by Don Ihde (Evanston: Northwestern University Press, 1974); and Mark C. Taylor, *Erring: A Postmodern A/theology* (Chicago: University of Chicago Press, 1984).

24 Richard J. Bernstein, "Hermeneutics and Its Anxieties," in Daniel O. Dahlstrom, ed., *Hermeneutics and the Tradition* (Washington, DC: American Catholic Philosophical Association, 1988), pp. 67-68.

25 For example, Constantine Passaris, *Understanding Canadian Immigration* (Toronto: Canadian Foundation for Economic Development, 1978); and Milly Cameron, ed., *Between Two Worlds: The Canadian Immigration Experience* (Montreal: Quadrant, 1983).

26 Keith A. McLeod, ed., *Multiculturalism, Bilingualism and Canadian Institutions* (Toronto: Urban Alliance on Race Relations, 1977), and Harold Palmer, ed., *Immigration and the Rise of Multiculturalism* (Vancouver: Copp, Clark, 1975).

27 Hugh MacLennan, *Two Solitudes* (Toronto: Macmillan of Canada, 1986; originally published in 1945).

28 Joseph Epes Brown, *The Sacred Pipe: Black Elk's Account of the Seven Rites of the Oglala Sioux* (Norman, OK: University of Oklahoma Press, 1953). The controversy over the authenticity of this account is taken up in John G. Neihardt, *Black Elk Speaks: Being the Life Story of a Holy Man of the Oglala Sioux* (Lincoln, NE: University of Nebraska Press, 1961).

29 Paul B. Steinmetz, S.J., *Pipe, Bible, and Peyote among the Oglala Sioux: A Study in Religious Identity* (Knoxville: University of Tennessee Press, 1990).

30 W.E.H. Stanner, "On Aboriginal Religion," *Oceania*, 30 (1960): 245-78.

31 See above, Chapter One, p. 13.

32 Omer Stewart, "The Peyote Religion and the Ghost Dance," *The Indian Historian*, 5 (1956): 27-30.

33 As, for example, pp. 50-55.

34 See Hazel W. Hertzberg, *The Search for an American Indian Identity: Modern Pan-Indian Movements* (Syracuse, NY: Syracuse University Press, 1971).

35 See the entire statement in Appendix 2, pp. 312-15.

Ten

Theoretical Epilogue: Vandersteene and the Understanding of Religion

> Go home! Egyptians resent Westerners who come here to
> study us when they can't study themselves.
> — Cairene after publication of *The Munshidin*
> *of Egypt: Their World and Their Song*

E gypt and Canada seem rather remotely connected. But for this
chapter they are. I have appended this theoretical epilogue to develop the methodological issues implicit or suggested in the main body
of the text. As will be seen, the study of Vandersteene draws some of its
inspiration from my work in Egypt, since the contemporary experience
of religion encountered there provided the framework for understanding his orientation to other traditions. Moreover, a challenge thrust
upon me in Cairo really set up the intellectual inquiry that became this
study.

I had attended a party attended by various literati and artists at the
pleasant, up-scale home of one of my former teachers in Cairo, and,
during the conversation, the subject of my recently published book
came up. There was some restiveness among the commentators. Some
thought the topic did not merit the attention of an Islamic scholar;
some lauded it as a pioneering study of a group that Egyptian scholars
and writers had failed to even acknowledge; some resented that a foreigner had to come to study the Sufi singers. One statement struck me
tellingly:

"Well, we really have mixed feelings about your book. On the one
hand, it has explored something no one else has done, and that's significant. But, on the other, we don't like people looking at our folk traditions. We get very tired of Westerners who can go anywhere in the

---

Notes to this chapter are on pp. 306-308.

292

world to study 'the natives' but who can't or won't look at themselves. Mostly I would say, 'Go home! Egyptians resent Westerners who come here to study us when they can't study themselves.' "

My reaction was, "Yes! Of course. Your point is reasonable. It is *natural that one should be able to apply one's insights at home!*" So I took the challenge seriously. If a career spent studying Islam is distorted when the only object of that study is but a particular group in a particular country, a career in religious studies is distorted if one cannot study one's own traditions. Moreover, it seemed only legitimate that the skills developed abroad could, indeed should, be applicable at home. I came to accept that my Egyptian friend was quite right—there is a moral issue involved if one cannot train one's analytic skills on oneself. *Dissonant Worlds* is my answer.[1]

In what follows, we look more closely at the theoretical issues which this study has raised: a closer look at what I have called interstitial religion and its manifestations in the Vandersteene case and a more incisive examination of the issues involved in interstitial leadership, along with some weighing of the ritual orientation of Vandersteene's approach. Finally I will draw out a few principles concerning religion in Canada arising out of Vandersteene's work.

Vandersteene and Interstitial Religion

Vandersteene *would not* have agreed with Geertz: "Understanding the form and pressure of . . . natives' inner lives is more like grasping a proverb, catching an allusion, seeing a joke—or reading a poem— than it is like achieving communion."[2] The instant insight accorded by a sudden grasping of a connection may help to know something about aboriginals, but the real core could only be experienced by the daily living in those regular patterns composing their life. One had to devise a means of living as the other, in the other's most meaningful activities. *One had to live in cohesion with the deepest values of the people in order to commune at their level.* In Vandersteene's view, this meant plunging into the religious world of the other.

The awareness of this truth came about slowly in Vandersteene's career. It surely arose first out of failure: he initially realized that Cree did not understand his descriptors, his symbols, his "language," his own sacred, that is, the Catholic mass. He came to see that they could not relate to the sacred as Euro-Canadians conceived of it. Even when he used terms laden with Cree sacrality, like Manitou, within a Christian context, he was not able to move the Cree deeply. He came to believe that another way of comprehending the Cree had to be found. Eventually he saw that everything from language to eating to humour

had Cree spiritual values within it; he came to hold that his empower-
ment could only come through engaging whole-heartedly even passionately in that sacred world of the other, *as it was encountered everyday
by the Cree*.[3]

How did he perceive the most sacred aspects of Cree existence to be
best engaged? Vandersteene probed this problematic in many ways, including (to name only the most important) language, social interaction,
cultural/religious activities (such as healing practices), art and sacred
ritual. Rightly or wrongly, (and this may be the vestige of European
values he retained) he came to the conclusion that Cree life was built
upon a "core" Cree character, and he would have to engage the Cree
through the most powerful expressions of that character.

Thus, first and foremost, Vandersteene grounds his reforms in a particular understanding of Cree psychology. The "core" of the traditional
Cree is not a set of beliefs nor a set of ethical principles, but the constant dialogue with the spirit world, begun initially through a vision
quest or dream and subsequently imprinted upon the inner being. Until that imprinting, the individual has no *personal* character. Thus one's
being becomes individualized by the spirit helper invading his experience; *ocitaw* takes up "abode" within, henceforth expressing a deliber-
ate destiny through the person. Yet this is not a fully known personna;
this character must undertake its own education in the world, and the
environment around the individual, including the social and religious
mores of the Cree, provides the training ground for the meaning one's
being possesses. Everything has the potential to teach something important to the person. But the learning from this world is always made
through the personality bequeathed by the spirit helper.

As individuals mature, and their inner lives are enriched by many
spirit helpers, they become far deeper and more spiritual. An inner
dialogue with one's spirit helpers sets the tone for a meditative life. For
Vandersteene the greatest Cree he knew reflected that depth: a quiet
dignity, a sense of selfhood unmolested by events, a mystical reliance
on an inner resilience and confidence. Thus, for the Cree, the soul of
the person presupposes multiple formulations and directionalities.
This was the *real Cree core of being*.

Vandersteene's confidence in "core" values likely derives from the
natural mysticism of Flemish mystic Jan Van Ruysbroeck (1293-1381),
for whom he had immense respect. Van Ruysbroeck, a simple priest
who retreated to the joys of mystical contemplation in the forest at
Groenendael, just outside Brussels, became one of the most celebrated
of Belgian contemplatives.

Van Ruysbroeck argued that there was a balance between all things, between living in the midst of people and living with God; he held that God was both existing and becoming, because, while the essence of God was at rest, the three persons of the Trinity spoke of action and process. This meant that the true nature of God is beyond our ability to grasp, and we have to be intellectually content with symbols and half-truths.

The ecstatic vision Van Ruysbroeck had of God was driven by his belief that love was the most compelling part of God, and constituted the element that unified the Godhead. Words were pointers, that intimated where the completion of being resided. When those who have achieved the fullness of inner insight are aware of the presence of God in their inner selves and conjoin the best of their intellects with this "spark" of God within, then they have the final experience of life, the superessential or "God-seeing life." Such life had usually been accorded the name of "true religion," but in fact, Van Ruysbroeck held that it could not be named, because reason required names (concepts). This does not mean that religion had no reasonableness about it, only that it could only be grasped in process.[4]

This core manifested itself in the individual through a rhythmic apprehension of life, by means of which one was more and more synchronized with the cosmos. In this way, ordinary life took on a *liturgical* tone. Thus we can see how Vandersteene could integrate Cree notions of the person with the perception of liturgical life derived from Van Ruysbroeck.

Vandersteene judged that the most fundamental tensions could best be resolved not by trying to overcome everyday dissonances but by encountering the sacred world of the other, in his case, the Cree, entirely *by means of* Cree forms. One is to become dual-positional in comprehending religion, that is, to be able to comprehend one's own religion through the forms offered by another. For him, the easiest means in this dual-positionality is ritual. Hence, he strives to find the basic ritualizing ingredients of Cree life and religion.

What was needed, then, was a Christianity founded explicitly on Cree cultural traditions, not a European Christianity with a Cree admixture. He crafted what can be called a Christo-Cree *interstitial religion*.

The question of the meaning of Vandersteene's interstitial religion is larger than just this singular missionary and his Cree problematic. It reflects, I believe, our collective encounter with the contemporary crisis of religious life. It also touches the heart of the Canadian vision of various religions in service to the common good. In the face of the failings and shortcomings of religion, even the problems of comprehending its truths seem to overwhelm the religiously aware. With so much diverse and divisive opinion about religion, whether one's own or others, how is one to judge the direction one should take? How is one to maintain the correct direction of faith when the objective signposts have disappeared? How can one live sensitively even humanly within a community, when that community comprises of various kinds of "the other?"

Religion, with its ultimate foundations for all life, makes absolute claims. Commitments to one's own tradition, by its very nature, privileges one's own religious answers. Yet those very answers relegate the other to inferiority. How can the deepest resources for good that is resident in religion presage such potential rejection? What is left but living with one's community by depreciating someone else's religion?

Vandersteene attempted to respond to these problems by developing a new kind of religious response, one based on a fundamental principle necessary in the Canadian Cree-Christian environment: *to act in such a way as to maintain the moral vision of God's creativity in religions.* He was governed by the conception that destroying another religion was destroying the work of God: "Every nation is an idea of God, every culture is an answer to that idea. Once it is supernaturally lifted-up by liturgy, Indian culture becomes eternal in God, even though it eventually disappears as any other human culture."[5]

It follows then that every religion is the creative expression of God through distinctive cultures, and each, through its own liturgy, finds a place of worship in God.[6] What must be done is to preserve the essential character of that religion by merging with it the critical distinctive of the Christian tradition. Out of this will come a genuine kind of local Christianity.

For Vandersteene, the cultural structures of Cree existence are foundational, and one must draw upon the sacred elements present there to formulate a new Cree Christianity. To use New Testament imagery, what is essential is the wine, not the wineskin. Discard the European wineskin that hampers access to the wine.

Vandersteene's view suggests that interstitial religion exists when the old forms, that is, European Christianity, are seen to be unable to carry the message, and before the proposed modifications have formulated a new and recognizably different religious expression, i.e., an institutional "Cree Christianity." Until this is in place, there will be an environment of transition.

Yet the fact that the religion can be envisioned, can be operated upon, can be described as the goal and can be said to be encountered in a new kind of ritual form indicates that it exists. It operates, in a way, like Heidegger's encounter with *being* — present but not able to be articulated. Interstitial religion thus suggests that encountering the "other" is a religious task that primarily functions in *process*, but which gives the conviction that what one encounters very powerfully *actually and truly is*.

From this overview, some characteristics of interstitial religion arising out of Vandersteene's work can now be sketched. The first is that the encounter upon which the proposed religion will be based is related to a cultural/religious form already in place, but the proposed expression cannot be conceived either as just an admixture of Cree elements nor satisfied with conventional Catholic Christian meanings. *It lives in the* process *of its being formulated and institutionalized*.

Secondly, a new religious reality exists as a possibility because the old is too culturally biased, and the essential coding of the experience cannot be done meaningfully by the other the way it is. Hence it has as yet no permanent configuration.

Thirdly, there is a liturgical fit which must be accommodated, else the power of encounter with the sacred will not be experienced for the Cree. For Vandersteene, working out the processes of this amounts to constructing a sacramental system that provides the opportunity for its participants to have a genuine encounter with God, as God is encountered by the foundational religio-cultural tradition.[7]

Fourthly, interstitial religion will be seen by someone outside to be purely sycretistic, not synoptic, that is, it will only appear to be an attempt to provide an outlet for culturally specific details, not alternative visions of the sacred; this is not its true purpose, however, because the cultural expression that fits the people arises out of their inner being, and has its own inner dynamic which must take its own intrinsic form to be acceptable. Moreover, the syncretistic view presupposes one cultural matrix, with all the assumptions deriving from one cultural system. Interstitial religion assumes that there are at least two, and consciously accepts that they will remain in existence.

Fifthly, basic processes can be seen at work in its formation, processes like the awareness of cultural tension and the need to resolve those tensions. Vandersteene knows how the tension can be resolved. He directs all his energies to its construction, and uses all his talents to promote it, selecting what he thinks will encapsulate it. It is not Cree as it is seen now, but Cree as it will be, complete with the lifting up of Christ's love deemed missing from current Cree liturgy.[8] The interaction between what was in place and what should be in place is governed by a sense of balance and reciprocity, indications of interstitial values operative in the process.

Finally, Vandersteene's work testifies to the importance of the interstitial to religious life, even to raising the issue of its being a permanent part of all religious life. Even while he was consciously a Flemish Christian, he passionately valued the religious mode of the other because it drew the deepest resources of his being toward its legitimization. He thus highlights the curious fact of interstitial religion: it strives to be superseded eventually by a permanent form — but prizes the distinctives it is attempting to integrate. Thus it is a kind of religious experience anticipating self-destruction, certainly a most unusual one among religion's intuitions.

Interstitial Religion and Leadership

It is evident that this approach to religion is based upon charismatic leadership; in Vandersteene's case, it is based upon attaining a special quality of leadership steeped in both Cree and Catholic Christian life. We turn now to the most important patterns of this leadership.

Steentje was shifting away from a text-based model of religious expression towards one of intuitive action, and hence he moved almost automatically toward the liturgical.[9] He did not believe he was creating a "new" religion; he held he was only setting up a Cree liturgical form of Christianity. Vandersteene saw it as the common "language" that the Church, indeed, the whole Church, shared with the Cree.

The medium of leadership in ritual reformulating situations brings us once again to Egypt. The fundamental role of ritual leadership forms a theme underlying my previous work, *The Munshidin of Egypt: Their World and Their Song*,[10] the book that raised the questions mentioned above. In that study, I was concerned with the phenomenon of a group of religious leaders who lived and worked in a religious environment where their position was clearly derivatory, but who, during the ritual situation, became specially charged with spiritual authority, so that they became absolutely indispensable. That is, they sang at the behest of the Shaikh of the Sufi order (the tariqa), and were decidedly controlled by him/her, but they were perceived as presenting a message from a higher source. That power could be named as God, or the Prophet, or the founder of the order, the Saintly Shaikh. The basic point is that the religious situation transformed the *munshidin* from those with decidely "second-order" authority, to those commanding the spiritual moment. The provisionary nature of their role appeared essential to their performance; indeed, one could say they revelled in it. Hence the organizational structure of the order, with its formal statuses and roles, did not encompass the entire meaning of religious leadership. It follows that one's role could be decidedly derivative from an organizational standpoint, and yet one could insist that that role was absolutely essential from a participational standpoint of the tradition. What gradually dawned upon me from the Egyptian Muslim context was that the religious authority of the ritual moment *may well* appear ephemeral to the analyst whose vision is pre-empted by organizational issues, but it is evidently absolutely essential *for the religious success of the group*. In that moment these people found their "calling" to be entirely fulfilling regardless of what the analyst thought of their organizational power. This has led me to believe that interstitial authority was a critical religious category that the status-minded analyst effectively ignored.

It struck me that Vandersteene was another type of interstitital leader: he was marginal insofar as Cree tradition was concerned, and his views ultimately isolated him from many of his Church colleagues. Yet he clearly believed that he had a calling to formulate a distinctive Cree Christianity, based upon the rituals of the *wikokewin*. He saw equivalence between himself and the shamans who brought the spirits into the presence of the people during the ceremony, except he would create a new liturgical form with Christian orientations.

In all of this he was aware of the special insights necessary to bring this about. Christian spiritual encounters with God were ritually similar to the encounter with the spiritual ancestors in the *wikokewin*. The meaning of death, sacrifice, community solidarity and ritual goals were all perceived to be equivalent. He evinced that the most elegantly patterned rituals found among the Cree were but the Cree equivalent to the long-standing European cultural tradition, only in their own distinctive form. What was needed was the prophetic ability to lead the Cree to it, and the political savvy to encourage his Canadian Church to accept the vision.

Vandersteene demonstrates that interstitial leadership rests partly upon a formal position within a tradition (i.e., the *munshid* is a Muslim Sufi, Vandersteene a Catholic missionary) and partly upon an alternative conception of the sacred encounter (the Sufi requires the ritual of *dhikr*, not accepted by the majority of Muslims as binding; the missionary must formulate his Christian life around Cree-identifiable characteristics). In the ritual moment theological concepts and intellectual distinctives are less dominant, presenting an occasion of fluidity where the spiritual person, in the form of the leader, must utilize his spiritual insights to lead in worship. In that moment, he is supreme regardless of what status he normally has. This is the triumph of the spiritual savant, not of the institutional priest.

From Vandersteene's perspective, no new "priesthood" was needed, since he did not see the reality the new liturgy would embrace to be any different than the old. What was needed was a religious skill—an insight into other symbols and uses more associated with Cree religious traditions, freeing them so that all their potential could be detected. In keeping with the religious ecologies of both European Christianity and Cree tradition, what Vandersteene held out for had a prophetic quality about it, and this accounted for the term often applied to him. But the role was constituted by a deep moral attitude about religious value in religions other than one's own.

Vandersteene and the Natural Liturgy of the Cree

We have seen that the vehicle he came to believe would centre him in the Cree world was liturgical in form; it was a "natural" liturgy, that is, a liturgy arising out of the deepest Cree cultural values. To those who fretted that this left an opening to superstitions Vandersteene had a sharp reply: "What is a superstition? It is sometimes something we just don't quite understand. There is no destruction in superstitions."[11]

Still, it is difficult to comprehend how any activity could be eliminated as being un-Christian under these guidelines. Yet we know that Vandersteene was no cultural purist: he worked diligently to change mourning customs in his missions. He evidently did not believe that everything Cree was good. Rather, he seemed predisposed to accept "natural" Cree rituals.

What can be "natural" about Cree ritual? Obviously he looked to his experience of the *wikokewin* as definitive. Such rituals would encircle the entire community, drawing upon their skills and abilities in both the religious and social spheres. It would constitute "an event," a significant expression that was powerful enough to bind all to participating regardless of personal differences. It would be expressed as Cree, because it revolved around the central feature of the Cree non-human beings whose ancestry coursed in their veins. It was natural in that it accepted and expressed all those ordinary values known among the Cree: eating, singing, drumming, dancing and honouring. It was natural because it was based upon Cree relationships, roles, orderings and livelihoods. It was natural because the process responded to Cree senses of time, place and activity. It was Cree because Cree specialists brought the event about, both by their initiative and through their gifts from the other world. In short, it was Cree because it had its genesis and motivations deep in Cree life.

Vandersteene and Archaic Religion

Yet I believe his vision failed because Vandersteene had misconceived interstitiality in the Canadian context. For example, all Cree were not disposed to understand themselves as "traditional." Some, like Nabis, explicitly rejected the Cree belief because it came in direct conflict with their religious experience. Some even turned against their own ancient tradition insofar as its concept of self-formation was concerned. On closer inspection, something very Cree in character was transpiring: seeking spiritual blessings from God in Pentecostalism was very much like seeking spirit helpers in the traditional Cree religion — each new spiritual experience added another level to the inner life.

At the time, Vandersteene chose to account for the sudden shift among the Cree as a rejection of the complexity of his Church for an essentially "surface" liturgy. Such behaviour, he supposed, arose out of the confusion of the people in the crossfire of Canadian secularity and diverse religions. He could not see that his Cree parishioners may well have regarded his particular vision of Cree interstitial religion as yet another attempt by a white man to construct a separate niche for them within Canada's religious environment, when they really wanted to be accepted and embraced by the white man for what they wanted to be, that is, Canadians like themselves with common religious motivations. They wanted to be individualist, even ecstatic, in their response with the divine, not regimented into a specific rite. Hence, *it was not institutional difference that these people wanted; it was to be regarded as sharing in the free common religiosity which everyone experienced within the pluralist Canadian reality.*

Thus, for Steentje's parishioners, the spectre of being marginalized Indians is resolved by the warm and emotional embrace of members of the white Protestant church, who accepted them as having common religious experiences. It was a direct way into the larger Canadian community. Since Vandersteene's Catholic Church no longer seemed to provide that way into the Canadian community, it could safely be abandoned. His vision really created a ghetto Church, which was fundamentally at odds with the Cree sense of being Canadian. My analysis concludes that he misjudged how connected Cree are to the religious life of other Canadians at a deep level, and how solidly they see themselves as an essential ingredient of the country's soul.

In order to come to terms with the deeper processes in action in Vandersteene from the Euro-Canadian side we will turn briefly to some of Eliade's views on the relationship of modernity to the "archaic" or the so-called "primitive." Eliade argued that until modernity had confronted its cultural past, it would never be able to understand its own current experiences. Like Vandersteene, Eliade thought there was something irreducible about archaic cultures, because out of them came many of the themes that feed the imaginary world of the soul today.[12] He also believed that modern people had to confront the "other," and specifically the other of primitive[13] myth and ritual, not just to understand that type of religion per se (which was not open to us anyway), but to comprehend the patterns that continued to percolate within our contemporary religious culture.

In his *Patterns in Comparative Religions*,[14] Eliade sought to show that modern experience always betrays patterned understandings, which were then subject to analysis. The sacred of "primitives" had a morphology, meaning that it had assumptions built into it about how the sacred operated and how they were to respond to it. This morphology could be read by modern people, bringing to awareness forgotten morphologies of the sacred which may now live in the subconscious.

Let us now consider, in the light of these aspects of the historian of religion's explorations, Vandersteene's emphasis on the original Cree culture and its application to his leadership commitments. Vandersteene believed that cultures were distinctive, developing out of idiosyncratic ways of encountering God. In this he was following the view common in Europe during his youth, and of Eliade's, that primitive cultures were an expression of the human spirit and should not be undermined by Christian dogma.[15] However, the longing for origins seems to be peculiarly European, so the distance from his Canadian colleagues was not of a superficial order, and perhaps not even fundamentally a disagreement over the treatment of the Cree people, but really was one of the psyche and its mythology. His whole experience since he had come to Canada had been to find the true origin of religion—to discover the primal reality resident in an untrammelled world. He sought that in the one place where the centre still held in Cree identity—the northern bush of Canada. Claims that Vandersteene was "outdated" really miss the mark: he was looking for a religious reality that was beyond the Cree to provide, indeed, probably that they never could have provided. He had not lived in the urban environment where Cree response had been manifold and acculturated. He had not acknowledged that the dramatic shift of aboriginal population is toward the urban environment, with its diverse religious character.[16] Rather, he argued that the aboriginal was not at home in the urban centre, and the lack of dignity and generally unfortunate circumstances which many encountered there were ultimately the result of a dislocation within their religious world. His search for renewal of Cree dignity and strength based on the traditional values of Cree religion for both urban and bush Cree as the only set of common concerns they both shared receives its power in his life from the European nostalgia for an ancient religious unity, a nostalgia generally identified as the "nostalgia for origins."[17]

Vandersteene held that religious ritual was the only explicit form capable of carrying and restoring correct relationships in the Cree world, and set about to create one that would provide it. He believed that Euro-Canadian culture was the principle evil buffeting the Cree, but, true to Cree conceptions, did not argue that a return to pagan forms of ritual was the answer. Instead, he envisioned a new ritual formula that would bring together the prime religious ritual of the West (Christian celebration of Christ's death and resurrection) and the central ceremonial of the Cree (the *wikokewin*) into a new ritual formula. He had in his own being to deal with the traumas and sacrifices necessary to bring this about, cultivating the potential out of his own initiative and his own imagination, given what he knew.[18] His own role was something akin to a trailblazer in the spiritual world, perhaps informed by Cree culture-bringer Wisakaychak. It was a bold attempt, but it fell short.

Vandersteene and Canadian Religion

Yet for all the failure of Vandersteene's liturgical vision, its interstitial nature still remains powerful. Vandersteene's insight that Cree culture must become the basis for any abiding institutional religious form for Church mission is widely acknowledged today, even if the precise meaning of that may differ. Taken in a larger sense, Vandersteene is really arguing that the religious values of the country's original peoples must be prized as an essential part of Canadian religious identity. Moreover, each religious "other" is part of a shared spiritual environment. Even in the face of incredible diversity, then, there is the sense that just beyond our striving to live with the other is a unifying religious vision that all share who inhabit this land. Encountering it leads us all to deeper understanding of our religious selves and thereby redefines our religious identity.

The more he became spiritually Canadian, the more the underlying power of the Canadian environment opened up religious depths to him. He thus became Canadian in a way that his European family could not comprehend. For example, Willem Vermandere tells of Steentje's confiding to him that the Cree had taught him that life was like a great river, full of whirlpools, but once you accommodated yourself to its rhythms, you would sail into the great ocean of God without

difficulty. The idea is expressed in a poem written within the first five
years of his mission, and after his early experiences in Little Red River:

> *River of Peace*
>
> The slow steady stream
> of driving water.
> But on the surface
> the playful splash
> of ever-changing wind.
> Exile
> if you're a canoe
> empty and light upon the water
> you toss hither and yon with the wind
> and you'll never see the shining lake
> in the land of Your Father
> But if heavy with concentration and longing
> you find the deep eddies
> you float through the wind
> in the steady safe flow
> of the current.
> Then the changing wind
> and the waves
> sing
> around your bow
> and every paddle stroke
> is no longer aching effort
> but surrender to joyful hope.

July 1955

The adoption of the river opens for us the problematic of the land,
geography and ecology in Canadian culture. For Steentje to accept natural metaphors for the meaning of life with his close friends indicates
that he appropriated a Canadian orientation long associated with the
literati, but which he apparently arrived at from his own feeling of
spiritual value. Very few of his poems do not have references to images
and metaphors drawn from nature or the environment around him.
Admittedly, he uses natural language to talk of Flanders at times, too,[19]
but his poetry has a freshness and familiarity with the countryside in
northern Alberta to which he related in a deeply held manner.

With the demise of the Soviet Union, Canada may now claim to be
the largest country in the world. The incredible variety and nature of
this vast expanse has often inspired poets and writers, but seldom have

these writers been concerned only with the land as a geographic entity; they have written of an environment, a shape and form that takes on a kind of presence. As such, weather, seasons and natural rhythms all integrate into the reality about which they speak. The result is that "the land" becomes a living force, influencing and challenging each Canadian in a different manner. Many of the writers speak of the reality they encounter with such awe that the whole attitude has been denoted as "geopiety."[20]

The place where one lives has attracted the attention of religion specialists like Gerardus van der Leeuw, but mostly for what it said about the general religious category of sacred space. They seldom look at one's environment as a totality within which one lives. They seem to imply that sacred space is only temple space, or that delineated as having direct religious import; the "space" of one's world is profane and therefore not subject to religious analysis. But in the Canadian case, the encounter with this ecology constitutes a foundational theme in Canadian identity, at least as it is seen through its writers.[21] Such a foundational character carries strong religious overtones; some might argue we have here a basic Canadian religious value. What has become of a reality that, starting with the terror of a storm, or of the anguish of the death of a relative in a blizzard, becomes a means of articulating hidden perceptions of the human condition? It becomes the kind of reality about which one can speak without being convinced that one knows exactly what the message is. It becomes a kind of spiritual terrain, from which images of a people are continually reflected, in a give-and-take of mutual discovery. It is a universe of meaning, a language through which existence is articulated. This is Vandersteene's example:

Northern Night

summer night
in which evening glow
flows into morning red

God's love blooms
tense awareness
of day and sun

on smouldering horizon
at once hidden and revealed
anguish subsides.

11 June 1976

This, then, brings Vandersteene into the heart of the Canadian human ecological scene. Insofar as these intimations reflect a Canadian consciousness, of something implicit in the Canadian experience, they reflect Vandersteene as being part of it. I think we can safely say that when he left this land in Slave Lake that day, the great river, the Peace, truly ran through his soul.

Notes

1 I am painfully aware that some aboriginals would argue that as a white I am as shut off from their views as any "other," and that the resentment is just as great for me attempting to speak for aboriginal traditions in this work as among the Egyptians. It should be clear that I do not hold to airtight definitions of "the other" which would grant acceptance of this argument. Constructions of the other seem to me to be as much made by human minds and cultures as concepts of identity and hence are also subject to other ways of seeing.

2 Clifford Geertz, "From the Native's Point of View: On the Nature of Anthropological Understanding," in P. Rabinow and W.M. Sullivan, eds., *Interpretive Social Science: A Reader* (Berkeley: University of California Press, 1979), p. 241.

3 A good example of such an approach is Rita Nakashima Brock, *Journeys by Heart: A Christology of Erotic Power* (New York: Crossroad, 1988).

4 See Evelyn Underhill, ed., *John of Ruysbroeck*, translated by C.A. Wynschenk Dom (London: John M. Watkins, 1951); John Ruysbroeck, *John Ruysbroeck: The Spiritual Espousals and Other Works*, introduced and translated by James A. Wiseman, O.S.B. (Mahwah, NJ: Paulist Press, 1985); and John Ruysbroeck, *Blessed Jan Van Ruysbroeck: The Spiritual Espousals*, introduced and translated by Eric Colledge (Westminster, MD: Christian Classics, 1983).

5 Vandersteene, "ATC."

6 Interestingly, Vandersteene's conflicts with his own principles arise most noticeably with the Protestants. The reason for this lay, I think, not in a personal crisis and his declining health, however important they were. Nor was it rooted in the ugliness of the Peace River missions. Rather it was in the uprooting of the Trout Lake church by the Alliance and Pentecostals. It was awareness that his notion of the Cree character would not predispose the Cree to his Church, *even to a Cree-ritualized Church*. Vandersteene must have realized that the Cree "essence" was even more complicated than he had assumed: his notion of a single Cree ritual arising out of a Cree cultural core was contradicted by the readiness of his parishioners to abandon his "interstitial" religion for what he thought was a simplistic Christianity.

7 On the face of it, however, there does not seem to be any reason why the quest for encounter need only be via ritual. It may be that Vandersteene's acceptance of the Cree notion of balance and reciprocity, which operates primarily in everyday life, with its liturgical sense, was the key. Nevertheless, there is evidently the belief that there was a tension between the goal of the quest, and its formulation *in process* which itself set up as a kind of ritual response.

8 Thus he goes beyond the Jesuits, whom he greatly admired, by not just downplaying those elements of Euro-Christianity that did not appeal to the Indians and foregrounding the similarities. His concern is much closer to the South American liberation theologians who argue that different kinds of people experience God in different ways. But it is not motivated by the same vision, because it does not make social liberation paramount.

9 At least this allows us to solve one problem: why he did not develop a Cree theology? Initially this was a puzzle to me because he obviously had the resources to rein-

terpret the Church's message, and follow in the pathway of liberation theology around the world. After all, his colleagues in South America had made impressive gains for their people by writing such works. Yet, there is no evidence that he tried to do this. If we accept that traditional theology was heavily committed to Greek notions of the self, and that made it difficult to formulate a theology built upon the process of encounter with spiritual forces in Cree tradition, it is evident that such a thing could not happen if he were to be true to Cree tradition.

10 Earle H. Waugh, *The Munshidin of Egypt: Their World and Their Song* (Columbia: University of South Carolina Press, 1989).

11 Vandersteene, "ATC."

12 I have not been able to determine whether Vandersteene had read Eliade, although it is difficult to believe he had never come across his views. One problem is that Vandersteene did not footnote his comments, so it is difficult to determine whether they are original or reflections of his reading.

13 This term has lost its usefulness because of the pejorative implications. Unfortunately we do not have a legitimate alternative, although pre-literate and aboriginal have sometimes been substituted. I have remained with the term because I am trying to reconstitute what Eliade said.

14 Mircea Eliade, *Patterns in Comparative Religions* (Cleveland, OH: World Publishing, 1963).

15 This idea is almost surely a legacy of the Enlightenment. For the church, however, the real beginning of this process only took place with the work of Fr. Wilhelm Schmidt, who argued that primitive people all had a high god, which he took as evidence of a pre-existing monotheism in the process of decaying under the influence of local gods. His views are summed up in his magnum opus, *Der Ursprung der Gottesidee: Eine historische-kritische und positive Studie*, 12 vols. (Munster: Aschendorff, 1912-56).

16 The shift to Canada's cities by aboriginal populations on a major scale is a recent phenomenon. Regina, Saskatchewan's largest city, is rumoured to have a majority Cree population. This notion was behind Clara Yellowknee's comment that Vandersteene was outdated. See Appendix 2, p. 312.

17 Thus the history of religions discipline, from the time of its pater, Max Müller, perhaps along with history, anthropology and psychology, has committed no little of its methodological energy to uncovering the earliest or primordial religious "form," as if finding that form will then provide the key to subsequent human expression. What seemed to be ignored was that the data which might provide that form was buried in a past that was irretrievable. What we do have available is already extremely complicated.

18 One element continued to elude, him, however, and that was the loving gift of Christ Himself. Cree ritual did not seem to provide any structural equivalent to someone in the spirit world destroying himself in order to set things right. There is, of course, a very good reason for this lacuna: Cree traditionally had no notion of equivalence between people. Persons were only and always themselves *ocitaw*, having been constructed by their own experiences and spirit helpers, so none could be "equivalent" in that sense. Secondly persons were also partly the tribe, having ancestors to whom they were connected, so the atomistic sense of separate self undergirding the Christian idea of human and divine could not apply. I sense that Vandersteene knew this and saw himself as somehow the bridge for the Cree.

19 See Tanghe, *Leven*, p. 39.

20 Dick Harrison, ed., "Introduction," in *Crossing Frontiers: Papers in Western Canadian and American Literature* (Edmonton: University of Alberta Press, 1979). Consider Stegner's vision of the prairies: "The drama of this landscape is in the sky, pouring with light and always moving. The earth is passive. And yet the beauty I am struck by, both as present fact and as revived memory, is a fusion: this sky would not be so

spectacular without this earth to change and glow and darken under it. And whatever the sky might do, however the earth is shaken or darkened, the Euclidean perfection abides. The very scale, the hugeness of simple forms, emphasizes stability. It is not hills and mountains which we should call eternal. Nature abhors an elevation as much as it abhors a vacuum; a hill is no sooner elevated than the forces of erosion begin tearing it down. These prairies are quiescent, close to static; looked at for any length of time, they begin to impose their awful perfection on the observer's mind. Eternity is a peneplain" (Wallace Stegner, *Wolf Willow: A History, a Story and a Memory of the Last Prairie Frontier* [Toronto: Macmillan of Canada, 1955], p. 7).

21 See my articles, " 'The Almighty Has Not Got as Far as This Yet': Religious Models in Alberta's and Saskatchewan's History," in Howard Palmer and Donald Smith, eds., *The New Provinces: Alberta and Saskatchewan, 1905-1980* (Vancouver, BC: Tantalaus Research, 1973), pp. 199-215, and "Naming the Currents: A Foray into the Nature of Religion in Canada," *Religious Studies and Theology*, 12, 2-3 (May-September 1992): 105-28.

Appendix 1

Chronology of Roger (Rogier) Vandersteene's Life

15 June 1918	Born to George and Julia Vandersteene in Marke, Belgium
June 1925	First Communion, attended primary school in Marke
May 1926	Refused to wave Belgian flag in primary-school parade
June 1930	Confirmation
June 1930-1933	College of St. Amand in Kortrijk, secondary education
November 1932	Life-threatening tuberculosis
May 1937	Decision to enter the priesthood, novitiate of the Missionary Oblates of Mary Immaculate (O.M.I.)
September 1938	One year of novitiate at Korbeek-loo
29 September 1938	First vows of the Oblates, studied at Oblate school in Velaines, joined the Flemish Youth Movement and took pro-German sympathies for Flanders' sake
September 1940	Entered Apostolic Seminary of the Oblates at Waregem
Winter 1940	Helped organize young artists' group at seminary
5 June 1941	First tonsure of the priesthood
12 July 1941	Minor orders for priesthood (at Tournai)
20 December 1941	Final orders (in Brugge)
19 July 1942	Sub-diaconate (in Waregem)
29 September 1942	Decision to become a missionary
19 December 1942	Diaconate (in Brugge)
11 July 1943	Priesthood (in Kortrijk) by Bishop A. Clabaut
Spring 1945	Became "Priest with the Black Heart" for his role in defending collaborationists
29 October 1945	Assigned to the Vicariate of Grouard in Northern Alberta
14 June 1946	Julia Vandersteene died, delaying planned voyage to America
September 1946	Sailed for North America
13 November 1946	St. Bernard's Mission in Grouard
19 February 1947	Assigned to Akitameg for language study with Fr. Floc'h
1 September 1947	Assigned as trainee to St. Martin's Mission in Wabasca
29 August 1950	Formally assigned to school in Fort Vermilion and the mission in Little Red River, began building house and chapel
23 December 1951	First mass in completed chapel in Little Red River
July 1954	Assigned to teaching and the mission at Desmarais/Wabasca

13 December 1954	Took strong stand against residential schools and white "church" policy to Indians
Fall 1955	Publication of *Wabasca*
Winter 1956	Beginning of extended furlough in Flanders (partially for the Oblates)
June 1957	Return to Canada and assigned to new project at Trout Lake
September 1958	Trout Lake school; begins revision of mass based on *wikokewin*
1960	Completes grotto to Virgin Mary at Trout Lake
March 1960	Calumet medicine pipe bundle transferred to him; becomes "medicine man"
1962	Begins building tipi church at Trout Lake
1962	Begins liturgical reform, drawings for catechism *Come Lord Jesus!* — eventually published in 1973.
January 1965	Death of father, returns for funeral
September 1968	Assigned to diocese for revision of diocesan mission; begins writing another book, entitled *And They Built Roads*
Winter 1972	On furlough, returns to Flanders and hailed as hero; speaking engagements constantly throughout Flanders
Winter 1974	Returns to diocese, transferred to Peace River Missions of Jean d'Or, Garden River, Fox Lake
Spring 1975	Completes Cree course for Edie Scott
Fall/Winter 1975	Diagnosed with cancer of the lung
7 August 1976	Dies in Slave Lake, in his 59th year; Willem Vermandere's folk song about Vandersteene becomes song of the year in Belgium.

Appendix 2

Evaluations of Vandersteene Collected during Research

Cree Comments

Cree evaluations of Vandersteene are highly nuanced. The following exemplify the range of opinions:

Jimmy Blessie, Elder, Garden River

I want to say something of Father and his medicine powers. We should keep in mind the true role of the medicine man. Every medicine man gets his powers from God, but the medicine man had to ask how to use those powers and the moment he didn't have the proper attitude, he could use them destructively. I can be tempted by these powers and it's really a temptation to use power against people who don't see and do things properly. But you can't. Father knew that; that's how he knew about the temptation of Christ.

Father came to understand some of our ways, that reconciliation with fellow humans was more important than saying mass, and was really reconciliation with God. Being in touch with God is a matter of being truthful and accepting. There are special moments in life, too, special moments like the nighttime is the time you feel the strongest connection to the person that has died.

Johnsen Sewepagaham, Son of His Old Friend and Chief in Fox Lake

His interest in natives comes out of himself and experiences. He was a great spiritual person, in terms of being in tune with spiritual values. He's an elder, someone we look up to as wise. I never personally thought of him as a medicine man. To me personally, he wouldn't talk about the pipe. It was too spiritual for him to talk about the pipe.

Notes to this Appendix are on p. 321.

Clara Yellowknee, Liaison Officer for Relocation Programme, Slave Lake

I think a lot of Indians sort of worshipped him. But Fr. Vandersteene, if he were here in Slave Lake would have been outdated. Trout Lake was an isolated community, and he fit there. He was kind of a comical priest, and that brought people to him. His soft-spoken way attracted people.

I think he knew people would eventually change. My parents, for example, were simple, God-fearing people, and along the way many Cree people have lost that. But, I guess it's the simple way that he saw in the Indian people.

Harold Cardinal, Cree Leader and Traditions Practitioner

He was just a great person and I felt very comfortable with him. I think, in a global sense, he was very much in touch with what was going on, although he might have seemed out of tune for some people. In the North American context, there is a movement that is comprised of young people from many tribes pursuing intertribal religion. For example, you have Sioux coming into Alberta to talk to the old Cree people to get the perspectives of traditional Indian religion. You have Cree that go to the Arapaho in Wyoming. Generally, throughout North America, this move-ment has been underway for the last 10 or 15 years. There are a lot of others, some college-educated, who are just like these young people. They are basically travelling to get a better understanding of their roots and an understanding of their religion and different ceremonies. Eventu-ally, they go back to their homes and to their own communities. I think now it's probably moving into another phase — between the Indians of the two Americas. Fr. Vandersteene had very much in common with that movement whether or not the two are synonymous or not.

As part of the local scene, he was part of a process in the community. I think he was going a bit further in trying to meld some of the Indian cere-monies with the mass and various Catholic rituals. Whatever mistakes[1] he made in terms of not following exactly the rituals have to be over-looked in terms of what he, as an individual, accomplished in his own thinking. I think if he had lived he would have progressed a lot further in his thinking. The Cree idea is that the process guides you to a particular place in your thinking to get help. It is a process that leads you to under-standing. I think in terms of what he wanted to accomplish perhaps he was never able fully to do while he was alive, within the church. There was too much opposition by the clergy. At his funeral, the bishop delivered the sermon to the people that were there. It was a very moving experience in many ways to hear the priest on behalf of all assembled issue a formal apology to the Indian people who were there for the manner in which they had been misunderstood and that they had direct-ly fought to suppress the Indian religion and Indian ceremonies.

When I was 16 or 17, I was probably more Catholic than the Pope, and, in a way, I resented the Indian ways. I think as I developed and in my search for knowledge then the validity of the Indian way of life be-came more and more real to me, too. I have since renounced my mem-bership in the Catholic Church in feeling my own release in terms of the Indian religion. Some say, "What if it's a lost cause? These are old and dead. It doesn't exist," I think that is the wrong perspective. I sup-pose the positon Vandersteene took symbolizes the kind of belief more and more people have of our religous beliefs. Indian culture developed over many centuries. In many ways what we are looking at is people having an opportunity to learn about life (assuming first of all that they choose to believe in God), and having it available to them to make their own decisions. It's an opportunity to use the environment as a place of learning about what God is all about. As we look out from season to season, we remember stories and legends, or whatever you want to call them, that utilize every blade of grass, the trees, the leaves, the sky, the air, that is, use the environment as it is. It is much like going into uni-versity and using the university to learn or using modern forms of communication to gain some information. I suppose then there is an Indian kind of resource and potential, and Indian religions have some-thing to offer by being a helper in the process. When a person begins more or less within a religious context, then that person finds values there, and then more insight. I think Vandersteene understood that.

Indian people are respectful of the ideals of other communities, and they put their own in a larger context. I think that is what we are trying to do, and I think that is what Fr. Vandersteene was doing. Try to bring that knowledge of the buffalo back so people can relate to it. It has been un-derground for too long. People should take the position that Indian religions are knowledge about human ways and that they are no longer a hindrance to living in the modern world. Moreover, they should not stop there, they should say something about how Catholic Christian-ity, and Judaism and any other religion, gives a pattern for how life should be lived. I suppose people don't really understand that.

I think one has to see the multidimensionality of Vandersteene to fully appreciate him. For example, he sensed the kind of vulnerability that people in isolated villages suffer. All communities are not the same. These people are not generally seen to be a certain type of com-munity with a certain need for land and resources. In some of these contexts, the notion of privately owning this land is so remote that it can't be comprehended. Why they hold that should not be an issue. It should be accepted. Yet their lifestyle is not part of the development plan. Hence, they are pushed out, and their lifestyle destroyed. There have to be ways to stop this social destruction. There has been an attempt to get governments to recognize that something needs to be done for the community. But if you look at it, it was not for the Indians that they put this road in, it was for business, for oil, for logging, etc., it was not for Indians to enjoy. That's why he opposed the road into Trout. Vandersteene took the best defence possible, that is, by keeping it isolated until the Indians themselves wanted to have a road.

Indian ceremonies and Indian lifestyle, he thought, were the best insurance in the long run to help the people survive the changes that were going on. His major impact was in terms of creating a certain kind of awareness within the Catholic Church. From the standpoint of Canadian politics, I don't think his impact any different than any other traditional priest. I think his real impact was in his being significantly different than his colleagues. He became part of the culture by the Indian way of doing things. The story of the bear is not important in the way he said it was. The bear is a constant and important symbol but it is not what he said it was within the Indian context. The same can be said about the Wisakaychak stories; this is a basic Cree conception. I think Wisakaychak plays a far more important role than just a few tales. I think in that regard he may really never have come to Cree knowledge about Wisakaychak. Our elders have an advanced understanding of Indian tradition and are able to draw comparisions between the philosophies of the natives and other peoples and certainly in northern Alberta there are elders who have been exposed to them. On another plane, the stories reflect the respective roles that Wisakaychak, like Jesus Christ, played.

On Vandersteene's notion of sacrifice as thanksgiving: It is very crucial not only in the traditional Cree lifestyle but in the traditional lifestyle of all travellers on the way. Burning some of the meat was a traditional way of expressing thanksgiving. He was right on the mark about that.

On the question of his limited knowledge of native religions: The art of learning is a process, and Vandersteene was travelling in that process. I don't think he had reached a place where he had a good grasp of everything. In part I don't think that was his fault, his problem was a limited geographical area. Yet he made maximum use of his geographical area. If you want to understand traditional native religion, you have to take a very broad perspective. The knowledge base in Alberta is vast, but it is just a piece of the knowledge base of the Indian in North America. The requirements of his mission didn't enable him to move that far amongst the Indian people.

He was not a nationalist; to make him into a Canadian nationalist would be to do him a disservice. He spent his time within the community, and he judged things from the community perspective, which is the Cree way. That was why he opposed the residential schools — they destroyed Cree communities. When he compared the relationships among family members in the communities with those who came from residential schools, it went against what he had seen in his exposure in the communities and, perhaps, against his view of what life should be. He tended to reflect native mentality, however, and he didn't take activist, political stances. Rather he held that one had to deal with the existing mentality; if it had not changed, then one should not go against it.

Art Lamothe, Former Priest, Colleague in Missions and a Métis

A number of Fr. Vandersteene's most characteristic works and views had a great and enduring impact on me in my first years as a missionary. His discourse indicated that he had made some level of cultural conversion to the Cree, and was integrating his Christian faith. For him, if Jesus could be incarnated a Jew and be the Son of God he could as well have been incarnated a Cree and be the Son of God. A singular divine historical moment chose Abraham that could have been another, but made the difference. There is a view of the sacredness of culture implied in this, though to me he never put it quite so.

He held that the moral implications of the gospel were revealed before the time of Christ and known to other cultures. The conscious love of Christ as supportive motive was awaited.

Despite this and what some people thought, he never said the local church would be better off to have local people running it. In this he was in my view very much a traditionalist, for he said he saw men in the community who should and would have been ordained men whom he felt were his equal, naming Julian Gladue in Trout Lake and Jimmy Blessie in Garden River.

One of his gems surely was his language ability. His perception of the beauty of the Cree language and his mastery of it was said by the Cree to be unique. It was a sign to natives that their language was able to stand well with or against any other language. His devotion to Cree was closely related to his Christianity. Cree was a "perfect medium for the Christian message": those are his words.

He did good things in combining hymns and native melodies. These were readily adopted and devoutly sang in Garden River and Jean D'Or. So it was with his rewriting of the Our Father, his picture book of the Creeds, his introduction of the drums in the mass. Yet in all this, to me there was a certain taste. The fault, if any, may be with me. It was

"I've done something for you," not "You have done something beautiful." Or "we have. . . ." The cultural irony of sending outsiders to eliminate, say, the *wikokewin* can only be outdone by a self-appointed outsider in the name of apostolic activity attempting to reintroduce it
when dead, asking himself, "Do I make these people go back or do I
make them go on." In this I saw Rogier as a romantic. He laboured
under this cross which I do not think he asked for. If a Christian Cree
rite does not see the light of day, his cultural work, to take nothing
from his concomitant religious endeavour, will be of little long-term
apostolic significance. To me, it does however cry in a wilderness;
cultures are to be sacred in Christ.

Fr. Vandersteene saw an apostolic structural conflict between native
communities and the residential school phenomenon. Being a man of
the communities, he of course sided with them. He wished there could
be a priest in each community and a school, etc., as needed. This he
saw as a completely separate though related issue to the highly jeop-
ardized humanity of the schools. He was at times a messenger from the
parents to children who had done nothing wrong but were held from
their parents for four and six months at a time. These, often cared for
by one staff who for survival reasons soon learned, at best, to steel
themselves against all, having usually been emotionally drained by the
simultaneous nurturing seeds of 30 or more children. He saw the van-
ity of it and tried to find good in what the schools were doing, yet they,
compared with the community men in mission country, had a virtual
monopoly on church resources. He, on business, seeking companion-
ship or spiritual solace, arriving with his dogteam as if from another
era to a twentieth-century compound, was a phenomenon and often
made to feel it.

From all of this, it must not be taken that he personally was a sad
man. To me he exuded self-confidence, spirituality, honesty, enthusiasm and joviality. Many of his admirers and critics may be willing,
sight unseen, to abandon their eternal rewards for his.

Family Comments

Vandersteene's family had deep connections to him, even if some of
them were no longer Catholics. He remained the centre of the family,
providing a connecting link between them that held throughout the
years he was away. Omer Tanghe, his friend and priest in Kortrijk,
noted that this decision to leave and go on the mission field continued
to haunt him, "Family was a cross he had to bear. They needed him but
it was a sacrifice he had to make." Yet it is clear that his family still
impinged on his consciousness, even at the mundane level of whose

house he would reside in while on furlough, as much as at the centre of a spiritual world they valued.

Jos, His Godchild, Brother and Devotee[2]

He remained an outsider in Canada, and allied himself with Indians as a way of overcoming that. He was not accepted by some priests and the Bishop, and so the Church never gave him much assistance. He used writing as a kind of therapy. He wrote to my children to carry on his work, but little Christie, who was 10 at the time, was the only one who said, "I'll go, Father." He was very disappointed. The fact is Roger was only very happy in Canada with the Cree and in Flanders.

He had a mystical relationship with plants. Yet he was lonely even in the bush. He was not satisfied with nature, so he was torn between people and nature. Thus he was not a mystic in the traditional sense. Take his art. It's dominated by the female form. There's a special sense of nature expressed through a woman's form, and even his secular sketches have a religious quality. Somehow, in his art he is giving life to this woman. His Virgin Marys are beyond sex to that of mysterious womanhood.

Eric, Younger Brother

I think he was a very difficult man. He certainly was a bit hard on me. He left his family with so many troubles. Mietje worked so hard for him when he came home, even staying up at nights to feed him. He just expected it. The least he could have done was to give her a painting. He never did.[3] He thought everybody should do things just because of who he was. He was such an idealist; he really terrified us.

Wilfried, Younger Brother

He was a missionary of the people and not a missionary of system, but the fact is that he could react to Cree problems where he could not react to the Flemish. He saw parallels between Flemish children educated in secondary school in French and when they spoke Flemish they were punished. When he saw this same thing in Canada, he was revolted by it. In some of his views on minorities, he was ahead of his time.

Roger found it easy to deal with people with a certain kind of status. He chose his associates carefully. But the fact is if Roger had stayed in Flanders he would have had problems with the Church. He needed opposition in order to function. He also would have opposed the Belgium government. He needed a platform or structure so he could say to someone, "You are wrong about this."

Mietje, Youngest Sister

All the members of the family had a devotion to Roger. He was the heart of the family. We all felt deeply for him in his work. I recall that he said that, after 10 years and only three converts, the Bishop told him to go somewhere else. Roger's response was that the Church's job was not numbers. But when he came home the last time, the fire was gone. I don't think he felt anxious about returning.

Colleagues in Mission and Priesthood

Fr. André Platteeuw, Childhood Friend and Flemish Priest

Roger was more an artist than a priest and more a poet than an artist. Thus, you can see something of his true personality in his poetry. Like all the Vandersteenes, Roger tried to hide his true feelings. Poetry opened up a way for him to address those feelings. He was a poet with a message, fighting with his language, and there is no essential differ-ence between him and other poets of his time; the earliest nationalist poets wrote in Flemish and they were writers about their personal experience, Verschaeve, Timmermans, Teirlinck. If you look closely, he does the same thing — they start out joyful, but they end up in tragedy.

As for his art, most of his paintings were functional; they were for his Church. Art was the servant of his missions and his message. You get some measure of him, though, when you realize that he had no for-mal training in art.

During World War II he was a mixture of a man who collaborates and one who wants the evolution of his people. To preserve and devel-op Flemish, he must work with the Germans. He was limited in what he could see by his loyalty to Flanders. Basically he was uncomfortable with minority situations; he wanted people to see there was another way to look at people. From that perspective he was critical of his Church in Canada. He denied three things which the Church believed: that the Cree had no God, that they lived badly, that they were sav-ages. Some of his criticisms are found in his book *Wabasca*; there are substantial differences between the French and the Flemish version of that book — the Flemish version is much more critical of the Church.

Despite what the family might say, Roger left a legacy for them: he left them with a higher public status. But they gave him much, too. Take music, for example. Beethoven really derives from the family influence, since his music is a kind of family tradition.

Fr. Jean-Paul Vantroys, French Priest and Fellow Missionary

Despite his criticisms of the Roman Church he was a very strong Catholic. I am sure he was a mystic, a Flemish mystic. He thought the cross was a stupid failure but from God's view it was a success. One has to be a Christian to understand it. In his talks he always came back to the fact that we must be like Christ, we must be poor, we must die in order to live. Fr. Vandersteene said, "I pray to God every morning that I won't be posted to a white parish," so that's why he enjoyed his life among the Cree. It was "natural" for him. He was a poet and very sensitive. He taught that if they became pagan again, go right back to what they had been in the old tradition again, then they at least could belong to something there. You cannot distinguish in him culture from religion. As it was, natives had no foundation.

I said to him, "You are a prophet." For me a prophet is a person who does something to symbolize a message of some kind. "No way," he said, "I am not a prophet." But I think God sends us men with messages; He doesn't want us to be copies of other men. I never had a talk with him but that I didn't become richer. I think he accepted to die because he believed that some day somebody else would harvest the crop. In that sense he was a natural mystic.

Archbishop Routhier used him because he had a program. Most of us just patch, a marriage here, a burial there, patching up the leaky old boat. But Vandersteene had a goal; he had a program for the natives as a whole. But I could not accept all his demands, living like the natives and all. I think he accepted over the years that we weren't going to leave our mission houses to live like the natives. I may have disagreed with him on some things, but I had a great deal of respect for him.

Archbishop Routhier, First Bishop

What made him a success, and an outstanding missionary, was his love of the people. I think there was something of the Fr. Lacombe in him. I don't think he would like to have been teaching in a school. Fr. Lacombe was sort of a roamer himself. He had Indian blood in him and he was not a man to stay in one place. He was the type where he was ready to do anything to reach his aims, which were good. Remember, Lacombe went to Ottawa and he would say, "I'm going to stay here until you say yes." Vandersteene was like that. He never bothered me in the sense that I gave him a lot of liberty because I trusted him very much and he never caused me any trouble. He contributed to Indians by helping them in their identity. He might have instilled a pride of what they are by his opposition to the schools, but I think that every man should be proud of what he is.

He was more intelligent than I. In any case he found in the ritual of the Indians all the points we have in the mass. But they don't have all these points in their religion. He lent a little of his imagination to the Indian rites. He said, "They have their own mass in their own way." That's the classic way I disagree with Fr. Vandersteene. Those rites don't have all the points of the mass. Maybe he can see more than me. But after 25 years with the Indians I think I can see something.

Sister Bernadette Gautreau, Teacher and Pastoral Associate at Jean D'Or Prairie

His work on the catechism was very important, but some of his pictures were very difficult in their symbolism. The girl on the cross has a mystical meaning, because the girl represents the Church. But such a mystical picture is a little too ambiguous for most people, including native people. It means something like Christ is reproducing himself in the Church, and His mystical body has a natural growth in the world. Or it may mean that the mystical body of Christ is already glorious in heaven, and that mystical body has to be reproduced in the world, in the physical Christ of the world. Hence Christ's suffering has to be applied to my life.

There is something very special about Fr. Vandersteene. It may seem strange, but among ourselves we don't talk much about priests who died in [the] past. It's really amazing how Fr. Vandersteene has stayed with us. He was a man of many colours, many talents, many dreams — a deep and spiritual man.

Fr. Virgilio Baratto, Priest in Mission

Fr. Vandersteene was an idealist. He certainly was idealistic about the hunter/trapper culture. But it's not there as a whole culture — less than five percent. But there is still a hunter/trapper mentality present among the Cree. A hunter may be hungry, but he takes some meat and puts in the trap to catch a bigger animal. So when he's in the city, he sits down, makes friends and uses that as basis to borrow five dollars. No matter how sophisticated a trapper gets, there is still that trapper inclination, and when crisis looms, the pattern reappears. Thus integration into Canadian culture will not be that quick. It often depends on the circumstances — one person changes quite a bit, while another might take a long time to change.

Fr. Camillo Prosdocimo, Priest in Assumption

We're crazy, we priests. Just like St. Paul. Day after day, the drunkenness, the welfare, the dwindling numbers in the Church, nothing appears to be happening. Vandersteene had less than he had before he started after 10 years of work. Still there is something beyond the drinking, the dirtiness, the ugliness of reserves — there's a goodness about the people. A wedding, with 150 people there to celebrate, with everyone participating in some kind of solidarity, this shows that we have built something. When they make this kind of people, it's not like in town, with an organized parish, everything set up and working well. Rather, it's to witness to them, with the conviction that the other person is equal to me. Never make a distinction between people, regardless. Drunkenness or sobriety is not a difference between people. If I met my father, it makes no difference to my spirit whether he is sober or not. In our Oblate ideal every man [*sic*] is as worthy as I, to live with, to share with the message of God. God loves him as much as he loves me. Life is like a walk, we are walking together. I ask you to give some of your meat, you ask me to fix your gun. God gave me some gift you don't have, we share. You don't like me. It doesn't matter, we walk here together. That's what Vandersteene loved.

Notes

1 The reference is to the construction of the church in Trout Lake with the door on the wrong end of the building.

2 Jos has transformed his house into a living museum of Roger, even to raising cactii, and having Roger's memorabilia on display.

3 Pol, Mietje's husband, informs me that, eventually, after one of the brothers had remonstrated with him about this, he gave her a painting.

Ode to Vandersteene

by Willem Vermandere

I had a friend in northern Canada
I say a friend, he was a brother, a father.
In the land of the Indians, Alberta
Roger Vandersteene was there, a father.

Children sit quiet, now listen to my song.
I tell you the story of Steentje.
He didn't have a wife, children nor fortune.
He had no strong physique.
Tiny he was.

But in his heart, he had a great vision:
I will the Indians teach about Jesus.
Yet that was above his power.
None wanted to be saved.

There stood his cabin by the river,
And he must go fishing and hunting
And very cold winter
Without food or fire.
He wrote in his letters, "I can't complain."

He smoked his pipe and listened well.
To the ancient Indian tales
Of the Great Spirit, who gives life to everything
And of the dead who come to seek us.

The river is a life-long trip.
Every curve lets people grow
Make sure that you're ready by the last curve,
That you're ready to pull into the vast ocean.

They hunted, otherwise there you die.
For days with dogs and toboggans,
Because the bear hide is massive and warm.
His fat and meat good to eat.

He wrote their language word for word,
And all their wonderful notions of mountains
and bush he had heard
And of the heaven we may expect.
Steentje became chief Cree Indian
Ayamihewiyiniw with the Spirit he was able to speak.
He had also a totem before his tipi,
Since there they are a sacred sign.

From the Buffalo Hills 'til Wabasca
With the Caribou huts far away
Around the huge lake of Athabasca
They called him "the little man with the big heart."

But now he has gone on his last trek
With his canoe he's rowed out to sea.
He was ready by the last curve.
And then he said:
"You have to bury me here."

I tell my children with my simple song
The story of Roger Vandersteene.
Without wife or children or fortune
He slumbers in the midst of his Indians, alone.

Appendix 4
Names of Informants

The following individuals were interviewed or were consulted, beginning in 1979.

Priests and Sisters

Baratto, Fr. Virgilio, Cadotte Lake
Bélanger, Fr. René, Falher
Berger, Sr. Jeannette, Jean D'Or Prairie
Bernard, Sr. Gloria, Garden River
Deharveng, Fr. Charles N., O.M.I.
Denise, Sr. Marguerite, Wabasca
Dérochers, Fr. P., Girouxville
Dufort, Sr. Therese, Trout Lake
Dumont, Sr. Claudette, Fort Vermilion
Filion, Fr. Robert, Grouard
Fillion, Br. Elphège, Desmarais
Forget, Fr. Joseph, Falher
Gautreau, Sr. Bernadette, Jean D'Or Prairie
Gendre, Fr. A., Slave Lake
Girardin, Sr. Gertrude, Fox Lake
Hernou, Fr. Paul (Maskwa), Trout Lake
Johnson, Fr. Jacques, Grouard
Joule, Fr. J., Joussard
Larve, Sr. Cecile, Garden River
Legaré, Mgr. Henri, McLennan
Mariman, Fr. Césare, Meander River
Marsan, Fr. J., McLennan
Michaud, Sr. Lorraine, Fox Lake
Montmigny, Fr., St. Albert
Plouff, Fr. Paul-Eugene, Fort Vermilion
Prosdocimo, Fr. Camillo, Assumption
Richer, Fr. Clement, Falher
Roué, Fr. Nicolas, Sturgeon Lake
Routhier, Mgr. H., St. Albert
Roy, Sr. Paulette, Jean D'Or Prairie
Vantroys, Fr. Jean-Paul, Wabasca

Cree and Métis

Alook, Dick, Fox Lake
Beaver, William, Slave Lake
Belcourt, Gordon, Edmonton
Blessie, Jimmy, Garden River
Buha, Beth Ann, Edmonton
Cardinal, Frank and Rose, Sucker Creek
Cardinal, Harold, Sucker Creek
Ghostkeeper, Louis and Veronica, Slave Lake
Gladue, Paul, Wabasca
Gray, Celestine and Harry, Trout Lake
Laboucan, Joseph, Wabasca
Lamothe, Arthur, Joussard
McLean, Mac, Buffalo Lakes
Nanooch, Joseph, Fort Vermilion
Noskiye, Emilia, Trout Lake
Ojay, Louis, Loon Lake
Okemow, Nabis, Peerless Lake
Sewepagaham, Johnsen, Jean D'Or Prairie
Sewepagaham, Julia, Trout Lake
Sewepagaham, Susie, Jean D'Or Prairie
Sinclair, Clifford, Slave Lake
Sinclair, Sarah, Trout Lake
Supernault, Dan, Pouce Coupe, BC
Yellowknee, Clara, Slave Lake

Others

Cook, George, Edmonton
Jackson, Dr. Mary, Peace River
Jaycocks, Mrs. Ruth, Grouard
Krynen, Dr. Wm., Edmonton
Le Culvez, Victor, Lac La Biche
Newman, Mrs. Pearl, Fort Vermilion
Peipenberg, Roy, Edmonton
Platteeuw, Fr. Andre, Brussels, Belgium
Scott, Edie, Eleske
Tanghe, Fr. Omer, Kortrijk, Belgium
Vandersteene, Anaïs, Eric, Etienne, Jaak, Johan, Jos, Mietje, Trees, Wilfried,
    Willy, various Flemish towns, Belgium
Woods, Dr. J. B., Slave Lake

Bibliography

à Jesu, Thomas. *De Procuranda Salute Omnium Gentium*. Antverpiae, 1613.

Abbott, Walter M., S.J., ed. *The Documents of Vatican II*. New York: Guild Press, 1966.

Ahenakew, Edward. *Voices of the Plains Cree*. Edited with an Introduction by Ruth M. Buck. Toronto: McClelland & Stewart, 1973.

Baldwin, Gordon C. *Talking Drums to Written Word*. New York: Norton, 1970.

Barrett, William. "Art and Being." In *Art and Philosophy: A Symposium*. Edited by Sidney Hook. New York: New York University Press, 1966.

Benedict, Ruth F. "The Concept of the Guardian Spirit in North America." *Memoirs of the American Anthropological Association*, 29 (1923): 28-85.

Bennabi, Malek. *Vocation de l'Islam*. Paris: Seuil, 1954. In English, *Islam in History and Society*. Chicago: Kazi Publications, 1988.

Bernstein, Richard J. "Hermeneutics and its Anxieties." In *Hermeneutics and the Tradition*. Edited by Daniel O. Dahlstrom. Washington, DC: American Catholic Philosophical Association, 1988, pp. 58-70.

Bhajan, Edward R. "Community Development Programs in Alberta: An Analysis of Development Efforts in 5 Communities, 1964-1969." M.A. thesis, University of Alberta, 1972.

Biggar, H.P. *The Voyage of Jacques Cartier*. No. 11. Ottawa: Public Archives of Canada, 1924.

Boff, Leonardo. *Church: Charism and Power*. New York: Crossroad, 1985.

Bouquet, Alan C. *The Christian Faith and Non-Christian Religions*. London: Cassell, 1958.

Bouyer, Louis. *Liturgical Piety*. Notre Dame, IN: University of Notre Dame Press, 1954.

Bowden, Henry Warner. *American Indians and Christian Missions: Studies in Cultural Conflict*. Chicago: University of Chicago Press, 1981.

Braroe, Neils Winther. *Indian & White: Self-Image and Interaction in a Canadian Plains Community*. Stanford, CA: Stanford University Press, 1975.

Brightman, Robert A. *ACAOOHKIWINA and ACIMOWINA: Traditional Narratives of the Rock Cree Indians*. Mercury Series, Canadian Ethnology Service Paper No. 113. Ottawa: Canadian Museum of Civilization, 1989.

Brock, Rita Nakashima. *Journeys by Heart: A Christology of Erotic Power*. New York: Crossroad, 1988.

Brown, Frank B. Review of *The Glory of the Lord*. *The Journal of Religion*, 65 (October 1985): 563-65.

Brown, Joseph Epes. *The Sacred Pipe: Black Elk's Account of the Seven Rites of the Oglala Sioux*. Norman, OK: University of Oklahoma Press, 1953.

Bryan, Alan L. "Late Protohistoric Cree Expansion into North Central Alberta." *Western Canadian Journal of Anthropology*, 1, 1 (1969): 32-37.

Buehrle, Marie Cecilia. *Kateri of the Mohawks*. Milwaukee, WI: Bruce Publishing, 1954.

Burckhardt, Titus. *Sacred Art in East and West*. London: Perennial Books, 1967.

Cameron, Milly, ed. *Between Two Worlds: The Canadian Immigration Experience*. Montreal: Quadrant, 1983.

Cardinal, Harold. *The Unjust Society: The Tragedy of Canada's Indians*. Edmonton: M.G. Hurtig, 1969.

Carême, Maurice, transl. *Anthologie de la poésie Neerlandaise*. Bruxelles: Asedi, 1967.

Carney, R.J., D. Evasiuk and W.H. Swift. *Report of the Northland School Division Study Group*. Edmonton, 1975.

Carrière, Gaston. *Histoire documentaire de la Congrégation des missionnaires Oblates de Marie-Immaculée dans l'Est du Canada*. Vols. 1-12. Ottawa: Éditions de l'Université d'Ottawa, 1957-75.

Choquette, Robert. "Les rapports entre Catholiques et Protestants dans le nord-ouest du Canada avant 1840." In *Western Oblate Studies*, Vol. 1: *Proceedings of the First Symposium on the History of the Oblates in Western and Northern Canada*. Edmonton: Western Canadian Publishers, 1990, pp. 129-40.

Clough, Shepard Bancroft. *A History of the Flemish Movement in Belgium*. New York: R.R. Smith, 1930.

Colledge, Eric, intr. and transl. *Blessed Jan Van Ruysbroeck: The Spiritual Espousals*. Westminster, MD: Christian Classics, 1983.

Consensus Report on the Constitution. Ottawa: Minister of Supply and Services Canada, 1992.

Conzemius, Victor. "Otto Karrer (1888-1976): Theological Forerunner of Aggiornamento." *The Catholic Historical Review*, 85, 1 (January 1989): 55-72.

Cooper, John M. "The Shaking Tent Rite among Plains and Forest Algonquians." *Primitive Man*, 17 (1944): 60-84.

Cox, R. *Adventures on the Columbia River Including the Narrative of a Residence of Six Years on the Western Side of the Rocky Mountains among Various Tribes of Indians Hitherto Unknown: Together with a Journey across the American Continent*. New York: J. & J. Harper, 1832.

Craik, Brian. "The Animate in Cree Languages and Ideology." In *Papers of the 13th Algonquian Conference*. Edited by William Cowan. Ottawa: Carleton University Press, 1982, pp. 29-35.

Cumming, Peter A., and Neil H. Mickenberg, eds. *Native Rights in Canada*, 2nd ed. Toronto: The Indian Association of Canada & General Publishing, 1972.

Dailey, R.C. "The Role of Alcohol among the North American Indian Tribes as Reported in the Jesuit Relations." *Anthropologica*, 10 (1968): 45-57.

de Jonge, Albert. *De Standaard*, during November 1990. Groot-Bijgaarden, Belgium, series section.

Delacroix, Mgr. S., *Histoire universelle des missions catholiques*, 4 vols. Paris: Grund, 1956-59.

De Ridder, André. *La Littérature flamande contemporaine (1890-1923)*. Paris: Champion, 1923.

_____. *Anthologie des écrivains flamands contemporains*. Paris, Champion, 1926.

Dewdney, Selwyn. *They Shared to Survive*. Toronto: Macmillan, 1975.

Dossogne, V.J., S.J. "From Caesar to 1814." In *Belgium*. Edited by Jan-Albert Goris. Berkeley: University of California Press, 1946, pp. 15-36.

Douglas, Mary. *Purity and Danger: An Analysis of Concepts of Pollution and Taboo*. London: Routledge and Kegan Paul, 1980.

Duchaussois, P., O.M.I. *Mid Snow and Ice*. London: Burns, Oates & Washbourne, 1923.

Ecker, Gisela, ed. *Feminist Aesthetics*. Translated by Harriet Andersen. Boston: Beacon Press, 1985.

Eliade, Mircea. *Cosmos and History*. New York: Harper Torchbooks, 1954.

_____. *Patterns in Comparative Religions*. Cleveland, OH: World Publishing, 1963.

_____. *Shamanism and the Archaic Techniques of Ecstasy*. New York: Bollingen, 1968.

Evans, James. *Cree Syllabic Hymn Book: Norway House*, 1841. Reprint, Toronto: Bibliographical Society of Canada, 1954.

Fisher, Anthony D. "The Cree of Canada: Some Ecological and Evolutionary Considerations." *Western Canadian Journal of Anthropology*, 1, 1 (1969): 7-19.

Foster, John E. "Le Missionaire and Le Chief Métis." In *Western Oblate Studies*, Vol. 1: *Proceedings of the First Symposium on the History of the Oblates in Western and Northern Canada*. Edmonton: Western Canadian Publishers, 1990, pp. 117-27.

Fraser, Nancy. *Unruly Practices: Power, Discourse and Gender in Contemporary Social Theory*. Minneapolis: University of Minnesota Press, 1989.

Frideres, J.S. "Education for Indians vs. Indian Education in Canada." *The Indian Historian*, 11, 1 (Winter 1978): 29-35.

Gadamer, Hans-Georg. *Truth and Method*. New York: Seabury Press, 1975.

Gazetteer of Indian and Eskimo Stations of the Oblate Fathers in Canada. Ottawa: Oblate Services, 1960.

Geertz, Clifford, ed. *Myth, Symbol and Culture*. New York: Norton, 1974.

_____. "From the Native's Point of View: On the Nature of Anthropological Understanding." In *Interpretive Social Science: A Reader*. Edited by P. Rabinow and W.M. Sullivan. Berkeley: University of California Press, 1979, pp. 225-41.

Gezelle, Guido. *Laatste Verzen*. Amsterdam: L.J. Veen, 1903.

_____. *Guido Gezelle's Dichtwerken*. 2 vols. Amsterdam: L.J. Veen, 1943.

Gill, Sam. *Mother Earth: An American Story*. Chicago: University of Chicago Press, 1987.

Goddard, John. *Last Stand of the Lubicon Cree*. Toronto: Douglas and McIntyre, 1991.

Goddard, Pliny Earle. "Notes on the Sundance of the Cree in Alberta." *Anthropological Papers of the American Museum of Natural History*, 16, 4 (1919): 295-310.

Goris, J.A., ed. *Belgium under Occupation*. New York: Belgium Government Information Center, 1947.

Grant, John Webster. *Moon of Wintertime*. Toronto: University of Toronto Press, 1984.

Greshoff, Jan. "Belgian Literature in the Dutch Language." In *Belgium*. Edited by Jan-Albert Goris. Berkeley: University of California Press, 1946.

Gutierrez, Gustavo. *The God of Life*. Maryknoll, NY: Orbis Books, 1991.

Haines, Francis. *The Plains Indians*. New York: Thomas Crowell, 1976.

Hallowell, A.L. "The Role of Conjuring in Saulteaux Society." *Philadelphia Anthropological Society*, 2 (1942): 89-96.

_____. "Ojibwa Personality and Acculturation." In *Selected Papers of the XXIXth International Congress of Americanists*, vol. 29, no. 2. Edited by Sol Tax. Chicago: University of Chicago Press, 1954, pp. 105-12.

Hamilton, George H. *19th and 20th Century Art*. New York: Harry N. Abrams, 1970.

Handelman, Donald. "Ritual Clown: Attributes and Affinities." *Anthropos: International Review of Ethnology and Linguistics*, 76 (1981): 321-70.

Harmer, John H. "Guardian Spirits, Alcohol and Cultural Defence Mechanisms." *Anthropologica*, 11, 2 (1969): 215-41.

Harrison, Dick, ed. "Introduction." In *Crossing Frontiers: Papers in Western Canadian and American Literature*. Edmonton: University of Alberta Press, 1979.

Hartt, Frederick. *Art: A History of Painting, Sculpture, Architecture*. 2 vols. New York: Harry N. Abrams, 1976.

Hernegger, R. *Macht Ohne Auftrag? Die Entstehung der Staats- und Volkskirche*. Freiburg: Olten, 1963.

Hertzberg, Hazel W. *The Search for an American Indian Identity: Modern Pan-Indian Movements*. Syracuse, NY: Syracuse University Press, 1971.

Hillman, Eugene, S.J. "The Formation of Lay Deacons." Photocopied handout.

Hirschfeld, Gerhard *Nazi Rule and Dutch Collaboration*. Translated by Louise Willmot. Oxford: Berg Publishers, 1988.

Hlady, Walter M. "Indian Migrations in Manitoba and the West." *Historical and Scientific Society of Manitoba*, Series 3, No. 17 (1960-61): 24-53.

Hoffman, Ronan. "Conversion and the Mission of the Church." *Journal of Ecumenical Studies*, 5, 1 (Winter 1968): 1-20.

Hood, Robert. "Some Accounts of the Cree & Other Indians, 1819." *Alberta Historical Review* (Winter 1967), pp. 6-17.

Huel, Raymond. "La mission Notre-Dame-des-Victoires du Lac La Biche et l'approvisionnement des missions du nord: Le conflit entre Mgr. V. Grandin et Mgr H. Faraud." In *Western Oblate Studies*, Vol. 1: *Proceedings of the First Symposium on the History of the Oblates in Western and Northern Canada*. Edmonton: Western Canadian Publishers, 1990, pp. 17-36.

Hultkrantz, Åke. *Prairie and Plains Indians*. Leiden: E.J. Brill, 1973.

Innis, Harold A. *The Fur Trade in Canada*. Toronto: University of Toronto Press, 1930.

Irwin, Lee. "Myth, Language and Ontology among the Huron." *Studies in Religion/Sciences Religieuses*, 19, 4 (1990): 413-26.

Jefferson, Robert. *Fifty Years on the Saskatchewan*. North West Historical Society Publications, Vol. 1, No. 5. Battleford, SK, 1929.

Jenness, Diamond. *The Indians of Canada*, 2nd ed. Bulletin 65. Anthropological Series No. 15. Ottawa: National Museum of Canada, 1958.

Johnson, Fr. Jacques. "Pilgrim's Reflections." *Falher Record-Gazette*, 26 January 1977.

Jungmann, Joseph A., S.J. *The Mass of the Roman Rite, Its Origins and Development* (Missarum Solemnia). Translated by F.A. Brunner, C.S.S.R. 2 vols. New York: Benzinger, 1951 and 1955.

_____. "Constitution on the Sacred Liturgy." In *Commentary on the Documents of Vatican II*. Vol. 1. Edited by Herbert Vorgrimler. Translated by L. Adolphus, K. Smyth and R. Strachan. New York: Herder and Herder, 1969.

Kandinsky, Wassily. *Über das Geistige in der Kunst*. Translated as *The Spiritual in Art*, a version of the Salier translation with F. Golffring, M. Harrison and F. Ostertag. New York: Witenborg, Schultz, 1947.

Karrer, Otto. "Die Eucharistie im Gespräch der Konfessionen: Vortrag 6.8.1960 beim Eucharistischen Weltkongress München." *Una Sancta*, 15 (1960): 229-50.

King, J.C.H. *Thunderbird and Lightning: Indian Life in Northeastern North America*. London: British Museum Publications, 1982.

Korp, Maureen. "Before Mother Earth: The Amerindian Earth Mound." *Studies in Religion/Sciences Religieuses*, 19, 1 (1990): 17-25.

Kossman, Ernest H. *The Low Countries, 1780-1940*. New York: Oxford University Press, 1978.

La Vois de l'archdiocese de Grouard-McLennan (photo-reproduced newsletter), 35, 6 (September 1976). McLennan, AB: Archdiocese of Grouard-McLennan.

Lacombe, Fr. Albert. *Dictionnaire de la langue des Cris*. Montreal: C.O. Beauchemin & Valois, 1874.

Lambe, W.K., ed. *Sixteen Years in the Indian Country: The Journal of Daniel William Harmon, 1800-1816*. Toronto: Macmillan of Canada, 1957.

Latourette, Kenneth S. *A History of the Expansion of Christianity*, 7 vols. New York: Harper & Bros., 1937-45.

Leflon, Jean. *Eugène de Mazenod, Bishop of Marseilles, Founder of the Oblates of Mary Immaculate*, 2 vols. Translated by Francis D. Flanagan, O.M.I. New York: Fordham University Press, 1966.

Lescelles, Thomas. *Roman Catholic Residential Schools in British Columbia*. Vancouver, BC: Order of OMI in BC, 1990.

Levaque, Yvon, O.M.I. "The Oblates and Indian Residential Schools." In *Western Oblate Studies*, Vol. 1: *Proceedings of the First Symposium on the History of the Oblates in Western and Northern Canada*. Edmonton: Western Canadian Publishers, 1990, pp. 181-91.

Lincoln, Bruce. *Emerging from the Chrysalis: Studies in Rituals of Women's Initiation*. Cambridge, MA: Harvard University Press, 1981.

_____. *Death, War, and Sacrifice: Studies in Ideology and Practice*. Chicago: University of Chicago Press, 1991.

Maccagno, Thomas. "Mission Possible: The Lac La Biche Mission Historical Society." In *Western Oblate Studies*, Vol. 1: *Proceedings of the First Symposium on the History of the Oblates in Western and Northern Canada*. Edmonton: Western Canadian Publishers, 1990 pp. 161-68.

Mackenzie, Alexander. *The Journals and Letters of Sir Alexander Mackenzie*. Edited by W. Kaye Lamb. Extra Series No. 41. London: Hakluyt Society, 1801. Reprint, Toronto: Macmillan of Canada, 1970.

The Mackenzie Basin: Proceedings of the Intergovernmental Seminar Held at Inuvik, N.W.T., June 24-27, 1972. Ottawa: Inland Waters Directorate, 1973.

MacLennan, Hugh. *Two Solitudes*. Toronto: Macmillan of Canada, 1986 (originally published in 1945).

Macquarrie, John. Review of *The Glory of the Lord*. *King's Theological Review*, 7 (Autumn 1984): 57-58.

Mandelbaum, David. "Changes in an Aboriginal Culture Following a Change in Environment, as Exemplified by the Plains Cree." Ph.D. dissertation, Yale University, New Haven, 1936.

_____. "The Plains Cree." *American Museum of Natural History Anthropological Papers*, 37, 2 (1940): 155-316.

_____. *The Plains Cree: An Ethnographic, Historical, and Comparative Study*. Canadian Plains Studies No. 9. Regina: Canadian Plains Research, 1979.

Martin, F.D. "The Aesthetic in Religious Experience." *Religious Studies*, 4, 1 (October 1968): 1-24.

Martin, Joel W. "Before and Beyond the Sioux Ghost Dance: Native American Prophetic Movements and the Study of Religion." *Journal of the American Academy of Religion*, 59, 4 (1991): 677-701.

McCarthy, Mary. "The Founding of Providence Mission." In *Western Oblate Studies*, Vol. 1: *Proceedings of the First Symposium on the History of the Oblates in Western and Northern Canada*. Edmonton: Western Canadian Publishers, 1990, pp. 37-49.

McLean, John. *Canadian Savage Folk: The Native Tribes of Canada*. Toronto, 1896.

McLeod, Keith A., ed. *Multiculturalism, Bilingualism and Canadian Institutions*. Toronto: Urban Alliance on Race Relations, 1977.

McManners, John, ed. *The Oxford Illustrated History of Christianity*. Oxford: Oxford University Press, 1990.

Meijer, R.P. *Dutch and Flemish: Two Literatures or One?* London: College University of London, 1973.

Memorian, Bro. "Roman Catholic Missions in Canada." In *The North American Indian Today*. Edited by C.T. Loram and T.F. McIllwraith. Toronto: University of Toronto Press, 1943, pp. 90-97.

Milloy, John S. *The Plains Cree: Trade, Diplomacy and War, 1790 to 1870*. Winnipeg: University of Manitoba Press, 1988.

Misner, E.G. "The Agriculture of Belgium." In *Belgium*. Edited by Jan-A. Goris. Berkeley: University of California Press, 1946.

Möhr, R.J. *Missionethnologie: Ein Wissenschaftliches Programm.* Nijmegen and Utrecht: Dekker & Van de Vegt N.V., 1956.

Moulin, Fr. Pierre. *Bulletin, Western Oblate History Project,* 18 (January 1992).

Müller, Werner. *Die Religionen der Waldlandindianer Nordamerikas.* Berlin: Dietrich Reimer, 1956.

Neher, Andrew. "A Physiological Explanation of Unusual Behaviour in Ceremonies Involving Drums." *Human Biology,* 34 (1962): 151-60.

Neihardt, John G. *Black Elk Speaks: Being the Life Story of a Holy Man of the Oglala Sioux.* Lincoln, NE: University of Nebraska Press, 1961.

Neill, Stephen C. *A History of Christian Missions.* Harmondsworth: Penguin Books, 1964.

————. *Colonialism and Christian Missions.* London: Oxford University Press, 1966.

Newton, Rev. William. *Twenty Years on the Saskatchewan, N.W. Canada.* London, 1897.

Nietzsche, Friedrich. *Beyond Good and Evil.* Translated by Walter Kaufmann. New York: Vintage Books, 1966.

Nock, David A. *A Victorian Missionary and Canadian Indian Policy: Cultural Synthesis vs. Cultural Replacement.* Waterloo, ON: Wilfrid Laurier University Press, 1988.

Oakes, Edward T. Review of *The Glory of the Lord. America,* 149 (December 1983): 436-37.

Oblate Fathers. *Residential Education for Indian Acculturation.* Ottawa: St. Paul's, 1958.

O'Meara, T.F. Review of *The Glory of the Lord. Theological Studies,* 45 (June 1984): 365-67.

Painchaud, R. *Un rêve français dans le peuplement de la prairie.* Saint-Boniface, MB: Les Éditions du Blé, 1987.

Palmer, Harold, ed. *Immigration and the Rise of Multiculturalism.* Vancouver: Copp, Clark, 1975.

Paper, Jordan. "The Post-Contact Origin of an American Indian High God: The Suppression of Female Spirituality." *American Indian Quarterly,* 7, 4 (1983): 1-24.

————. *Offering Smoke: The Sacred Pipe and Native American Religion.* Edmonton: University of Alberta Press, 1988.

Parnell, Ted. *Disposable Native.* Edmonton: Human Rights and Civil Liberties Association, 1976.

Passaris, Constantine. *Understanding Canadian Immigration.* Toronto: Canadian Foundation for Economic Development, 1978.

Pentland, David. "A Historical Overview of Cree Dialects." In *Papers of the Ninth Algonquian Conference.* Edited by W.Cowan. Ottawa: Carleton University Press, 1979, pp. 104-26.

Pôle et Tropiques: Revue apostolique des missionaires Oblats de Marie Immaculée. Gemmenich, Belgium.

Pollock, Griselda. *Vision and Difference: Femininity, Feminism and the Histories of Art.* New York: Routledge, 1988.

Preston, Richard J., and Sarah C. Preston. "Death and Grieving among North-
    ern Forest Hunters: An East Cree Example." In *Coping with the
    Final Tragedy: Cultural Variation in Dying and Grieving*. Edited by
    David R. Counts and Dorothy A. Counts. Amityville, NY: Bay-
    wood Publishing, 1991, pp. 135-55.

Rahner, Karl. *Lexikon für Theologie und Kirche*. 11 vols. Friburg, 1957-67.

Ralph, Julian. *On Canada's Frontier. Sketches of History, Sport, and Adventure and
    of the Indians, Missionaries, Fur-Traders, and Newer Settlers of West-
    ern Canada*. New York: Harper & Brothers, 1892.

Ray, Arthur Joseph. *Indians in the Fur Trade: Their Role as Trappers, Hunters, and
    Middlemen in the Lands Southwest of Hudson's Bay, 1660-1870*.
    Toronto: University of Toronto Press, 1974.

Ray, V.F. "Historic Backgrounds of the Conjuring Complex in the Plateau and
    the Plains." In *Language, Culture and Personality: Essays in Memory
    of Edward Saper*. Edited by L. Spier et al. Menasha, WI: Sapir
    Memorial Publication Fund, 1941, pp. 204-16.

Ricoeur, Paul. *The Conflict of Interpretation*. Edited by Don Ihde. Evanston:
    Northwestern University Press, 1974.

Ridington, Robin. *Swan People: A Study of the Dunne-Za Prophet Dance*. Mercu-
    ry Series, Canadian Ethnology Service Paper No. 38. Ottawa:
    National Museum of Man, 1978.

Rogers, E.S. "Plains Cree." *The Beaver* (Autumn 1969), pp. 56-59.

Rousseau, Dom Olivier, O.S.B. *Histoire de mouvement liturgique*. Paris, 1945. In
    English, *Progress of the Liturgy*. Westminster, MD: Newman Press,
    1951.

Russell, Dale R. *Eighteenth-Century Western Cree and Their Neighbours*. Hull,
    QC: Canadian Museum of Civilization, 1991.

Ruys, Manu. *The Flemings: A People on the Move, A Nation in Being*. Translated
    by Henri Schoup. Belgium: Lannoo, Tielt and Bussum, 1981.

Sacerdotal Communities of Saint-Severin of Paris and Saint-Joseph of Nice,
    The. *The Liturgical Movement*. Translated by Lancelot Sheppard.
    New York: Hawthorn Books, 1964.

Sargent, Daniel. *Catherine Tekakawitha*. Toronto: Longmans, Green, 1936.

Schmidlin, Joseph. *Catholic Mission History*. Translated by Matthias Braun,
    SVD. Techny, IL: Mission Press, 1933.

Schmidt, Wilhelm. *Der Ursprung der Gottesidee: Eine historische-kritische und
    positive Studie*. 12 vols. Münster: Aschendorff, 1912-56.

Sertorius, Lili. *Literarisches Schaffen und Volkstum in Flandern*. Berlin: Verlag
    "Das Deutsche Volk," 1932.

Sherzer, Joel. "Areal Linguistics in North America." In *Current Trends in
    Linguistics*. Edited by Thomas A. Sebock. The Hague: Mouton,
    1973, pp. 749-95.

Skinner, Alanson. "Political Organizations, Cults, and Ceremonies of the
    Plains Cree." *Anthropological Papers of the American Museum of Nat-
    ural History*, 11, 6 (1914): 513-42.

_____. "The Sundance of the Plains Cree." *Anthropological Papers of the
    American Museum of Natural History*, 11, 6 (1914): 282-93.

Smith, James G.E. "Preliminary Notes on the Rocky Cree of Reindeer Lake." In *Contributions to Canadian Ethnology*. Edited by D.B. Carlisle. Mercury Series, Canadian Ethnology Service Paper 31. Ottawa: National Museum of Man, 1975, pp. 171-89.

————. "On the Territorial Distribution of the Western Woods Cree." In *Papers of the Seventh Algonquian Conference*. Edited by W. Cowan. Ottawa: Carleton University Press, 1976.

————. "Western Woods Cree." In *Handbook of North American Indians*. Vol. 6: *Subarctic*. Edited by J. Helm. Washington, DC: Smithsonian Institution, 1981.

Sotemann, A.L. "Martinus Nijhoff's Poetry in Its European Context." In *Nijhoff, Van Ostaijen, "De Stijl": Modernism in the Netherlands and Belgium in the First Quarter of the 20th Century*. Edited by Francis Bulhof. The Hague: Martinus Nijhoff, 1976, pp. 95-116.

Stanner, W.E.H. "On Aboriginal Religion." *Oceania*, 30 (1960): 245-78.

Stegner, Wallace, *Wolf Willow: A History, a Story and a Memory of the Last Prairie Frontier*. Toronto: Macmillan of Canada, 1955.

Steinmetz, Paul B. "The Sacred Pipe in American Indian Religions." *American Indian Culture and Research Journal*, 8, 3 (1984): 27-80.

————. *Pipe, Bible, and Peyote among the Oglala Sioux: A Study in Religious Identity*. Knoxville: University of Tennessee Press, 1990.

Stewart, Omer. "The Peyote Religion and the Ghost Dance." *The Indian Historian*, 5 (1956): 27-30.

Stillman, Clark, and Frances Stillman, transl. *Lyrica Belgica: Guido Gezelle, Karel van de Woestijne, etc.* New York: Belgium Information Centre, 1963.

Streuvels, Stijn. *Langs de Wegen (Along the Roads)*. Translated by Edward Crankshaw. Boston, MA: Twayne Publishers, 1976.

Strynadka, Arnold. *The Native People*, October 1971, p. 16, col. 2.

Tanghe, Omer. *Little Big Man, My Brother*. Kortrijk; Lanoo, 1973.

————. *Leven en sterven in de missie der eenzamen*. Amsterdam: Lanoo, 1978.

————. *As I Have Loved You: The Life of Catherine de Hueck Doherty*. Dublin: Veritas Publications, 1988.

Tarasoff, Koozma J. *Persistent Ceremonialism: The Plains Cree and Saulteaux*. Mercury Series, Canadian Ethnology Service Paper No. 69. Ottawa: National Museum of Man, 1980.

Taylor, Mark. C. *Erring: A Postmodern A/theology*. Chicago: University of Chicago Press, 1984.

Theunis, George. "In the First World War." In *Belgium*. Edited by Jan-A. Goris. Berkeley: University of California Press, 1946, pp. 53-65.

Trottier, Alice, F.J., ed. *Journal d'un missionnaire-colonisateur, 1890-1897*. Edmonton: Le Salon d'histoire de la francophonie albertaine, 1984.

————. "Les Oblates et la colonisation en Alberta," In *Western Oblate Studies*, Vol. 1: *Proceedings of the First Symposium on the History of the Oblates in Western and Northern Canada*. Edmonton: Western Canadian Publishers, 1990, pp. 107-16.

Underhill, Evelyn, ed. *John of Ruysbroeck*. Translated by C.A. Wynschenk Dom. London: John M. Watkins, 1951.

Van der Plas, Michel. *Mijheer Gezelle*. Amsterdam: Ako, 1991.

Van Nuis, Hermine J. *Guido Gezelle: Flemish Poet-Priest*. New York: Greenwood Press, 1981.

Vandersteene, Roger, O.M.I. *Wabasca: Dix Ans de Vie Indienne*. Translated from Dutch by Jacques De Deken, O.M.I. Gemmenich, Belgium: Éditions O.M.I., 1960.

_____. "Among the Cree." Talk given to Daughters of Wisdom Conference, Red Deer, AB, 1965.

_____. "Some Woodland Cree Traditions and Legends." Edited by Thelma Habgood. *Western Canadian Journal of Anthropology*, 1, 1 (1969): 40-64.

_____. *Wanneer gij uw ogen op God gericht houdt: Brieven aan een religieuze*. Kortryjk, Belgium: Di Riemaeker pvba, 1977.

_____. *Levensvervulling*. Edited by Gabrielle Demedts. Roeselare: Hernieuwen-Uitgaven pvba, 1979.

_____. *La catechèse des enfants Indiens*. Grouard: N.p., n.d.

_____, in collaboration with Margaret Denis, S.O.S. *Come Lord Jesus! The Story of the Church*. Ottawa: Canadian Catholic Conference, 1973.

Vantroys, Jean-Paul. *La Voix*, 35, 6 (September 1976).

Vennum, Thomas, Jr. *The Ojibwa Dance Drum: Its History and Construction*. Smithsonian Folklife Studies Series No. 2. Washington, DC: Smithsonian Institution, 1982.

Von Balthasar, Hans Urs. *The Glory of the Lord: A Theological Aesthetics*. Vol. 1: *Seeing the Form*. Translated by E. Leiva-Merkakis. Edinburgh: T. & T. Clark, 1982.

Vriens, L., A. Disch and J. Wils, eds. *A Critical Bibliography of Missiology*. Translated by D. Tummers. Nijmegen: Bestelcentrale der V.S.K.B., 1960.

Waugh, Earle H. "'The Almighty Has Not Got as Far as This Yet': Religious Models in Alberta's and Saskatchewan's History." In *The New Provinces: Alberta and Saskatchewan, 1905-1980*. Edited by Howard Palmer and Donald Smith. Vancouver: Tantalus Research, 1973, pp. 199-215.

_____. *The Sacred Circle*. National Film Board/University of Alberta film production, 1979.

_____. *The Munshidin of Egypt: Their World and Their Song*. Columbia: University of South Carolina Press, 1989.

_____. "Vandersteene's Art: Christian Interaction with Cree Culture." In *Proceedings of the Fort Chipewyan and Fort Vermilion Bicentennial Conference*. Edited by Patricia A. McCormick and R. Geoffrey Ironside. Edmonton: Boreal Institute for Northern Studies, 1990, pp. 118-27.

_____. "Naming the Currents: A Foray into the Nature of Religion in Canada." *Religious Studies and Theology*, 12, 2-3 (May-September 1992): 105-27.

_____, and K. Dad Prithipaul, eds. *Native Religious Traditions*. Waterloo, ON: Wilfrid Laurier University Press, 1979.

Whitford, Frank. *Expressionism: Movements of Modern Art*. London: Hamlyn Publishing Group, 1970.

Wiseman, James A., O.S.B., intr. and transl. *John Ruysbroeck: The Spiritual Espousals and Other Works*. Mahwah, NJ: Paulist Press, 1985.

Wolf, R. "American Anthropologists and American Society." *Western Canadian Journal of Anthropology*, 1, 3 (1969): 10-18.

Worsley, P.M. *The Trumpet Shall Sound: A Study of "Cargo" Cults in Melanesia*. London: MacGibbon and Kee, 1957.

Zuern, Theodore F., S.J. "Indians Must Be Indians." *The Catholic Digest* (April 1969), pp. 76-80.

Index